VOICES OF VICTORY

VOICES OF VICTORY

Powerful eye-witness accounts of the battle to take Germany, February 1945 to VE Day

GERAINT JONES

MACMILLAN

First published 2025 by Macmillan
an imprint of Pan Macmillan
The Smithson, 6 Briset Street, London EC1M 5NR
EU representative: Macmillan Publishers Ireland Ltd, 1st Floor,
The Liffey Trust Centre, 117–126 Sheriff Street Upper,
Dublin 1, D01 YC43
Associated companies throughout the world
www.panmacmillan.com

ISBN 978-1-0350-7004-6 HB
ISBN 978-1-0350-7006-0 TPB

Copyright © Geraint Jones Media Ltd 2024

The right of Geraint Jones to be identified as the
author of this work has been asserted by him in accordance
with the Copyright, Designs and Patents Act 1988.

All rights reserved. No part of this publication may be reproduced,
stored in a retrieval system, or transmitted, in any form, or by any means
(electronic, mechanical, photocopying, recording or otherwise)
without the prior written permission of the publisher.

Pan Macmillan does not have any control over, or any responsibility for,
any author or third-party websites referred to in or on this book.

1 3 5 7 9 8 6 4 2

A CIP catalogue record for this book is available from the British Library.

Map artwork © ML Design

Typeset in Adobe Garamond Pro by Palimpsest Book Production
Printed and bound by CPI Group (UK) Ltd, Croydon, CR0 4YY

This book is sold subject to the condition that it shall not, by way of
trade or otherwise, be lent, hired out, or otherwise circulated without
the publisher's prior consent in any form of binding or cover other than
that in which it is published and without a similar condition including
this condition being imposed on the subsequent purchaser.

Visit **www.panmacmillan.com** to read more about all our books
and to buy them. You will also find features, author interviews and
news of any author events, and you can sign up for e-newsletters
so that you're always first to hear about our new releases.

Dedicated to my *Taid*, Beuno Thomas, Royal Air Force; Uncle Richard, Royal Engineers; Auntie Lowry, Women's Royal Naval Service; Uncle Orwel, Merchant Navy; Auntie Alice, Queen Alexandra's Imperial Military Nursing Service; and all others who paid for our peace at the price of their own

CONTENTS

Glossary   xi

Introduction   1

Chapter 1: The Loneliest Club in the World
Plans, Preparations and Soldiers
Christmas 1944 – 7 February 1945   7

PART 1: Operation Veritable

Chapter 2: Highlanders
51st (Highland) Division in the Reichswald, and
on the Gennep–Goch road
8–12 February 1945   27

Chapter 3: Break-In
15th and 43rd Divisions at the Siegfried Line and Kleve
8–12 February 1945   41

Chapter 4: One of the Most Unpleasant Weeks of the Entire War
The Battle of the Reichswald Forest
8–18 February 1945   61

Chapter 5: Moyland
15th (Scottish) Division on the road to Kalkar
12–17 February 1945   83

Chapter 6: Goch
12–22 February 1945   95

Chapter 7: Iron Sides
3rd Division enter the battle
26 February – 1 March 1945   111

Chapter 8: Another Taste of Hell
The 53rd Division's push from Goch to Alpen
26 February – 8 March 1945   127

Chapter 9: Reaching the Rhine
Operation Blockbuster
26 February – 12 March 1945   143

PART 2: Crossing the Rhine

Chapter 10: Operation Plunder
British plans and preparation for the crossing of the Rhine   159

Chapter 11: Operation Turnscrew
The 51st (Highland) Division's battle on the Rhine
23 March – 1st April 1945   165

Chapter 12: Operation Widgeon
No. 1 Commando Brigade at Wesel
23–25 March 1945   177

Chapter 13: Operation Torchlight
The 15th (Scottish) Division's battle on the Rhine
23–28 March 1945   193

Chapter 14: Red Devils
3rd and 5th Parachute Brigades during Operation Varsity
24–25 March 1945   203

Chapter 15: Nothing Is Impossible
Glider pilots during Operation Varsity
24–25 March 1945   219

Chapter 16: Mass Murder
2 Ox and Bucks during Operation Varsity
24–25 March 1945   233

PART 3: The Race to Victory

Chapter 17: The Mosaic of Victory
Clearing the Dutch/German border
27 March – 11 April 1945   257

Chapter 18: For Valour
The Teutoburg Forest and Ibbenbüren
1–7 April 1945   281

Chapter 19: More Bloody Bridgeheads
VIII Corps on the River Weser
27 March – 9 April 1945   293

Chapter 20: For Freedom
Actions on the River Aller
9–15 April 1945   317

Chapter 21: Liberation
The liberations of Belsen and Fallingbostel
12–16 April 1945   345

Chapter 22: Die-Hards
XXX Corps' capture of Bremen
13–27 April 1945   361

Chapter 23: Final Days
*XII Corps' capture of Hamburg, and VIII Corps' race to Wismar
15 April – 3 May 1945* 381

Chapter 24: Victory in Europe
*The final days the of war in Europe, and the first of peace
May 1945* 397

PART 4: After War

Chapter 25: The Price of Victory 413

Epilogue 427
Notes 431
Bibliography 445
Acknowledgements 449
Picture Acknowledgements 451
Voices from the Imperial War Museums 453

GLOSSARY

Regiments and military formations

Argylls	Argyll and Sutherland Highlanders
Armd	Armoured
Bty	Battery
BW	Black Watch
Camerons	Cameron Highlanders
Cameronians	Cameronians (Scottish Rifles)
CCS	Casualty Clearing Station
CDO	Commando
Cheshires	The Cheshire Regiment
Coy	Company
DCLI	Duke of Cornwall's Light Infantry
Devons	Devonshire Regiment
Div	Division
DLI	Durham Light Infantry
Dorsets	Dorsetshire Regiment
East Lancs	East Lancashire Regiment
East Yorks	East Yorkshire Regiment
Fife and Forfar	Fife and Forfar Yeomanry
Gordons	Gordon Highlanders
HLI	Highland Light Infantry
KOSB	King's Own Scottish Borderers
KRIH	King's Royal Irish Hussars
KRRC	King's Royal Rifle Corps
KSLI	King's Shropshire Light Infantry
Mons	Monmouthshire Regiment

Ox and Bucks	Oxfordshire and Buckinghamshire Light Infantry
RA	Royal Artillery
RAF	Royal Air Force
RAMC	Royal Army Medical Corps
RASC	Royal Army Service Corps
RDG	Royal Dragoon Guards
RE	Royal Engineers
Recce	Reconnaissance Regiment
REME	Royal Electrical and Mechanical Engineers
RM	Royal Marine
RTR	Royal Tank Regiment
RWF	Royal Welch Fusiliers (pronounced 'Welsh')
SAS	Special Air Service
Seaforths	Seaforth Highlanders
SLI	Somerset Light Infantry
SOE	Special Operations Executive
South Lancs	South Lancashire Regiment
Sqn/Sdq	Squadron
Staffs Yeomanry	Staffordshire Yeomanry
Suffolks	Suffolk Regiment
Welch	Welch Regiment (pronounced 'Welsh')
Wilts	Wiltshire Regiment

A number before the abbreviation of a regiment denotes a battalion within it. For example, 2 East Yorks represents the 2nd Battalion, East Yorkshire Regiment.

Companies/squadrons within a battalion/regiment are for the most part named by letter. For example, A Coy, 2 East Yorks represents A Company, the 2nd Battalion, East Yorkshire Regiment.

General Terms

'55s'	A 4.5-inch medium field gun that fired a 55lb (25kg) high-explosive (HE) shell.
88	Also referred to as 88mm. A German

GLOSSARY

	anti-aircraft and anti-tank gun that fired an 88mm shell.
AP	Armour Piercing
APC	Armoured Personnel Carrier
ARV	Armoured Recovery Vehicle
AVRE	Armoured Vehicle, Royal Engineers
AWOL	Absent Without Leave (pronounced 'a-wall')
Blighty/Blighty wound	A wound or injury that would necessitate evacuation to Britain
Bofors	A British anti-aircraft gun
Bren	A magazine-fed machine gun
Bren carrier	A tracked vehicle used to carry men and equipment
Brew up	To make tea, or to describe a tank/vehicle catching fire and/or exploding
Buffalo	A tracked, amphibious assault vehicle
CO	Commanding Officer
Crocodile	A Churchill tank equipped with a powerful flamethrower
CSM	Company Sergeant Major
DCM	Distinguished Conduct Medal
DD tank	An amphibious tank
DSO	Distinguished Service Order
DUKW	A particular model of amphibious truck (pronounced 'duck')
FOO	Forward Observation Officer
Hamilcar	A large glider model used for carrying heavy equipment
HE	High Explosive
H-Hour	The time that an attack, or other form of military operation, is set to begin
Horsa	A British troop-carrying glider
HQ	Headquarters
Kangaroo	A variant of armoured personnel carrier
LAD	Light Aid Detachment
MC	Military Cross
MG	Machine Gun

MID	Mentioned in Despatches
MM	Military Medal
Moaning Minnie	British slang for the German multiple-barrel rocket launcher
NCO	Non-Commissioned Officer
OP	Observation Post
Panzerfaust	A single shot, man portable anti-tank weapon
PIAT	Projectile, Infantry, Anti-Tank. A man portable anti-tank weapon
POW	Prisoner of War
RAF	Royal Air Force
RAP	Regimental Aid Post
RHQ	Regimental Headquarters
RSM	Regimental Sergeant Major
Sapper	A military engineer. Also used as the equivalent rank of private in the Corps of Royal Engineers
Schu-mine	A form of anti-personnel mine used by the German military
SP	Self-propelled (gun). Turretless, tracked and armoured vehicles equipped with a powerful gun, and used by the German military
Spandau	A generic term, used by British soldiers, for enemy machine guns
SS	*Schutzstaffel*, a Nazi paramilitary organization
Stonk	A bombardment of shells and/or bombs
TA	Territorial Army
Universal carrier	An upgraded model of the Bren carrier, used to carry men and equipment
VC	Victoria Cross
Volkssturm	The German national militia established in September 1944, and made up of males aged sixteen to sixty who were not already in military service
Waffen-SS	The *Schutzstaffel*'s combat branch
WASP	A Universal carrier equipped with flame-thrower (pronounced 'wasp')
Wehrmacht	German Armed Forces

INTRODUCTION

On 8 February 1945, nineteen-year-old Ray Ashton crouched beside his comrades in a muddy field in Holland. Having landed in Normandy in June the previous year, and having fought in countless actions during the eight months of the advance across North West Europe, the prospect of facing death was nothing new to Ray, nor was the loss of friends and comrades. But today was different. After more than five years of bloodshed in Europe, the British army was poised to make its final, decisive campaign against Nazi Germany, and into the very heart of the Reich itself.

It began with the largest British bombardment since El Alamein. More than a thousand guns and mortars hurled high explosives onto German soil, reducing buildings to rubble and shredding both trees and men. Tanks, lined up in their hundreds, fired until their barrels wore out. Machine-gunners, piles of empty shell cases at their elbows, sent a million bullets arcing through the air.

'It was a frightening thing,' said Ray. 'The noise was indescribable. But what it must have been like to have been on the receiving end, I can't imagine.'

As the barrage crept forwards from the enemy's frontline, the British infantrymen cracked jokes, offered prayers, and shared one last look with their mates.

Whistles blew. Orders were echoed. The soldiers rose from the cold ground and advanced on their enemy.

'I can remember these Germans, initially, coming out in droves, carrying wounded on doors and one thing and another. White-faced, shaking, and in a terrible state.'

With such a beginning came the hope that the end of the war was weeks, perhaps days, away.

'You think it's all over. You think it's going to be a walk-over. It never is.'

It was hoped that the 'break-in' to Germany, Operation Veritable, could achieve its aims in a matter of days. Instead, in the face of a determined enemy and the grim conditions of winter, it would take the army four bloody weeks to advance a distance of thirty miles.

Many more battles were to follow, but two months later, when Germany offered its unconditional surrender, the British Liberation Army (BLA) had pushed more than 300 miles into their enemy's territory, the tenacious enemy exacting a heavy price for every yard of the British advance. From eighteen-year-old 'raw recruits' to 'old soldiers' who had been at Dunkirk, 6,000 British soldiers would fall during the campaign, many of them within weeks, and sometimes days, of Victory in Europe.

That moment, when it came, was not always celebrated.

'It was a time for reflection, really,' said platoon commander Vic Sayer. 'I always think when I see these pictures of celebrations in Piccadilly Circus, it wasn't quite like that in a battalion. You thought of all the men (that you'd lost). It had been a hard slog from Sword Beach to Bremen.'

'We'd suffered quite a lot,' said nineteen-year-old James Campbell, an infantryman who had fought since Normandy. Two days after the end of the war, these 'originals' of his battalion were due to be addressed by their commanding officer (CO), but when the CO saw how few remained, 'he burst into tears and dashed off the parade ground'.

Less than a quarter of the battalion was still standing.

The purpose of this book is to tell the stories of men like James, Vic and Ray in their own words – the young men who trudged through mud, slept in rain, killed the enemy, and lost their friends.

'This is just a rifleman's tale,' said Tom Gore, who would turn twenty a few days before VE Day. 'Maps and the bigger things was left to the generals, and the colonels, and the company commanders. Little things, when you're in the infantry section, sticks in your mind. It's not the bigger picture, it's just the infantry section. That is your comrades – your section.

'You do anything for your comrades. You didn't care what happened to anyone else, really. You hardly ever knew what the rest of the battalion was doing. And even down to platoon you never knew what the other platoons were doing, actually.'

The British campaign in Germany has been largely overlooked by both history and our nation. As such, I am deeply grateful to three former British army officers turned historians. Tim Saunders has covered the Battles of the Reichswald and the Rhine in great depth, and John Russell has done the same for the battles that took place on the Rivers Weser and Aller. Patrick Delaforce, who was present for several of these actions, and more, later wrote a number of campaign and divisional histories that included this period. I owe a debt to all of these authors among many others for laying the groundwork on which I have been able to place these personal accounts, and to the late Max Arthur, for introducing me to what I believe is the true essence of history – the stories of those who were there.

'Records is not individuals,' said Tom Myers, a decorated soldier of the Durham Light Infantry. 'You can find more talking to a man than you can reading a bit of history about him on paper.'

Tom's story is one of the thousands recorded by the Imperial War Museums, who have kindly provided the majority of first-hand accounts used in this book. The museums' sound archive is nothing less than a national treasure, and I am certain that I am not alone in my gratitude for the tireless work of the interviewers and archivists who have ensured that the voices of these heroes will always be with us.

War is a human endeavour, and as such there is only so much we can learn from 'maps with red and blue arrows and oblongs'.[1] It is who and what those markers represent that makes war so terrible – millions of lives, and millions of tragedies. Without these stories we are no longer remembering *war* – we are simply recording the movement of armies. With that being said, it is also true that oral histories have their own 'failings' – humans make mistakes. Neither our actions, nor our memories, are infallible.

'I may forget the details, but the general experience sticks in your mind,' said tank crewman Austin Baker. 'It's something you never forget, really.'

With that in mind, this book is primarily about the *experience* of the soldier, and I am allowing them their opinions. As an example, many British tank crewmen believed that their Shermans and Churchills were inferior to the German Tigers and Panthers, and while there may be a case to be made that the Sherman was the more successful tank overall in the war, that is scant comfort to the eighteen-year-old trooper convinced that a Tiger is about to turn his tank into a bonfire. And so, while additional sources have been used to keep the reader abreast of the developments in the campaign, what a soldier *recalled* and what he *felt* is the main purpose of these pages.

The majority of the personal accounts in this book come from the 'other ranks', which outnumber those of officers for several reasons. Firstly, because they outnumbered them in the army. And secondly, because their individual actions are often less documented. Unless an 'other rank' had performed some action worthy of a gallantry award, it is unusual to find them named in regimental war diaries, or in the later histories that followed.

'They never mention your name unless you were a lieutenant,' said Charles White, whose own deeds, but not name, had been recorded in the regimental history. From private to general, I believe the courage and sacrifice of all should be recalled equally. As was proved during the Battle of Germany, death does not distinguish by rank and class, and neither should history, nor remembrance.

And it is remembrance that is the driving force behind this book – for myself as author, and for those who told their tales. As a nation we have a proud tradition of honouring our war dead, but we often know little of these men because their stories died with them. We can, however, learn more of their lives through the experiences of their comrades, who deserve to be remembered in their own right, for no soldier who fought in this war served without sacrifice. They were separated from their families, lived in conditions that would be hardship enough without the threat of death and wounds, and gave years of their prime in service of their country. Some were able to transition seamlessly back into civilian life – many said the war even benefited them – while a number were left physically and mentally scarred for life.

'I personally don't like to talk about the war,' said commando John Carney. 'I know I've talked now, but I've talked because I was asked and that was it.'

When a voice quivers during an interview, or tears flow, one is reminded that these veterans were not superheroes, but ordinary men who were called upon to do extraordinary things, and did not fail. They do not tell their tales for glory, but because they want those of us who follow them in life to remember the lessons of history, and to hold dear the memories of their comrades, and the sacrifices that they made.

'For people to turn around and say, "Oh, they want to forget all that," that annoys me, because anybody that has experienced it can never honestly say they forget it. Anybody who served in the front, or in anything connected with the aftermath of the frontline – that includes medical services and that – will never forget it.'

These were the words of Joe Abbot, who served in the Royal Armoured Corps, one of the army's three 'teeth arms' (the others being the Royal Artillery and the Infantry). I have focused on accounts given by soldiers from these branches because it was they, by and large, who suffered the greatest privations in the field, and they who had to close with and kill the enemy. They did not win the war alone, and I do not seek to downplay the role of any other branch, or that of soldiers in other theatres of the war. The final defeat of Germany was a truly colossal undertaking, the likes of which had never been witnessed in Europe before and, God willing, will never be witnessed again.

Geraint Jones

CHAPTER 1

The Loneliest Club in the World

Plans, Preparations and Soldiers
Christmas 1944 – 7 February 1945

'Normandy was an exciting adventure. We were green kids, going in. It was what we'd been waiting for to get a go at them, it was all exciting.

Feelings were different (now). We were living on our nerves. We'd had enough. We'd lost so many men, and good friends. We'd seen so many go, and so many new ones come. It was going to be our turn soon. It was the inevitability of it all. It was just a matter of time until you got yours.

None of us expected to live.'

Ronald 'Ronnie' Henderson,
13th/18th Royal Hussars

Perhaps nowhere are the comforts of home, and the milestones of life, more appreciated than on a frontline of war.

'They sent me out on a patrol down the riverbank on Christmas Eve,' said Fred Cooper, a Londoner in the 2nd Battalion, King's Royal Rifle Corps, who were holding positions on the River Meuse. 'We got down the riverbank, and we was laying down, and all of a sudden, it must have been a recording of a German choir, and it blasted out across the river. It had a strange effect on us, you know.

Conscious of the fact that the Germans were aware that it was Christmas, and so were we.'

Fred had been called up for service in November 1939, at the age of twenty. He had gone to war willingly, eager to get to grips with his nation's enemy.

'I think people of my age had a different attitude compared to the older generation that had suffered all the hardships and deprivation and misery and grief of the First World War.'

Fred saw his first action in 1942, and fought at El Alamein. He was later wounded in Normandy and evacuated to England, but longed to rejoin his comrades.

'The lads that I'd been with in the desert, in Italy, and in Normandy, you felt part of a family. And if you wasn't with 'em – as much as when you're out there you wanna get home – you feel like you're a coward. You're duckin' out, or somethin'. Within a week I was on my way. And when I got there, surprisingly enough, they were no less than two hundred yards from when I'd left them.'

Fred was one of the 'old soldiers' who formed the spine of the British Liberation Army's divisions. These were the veterans who could spot an ambush and 'smell' an enemy, and while they were not invincible, they were entirely invaluable.

After more than seven months of near-continuous battle, the highly trained British Liberation Army that had landed in Normandy no longer existed. Tens of thousands of casualties meant tens of thousands of replacements, and these arrived fresh out of four months of training, and without the benefit of the extra time spent honing skills and gelling with their comrades as a fighting force. They were green and raw and would rely upon the experience of canny veterans to survive, some of whom were only teenagers themselves.

Some seventy miles south of Fred Cooper, in the Ardennes, nineteen-year-old Bob Atkinson was enjoying a break from his frozen trench, eating Christmas dinner in a school classroom.

'We got turkey and all this, but it were tinned stuff. To get owt was alright. I think we got one bottle of beer per man. It was a hot meal. You got a hot meal and it was served on't tables in school rooms. That was summat. Better than eatin' out a mess tin.'

From South Ulverston, Bob had left school in August 1939 at the age of fourteen and was employed by the Post Office at the onset of the war. He delivered call-up papers in the mail, and knew that his own would eventually come.

'Me mother was worried, and I think me dad calmed her down by saying, "Oh, it'll all be over soon." But he knew it wouldn't be over soon. They'd said that about (the) First World War.'

Bob's family was no stranger to battle. His grandfather had fought in the Boer War, and his father in the First, where he was wounded three times, and gassed. Bob's own campaign began in Normandy and led him across North West Europe with the 1st Battalion, East Lancashire Regiment. He carried a Bren gun, but more often than not it was a shovel or pick that he was using in anger, digging narrow slit trenches in which the infantryman lived, slept and fought.

'I dug more holes than borough council,' Bob laughed.

During their time in the Ardennes, Bob's battalion suffered many casualties from frostbite, trench foot and shrapnel.

'The weather was bad. Murky. Mists. Freezing. Snow. Try going through trees with snow on the branches. It was down the back of your neck. No proper clothes for it.'

More men were lost in an attack on Grimbiémont on 7 January.

'The company I was with was down to about twenty-five or thirty men out of well over a hundred. There was no corporals, sergeants, nothing.'

Five years into its second world war, Britain was running out of men.

Scraping the Barrel

Corporal John Dobbs and Sergeant Tom Myers would be going into Germany with the 9th Battalion, Durham Light Infantry, and the stories of how they came to be there are emblematic of the British Army's casualty replacement needs, and man-power shortage, in the latter stages of the war.

Tom, a miner from Spennymoor, joined the territorials in May

1939 and went to France with 10 DLI on two occasions – the first in 1940, as part of the British Expeditionary Force, and the second in June 1944. On the 31st of that month he suffered wounds to his throat and side, and was evacuated to England.

John, who was orphaned as a child, was conscripted into the South Wales Borderers in 1940. The day after the D-Day landings he was informed that his battalion was being broken up to provide replacements to those now in Normandy.

John arrived in France in June and was drafted into 10 DLI. His time with the battalion came to an end in August, after an attack on the Mézidon chateau resulted in large numbers of casualties. 'I think I was about the only corporal who came back,' he said.

John lost several friends in the bloody action, some of whom had been with him for four years. 'It's like a family being broken up.' 10 DLI's casualties were by this time so heavy that it was disbanded. 'Those of us who survived were sent to the 9th Battalion.'

Meanwhile, Tom Myers had recovered from his injuries and returned to France in September with a draft of sixty other Durhams. When Tom, the senior NCO present, was told to take the draft to join the Green Howards he ignored the order and instead reported to 6 DLI, who were the nearest battalion belonging to his regiment. He was fortunate that the CO was glad of the men, and that he shielded Tom from the fallout. Tom was clearly a well-trusted leader, and was made acting Company Sergeant Major of A Company before the month's end.

Two months later, after more fierce fighting in Holland, the 50th Division – of which both 6 and 9 DLI were a part – was broken up.

'The 6th and 8th (Battalions) were sending some (men) back as a small cadre to train people in England,' said Tom, who was himself asked to train a number of sergeants before they left. Many of those holding the rank had landed in Normandy as privates. They had been promoted several times to fill dead men's shoes because of their leadership abilities, but had never been trained on the methods of instruction, and other duties of a Senior NCO.

While a nucleus of 6 and 8 DLI would return to England, the

9th would join 7th Armoured Division – the Desert Rats – themselves one of the longest-campaigning divisions in the army. Tom agreed that the decision to disband 50 Division was the right one, and that many of the division's old soldiers had reached the end of their endurance.

'They were all tired. They'd had enough. You can only do so much. I mean, put a boxer in a ring and he can only go on and on so long, and at the time he's gonna get worn down, and he's gonna get wavy. And he'll know he's gonna get a good hiding, sometime.'

Tom recalled stories of men who did not believe their luck could continue to carry them from Dunkirk, and through North Africa, Italy, and from the invasion of Normandy to the end of the war. Personally, he was not overly concerned about the disbandment.

'50 Division, in a way, to some it meant summat. To others it meant nothing. It was the battalion that counted. Your company. Then your platoon. Then your section. And as I've said before, the frontline's the loneliest club in the world.'

Tom now had the opportunity to leave that club and see out the war as an instructor in England. Instead, he volunteered to transfer to the 9th Battalion.

'I wasn't worried about war. It's not that I wanted to go and kill anybody, or shoot anybody, or be killed. It just had become part of me life then.'

Tom and forty others from 6 DLI joined B Company, in the 9th Battalion, and it wasn't long before he showed both his experience, and courage. On 21 January, in action at St Joost, Tom was returning from Company HQ and found himself cut off from his platoon by around twenty of the enemy. And they were coming his way.

Tom allowed the enemy soldiers to approach to within fifteen yards before opening fire with his Sten gun, killing and wounding eight or nine. The remainder retreated behind a house.

Tom waited for them to appear once more then threw three or four grenades, causing more casualties and the rest to disperse. He then continued on to his platoon, running into two German soldiers and killing them at point-blank range. Single handedly he had broken the encirclement of his platoon, for which he was awarded the Distinguished Conduct Medal.[1]

John Dobbs was injured in the same action, but returned to the battalion in March. With Britain so desperate for men, only the most serious wound could end a soldier's war and a man might spend as long in hospital as he had in training before being returned to the frontline. Others tried to get back almost immediately, and had what today might be labelled as 'separation anxiety'. For the soldiers, this was simply the bond of comradeship.

David 'Dai' Edwards, a twenty-one-year-old from Abergavenny, had been wounded in Normandy while serving with the 2nd Battalion, Monmouthshire Regiment.

'There was this feeling, *I've got to get back there.*'

And though this was true of many soldiers, there were others who were determined to ensure that their war was over.

'We'd had these examinations, and we knew we were being prepared to go back as soon as we possibly could. One evening, I could hear – I'm reluctant at times to tell people this, but it's as it was – I could hear this thump, thump, thump in the next room.

'I walked in, and there was one of the fellas, and he had a bucket of water, and he had a towel, and he'd knotted the end of the towel and that was in the water. He was smashing his knee, and it's no exaggeration to say his knee was black and blue.

'I said, "You'll ruin your knee." And he said, "I don't care. I'm not going back."

'That affected me tremendously. I thought, *Well, you're a bit of a swine.*'

Less than one per cent of the British Army's battle-casualties and injuries in North West Europe came from self-inflicted wounds,[2] and the morale of the army was considered high. This related to the soldiers' willingness to go into battle, and did not mean that they always accepted their lot without complaint.

After Dai passed his medical examination he was informed that he would be sent to a different battalion than the one that he'd left. To this he strongly objected, but his words seemingly fell on deaf ears. He was told: 'You are a soldier. You will go where you're posted.'

'I didn't like that one little bit. I was very resentful.'

On the back of a lorry heading to the front, Dai saw biscuit tins with holes punched in them, the light of hurricane lamps glowing within. A downward-facing arrow signalled that one was travelling to the rear, while an upward-facing arrow meant the direction of the frontline.

'Then it was getting light. I saw a couple of fellas at the side of the track, and when we got near enough I could see that one of the fellas had the Monmouthshires (insignia).'

Dai was elated.

'It turned out to be our battalion, and I got back to the same company, same platoon.'

Tom Bryan, 7 Somerset Light Infantry, was one of three brothers serving in the army. It was common for all of a family's siblings to be serving in the latter stages of the war, particularly for men.

'There was so many (brothers) getting killed that they used to put them in different battalions so that they stood a better chance.'

Tom had been one of the thousands of casualties suffered at Hill 112, in Normandy, and rejoined his company at Nijmegen. He had only been gone a matter of months, but was shocked to see how few of the Normandy men remained.

'There was only about five or six of them left. Most of them had been killed or wounded. This Lance Corporal (George Dodd), as soon as he seen me he was crying his eyes out, I'll never forget it.

'I said, "What are you crying for, Corp?" I knew him well.

'"Oh," he said. "A lot of our lads got killed like, you know. Seeing you, I was overcome."

'I said, "Don't worry, son, I'm still around, like."'

Tom would survive the war. Lance Corporal George Dodd, twenty-nine years old, did not. He was killed outside of Bremen, three weeks before peace.[3]

Sergeant Harry Simpson, from Leeds, had joined the army a few months before the war, and served in 7th Battalion, the Black Watch. By the end of 1944 he had already been wounded several times on several continents, and he recalled one 'laughable incident' in hospital after his most recent injury, which had been caused by shrapnel in the Ardennes.

'The staff-sergeant came down from the Medical Corps, he says, "Now listen. In a short while the matron will be coming in to see you. When she gets to the end of your bed you must be laid to attention."

'I says, "Attention be buggered! We're in a hospital. Don't be bloody daft."'

Harry was soon after taken to Amiens for convalescence, but he was eager to get back to his comrades.

'The Doctor says to me, "I'm afraid you're not going back to your unit. This is the fourth wound you've had, and I can't send you back."

'I said, "Be buggered! If you don't send me back, I'm going back on me own, I'll tell you that now!"'

Harry's subtle diplomacy did the trick. He rejoined the 7th Black Watch in the Nijmegen area, where they were preparing to take part in the invasion of Germany.

'By God, we had some times there. Good and bad.'

Britain's Khaki Melting Pot

It was something of an uncomfortable moment when Victor 'Vic' Sayer arrived at the 2nd Battalion, King's Shropshire Light Infantry, in late December 1944. Vic, a Second Lieutenant, was to take over command of 13 Platoon from its sergeant, who had been leading the platoon 'with distinction' for some time.

'And I thought, God, he's going to resent me coming in. But he didn't. If he did, he didn't show it, and I was made very welcome by the platoon. It was very democratic in those days.'

This more 'democratic' approach to military leadership was the result of the BLA being largely a citizen army. Junior officers like Vic, who was twenty years old, were often in command of men who were both their senior in age and experience, and while this is the norm in the army, it can come under particular strain when a large number of the soldiers are conscripts rather than volunteers.

'It's a difficult job to keep men under control in a platoon like that,' said Aubrey 'Bruce' Coombs, 6th Battalion, Royal Welch Fusiliers. 'People don't know what it's like. I respect an officer who's been a platoon commander more than anyone else in the back. He's the man who had to keep the platoon in order, and keep everything going.

'Every one of them was brave, I never knew one who wasn't. You know, you looked up to them. You looked for leadership.'

The attrition of junior officers was so high that NCOs often had to step up and command platoons, such as had been the case for Vic Sayer's platoon.

'The sergeants that we had were exactly the same as officers,' said Bruce. 'They should have been made officers. Jimmy Wiley was in charge of the platoon without an officer for a long time until he got killed, and we all looked up to him because he was a brave man.'[4]

Tank crews, spending endless hours in the confines of their armour, got to know their own officers especially well.

'You get to know officers by living with 'em,' said Denis Whybro, 1st Fife and Forfar Yeomanry. 'I had all the confidence in the world (in mine).'

Denis would be on first-name terms with his officer inside of their tank, but referred to him by rank or 'sir' outside it.

'When you sleep with 'em, eat with 'em, you get like a family.'

The army brought together men from all corners of Britain, which came with some peculiar difficulties – particularly for an Englishman serving in a Scots regiment, like Denis.

'They were a bit fiery, and you can't understand some of them. There was a bloke called Williams, I knew him all the time I was in the Fife and Forfar, but I never could understand him.'

The British class system was also strongly felt in the army. As a generalization, those from the upper and middle class served as officers, while the working class made up the other ranks. There were, of course, exceptions.

'I was right in the middle (of the 'Great English Class System'),' said Stewart Irwin, Rifle Brigade. 'I was, I suppose, a typical middle-class boy when I went into the army.

'My first evening in barracks, I was standing by my bed, and a tiny Cockney looked me up and down. "You long cunt," he said, which was a good start. There was a lot of resentment because of the way I spoke. There was quite a lot of it, and this didn't really disappear until we went abroad, and they realized that they had to depend on me for their lives, and all the rest of it.

'Once I was having a meal and somebody shouted at me, "People like your father put my old man out of work!" and things like that. As you can appreciate, the thirties weren't far behind. There was a lot of resentment.

'You'd be called "college boy" and "professor", and all the rest of it.

'And of course, as far as the officers were concerned, they didn't like me being a ranker. They thought that I ought to have gone into officers' training and become an officer.

'I wasn't interested. Not remotely interested. I was an art student.'

Stewart pointed out that both his treatment by officers and enlisted was not universal, and many treated him perfectly amicably. Attitudes to the war itself also differed.

'You got one or two death and glory boys, I called them, who were absolutely dead set on getting a medal, and they went right across the board. Right through the officers, and right through the men, right down to the ordinary rifleman. But the general attitude was "let's get this over and done with as fast as possible, and get back into civilian life".'

Preparation

The willingness of Britain's soldiers to fight, the training that they received before the battlefield, and the leadership that they received on it were all keys that could unlock a final victory in Germany, but only if applied in combination.

'If you're not trained, you're not an army,' said Denis Whybro, 1 Fife and Forfar. 'I don't think you can do anything unless you have absolute confidence in the troops you command.'

Soldiers, with their lives on the line, also needed to have this confidence in their commanders. Bob Atkinson and the men of A Company, 1 East Lancs, had full trust in theirs.

Born and raised in Clapham, Major Ferdinand 'Joe' Cêtre was the son of a French father and German mother. Nicknamed 'Stalin' for his thick black moustache, Joe was a pre-war regular soldier and joined the British Expeditionary Force in April 1940, earning a Military Cross during the battalion's rearguard actions at Dunkirk, and a second during fighting in the Ardennes four years later. He was a highly respected officer, and treated his men accordingly – giving them the utmost preparation to survive the coming battles in Germany. This was particularly important given that the East Lancs received a draft of 284 replacements prior to Operation Veritable, as well as thirty-five returning casualties – almost a third of a battalion's full strength, and a testament to the painful experience of the East Lancs in the Ardennes. They had since been quartered in Helmond to prepare for their next campaign.

'It was a period of intensive preparation, and we were there quite a long time,' recalled Joe. 'From the eighteenth of January to the sixth of February, this was preparation in every way. We were brought up to strength, to thirty-seven officers, 914 other ranks, which was over the Battle Strength of a battalion, normally 800 or so.

'A lot of things went on. A lot of exercises. Soldiers weren't just left lying around sleeping, and one thing or another. There was some very tough exercises on ground similar to the Reichswald, and on objectives which we considered we might have to tackle, and one of those was carried out in a howling gale.

'There were a lot of studies of air photos and periodic bringing up to date with intelligence information as to what the Germans had in (the Reichswald), and table exercises to work out tactics and the conduct of operations, and in fact it was altogether a very intensive period.'

'We were doing training because we had that many reinforcements,' said Bob Atkinson, who served under Joe in A Company. 'About twenty-one, twenty-two of us had been in action. (The rest) were straight from England. There might have been a few wounded that had come back, but the sixty that I saw, I don't think there'd be above four that had been in action. They were raw recruits.'

1 East Lancs were one of the three English and Scottish battalions in the 53rd (Welsh) Division, replacing the three Welsh/Welsh Border battalions sent to join 11th Armoured Division in 1943. At first these 'non-native' battalions in the Welsh Division served together in one brigade – wryly referred to as the International Brigade – but the division was further reshuffled in August 1944, mixing 'international' and Welsh battalions in the same brigades. This was to avoid mass casualties being inflicted upon villages, towns and counties in a single day, as had befallen the division that July, at Évrecy in Normandy.

Nineteen-year-old Bruce Coombs, 6 RWF, had taken part in that bloody battle.

'I should have listened to my father,' he laughed. 'I shouldn't have volunteered. But he'd done the same as me. He volunteered. You don't listen to your father and mother, do you?'

Bruce recalled the battalion's planning and preparation in late January, after they came out of the Ardennes.

'You used to get (briefings) with aircraft photographs and all, you know? Showing you where all the ditches were, and trenches were, and things like that. You'd be behind the line, waiting to go up, and then the officer would get called back to HQ for a briefing. Then they'd come and call sergeants, and he'd get a briefing, then he'd brief us then. It was pretty well organized.'

But although at times the men would be given specifics about a coming action, they were often in the dark about the bigger picture.

'We didn't know where we were going, but the Dutch people did. They told us, you're going up to Nijmegen tomorrow.'

This was the assembly area for the coming battle, where the mass of troops gathering was a familiar sight for the army's experienced soldiers.

Nineteen-year-old Tom Gore, from Devon, had returned to the 9th Cameronians (Scottish Rifles) after being wounded in Normandy. As his division, the 15th (Scottish), got near to Nijmegen, 'we heard the rumble of the guns again, and the military presence was really big. We passed 51st Highland Division. 53rd Welsh Division. 43rd Wessex.'

Each of these divisions numbered some 15,000 men, but only around half were infantry soldiers. As well as a headquarter and logistical element, the infantry divisions had their own artillery, reconnaissance, and engineer contingents, all of which was to support the division's three infantry brigades, made up of three battalions a piece. It was they who bore the brunt of the division's fighting and, consequently, its casualties.

'The platoon I left in Normandy was virtually non-existent now,' said Tom. 'The only person I knew, he was a corporal in Normandy. He was now the platoon sergeant. Sergeant Rose.

'We ended up at a windowless school with a load of Guards Armoured tanks. So we laid our blankets on the floor, slept on the floor.

'The next day we were briefed. And obviously this was to be the big one.

'It was the Siegfried Line.'

The Plan

Ian Hammerton had joined the Territorial Army in 1938, when war seemed all but inevitable, and in early September 1939 he was working at a bank in London. 'One could just see the newspaper sellers with their placards with "War About to Be Declared", and "TA call-up". So that was the end of banking.'

Ian's regiment – the 22nd Dragoons – were equipped with tanks fitted with chain flails for clearing paths through minefields. On D-Day Ian had been one of the first men to land on Juno Beach, and he would now be one of the first to lead the break-in to Germany. The significance of the moment was not lost on him.

'The Siegfried Line had played such a big role in the army right from 1939 – "We're going to Hang out The Washing on the Siegfried Line."'

The defiant lyrics of this popular song might have helped the nation's morale, but the reality of breaking through this fortified line was daunting. In November 1944, in order to clear a enemy salient on the front, Operation Clipper had been launched on a portion of the Siegfried Line in the area of Geilenkirchen. The two-week operation cost 2,000 Allied casualties, leaving Ian and other soldiers in no doubt about what lay ahead for them in Germany.

'I do know that several members of my troop, particularly the older members, were not at all keen to go on leave before that. They said they wouldn't be able to bring themselves to come back, and some of them deliberately refused to go on leave for that reason.'

The offensive into Germany's Rhineland – known as Operation Veritable – was to be the largest operation mounted by the 21st Army Group since Normandy. Field Marshal Montgomery detailed General Crerar and the First Canadian Army to lead it, supplying numerous British divisions and brigades to bolster its strength. The two nations' armies had a long history of working side by side, and the trust and respect between them was implicit.

Crerar's plan was to deploy his troops south-east of Nijmegen on the Dutch border, attacking on a five-division front through the natural corridor formed by the Maas and Rhine rivers. Blocking much of their route was the more than thirty square miles of the Reichswald Forest, which the enemy considered impassable to tanks and large formations of men, but through which Crerar would push both armour and infantry.

To the north of the Reichswald was a stretch of open land around 5,000 yards deep which led to the town of Kleve – this was where the First Canadian Army planned on punching through the German defences, and sending armoured columns racing to seize bridges on the Rhine in the area of Xanten and Wesel.

Four days before the operation began, Crerar told his commanders that, if everything worked in their favour, he would not be surprised if their armour reached the Rhine in a matter of days. 'On the other hand, if conditions are against us, the battle may well last three weeks.'[5]

American soldiers would also fight in the Rhineland. A day after the First Canadian Army launched Operation Veritable, the Ninth US Army would launch Operation Grenade from the south, in the area of the Roer, in order to squeeze the German forces in a pincer move, and finish them off with the Anglo-American forces side by side on the Rhine.

The bulk of the German forces in the Rhineland were a mixture of infantry and paratrooper divisions. These formations were already understrength at the beginning of the battle, but the paratroopers in particular were well-equipped, and highly motivated soldiers. The German soldiers also possessed a large amount of automatic weapons. Some, like the Schmeisser, were personal weapons, while others were crew-served machine guns – variants of the latter were collectively known as spandaus by the British soldiers, a carry-over from the First World War.

The enemy's reserves in the Rhineland comprised of the 116th Panzer Division, a division of paratroopers, and a division of Panzer-Grenadiers. They were supported by a large concentration of artillery but had little in the way of air support – something that the Allies had in abundance, so long as the winter weather permitted. What the Luftwaffe did have, however, was the world's first jet fighter, and these would terrorize many a British soldier in the coming weeks.

The frontline of the German defences was made up of trenches and strongpoints fronted by minefields, but the defence of the Rhineland depended on depth – stretching back for miles to the banks of the Rhine were fortified buildings, villages and towns that would need to be taken, often at the point of the bayonet.

Allied success would lie in careful reconnaissance, a massive build-up of artillery, armour and infantry, and, most importantly, the willingness of those men to risk their lives and use violence to achieve their aims.

Once briefings had been completed, the troops had nothing to do but prepare their kit, check their weapons, and think. This was the time when doubt and worry could enter a soldier's mind. Perhaps aware of this, the officers of Tom Gore's company made sure that the men were kept occupied, and entertained.

'Come the night, we had a sort of company concert.'

The show was put on by three of the company's officers, though Tom could not recall their names.

'Officers didn't stay long. They came and went,' he explained, referring to the high rate of casualties among platoon commanders. 'Two of these officers was missing when we came out of the Siegfried Line. Ours was the only platoon with an officer.'

'Blue' entertainment was provided by one of the enlisted ranks.

'Rifleman Baker was a Cockney, and he was telling dirty jokes. The door opened and the padre walked in, so we had to pack up that and we had a sing-song. We went to bed that night and the planes started to come over.'

This was a force of 285 Lancaster bombers headed for Kleve. General Brian Horrocks, commanding the British XXX Corps, recalled making the decision to order the attack.

'One day Crerar visited me and said that, in addition to the whole of the Tactical Air Force being able to support the attack, the "Heavies" from Bomber Command were at my disposal. He then said, "Do you want Cleve taking out?"

'I knew that Cleve was a lovely old historic Rhineland town. Anne of Cleves, Henry VIII's fourth wife, came from there. No doubt a lot of civilians, plus women and children, were still living there. Their fate depended on how I answered Crerar's question, and I simply hated the thought of Cleve being "taken out".'[6]

Knowing that Kleve was the hub through which German reinforcements would come, and that it was a crucial objective to seize before reaching the Rhine, General Horrocks decided that 'the lives of my own troops must come first. So I said "yes" – the most terrible decision I have ever had to make in my life, and I can assure you that I felt almost physically sick when, on the night before the attack, I saw the bombers flying overhead on their deadly mission.'[7]

Richard Dimbleby, a correspondent for the BBC, was flying on Kleve in a Lancaster of No. 153 Squadron:

'There is the town, the junction we're attacking, lit like London on its brightest day, but not lit only by the light of flares – the lights of bombs that are bursting, and incendiaries that are bursting too. There ahead of us are great clouds going up into the sky, and red fires growing thick and crimson inside them.

'If my voice is strained, and if perhaps I'm not speaking as fluently as I should, you must forgive me. I had no idea we were going to see anything like this.'[8]

'The scene ahead was fantastic,' said Flying Officer Roy Yule DFC, a pilot in No. 626 Squadron: 'Red and yellow tracer shells were crisscrossing from the flak batteries outside the town. They seemed to be coming from eight different positions and looked like 20mm and 37mm, which are nasty blighters at the height we were at. Strings of bombs were falling through the cloud from the Lancs above. Flashes from the exploding blockbusters on the ground were blinding. A stricken Lancaster crashed on its run-in, blowing up with its full bomb load.'[9]

The use of these massive Blockbuster bombs seemingly went against General Horrocks' request that only incendiaries be used on Kleve. Instead, more than 1,300 tons of high explosive were dropped on the historic town, which had already been bombed several times before, and 80 per cent of it lay in burning ruins. The majority of the civilian population had already been evacuated, but a hundred Ukrainian forced labourers, locked in the town's prison, were killed in the bombing.

As the explosions of the raid rumbled in the distance, the soldiers waiting to attack from Holland tried to snatch what sleep they could, but the anticipation of action must have made this a near-impossible feat.

'Blanket rolling was half past one,' said Bob Atkinson. 'You rolled up your blankets and took them to a truck. Then you got breakfast, two o'clock I think it was, something like that. Then you waited for your moving-off time.'

Lieutenant Ian Hammerton would be at the head of the advance.

'On the morning of the do we were up at about three o'clock in the morning, and I can remember cold bacon sandwiches. *I hate cold bacon sandwiches*, especially at that hour of the morning.

'We moved up into Groesbeek, did our final radio checks and everything there, and then the word: "Go!"'

PART I

Operation Veritable

The Battle of the Reichswald and Rhineland

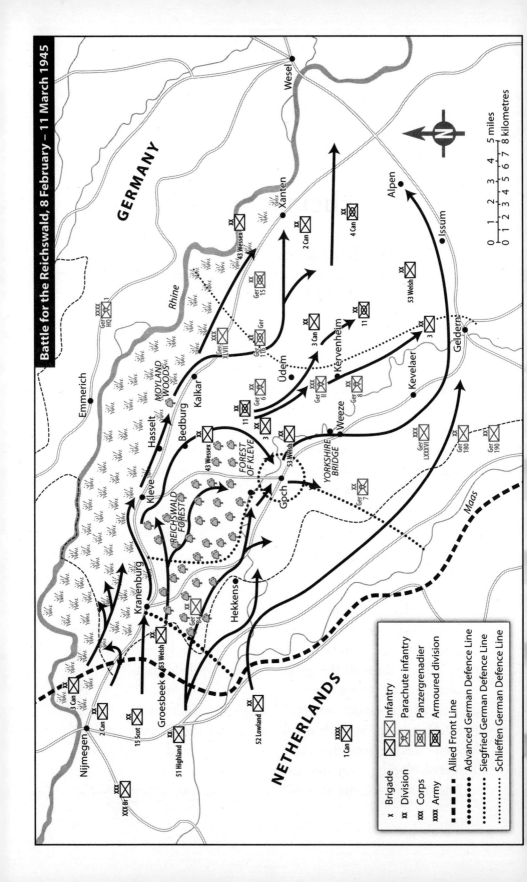

CHAPTER 2

Highlanders

*51st (Highland) Division in the Reichswald,
and on the Gennep–Goch road
8–12 February 1945*

'They realized that they couldn't withstand the heavy barrage. We couldn't hardly stand it either, but we had to. And then they came running out in panic. Unfortunately for them, some of them still had their weapons in their hand. You just shot them, and they fell in front of us. The colonel says to me, he says, "Simpson, shoot that man." And there's a man running towards him, his arms are flying all over the place. But we didn't realize he was giving himself up, and we just shot him. Down he fell.'

Harry Simpson, 7th Battalion, The Black Watch

Darkness is descending on the Reichswald.

It falls more like fog than night. The space between the trunks fills and blurs, the density of trees seeming to multiply as though one is looking through the grubby lens of a kaleidoscope.

Gone are the ordered rows of trees that stood here eighty years ago. Instead, I meander between saplings and thick beech, a carpet of mulching leaves beneath my boots, the occasional sharp snap of a branch cracking beneath a clumsy foot. The ground is steeper than I expected, sloping away into the gloom.

After a time I come to a clearing, mist draped across it like a cobweb. It is no wider than fifty yards, no longer than a hundred, but in the winter dusk it's impossible to pick out the kind of shapes that might threaten your life, if someone had a mind to end it.

I come to the evidence of such times. The ground is dropping away now. A few hundred yards distant, lights flicker, the sound of traffic dampened by the woods. Cutting through the ground is a zigzagging pattern, a trough for leaves, but eighty autumns have not erased the marks of war. I tread through trenches, and weapons pits – all looking down the slope, a perfect killing ground.

Whether or not men fought and died in this exact position I do not know, but it would be hell to defend, and worse to attack. And in the moments between: cold, wet, miserable, disorientating, claustrophobic and lonely.

Standing on the lip of a trench, I understand – as much as I will ever be able to – the words of General Brian Horrocks, and his recollection of visiting his soldiers in the Reichswald:

'I almost stumbled over two young soldiers crouching in a very muddy trench. They were all alone and could see none of their comrades. Here, I thought, is the cutting edge of this vast military machine.'[1]

Ronald 'Ron' Hann, a platoon sergeant in C Company, 5th Battalion, Queen's Own Cameron Highlanders, had been on that cutting edge since El Alamein. More than three years later, in the early hours of 8 February, he noticed several signs in an otherwise ordinary field as he marched towards the frontline. They were marked: 'HD Cemetery, which meant (that it was) our divisional cemetery.'

Ron was looking at the ground in which he and his comrades might soon be buried.

'War is death, and that is something you have to live with.'

The mission of Ron's division during the opening stage of Veritable was 'to capture the high ground to the north of the (southwest) corner of the Reichswald Forest. It was then to swing south and occupy that part of the forest and to hold down any attempts by the enemy to move troops north in that area.'[2] They would be aided in doing so by a mass of artillery, elements of the Guards

Armoured Division, specialist armour of 79th Armoured Brigade, and tanks of the 34th and 8th Armoured Brigades.

'Our brief was that we would be shooting in the infantry of the 51st (Highland) Division,' said tank crewman Ronald Mole, 4th/7th Royal Dragoon Guards. 'It was a moonlit night. It was crisp. And round about twenty past four, out there in the forest, a piper started playing a dirge with his foot on a log. It made my hair stand on the back of my neck, and he was on my side! I don't know what the Germans felt like, just over the other side in the forest.'

At 0500 hrs, the guns began to roar.

'We had the biggest fire plan – barrage – that we'd ever fired anywhere,' said Edward Palmer, of the 52nd (Bedfordshire Yeomanry) Heavy Regiment, Royal Artillery. 'An absolute, solid mass of artillery to blast our way (in).'

'The battalion rises to the reverberating noise of fierce and unending fire,' wrote the war diarist of the 7th Black Watch.[3]

Serving in this battalion was Sergeant Harry Simpson, who had rejoined B Company after being wounded in the Ardennes. 'I went back to my old platoon, 10 Platoon.'

Even an old hand like Harry – who was twenty-three – was impressed by the weight of the barrage that opened the battle.

'We had an artillery support there which in my estimation equalled El Alamein. Not as long as El Alamein, but it was an intensity, by God. The ground I stood on was shaking. Even the trees were shaking.'

The fire of the artillery was bolstered by that of hundreds of tanks, parked cheek by metal jowl in long armoured lines.

'After two hours of firing, the rifling of our barrels were gone,' said Ronald Mole. 'Finished. The idea then was to go back and get new barrels. The air was absolutely foul with cordite fumes. It didn't take long to be overcome by these fumes. As long as you were able, you were firing and getting rid of as many shells as you could. It was just a solid wall of steel behind which the infantry were advancing.'

The tanks' crews would rotate, taking turns loading, firing and handing up ammunition from beside the tank. Ronald was passing a shell up to his officer when 'there was just a soft swish, which apparently came from a sniper that had been stuck in a tree for I don't know how long, and it struck the shell that Captain Martin was holding.'

The tank round exploded, causing Captain Martin to suffer multiple fractures. The blast also caught Ronald in the face, and threw him 'two or three feet': 'I lost all interest in the war then, as you can imagine.'

As Ronald, his officer and other casualties were taken away from the front for treatment, the infantry were making their way forwards to their forming-up points and start lines, where they would await an H-Hour of 1030 hrs.

Harry Simpson and his men had got into position, and were watching the barrage fall, when one of the NCOs reported that a soldier had taken off and run to the rear. Harry looked around and saw a farm building that was a likely hiding place. He found the deserter just as the man placed one hand over the muzzle of his rifle and pulled the trigger with the other.

'He put a bullet through his (hand), and I threw a bayonet. Fortunately it didn't stick in him. Fortunate for him,' Harry added.

The self-inflicted wound would keep the man out of the battle, and Harry returned to the start line without him. Private Macdonald, an old soldier who had earned a place in the rear echelon of the battalion, was brought up to replace the deserter.

'And he took his place, never a word. A wonderful soldier, were Mac. Only a little chap – he only stood about five foot two – but by God, what a soldier he were.'

At 1046 hrs, the battalion's H-Hour, Harry put a whistle to his lips and blew.

As their own artillery roared overhead and crashed into the Siegfried Line, the 7th Black Watch rose up from the ground and advanced. Such was the devastation of the barrage that the Highlanders found it difficult to navigate, as many of the features that they had learned from aerial photographs and model pits were now just splintered trees and demolished buildings. 10 Platoon's objective was a farmhouse that 'was just rubble'. They were about a hundred yards short when the enemy opened up, pinning the platoon down and preventing any further advance.

'I thought, *Oh, bugger this*,' said Harry. '*I might as well die bloody standing as led down here*, so I jumped up, put a hand in a little bag of hand grenades that I had with me. I took one out, pulled the pin out and ran forward. I threw a grenade and carried on running to where it had exploded. There was a machine-gun nest there, finished.'

The rest of the platoon rushed up to join Harry. 'Corporal Mills ran up on my left, followed by little Macdonald. And I'm stood there like a bloody fool waving them on.'

Bullets began to tear through the air.

'I got a bullet through the foot,' Harry said nonchalantly. 'Corporal Mills got a bullet through him, and Little Macdonald, he just stood there, he lifted his hand up, and he says . . .' At this moment in the interview, Harry's tone changes completely. He is no longer the confident, matter-of-fact stoic who had spoken for hours, but the young soldier who saw a friend die, and the old man who knows the value of life as only someone who has lived a long one can.

He begins to cry. His voice breaks. But his words do not fail him.

'Little Macdonald lifted his hand up, and he says, "Cheerio, Ginger." Poor little bugger. He had a bullet through his heart. Poor little bugger, he should have been left out of battle. And he died all for that bastard deserter.' Harry's voice now hardens. '*All for that bastard deserter.*'

He softens just as quickly, moved by the memories of a great friend and comrade. 'He took that deserter's place. Little Mac, the great little soldier.'

Little Mac – Thomas Macdonald – was twenty years old when he was killed.[4]

'He'd been left out of battle because he'd done so much, and always in it with a bloody good heart. He finished up laying dead in the Reichswald.'

With the 1st and 7th Battalions of the Black Watch on their

objectives, the Camerons and Gordons pushed further into the forest before dawn the next day. A number of close-quarter actions followed, where tanks fired point-blank into the dugouts of the enemy, and the Highlanders charged with fixed bayonets, and even shovels.

Lieutenant Ross Le Mesurier, an officer of the 5th Camerons, gave an account that is emblematic of the fierce fighting that day:

'My head was creased by a bullet, then a piece of shrapnel hit my back. The day dragged on, our progress was slow and darkness came early. Our company wireless operator was badly wounded and in great pain. His uncontrolled moans seemed to draw gunfire.

'I cocked a phosphorous grenade to throw it. It was hit by a bullet or piece of shrapnel and burst in my face, which was covered in blobs of burning goo. I rubbed handfuls of snow mixed with mud on my face to stop them burning.

'Some Germans started advancing towards us. A few of us charged them, firing from the hip. My Sten gun jammed so I freed my shovel. I hit one with the shovel blade in the neck. He hit the ground in a heap.'[5]

The battlefield rang to the sound of shouts and screams, gunfire and blasts, and even music.

Major Martin Lindsay served in the 1st Battalion, Gordon Highlanders. The thirty-nine-year-old had something of a national reputation as an explorer, having travelled from west to east Africa through the Congolese rainforest, and as the leader of an Arctic expedition during the 1930s. He recalled how he made use of pipers to link up with another unit.

'I was afraid that some enthusiast in the moonlight might shoot at us, so I passed word back to the two pipers with Company HQ to play the regimental march, and before long we heard the distant strain of "Cock o' the North".'[6]

Martin believed that the battle on the Siegfried Line was one of the most important battles in the long and distinguished history of the Gordon Highlanders, and that their casualties were relatively light. He credited this to the Royal Artillery battery that supported them, sometimes to the tune of 830 rounds per gun in a single day

– the equivalent of more than one shell every two minutes for twenty-four hours.[7]

The gunners of the Royal Artillery saved countless British lives during the campaign, and perhaps nowhere was this more true than at the fortified village of Hekkens.

Hekkens

Alfred Leigh, 2nd Battalion, Seaforth Highlanders, had been keen to take part in the war, feeling the call of both adventure and duty. He saw his first action in Normandy, and was an experienced soldier by the time of the 'grand slam' that was the Reichswald battle. His battalion was held in reserve on 9 February, and that afternoon they were moved to the forward assembly area on the edge of the forest, which was still under intermittent mortar fire. As they passed down the main axis of advance into the forest, the battalion came under machine-gun fire and were ordered to dig in and await morning.

'We lost one or two lads going into the forest by shelling. At the edge of the forest we dug in. Smithy and me, we heard this bloke shouting, "Help me, help me!" We didn't know if it was a Jerry or what it was.'

The experienced soldiers knew that the enemy could be trying to lure them into an ambush, but then 'the sarge come and said, "Give us a hand with a stretcher." One of the lads had been shot through the stomach, so we carried him back.'

Alfred's battalion went into the attack the next day. Their objective for 10 January was the crossroads of the Hekkens–Kranenburg road. Once seized by the 2nd Seaforths, 5th Camerons would push through and take positions astride the next lateral road, while 5th Seaforths would turn south and attack Hekkens.

The advance of the 2nd Seaforths began at 1130 hrs, with C Company in the lead, supported by a troop of tanks. Artillery fired onto the immediate objectives and those behind it.

'We had three Churchills going up the road,' said Alfred, who was with C Company and at the head of the advance. 'I'll never forget the smell of pine. I still smell that pine to this day.'

The forest – which before had been 'dead quiet. Silent. Eerie. Ghostly' – was now filled with a riot of noise.

'All of a sudden he struck us with mortars and all that, and what with the mortars striking the trees and all that, the shrapnel came down, and Corporal Andrews, he got wounded in the 'ead. I think another lad got wounded in the backside, and one or two more, and Smithy, my mate – he'd been through North Africa, so he'd seen a bit – a lump of shrapnel went right through his mess tin.'

It was one too many close calls for Smithy, who had been in and out of action for almost three years.

'He went bomb-happy,' said Alfred. 'I never saw him again.'

The leading companies were still 600 yards short of their objective when they came under this shell fire. Undaunted, they pressed forwards towards the crossroads. They then came under considerable small-arms fire from the enemy dug in around the road, and an anti-tank gun opened fire on the leading tanks.

The Seaforths met force with force.

'We did a bayonet charge,' said Alfred. 'The Churchill tank was behind us. I turned around and that got knocked out. To the left of me I saw the platoon officer go down. A young chap called Stronach, I heard him screaming out for his mother.'

Private Stronach had been hit by a mortar, the bombs bursting in the trees and raining down shrapnel. The slim chance of escape was to get below ground.

Alfred and Peter McGrory, who had served with the Eighth Army in the desert, began to dig into the sandy soil of the forest. The picks that they carried proved useless, and both men were digging with their hands when Peter pointed out a German close by. Alfred raised his weapon and fired, but soil jammed the mechanism, and the enemy soldier vanished from view. It was at this time that the pair realized that they were about thirty yards ahead of the rest of the company.

'I thought, *We're in a right state here*. So Peter said, in soldier's language, "Bugger this, we'll go back."'

Peter moved first. Alfred followed. He overtook his friend and dived for cover behind a bank of earth.

'Peter must have been a couple of seconds behind me. A mortar bomb busted on the trench, and he got wounded on the back of the 'ead.'

Alfred was unhurt, but not unshaken.

'I was in a bit of a state, then. I could hardly hold a cigarette. Anyway, the lads said, "Peter's been wounded." I said, "Oh, strewth." I couldn't believe it like, you know?'

Still shaking with nerves, Alfred found the nearest officer, who carried morphine. He then returned to his friend to administer what aid he could.

'I rolled his sleeve up, but for the life of me I couldn't put that needle into his arm. It was like rubbery, you know?'

Owing to the bravery and leadership of Alfred's sergeant and stretcher-bearers, Peter was then evacuated along with many other casualties.

'Sergeant Ross, our platoon sergeant, he did wonderful work in the forest by getting the wounded away.'

With the enemy's attention fixed on both C and D Company, the remainder of the 2nd Seaforths were able to push up onto their flanks and take positions across the road. The 5th Cameron Highlanders then launched their own attack at 1530. Their objective was the next road beyond the Seaforths.

Sergeant Ron Hann, 5th Camerons, was at the head of his battalion's push.

'We lost a lot of men, and (the Germans) lost quite a lot more, because there was bodies everywhere. There was a lot of slaughter there. It was pretty, well, pretty horrific as far as life and limb was concerned. Of course, what made it worse as far as the man on the ground was concerned, we could not use artillery – not accurately, anyway – nor air cover. Not in the forest. We weren't sure who was who. It was more or less getting towards the hand-to-hand stuff.'

'We went to cut a road, and oh my God, the machine-gun fire was terrific. They were firing onto this main road with machine guns. We sort of scrambled across, and took quite a few Germans prisoner. They threw their rifles in the air when they seen us in amongst them.'

With the road under withering fire, Ron's platoon was cut off from the rest of the battalion.

'We had flame-throwing tanks further back, and if we could get a contact, they could come and winkle the Germans that were pinning us down. We were just lying on the ground. We had no trenches, and they were more or less surrounding us.'

Ron was asked by the platoon commander to make a dash to the rear and find the supporting tanks.

'I thought, *Well, if I get up, I'm going to get shot. If I stop down here, we'll probably all get killed.* So I then said, "I'll have a go and try and get out. Try and get back across the road."

'I made a dash for it, but I didn't get far. I saw the German's head among the bushes, and he fired what I was told later was a Panzerfaust.'

These were handheld anti-tank projectiles that were both easy to fire, and lethal.

'Fortunately it landed, I think, three or four feet in front of me, which of course blew a lot of the guts out of me leg, out of the lower part of the left leg, and I was filled with shrapnel in the other leg, and hands, and in my face. Of course, that was it. I was down.'

A stretcher-bearer rushed out for Ron and was allowed safe passage by the enemy.

'They stopped firing. The Germans didn't fire at all at him, they let him go, and he came across from over the road and he dropped down beside me.'

Ron remembered the man's words: 'I don't know how the hell you're going to get out. I'm the only stretcher-bearer left.'

The Germans again held their fire as the stretcher-bearer helped Ron to the rear. Ron was then placed down behind a hedge, where a medical officer was working on 'a lot of these fellas. He was going along, taping people up and whatever. Doing what he could.'

Ron was eventually loaded onto a jeep and taken to a Canadian casualty clearing station near Nijmegen.

Harry Simpson, 7th Black Watch, had remained with his company despite his wound, and witnessed the Seaforths pulling back after their action at the crossroads.

'They'd been battered bloody stupid. Uniforms hanging off them. Limbs missing. What a state they were in. And then we were informed that we were to go and try and capture the same place.'

Harry's company commander, Major Peck, drew his men together.

'He said, "Now, I know you're all worried about seeing those lads, what's left of the Seaforths coming back. But," he says, "have a heart. Because we'll get reinforcements, and it will be only shell fire."'

Whether or not Harry believed this, he was stoic about what lay ahead.

'It was your job to do,' he said simply.

And as the 7th Battalion advanced, it soon became clear that there was more than shell fire to greet them. Indeed, the enemy used tactics that surprised even a veteran like Harry.

'I've never seen anything like this before. You saw something new (in battle) every time. We're just advancing in open formation when we heard, "Watch out, you better watch your bloody backs." Turned around – *what the hell am I looking for?* And when you turned around, you either saw it or you did not see it.'

What Harry saw was that 'the enemy had dug in slit trenches and they had covers on top. The top cover was like bread trays, full of soil and turf. And when they heard you walk past, and everything was silent to them, they popped up sharp, fired like bloody hell, and pulled it back over them.

'When we saw our chaps being shot in the back, we lost our temper. We thought, *Alright, well, this is it. No prisoners.* So we shot the lot.'

Then they came to Hekkens.

'It was a village surrounded by gun emplacements encased in concrete pillboxes. It was just like pictures we'd seen of the First World War.'

The artillery barrage that fell on Hekkens was also one that would have been familiar to veterans of the trenches. Fourteen medium, four heavy and four field artillery regiments 'softened up' the enemy's defences. A Company followed closely on the heels of the shelling, and were upon many of the defences before the German soldiers had come out of their dugouts.[8]

The 1st Fife and Forfar Yeomanry were also in support. Ivor Evans, a Welshman in a Scottish regiment, was the driver of a Crocodile flame-throwing tank.

'We were being mortared, and we were shut down. We'd closed all the hatches down. And I was looking through the periscope. And this one infantry bloke, jumping into a slit trench, and somebody had put a mine in the bottom of it, and he was blown up in front of me there. Right close to me.'

Denis Whybro served in the same regiment. Towing a trailer full of flammable jelly, the Crocodile tanks could become a funeral pyre for the crews if they were struck by a shell, or bazooka. It was a terrible thought that Denis pushed from his mind.

'You seem to overcome fear. You never thought about it at the time. You was too busy. You gotta keep your wits about you. You're keyed up, but you gotta know your job. Ain't no good thinkin' too much.'

With this in mind, Denis made a point of never looking closely at the destruction that their Crocodiles caused.

'If you got caught in the pillbox, you was dead, because (the flames) bounced round that like a rubber ball.'

The war diary of the 7th Black Watch records that some 100 prisoners were taken during the action at Hekkens, which lasted less than one hour, during which 'a considerable number of enemy (were) killed.'[9] Little of the village remained standing. Harry Simpson described the scene as 'Tree trunks, collapsed houses, rubble.'

Alfred Leigh's unit, the 2nd Seaforths, were pulled out of the line to re-group. Their casualties, particularly among NCOs, were so high that the battalion would require three days to reorganize. The battalion's badly injured were evacuated to Britain, but the wounds of some could not be survived.

'I found out that Peter died,' said Alfred.

Peter McGrory, twenty-nine years old, succumbed to his wounds on 23 February, and was buried in his hometown of Paisley.[10]

Nineteen-year-old Alfred Stronach, the soldier that Alfred had heard crying out for his mother, did not survive the battle at the crossroads.[11]

Stanley Whitehouse, 1 Black Watch, was told by a stretcher-bearer that men who cried for their mother were often fatally wounded.

'If one man was calling "stretcher-bearer" and another crying out for his mother, he invariably gave preference to the man asking for the stretcher-bearer. Experience told him that a soldier calling for his mother was usually severely wounded and probably dying anyway. It was strange how men of all nationalities, when badly hurt, cried out for their mother, never their father or their wife, always their mother. I had heard badly wounded Germans calling out "*Mutter, Mutter*", and it was often the last word they ever uttered.'[12]

Ron Hann, 5th Cameron Highlanders, had survived his own wounds and was evacuated by air to Swindon, and then taken to hospital in Cardiff. When Ron awoke from surgery, he spoke to a young female nurse who was making the rounds.

'I said, "Oh my God, my foot's sore." She pulled the (bed clothes back) and had a look.'

Ron also looked down.

'I said, "It's not there."'

His leg had been amputated.

Ron was visited soon after by the surgeon. '"I'm sorry," he said, "because we always like to warn people that we are going to take it off. In your case I hadn't time. If I'd left it on till the next day, it might have been too late for you."'

Ron's answer was stoic. 'Fair enough. If you had to take it off, that's fair enough.'

He was twenty-two years old at the time, and was told that he had not been expected to live through the night. 'I said, "Oh well, I'm still here anyway." We're now, what, fifty-five years later? And I'm still here,' he chuckled.

Twenty-five years after Ron's interview with the IWM, at first glance one would not recognize the battlefield on the southern side of the Reichswald for what it once was. The villages and farms are tidy to the point that they'd pass a regimental sergeant major's inspection, but a short walk up a steep hill into the forest, and the scars of war cannot be hidden – deep trenches, craters and concrete bunkers are overgrown with shrub and vines, filled with leaves, but unmistakable. Where men once killed each other with bullets and bayonets, shells and shovels, the occasional figure appears walking a dog, or with a grandchild, and BMX trails cut through defences that had been built to hold tanks in check. The wind gently shakes the trees, birds call to each other from the boughs, and not even the history of the forest can dim its winter beauty.

As a visitor in the eightieth year of peace, one cannot imagine the hell that had once existed in this place. And this, I am certain, is what the Highlanders would have wanted.

CHAPTER 3

Break-In

*15th and 43rd Divisions at the
Siegfried Line and Kleve
8–12 February 1945*

'(Herbie) was just about done in. He was the only one who'd got up from that lot. They weren't all killed. One was killed, one was badly wounded, and the rest were wounded with wounds enough to take them back.

That shook Herbie up quite a bit. He was weepy, and I put him down the cellar, and there was some civilians in there including a German girl, I suppose she was about sixteen, and she held his hand.'

Alfred Wooltorton, 2nd Battalion,
Argyll and Sutherland Highlanders

In the early morning of 8 February, Tom Gore and his comrades in the 9th Cameronians were moving towards their start line when they came up against an imposing force – the regimental sergeant major (RSM), who ordered the men to do up their chinstraps and buttons, and generally smarten themselves up.

'You'd think you were going to a big parade instead of going to move up under the artillery barrage!' said Tom. His march continued over rolling hillsides and through woods, the dark skies of pre-dawn lit by the brilliant flashes of a thousand guns.

'Army Group Artillery, right the way down to Vickers machine guns, were all belting off,' said Ray Ashton, of the 1st Battalion Middlesex Regiment, whose machine guns and mortars were firing as part of Operation Pepperpot. This supplementation to the traditional artillery barrage included anti-aircraft guns firing at ground targets, mortars, tank guns, anti-tank guns and machine guns, the aim to saturate the enemy-held area with fire, and deny them the freedom of movement to reinforce, and resupply. The psychological impact was also massive. Coupled with the heavy guns of the artillery, it was 'shock and awe' long before the term was coined.

'It was a frightening thing to listen to,' said Ray. 'You couldn't hear yourself speak. You had to shout in your neighbour's ear to make yourself heard. You almost felt sorry for (the Germans) really, you know?'

Ray's commanding officer, Lieutenant-Colonel John Hall, and his driver Stanley Hardman were both killed in these initial moments of the barrage when their jeep 'ran over some seventy-five grenades'.[1] They were both married men in their mid-thirties.

The majority of the casualties taken by 21st Army Group that day would be caused by enemy shells, bullets and mines at the head of the advance, but others died behind the frontline. Viscount Elveden, also known as Arthur Guinness, was a major in the Royal Artillery and part of the Guinness brewing family. He was killed in a V-2 strike near Nijmegen, the Dutch town through which supplies and soldiers were flowing to the front.

The task of punching through to Kleve, made via the narrow strip of farmland above the Reichswald, had been given to the 15th (Scottish) Division. They were to capture the village of Kranenburg, breach the Siegfried Line defences, capture the high ground of the Materborn feature that overlooks Kleve, clear and hold the town itself, and despatch strong mobile columns to capture, if possible, the villages of Üdem and Kalkar, and clear the Emmerich road up to the west bank of the Rhine. They were supported by 2nd Household Cavalry Regiment, 6th Guards Armoured Brigade, flame-throwing tanks of 141st Regiment Royal Armoured Corps, 6th Assault Regiment Royal Engineers, 1st Canadian Armoured Personnel Carrier Regiment, 49th Armoured Personnel Carrier Regiment, and specialized tanks of the 22nd Dragoons.

Lieutenant Ian Hammerton, 22nd Dragoons, commanded a troop of flail tanks, their spinning chains designed to strike and detonate buried mines, clearing lanes through which men and armour could then advance.

'I think I was leading that day, and as we came out from behind the farmhouse where the start line was, we went slap into a whopping great hole in the ground.'

Ian quickly swapped tanks with a more junior commander so that he could resume the mission.

'We set off down the forward slope, flailing away. We saw something move behind the haystack and we brought both guns to bear on it and blasted the haystack to smithereens. It turned out to be some chickens,' he laughed.

Ian then heard over the radio that there was enemy armour in the area. Nonetheless, he continued to flail up to a level crossing on a railway line, and luck seemed to be with him.

'We didn't touch a solitary mine.'

With the first lane now open for the Guards' tanks, Ian decided to flail back and create a second gap. Again he found no mines, but the rest of B Squadron were not so lucky.

'They all had terrible trouble from mines and from the very soft ground, and not all the lanes succeeded. From then on things got a bit hectic. We followed the Guards along on call. They didn't come across any terribly stiff opposition, but we were ordered not to use the road because it was to be used for troops who were directly involved, so we were told to keep to the fields.'

Film held by the Imperial War Museums shows flail tanks churning through mud, and infantry – seemingly in good spirits – riding on the top of Churchills. The long line of tanks seems unbroken, and ahead of them lies an equally solid wall of trees.

Evident in the fields are the skeletal remains of gliders that had borne the American 82nd Airborne Division to battle at Groesbeek five months earlier. More infantry follow on, some of them carrying stretchers for the inevitable. A few tanks are already immobile and listing in the mud, either casualties of mines, or weather. Thawing snow, coupled with deliberate flooding caused by the enemy's destruction of dykes and gates along the nearby major rivers, meant that the ground was saturated with water, if not flooded completely.

Ian Hammerton recalled that it took the whole day to get the squadron across the fields. 'Or (the) remains of the squadron, because a number of tanks had been knocked out on mines. And it was just an ordinary small-size field. The only vehicles that would get us through were the Guards' recovery Churchills. We had to haul each tank through.'

The bombardment had been massive, the tanks were numerous, but the coming battle would be decided by the infantry, who slipped and trudged their way through mud, hedgerows and shattered forest, and all the while in the face of the enemy.

It wasn't long before they found them.

'I can remember these Germans, initially, coming out in droves,' said Ray Ashton. 'You think it's going to be a walk-over. It never is, of course. They were very quick at recovering. In a short space of time, we encountered opposition. Stiff opposition.'

The Poor Bloody Infantry

Mines were beginning to claim lives, and limbs, as the infantry advanced across the fields. The war diary of the 2nd Argylls recorded that their B Company were held up for a time in a thickly sown minefield, causing them to fall behind the creeping barrage. One of the company's NCOs, Sergeant Page, attempted to lead his platoon across but trod on a mine which blew his foot off. By the time a safe gap was found, B Company had lost one man killed and six wounded.[2]

To the left of B Company was A Company, where twenty-two-year-old Alfred 'Alf' Wooltorton served as the platoon sergeant of

7 Platoon. The attrition rate among junior officers was so high that for a while Alf had commanded the platoon himself, but a new lieutenant had arrived in time for Operation Veritable. Alf had also received a corporal who had been serving in the rear echelons, but who had committed some transgression worthy of a ticket to the frontline.

Alf's new officer, Lieutenant David Hutton, was the son of a former RSM in the Argylls. 'He was younger than me. He was twenty year old. Nice young man.'

As they continued to press on towards their objectives outside of Kranenburg, Alf found himself in a position familiar to many a platoon sergeant – that of reigning in an enthusiastic, and no doubt brave, young officer.

'Lieutenant Hutton was pretty keen and I had a job to get him to realize we were moving forward in steps (with the artillery), and they put down white smoke markers as a guiding line where you should not move before, and he was getting a little in front of them at times.'

One of these smoke shells dropped short and struck the new corporal. By some miracle it impacted on the entrenching tool carried on his back.

'Well, he let out an awful yell. Had it been another inch or two to one side, it would have gone through him, I think.'

The corporal was collected by stretcher-bearers and taken to the rear. The rest of the platoon pushed on, crossing a large minefield that had been laid by US paratroopers in their defence of Groesbeek in earlier months. The mines had been laid on the surface, and posed little issue in daylight. Alf's first objective was also easily overcome.

'There was one large earthworks which we had to take. They had the white flag up, and I can remember feeling very angry at (our) tanks. They fired. I mean, these poor paratroopers, they'd been there all night, they'd had all this pounding overnight, and I didn't think they deserved being shot at. The flag went down because the guy (who was holding it up) was hit.'

Alf was told to take up a defensive position while the company commander, Lieutenant Hutton, and their batmen went to look around the nearby farm buildings.

'They'd only just gone in and all hell let loose on the farm. They took an enormous salvo of shells. After about five or ten minutes, Lieutenant Hutton's batman came out. He was a Lancastrian called McIntyre.

'He dumped himself aside me and he says, "Wee Hutton has had it, Wally. You're in charge now." I said, "What's happened?" He said, "Well, he's so badly hit he can't survive. He's got an arm hanging off, and a leg badly (wounded)."'[3]

The company commander had also been wounded, and required evacuation. Alf gathered up his platoon and joined up with the rest of the company at the edge of Kranenburg, which had been wrecked by artillery, and told the Company Sergeant Major about what had happened.

'Sergeant Major pointed out to me that we'd got to get to the other side of the small town, down the railway line. There was a Spandau up on a highpoint and that was raking the railway line.'

The troops put down a smoke screen and were preparing to move when four figures came running out of it carrying 'something'. The 'four figures' were enemy prisoners of war (POWs). 'Something' was a wounded British soldier.

'I knew (him) but I didn't know his name, so I said, "Are you alright, Jock? Do you want a drink?"'

Alf was taking his water bottle out when one of the POWs tapped him on the shoulder, then pointed to his own stomach. Alf immediately recognized the gesture for what it meant – the British soldier had been hit in the gut, and could not be given liquids. The POW, who was likely a seasoned soldier, then took the water bottle from Alf's hand, and gently wet the wounded man's lips.

'I thought, in the midst of all this, there's someone with a bit of humanity about 'em. I don't know whether he survived or not because I don't know his name. But that was just one little incident in a day which I think was one of the worst that I've ever remembered.'

Still under fire, Alf's company were able to move down the

railway line and into a 'big old factory that was between us and our final objective.' The enemy machine gun position continued to rake the building, showering glass from the windows. Sergeant Major Green had by this time taken command of A Company, and led them out, telling Alf to follow on behind and ensure that all the men were out.

'I was last one out of the factory. By that time they'd gone across one meadow, and they were about three parts the way across another. As I got near the fence between the two meadows I can remember seeing my PIAT man who was right up front suddenly go up in the air. He'd stepped on a Schu mine.'

Alf was sent forward by Sergeant Major Green to find a way ahead, but he soon came to a barbed-wire fence adorned with signs that read '*Achtung Minen*' – 'which didn't take much interpreting. So I stopped, held my hand up, and (CSM Green) came up. He said, "What's up?" and I told him.'

Alf was awed by what happened next.

'The old boy, he didn't say a word. He always carried a rifle, and he put that over his shoulder and he got up and he walked right across through this area. Nothing happened, fortunately, and he stood there and just sort of calmly called us over.'

It was one brave act among many for Company Sergeant Major Green that day. He was awarded the Distinguished Conduct Medal (DCM), which ranked one grade lower than the Victoria Cross.

As dusk was falling, Alf was given charge of evacuating 'two bodies. I don't know if they were bodies, if they were alive, or dead. Difficult to say. We were told they were from another company, we were to look after them, and bring them (back).'

His men collected doors from nearby buildings, and with the two casualties placed upon them, they set out across a ploughed field that Alf hoped would be free of mines.

'It was pretty heavy-going and there was a lot of moaning going on. I was carrying about six or seven rifles from the people who were carrying the doors.' In the end Alfred got so fed up of the moaning that he told the men to put the makeshift stretchers down. He then gave them the kind of dressing down that has been perfected as an art by British Army sergeants, concluding with the truth that it could be them carried on a stretcher one day.

'Well, that shut them up a bit.'

Nineteen-year-old James Campbell served in the same battalion as Alf. James was an old hand himself, and had been wounded in the vicious fighting at Hill 112, Normandy. At Kranenburg he waded through waist-deep water while under fire to reach his objective.

'Twice we were shelled by our own artillery, and it inflicted quite a number of casualties on us. Particularly, a very good friend of mine from the carrier platoon, Sergeant Stevenson, he got hit very badly. We loaded him onto one of my carriers to take him away, and unfortunately he died in the hospital. We had quite a few killed that day.'[4]

Despite this 'friendly fire', James refused to bear a grudge against the artillerymen.

'All credit to them because they never let us down.'

Donald Newsom was another nineteen-year-old veteran of Normandy and beyond. His battalion, the 10th Highland Light Infantry (HLI), were on the left flank of the Argylls and had been given the task of clearing Kranenburg. They too were confronted by minefields, but orders came over the radio to press on with the attack regardless.

'I think it was very much the wrong decision,' said Donald, who would later be awarded a Mention in Dispatches for his part in leading the company through the minefield. 'Men were blowing up either side of me, and they were coming back minus their legs. You just didn't know whether the next step you took you were going to get blown to smithereens.'

Larger mines had also been buried along the front to take out vehicles, and claimed the tank of Lieutenant David Scott-Barrett, Scots Guards. A further eight Churchills had been similarly disabled, or become bogged down in the mud, and only one remained to support the HLI's attack into Kranenburg.

Knowing that the armoured support was vital, Lieutenant Scott-Barrett immediately got out of his own ruined tank and ran through a minefield strewn with the bodies of infantryman. He then led his one remaining tank on foot, acting as a liaison between its crew and the infantry.[5]

The tank was commanded by Sergeant Lewis Aitken, who led the infantry into Kranenburg, engaging machine-gun posts and snipers along the way, and placing the tank in a vulnerable position for possible anti-tank gun and Panzerfaust ambush.

The citation of Sergeant Aitken's Military Medal (MM) noted that 'The Infantry Company Commander reported that the effect of his supporting fire undoubtedly did much to force the enemy to surrender, that the way in which he fought his tank was quite magnificent and that his action undoubtedly saved the infantry many casualties.'[6]

Lieutenant Scott-Barret was himself awarded the Military Cross (MC). Both the Military Medal and Military Cross were of the same grade, but awarded to other ranks and officers, respectively.[7]

High Ground

As the HLI were fighting their way into Kranenburg, the 9th Cameronians were to seize the Galgensteeg Ridge, an area of high ground overlooking the town. They did so on the heels of the creeping barrage.

'And then it lifted,' said Tom Gore, 'and there was a lot of shells falling in amongst us, and we never knew whether it was our barrage firing short, or the enemy firing back, but there was the usual cry. "Stretcher-bearers! Stretcher-bearers!"'

At 1440 hrs the battalion's war diary recorded 'own artillery falling short and number of casualties'.[8]

Tom's platoon also began to encounter the enemy's dead and wounded.

'About six Germans, wounded, (were lying on stretchers) across the road with their medical orderly there. Someone had given them a cigarette, but they never had no matches. So I give the medical orderly a box of matches. I suppose it was the sort of human thing to do. There was one of the tanks on fire behind us. There was a hell of a lot of activity behind us. Of course, the inevitable stretcher-bearers.'

Tom's platoon was then halted by the equally inevitable minefields. Like many brave deeds in war, what happened next went unrecognized by official award, but not by the men who were there to see it.

'He was a great leader, Sergeant Rose. He shouted in his Scots language, "Get yourselves spread out or you'll all get 'effin killed." He stepped over the wire into the minefield, and we all followed. We picked our way over the minefield.'

Other parts of the battalion were not so fortunate. B Company entered a minefield and suffered many casualties, the majority of whom had their legs blown off. The battalion's war diary recorded: 'Those that survived bore their painful evacuation with the utmost courage.'[9]

The minefield behind them, the Cameronians pushed onto the Galgensteeg Ridge.

'We put an attack in onto the top of the 'ill,' said Tom. 'Halfway up the 'ill there was a little farmhouse. Rifleman Davies went in, and all of a sudden he came running out. With instinct we all run after him and ended up in a heap on the floor.'

An explosion soon followed, and then Davies gave his explanation.

'He had thrown a hand grenade in the house, and (the house) had been fortified. Someone had put chicken wire in the window, and the grenade had (bounced) back at him. That's why he ran. So that was another lesson we learned. We never let Rifleman Davies throw a grenade again 'less we could help it.'

Perhaps another lesson that Tom and his comrades had lived to learn was this: that the civilian dwellings in the area were not just close to the Siegfried Line, but part of it.

'A lot of them were bungalows,' said Ray Ashton, Middlesex Regiment, 'fairly modern bungalows, and a lot of them had cellars. The cellars were all built slightly above ground so they formed pillboxes. There was slits in the walls of the cellars, bungalow perched on top. Looked like quite innocuous houses, but were in fact fortified houses.'

The enemy defences on the Galgensteeg Ridge had been lightly manned, and the 9th Cameronians consolidated their position on the high ground. The war diarist of 2nd Argylls recorded that by '1700 hours the Cameronians on our right had cleared the high ground and life became more peaceful around Kranenburg. There was no sign of a counter-attack (. . .) and by darkness the battalion was securely dug-in for its first night on German soil.'[10]

As darkness fell there were mixed feelings amongst the division's officers. Though both the Galgensteeg Ridge and Kranenburg had been seized, the condition of the terrain had been treacherous at best, and there was severe concern as to whether or not the 15th (Scottish) – and the 43rd Wessex waiting to push through them – could continue on schedule.

The next day, General Brian Horrocks, their corps commander, made one of his 'worst mistakes of the war'.[11]

Kleve

There is an old saying in the army that no plan survives contact with the enemy, but to historian Tim Saunders, a more fitting adage for the attack on the Siegfried Line was that no plan survives contact with the mud.[12]

'The weather was utterly appalling,' said Douglas Goddard, an officer in the 112th Field Artillery Regiment, Royal Artillery. 'Constant teeming rain. The whole area was flooded. We fought the battle along elevated roads with rivers both sides, lakes both sides, which meant that the German defence was extraordinarily effective because you couldn't deploy. We could not move around the flanks because of the water.'

Despite these conditions, the first day of Operation Veritable had gone as well as could be expected for the 15th (Scottish) Division. The crucial town of Kranenburg had been taken, as well as the high ground to its south. The defences of the Siegfried Line now lay ahead, as did the high ground of the Materborn feature that bordered Kleve, and the town itself.

15th Division would continue the attack with the support of

Grenadier Guards tanks and specialist vehicles of 79th Armoured Division, such as flail tanks and AVREs, which carried the equipment necessary to breach and bridge the deep anti-tank ditches. The assaulting battalions of infantry would be carried into battle by Kangaroos – a Sherman chassis, without a turret, used as an armoured personnel carrier.

The attack was planned for the evening of the 8th, but trouble with moving through the mud delayed this until 0500 the following morning. Conditions, rather than enemy action, continued to be the greatest hindrance to the advance, but by 1000 hrs 44th (Lowland) Brigade had broken through the line, and were on their objectives on the western side of the Materborn. Due to the difficulties in bringing up the reserve brigades to push through them, 44th Brigade were then ordered to continue on to the Materborn itself. Colonel Richardson, the commanding officer of 6th Battalion, King's Own Scottish Borderers, recalled that the enemy infantry did not offer much resistance, and were overcome with the aid of flame-throwing tanks.[13]

The battalion's war diarist noted that 'the Boche reacted very strongly during the night with patrols, one infiltrating into C Coy (Company) area, who immediately drove them out.' A further enemy patrol overran a platoon of machine-gunners, 'knocking out three guns'.[14]

Ray Ashton was with the Middlesex Regiment, who were providing mortar and machine-gun support for the 15th Division.

'There was some houses on our left, which was flooded land. We got fired on from one of these houses, so we fired back, but there was a tank, a Cromwell tank, by the side of the road, and he said, "Don't worry, I'll clobber that for you." He let fly and knocked the chimney off, and put one through the top of the house.'

A white flag came out and a few Royal Engineers set off to the house with a rubber dingy. 'Got about halfway, and the Jerries opened up again,' Ray said.

It was likely the final act of the enemy soldiers as the tank took retribution and 'simply knocked this blooming house to pieces. And that was just one of the incidents really on the Siegfried Line.'

As darkness descended, Ray and his comrades searched for a safe place to spend the night.

'We drove into a farmyard and jumped out (of) the carriers, and took cover in what were ready-prepared German trenches, which is a thing we never did, because Germans were notoriously lousy. But on this occasion it was pitch black, there was a lot of enemy fire, (and) we took what cover we could. I can remember seeing these burning buildings, vehicles, all around, and tanks getting hit. I remember one particular tank, it glowed red in the dark. I don't think the chaps got out.'

As 44th Brigade secured the Materborn, 15th Reconnaissance Regiment began to search ahead for routes that could be used for the 43rd (Wessex) Division to pass through and seize the Goch Escarpment, some six miles to the south of Kleve.

The 15th Reconnaissance Regiment's war diary recorded that 'During the night several recce parties from 43 Div called in at Regimental HQ. These recce parties appeared to be under the impression that CLEVE was in our hands and it was merely a matter of motoring through and signposting routes without any form of protection whatsoever. The majority of these recce parties were persuaded that there were large quantities of the enemy still in the area.'[15]

XXX Corps Headquarters were also under the impression that 15th (Scottish) were either in Kleve, or close to being so. The reality was that they were still on the Materborn feature and strung out along the muddy routes trying to reinforce it. It was the kind of misunderstanding that can turn the course of a battle.

XXX Corps Commander, General Horrocks, now ordered the 43rd Division to move through 15th Division. Though he would later regret the decision, it was made with the best of intentions. Horrocks did not want to give the reeling enemy time to recover, but the arrival of this fresh division into the already existing congestion caused by the mud and flooding meant that the 43rd and 15th Divisions became jammed together on the solitary road, and their units disorganised.[16]

John Corbyn, a lieutenant-colonel in his early thirties, was the commanding officer of the 4th Wiltshires and at the head of the 43rd's advance.

'I was told that some armoured cars had got to the edge of Kleve and had to go back because there was enemy fire. So we went along the road to Kleve and we were helped to some extent by the use of artificial moonlight, supplied by searchlight units, shining the lights on the clouds above, which provided a certain amount of lighting in (an) otherwise extremely black, storm-tossed night.

'(Kleve) had been bombed by the RAF, so the roads and the houses were in a pretty bad way. The other great obstacle was the embankments of the Rhine had been knocked down so the countryside was flooding. The water was rising, and it was raining, and it was dark and the maps were not at all good.

'We got to where the armoured cars were held up, and there were roadblocks here. We had to get out of our vehicles, dig out some very gallant Germans, who had been left behind with an anti-tank weapon to take at least one tank with them when the moment of departure to the next world came.'

The armour supporting 4 Wilts belonged to the Sherwood Rangers. Nineteen-year-old Ernie Leppard, from Battersea, was a member of a Sherman tank crew.

'It was all pitch dark then suddenly illuminated with gun flashes, then we come to this defended position which was like a gamekeeper's house. The Germans were firing back so we just lined up and blasted the place out of existence.'

Armoured bulldozers worked to fill craters in the road caused by the RAF's bombing raids, but the going was slow, and the column of Sherwood Rangers and 4 Wilts were ordered to halt in the south-eastern suburbs of Kleve at 0520 hrs on the 10th.

After a long night of action, Ernie and his crew were ready for breakfast. He jumped down from his tank to rummage for plates and cutlery in the nearby houses as the rest of the crew brewed tea outside of the tank. Ernie found what he needed, and a live chicken to boot. He returned to his tank moments before 'all hell let loose' and enemy small arms and shells smashed into the British column.

'My tank, being the lead tank, was the first one to be knocked out. It had been hit by an 88 when our co-driver was still inside it and he was killed. The second shot, straight through the front. Another one went straight through the co-driver's hatch, and another one went in and ricocheted straight up through the roof where I would have been sitting if I had been in that tank.'

The four surviving members of the crew took cover in a nearby basement as the battle raged around them. They were soon joined by others, their own tanks lost. Enemy armour was in Kleve, and the Shermans were outgunned.

Lieutenant David Render, Sherwood Rangers, had gone into action in a Dingo scout car, and spent the night feeling vulnerable outside of a tank. He felt a lot worse when he came within twenty yards of a massive Jagdpanther tank destroyer, its 88mm gun pointing straight at him.

'It was like something out of a slow-motion film and I think I might have got as far as saying "shit" before I was stunned by the flash of the trace in the back of the amour-piercing round that shot less than a foot above the top of my head.'[17]

The Jagdpanther could not depress its gun low enough to hit the diminutive Dingo, which stood less than 5 feet tall.[18] Such were the fine margins between life and death.

Eric Wheeler, 4 Wilts, recalled the confused nature of the fighting that day.

'It was just chaos and confusion half the time. We were fighting them, and they were fighting us. It was said afterwards they didn't know who was more surprised. The Germans on seeing us, or us on seeing the Germans. Things were a bit chaotic for a few hours.'

According to the historian of the 43rd Wessex, the commander of the Wehrmacht's 84th Division, Major-General Fiebig, 'found himself personally involved in the fighting with 129 Brigade which had superimposed itself around his headquarters in Cleve. He was apparently endeavouring to deploy west of Cleve and Materborn what was left of his own division and 6th Parachute Division, supported by tanks and SP guns of 116 Panzer Division. These fresh troops had only just arrived and found themselves faced by a situation as vague and confusing as that confronting 129 Brigade. Both sides had reacted with equal violence.'[19]

William Hanna was no stranger to such action, having landed on Gold Beach with 50th (Northumbrian) Division. He had since been reassigned to the 43rd (Wessex).

'We were based on a crossroads within Kleve itself, and my section was in a house right on the corner. During the day, no way you could go out on that crossroads, because the snipers were there. They would have had you. The Germans had a lot of snipers there, in the rubble.'

William, himself a sniper, was led by a new lieutenant fresh from England.

'He'd just joined the battalion and this was his first encounter with the enemy. He wanted me to take him round to show him where the enemy positions were. I says, "No bloody way." I said, "If you put your head out on that crossroads there, your mum won't see you again, cause Fritz will have you between the eyes."

'He wouldn't take any notice of me. So out he went, on his own. And, of course, within two steps, down he went. He was shot. And, of course, then it meant me and my chaps had to go out and retrieve the body, because we didn't know if he was dead or alive, and we couldn't just leave him there. That was a typical example of a young subaltern who was a real VC-wallah who wouldn't listen to seasoned soldiers.'

William's own war came to an end soon after.

'I was coming back from a sniping task. I got up to run across an opening, and I got shot through (the side of the knee).'

43rd Division's 214th Brigade were released into the battle later that day, but it was dark before they launched from Nütterden, a village on the other side of the Materborn. Arthur Jones was an experienced member of 5th Battalion, Duke of Cornwall's Light Infantry (DCLI), and served in the anti-tank platoon. Advancing under shell fire across the muddy fields, it wasn't long until his Bren carrier slipped a track.

'We decided we'd have to dig in around the carrier. The trenches were filling up with water. It was like digging into liquid mud.'

Being an old soldier – and a tired one at that – Arthur was able to fall asleep in the appalling conditions.

'The next minute I woke up and I was buried. A Churchill tank had gone up through and squeezed the ground, and just pushed the side of the trench in on me.'

Arthur's comrades came to his aid and dug him out with shovels.

'Good thing I had me steel helmet on. They'd have took me head off,' he chuckled. 'Clanking across the top of me 'ead with these shovels. That was something to remember.'

The battle for Kleve continued to rage through the night, and if there was one commonality in accounts given by those who were there, it was 'chaos'.

Ernie Leppard and other stricken tank crewmen spent an uncomfortable day and night in a basement, wondering if the tracks they could hear outside belonged to friendly or enemy tanks.

'One of our blokes had gone completely bomb-happy so we had a job keeping him quiet. He was crying and screaming. His tank had got hit, and he was slightly wounded, but he had gone off his head.

'Next morning we rescued some rations from our tank which was just across the road. Sergeant Major come round about midday (and said) we had to move quickly because German defences had flooded the road from Nijmegen to Kleve. I was a bit annoyed because I had some loot in the turret which I'd forgot.'

In the early hours of the 11th, 6 KOSB were ordered into Kleve to take over from 129th Brigade of 43rd Division, which included the 4th Wiltshires. 6 KOSB's war diary recorded that 'There was a certain amount of confusion as to location of own & enemy troops.'[20]

James Wilkinson was with the 'Kobs'.

'When we got into Kleve, we turned around a bend in the road and there's about thirty Germans standing there with picks and shovels digging in positions. They dropped their shovels and put their hands up.'

That night the battalion sent patrols into different areas of Kleve, 'reporting no sign of the enemy'.[21] That same evening, 15th

Reconnaissance Regiment recorded that the town was 'now firmly in our hands'.[22]

The following day, Tom Gore and the 9th Cameronians entered the 'completely flattened' city. The rain was still pouring, and with their water carts held up in the massive traffic jam that stretched back from Kleve, the men filled their bottles from the run-off of gutters.

'I always remember it because the bottom of the mess tin was full of grit from the roofs.'

The Cameronians and other units were put into billets to await their next battle. Such accommodation was hard to find following the destruction of the city, and many would come to lament the use of the heavy bombers – not only because of the deaths of civilians, but for the difficulty that the damage caused the advancing army. Masses of rubble needed to be cleared from the roads, and deep craters could not be easily bypassed due to the flooded fields. 214 Brigade's commander went as far as to call it 'oafish stupidity', and lamented that the lessons of Caen, in Normandy, had not been learned.[23]

Once they were settled into their accommodation, Tom Gore left his platoon to find a suitable place to answer a call of nature, and watched British artillery at work as he walked.

'A German plane appeared from nowhere, dropped a bomb on these artillery pieces, and silenced them. Then our planes arrived and there was a dogfight. The German plane came right overhead with smoke pouring out of him, and crashed further into town, and the pilot was floating down on a parachute. You could clearly see him. I thought about going after him, but I decided that the mission I was going on to tend to nature was more important.'

Other soldiers, now on the enemy's soil, were taking the chance to look for 'souvenirs'.

'The first house we went in in Germany, we went a bit berserk,' said Len Watson, 15th Reconnaissance Regiment. 'There was all these swastikas in the place. I remember after we'd had a meal in there we flung all the pots out of the windows. We had a guy called McManus, from London. He came out dressed in an evening dress.

'I never bothered with souvenirs. A lot of lads did. Armstrong, our sergeant, he was forever bringing stuff back onto the carrier, and about three days later I'd sling it off.'

There was little time for Len and other soldiers to explore, as they were soon pushed into further battles. It had been hoped that by going through Kleve a bridge over the Rhine might be seized in the first few days of Operation Veritable, but four days had now passed, and the force was held up some sixteen miles from the bridge at Xanten, and twenty miles from the bridge at Wesel. Worse still, it was clear that it would be some time before the Ninth US Army could launch Operation Grenade – German forces had opened the sluice gates of the Roer dams, meaning that there could be no US advance until the floods subsided. The full weight of the enemy's reserves could now be focused on the British and Canadian forces, including units stripped from the sector facing the American troops. Flooding and mud also restricted the Anglo-Canadian ability for resupply, reinforcement and casualty evacuation. From the lips of old soldiers who slipped in the mud, and shivered in the ruins of Kleve, might have come the muttered words of 'bloody disaster'.

Only a matter of miles to their south-east, the 53rd (Welsh) Division were enduring what General Horrocks described as 'one of the most unpleasant weeks of the entire war'.[24]

It took place in the Reichswald Forest.

CHAPTER 4

One of the Most Unpleasant Weeks of the Entire War

The Battle of the Reichswald Forest 8–18 February 1945

'The only breaks you had (were) when you went in and captured your objective. Another battalion goes through, and then you more or less get a little bit of a break then, before you move forward again, but it's mentally affecting you. You always knew. You wanted to stay where you were. Everybody did, you know? You didn't like the idea of somebody coming (and saying), "Alright, get your kit on, we're going forward again." You didn't like that. Nobody did. And if they did say it, they're liars, because you always had that horrible steel in your stomach. I think the longer you're there, and you see boys being killed – boys been there a couple of weeks, a week, or a day – you always fancy, why has your turn not been called up on, you know? So I think it did affect you. It took a terrible strain.'

Aubrey 'Bruce' Coombs, 6th Battalion,
Royal Welch Fusiliers

Night had fallen on the first day of Operation Veritable when Major Joe Cêtre MC led A Company east from Groesbeek at the head of the 1st East Lancs. Lit by burning buildings and searchlights in the sky, the road was thick with soldiers and supplies going one way, prisoners the other, their spirits shattered by the opening barrage that day.

'They were like zombies,' recalled Joe. 'They looked as if they hadn't shaved for a week. Their eyes were hollow and absolutely burned out. And they were just shambling along, completely exhausted.'

Bob Atkinson, of A Company, remembered passing artillery crews busily feeding their hungry guns.

'We were marching down this road, and they were just above us. (The noise was) terrible. No wonder I'm not so good with ma lugs,' he chuckled.

Shells were also falling on the British column, two of the East Lancs' vehicles suffering direct hits, which further delayed progress. Eventually the track became nothing but a muddy quagmire, and the supporting tanks were unable to follow.

'By the time that we had reached the outskirts of the forest the barrage had lifted,' said Owen Butcher, a nineteen-year-old sniper from Witham. 'It was pitch black. (We were) going into the unknown.'

The battalion's start line at the edge of the Reichswald had been gained by 71st Brigade, whom the East Lancs now pushed through, A Company in the lead. The searchlight beams of 'Monty's Moonlight' shone against low-lying cloud to create an illuminating effect on the ground below, but struggled to penetrate the canopy.

'At least you could see where the stumps were,' said Joe Cêtre. 'The Germans, in their orderly way, had created all these rides and paths in a very methodical way, where presumably they haul the lumber when they cut it, which made it rather easy for operational purposes to divide (the forest) into a grid.'

This was as far as 'easy' went when it came to the Reichswald. Moving through a forest at night is a difficult proposition at the best of times, and the soldiers were encumbered with heavy kit, carrying weapons, and battling against both an enemy and the winter elements. Joe recalled 'thawing snow. Constant rain. A lot of the time we were up to our knees in leaf mould, and mud. And also, of course, the destruction of the trees and so on by artillery created additional obstacles. We couldn't go in a straight line because of the wreckage and the craters and everything.'

The battalion's first objective was the forest track named 'Kentucky'.

'The artificial moonlight shed its light on this Kentucky road. It almost looked like a sort of stage in a theatre. Along this eerily lit road trudged a Fordson tractor, loaded with some heavy shells, dragging a gun. It was unbelievable. I don't think they knew we were there.'

That soon changed.

'D Company dealt with that lot. There was some Germans in the trenches, too, and they suddenly came to.'

Bob Atkinson recalled the nature of the enemy's defences. 'They were like First World War positions. They were all wooded up the sides, bunkers behind with wood and soil, wood and soil.'

'There was a lot of Spandau fire,' said Joe Cêtre, 'and B Company, the next company, passed through. 10 Platoon went into (the first positions) and there was hand-to-hand fighting. And then they went into the second one, where they met stronger opposition. There was really quite a lot of fighting there. Really close. And we had some casualties.'

Four of the East Lancs were killed, and five wounded.

With the German defenders either driven out, killed, or taken prisoner, the battalion consolidated its position on Kentucky.

'By now it had got far into the night,' said Joe, 'and the battalion spent the night on the position in all-around defence, soaked to the skin.'

The men of the East Lancs peered from their positions into the black forest, their ears straining to hear footsteps or voices that might be muffled by the pouring, cold rain. Then came dawn. And with it, the enemy.

'The Germans at that stage were beginning to react more vigorously, with sniping and machine-gunning,' said Joe. 'The night before I think they were equally as confused as we were.'

Things got worse when the East Lancs heard the unmistakable sound of tracks.

'We could hear this tank coming,' recalled Bob Atkinson. 'It come along this road and somebody said, "It's a Panther!" It was a nerve-shredding moment for the soldiers, then one man called out, "Don't fire, don't fire!"'

The tanks were friendly Churchills that had arrived to support them. '(They) had to go right round,' said Joe Cêtre, 'and joined us on the morning of the 9th, which considerably increased our firepower.'

'Now that the Churchills were here, (A Company) attacked to relieve the pressure on B Company, and establish themselves on B Company's right.' With the help of the tanks, and a 'short, sharp, artillery bombardment', A Company fought through the enemy's trenches.

'There was two or three lines of defences,' said Bob Atkinson. 'We were having to take one after t'other. They were going in with fixed bayonets, but me being a Bren gunner, I was just firing Bren. Giving them a taste of lead.'

'It was a complete success,' said Joe Cêtre. 'One of the subalterns of A, Stewart, did a magnificent job, and having got the first set of trenches, then rushed into the second, killing quite a few with his own Sten.'

Eighteen enemy were killed and forty prisoners taken. A Company lost one man killed and another wounded. The Germans replied to the attack with artillery, which caused 'quite a few casualties'.

By nightfall on 9 February, the East Lancs had firmly established themselves in the forest, but their greatest challenge still lay ahead.

No Equal

The East Lancs remained in position on Kentucky during 10 February, as 71st Brigade pushed through them to clear the eastern edge of the forest. Joe Cêtre's notes for the day number only a few words, but speak volumes: 'Cold. Wet.'

THE BATTLE OF THE REICHSWALD FOREST

With the ever-present threat of snipers and shelling, it was not possible for the men to get out of their positions to warm up, and so a miserable day passed second by second, rain drop by rain drop. The battalion did receive a message of congratulation from their divisional commander for the previous day's action, however. 'That sort of cheered us up,' said Joe.

Orders were also received. The battalion was to secure a bridgehead over a further road, Utah. On 11 February, at 0700 hrs, the East Lancs moved off along Kentucky as its main axis of attack. The order of march for the companies was D, A, B, C. They soon met the enemy.

'We had encounters of Germans on the way,' said Joe. 'We're having them the whole time. And D Company was engaged in a lively battle.'

A Company moved to D's right to form a two-company front, and the fighting continued. 'All these were small battles involving platoons,' explained Joe. 'Even individuals. As I say, you might be behind one tree, and the German might be behind the next. It was that sort of battle.'

The battalion reached its first objective, Utah, but took casualties from heavy shelling. B Company now sent forward a patrol to investigate a trench system on the other side of Utah, and found it unoccupied. This seemed to corroborate intelligence received by the commanding officer, which had it that the Germans were pulling out of the forest.

'The thing to do now was to make an all-out dash for Virginia before nightfall,' said Joe.

With the battalions on their flanks still engaged in their own battles on Utah, the East Lancs were told to press forward 'while the light stood. And this, remember, would have been about two-ish or more on a February day.'

Only a couple of hours of daylight remained.

'You must get the idea that it's pressure, now. Rush, rush. Rush against the failing light. D Company immediately pushed in with tanks to occupy the trench system, followed by the rest of the battalion, C, B and A. But the enemy did move into the trench system in increasing numbers. It appears that they'd been taken off balance a bit, and didn't expect us to follow quite so quickly, or quite so closely, after the initial encounter, and they were now beginning to realize that, unless they did something, we'd get the forest. This rather contradicts the information that the CO got, that they were pulling out. In fact they were doing quite the contrary.'

This left the commanding officer of the East Lancs with two options:

'One, to really get the battalion consolidated in that area, or push on. The disadvantage of consolidating (on Utah) would have been to allow the enemy to really build up, and then you'd have a major task.'

Instead, the CO acted to maintain the initiative before the Germans could reorganize, and pushed the battalion onwards to Virginia. This action provoked a 'violent reaction' from the enemy.

'D Company pushed on and arrived at a clearing where the enemy was quite strong. This place opened up like a hornet's nest. There was Spandaus, they were shelling, and they shelled very heavily along Maine, because that was the route we were coming down, and they observed that.'

D Company was in danger of being surrounded, and decisive action was needed. A barrage of smoke was laid down by the artillery, enabling the rest of the battalion to make a swift move across the clearing to support D. They did so 'with surprisingly few casualties', said Joe.

'The enemy fired from various directions, and one of our tanks was knocked out. This was about half past four, a winter evening about to set in. C Company was now in the lead and found themselves confronted by another clearing, and opposition in front with mortars, (machine guns), anti-tank guns.

'The 1/5th Welch could be heard battling out on our left. They were also having problems. Also, the Germans began infiltrating a trench system. A forest being as it is, you get round people. You get behind people. So, the situation was rather tricky.'

After liaising with both the artillery and tanks to provide fire support, 'C Company got onto its objective they were clearing. B Company was on the flank giving support.'

C Company then came under heavy and accurate fire from a previously undetected machine-gun position. The Spandau was in enfilade, meaning that it could rake the entirety of C Company with its automatic fire. It was a critical moment in the battle, with dozens of lives on the line.

Recognizing the danger, Colour Sergeant Wilfred Linton ran through heavy fire to the threatened flank and assaulted the position alone, killing three of the enemy and putting the machine gun out of action. C Company, their flank secure, were now able to take their objective. Joe Cêtre recalled an estimated thirty enemy dead, a handful of prisoners, and two East Lancs casualties.

'But had (Linton) not taken that initiative, the tale might have been written differently.' The 'courage and presence of mind' of Colour Sergeant Linton, who had acted entirely on his own, was later recognized with the Military Medal.[1]

'We now come to A Company,' said Joe Cêtre, who commanded this body of men. 'We advanced in the lead, at dusk, for Virginia.'

They did so with the support of a troop of tanks. With their movement and view limited by the forest, the armour relied on the infantry to protect them from ambush.

'Quite suddenly I heard a bang,' said Joe, 'a very loud one, and before I knew what happened I saw a couple of Germans rushing through the woods. They'd been a little bazooka party (and) had a go at one of the Churchills, but they missed.'

Pressing on relentlessly through the rain, and difficult conditions underfoot, A Company and the supporting tanks reached Virginia and took positions on a track junction known as 'Dead Horse Corner'. The four dead animals on the track were some of an estimated 750,000 horses killed in German service during the Second World War, its military relying heavily on the animals for transportation and supply. Joe and other old hands in the battalion were well used to such sights, and scents, though owing to the rain and snow, 'the smell wasn't what it would have been in Normandy'.

The East Lancs were now upon Virginia, and night was upon

them both. The order came to 'dig in and hold', and Joe formed his company into a 'very tight defence'.

'It was a question of two platoons forwards, and one back. Dig, dig, dig. We'd no sooner started (this) when a German patrol walked straight up the path, completely oblivious that we were there, and a short, sharp fight developed. Grenades. Possibly the bayonet. Grenades, machine guns, everything. It was hard to see what was happening. I think they must have been about twenty strong. They must have got the fright of their lives. Well, we probably did too.

'One of ours was killed, and Sergeant Wilson was wounded, and I think Corporal Brian took over, and did magnificently.'

Now in darkness, A Company continued to dig for their lives.

'We could hear, in the distance, the sound of tracks, and Germans shouting.'

It appeared as though the enemy were building for an attack, and the East Lancs were perilously alone, having outdistanced the rest of the brigade, the other battalions held up by their own battles. Joe was very aware of their isolation as 'Germans started infiltrating in the rear. We soon found the casualties couldn't be evacuated beyond the Regimental Aid Post. And also, of course, if this prolonged for a certain amount of time, we couldn't get things through. Ammunition. Food. Supplies. We had the tanks forward with us, so that was a consolation, but we were in a rather sticky position.'

Behind Joe's position at Dead Horse Corner was the battalion's Forward Observation Officer, Captain Lester. His communications with the artillery were 'a great comfort', but such radio contact in the forest was tenuous at best.

'Cable gets cut by shelling,' explained Joe. 'Atmospherics and so on (affect the radios). And also batteries are wearing down.'

The enemy began to make probing attacks all along the East Lancs front, but particularly on the left flank of the battalion.

'Occasionally we saw a figure, or a face, and that was shot at. If things got too hot, we got in touch with the (artillery), and they put down fire. Sometimes the fire was very nearly on top of us, but that didn't matter. We were dug in.'

'We made like a block defence,' said Bren gunner Bob Atkinson. 'All-around defence, and Germans come and counter-attacked. They were coming through the woods. You couldn't see what you were doing.'

The trees of the Reichswald had been planted in rows, meaning that visibility 'through' them was sometimes possible from one vantage point, but not another. As the enemy advanced, Bob and his comrades close by relied on warnings and range distances shouted over by the men on their flanks.

'D Company shouted us, "Hundred yards, Jerry's coming!"'

Vicious close-quarter fighting ensued.

'We stopped them. We repulsed them. But they got within twenty-five yards.'

The ammunition that the men had carried with them into the forest was running out fast. Bob recalled that stretcher-bearers were used to bring more up to the men, which would be a violation of the Geneva Convention.

The night became 'an unbroken series of infiltration attacks,' said Joe Cêtre. 'Particularly between A and C, because that was the dense part (of the woods).'

Captain Lester, the forward observer for the artillery, 'did a wonderful job. He was constantly being shelled. I mean, the Germans knew where we were. We were being shelled, too.'

One can only imagine the scene. The flashes of explosions lighting the trees, branches sent tumbling, splinters flying. Men desperately working the actions of their weapons, hands cold and slippery from rain and mud. Shouts of warning, of orders, and for 'stretcher-bearers!' The bark of firearms, the crump of grenades and the screams of the wounded.

'A very uncomfortable night,' Joe Cêtre said simply. 'Very uncomfortable. Mind you, this wonderful quartermaster somehow infiltrated through the Germans and got through to us. We got a hot meal. He was an old soldier, too. He wasn't just a sort of administrative type. He was a soldier.'

Bob Atkinson remembered the moment differently. 'First thing they brought to us was some cheese sandwiches, and it was one slice of bread with some cheese in. That was what we got, and we'd been, I'd say, twenty-four hours or so without (food).'

Whatever the contents of the meal, it was at least food in the belly for men in a battle far from over.

'The pressure increased not only on us, but on the other companies too,' said Joe Cêtre. 'By midday (we had) almost complete failure of wireless communication with Brigade, and very sketchy with the gunners. We still had the tanks. Nothing more we could do except shoot it out.'

In the early afternoon, 'the enemy made a particularly strong infiltration attack between A and C companies, and also put pressure on C and D. All companies were committed.' This meant that the entire battalion was now engaged in repulsing the attacks. The reserve company, supported by a troop of tanks, was pushed into position between A and C, while the carrier platoon was placed under Joe's command and sent to strengthen the position between A and D, B and C companies then made a 'short sharp counter-attack' to help relieve the pressure.

'It was a question of backs to the wall, if you like,' said Joe. 'And things looked a bit black.'

There must have been an incredible sense of relief when communications were established with the other battalions in the brigade, who were now pushing the enemy back.

'Things started looking up,' said Joe.

They looked even better when those two battalions, 1/5th Welch and 7th Royal Welch Fusiliers, secured the flanks of the East Lancs, and 71st Brigade came up and began to push through them.

'The (Highland Light Infantry) came through with the (bag)pipes blazing,' recalled Bob Atkinson. 'It was rather good to hear them.'

Bob had been in position for so long that his knees and feet had sunk deep into the mud, and he needed the help of his comrades to pull him free from the forest's grasp.

'Early the next morning, they come up with food, and we got our rations that we'd missed, so we were having porridge and pudding in one dixie. We had it all to eat, and we thought we'd clear it, but you can only get through about half of it.'

After a short 'rest' in the mud and rain, the battalion moved to the north-east corner of the Reichswald Forest.

Owen Butcher was given the unenviable task of collecting the bodies of the men who had fallen in the previous action. 'I went back into the Reichswald with a padre, and a colour sergeant, to remove the bodies. I wasn't particularly keen, although I didn't have a choice. You do as you're told.

'The lorries parked on the track. You're just wandering around, looking where you think different companies were, and where people are going to be lying. A lot of the casualties at that point were from shells bursting in the trees. I mean, sometimes there was complete bodies. Or sometimes there was parts of bodies. It wasn't the best of jobs. I think today you'd want counselling. Might even want compensation.'

The East Lancs suffered 142 casualties in the Reichswald, with twenty-three killed in the first three days of the battle. Some were draftees of eighteen, while others were old soldiers who had been with the battalion since before Dunkirk. Their CO, Lieutenant-Colonel Allen, later spoke with a reporter from the *Yorkshire Post* about the experience of his battalion at that time.

'We were cold. We were wet. We were hungry. And we kept on fighting.

'It was bloody. Observation was from one tree to the next. We were behind one tree and the Bosch was behind the next. A terribly wearing business for the men. Psychologically, and mentally. It was nearly all bayonet, Sten, and grenade fighting. The Bosch reserves fought very well, stubborn, and had to be dug out with the bayonet.'[2]

Major Joe Cêtre was equally proud of his men through the war.

'The quality of the soldiers couldn't be better. They were really the salt of the earth. They were splendid men, right back from the days of Dunkirk, when they were all regular (soldiers).

'Later on in the fighting, we didn't have the regulars, but the National Servicemen who took their place had the same qualities. And the endurance – not only the endurance, but the fighting qualities – in spite of all conditions, they always showed.'

Referring specifically to the Reichswald, Joe continued: 'In conditions of the thaw, mud, incessant rain, transport bogged down, a lot of the kit and equipment, mortars and ammunition, having to be humped manually, with hardly any rest, erratic feeding, soaked to the skin, (they) still managed to fight doggedly on. And to reach the final objective, after five days of continuous fighting, I think that there is no equal amongst any other soldiers in the world, in what the British soldier did, and can do. And the Lancastrian soldier at that.'

A Rough Old Cup of Tea

Major Cêtre's interview was a rarity in the degree of detail he was able to recall when describing the actions of the Reichswald. More often soldiers' tales came as stark snapshots, pinned to memory by a particular emotion, or sense. All battles are chaotic, all killing is primitive, but perhaps this is never more so than in our primordial home.

'It was terrifying at night,' infantryman Roland Dane, 7th Black Watch, said of the forest. 'You'd hear the sounds, and your nerves are taut all the time, because you never knew when there was a German patrol coming through, and you'd hear clicks and rustles of the trees. Water, dripping. And at night they magnify. It was your imagination that was working.'

'The forest was eerie,' recalled Cyril Handley, 9th Royal Tank Regiment (RTR). 'It got to you. The forest itself got to you. You never knew what was going to happen. You didn't know who was where.'

'It was like looking into a tunnel that you can't see the other end of,' said Joe Abbot, 53rd Reconnaissance Regiment. 'Just blackness, and all trees, and mud underneath.'

From bullets to blades, there were many ways to die in the Reichswald.

'A lot of casualties were caused by air bursts and shells hitting trees,' said Fred White, 1st Battalion, Oxfordshire and Buckinghamshire Light Infantry. 'Jerry wasn't daft – he had all those spots marked.'

'You were taking it and not giving it half the time,' said Dai Edwards, 2nd Monmouthshires. 'We endured it, mainly. It's the same as Normandy. We very rarely saw the enemy at all. Fellas were being killed (who) had never seen an enemy soldier, especially if you were being shelled.'

Raymond 'Ray' Chandler, of the same battalion, agreed that soldiers rarely saw the enemy until they started firing. 'The weather didn't help at all. The German soldier, although he was retreating and on the losing end, he was a very good soldier. He didn't give up very easily.'

Ray fought many actions in the forest, but he didn't know if he'd killed his enemy.

'I don't know. I honestly don't know. I fired at them. I've always assumed that I hit them, but I never stopped to have a look. I honestly don't know.'

As well as the danger of artillery, mines and small arms, the German defenders of the forest had anti-tank guns and armour, and the deadly handheld Panzerfausts.

'Once we were in there, all the soldiers wanted to get off (the Bren carrier),' said Ray, 'and they'd walk, but I had to stay in there and drive. I heard a *whoosh*, and they all tell me that it was a German handheld rocket launcher. Thank God he missed. It went over the top of me.'

'Why did they get out and walk?' Ray was asked.

'It was blooming safer,' he laughed back.

Bruce Coombs, 6 RWF, was an experienced soldier who had fought since Normandy.

'It wasn't very nice,' he said simply of the Reichswald. 'I don't remember taking my boots off, going through the forest. An infantryman never took his boots off, unless he was in the rear. When you did take them off your socks were marked on your feet. The stitching.

'You sleep in your trenches if you're in the actual front. You never had no blankets or nothing like that. You just get your head down and sleep.'

'You got so tired, to keep awake was incredible,' said Dai Edwards. 'You'd fall asleep in anything. It didn't matter if the ground was muddy, or wet. (Lack of sleep) was the main thing. It was so debilitating. I think you began to imagine things.'

Robert Smith was a sapper in the 282nd Field Company, Royal Engineers, who had the impossible task of trying to turn the few muddy tracks into serviceable roads.

'We tried to overcome this problem by sinking tree trunks and rubble and goodness knows what, but it just sunk into the mud, and it was just a waste of time. We as engineers could do very little to assist, try as we may. We just had to follow up on foot, leaving all our transport behind. The whole of the first few days was purely a footslog by the infantry.'

In times of danger and gruelling conditions, soldiers often relied on a few 'characters' to keep their spirits high.

'One night it was tipping down with rain,' said Thomas O'Brien, Royal Army Service Corps (RASC), whose elder brother had been killed earlier in the war, 'and these infantry boys was there, the RWF I think. We was in a farm, and they were going (to attack) in the morning. This bloke started up with a mouth organ, and he started playing, "This is the lovely way, to spend an evening".'

'Don't matter what company it is, you'll always get a comedian,' said Fred White, who was known as 'Chalky' to his mates. 'And while you've got a comedian, your morale's high. If you've got no comedian, you're right at the bottom.'

Tea was also essential for the soldier's morale.

'Edgar, my mate, he had to tell my kids about the day I gave him a cup of tea. Because it was the unwritten law. If you were in action, no matter who it was, if you wanted a cup of tea, and you were brewing up, they could have one. That was unwritten law.

'Edgar joined us in the Reichswald, he'd just come back off leave. What a place to come back to! From Whitney to the Reichswald. So he said, "Mate, cup of tea, Chalky?", so Chalky makes a cup of tea. He took a mouthful and he said, "Blimey, this is rough. Where'd you get the water?" I said, "From a ditch." I won't tell you what he said, but he loves telling my kids this. Yeah, "Your old man and his ruddy water out the ditch." I said to him, "Well, you drunk it?" He said, "Yes, but it was a rough old cup of tea."

Tanks in the Trees

The Wehrmacht did not believe that the Reichswald would be passable to tanks, but General Crerar was determined to push armour through along with his infantry.

'We had to knock the trees down as we went through,' said Charles Poulter, who had been drafted in 1942, and served with C Squadron, 9 RTR. 'Keep away from the tracks, because they were mined. We had to push the trees down and travel like that until we reached the end of the forest. That took a week to ten days to do that.'

During that time the tanks covered a distance of some seven miles – a far cry from some of the rapid advances that had been made following the Battle of Normandy – and the attrition rate of the vehicles was incredibly high.

'Out of the fifty tanks that had left (the start line), I think it was only twenty tanks that reached the end (of the forest).'

Charles's own tank was one of those that did make it, and his troop was ordered onto a track junction to support the nearby infantry.

'Each tank was on the T-junction, each with their backs facing one another, looking down each side of the junction. The infantry were dug in on the sides of us in the forest.'

That night the troop was visited by the squadron's second in command, 'Captain Leek, and Trooper Paget, they came round with a rum ration, which was welcome because it warmed us up a little bit.'

Each of the tank's crew would spend one hour on guard duty in the commander's position, while the other four tried to sleep within the confines of the armour. One night, shortly before midnight in the pitch-black forest, Charles was relieved from the duty by his sergeant, Reg Mead. Charles moved down into the tank, but before he could fall asleep he heard someone moving on the top deck.

'And they said, "Are you alright, Jock?" in broken English. And when somebody said that I gathered there was a problem, but before we could do anything about it, there was a machine gun, a German machine gun, fired. Automatic fire.'

Charles quickly pulled Sergeant Mead down into the turret, but it was too late.

'I knew what had happened to him when I pulled him inside, cause blood was everywhere. I closed the hatches, and at least that stopped a grenade or something being thrown inside the tank. We couldn't fire any guns, we were just helpless inside, cause the infantry that were around us, and our own crews were so close together. Then I heard a bit of a thud from outside.'

The next morning Charles was able to piece together the events of the night before.

'One of the German infantry had gone in front of the tank, and fired a bazooka at the tank, and that bazooka had luckily enough struck the thickest part of the tank, and it had scooped a big churn of the armour out of the front.'

Sergeant Alfred 'Reg' Mead had been killed outright, shot in the back of the head by the German infiltrators.[3]

'The commanding officer said to me, "Get a couple of the lads and lift him out the tank. Go through his pockets. Get all the information in his pockets, and let me have them."'

This was so the officer could know the names and addresses of Reg's loved ones, and write to them with his condolences. After Reg had been taken from the tank, the decision was made to wait for a padre before burying him.

'Suddenly one of our own infantry came through the trees. (He) spoke to our commanding officer and said there was a counter-attack coming in just the other side of the clearing.'

The commanding officer told Charles to stay where he was with his tank. He would take the others to deal with the counter-attack, and then return to see to Sergeant Mead.

'And I knew by what he said that's what he's going to do, because we relied on him, and trusted him.'

Indeed, the officer was true to his word. When the troop had returned, and a padre had been found, the soldiers buried their comrade, Reg.

'We had a quick service. Another spare crew came up, and we carried on.'[4]

The enemy made the British soldiers pay dearly for their advance through the forest, but a 'friendly' bullet was just as deadly. With so many men fighting in such difficult terrain, and often at night, 'friendly fire' incidents were inevitable.

On 9 February, Raymond Wigmore, 1 Ox and Bucks, was going into an attack in the Reichswald. The infantry were being supported by tanks, but these soon became bogged down in the viscous mud.

'We were catching up with the barrage, and we had to stop. I was stood by the lieutenant, shoulder to shoulder. One of these tanks had managed to get out of being bogged down, and it was firing the BESA machine guns. We used to call them Beezers.'

The tanks were firing long bursts over the heads of the infantry, but as one hit a dip in the ground the nose of the tank dipped down, and the aim of the gunner with it.

'It shot the platoon commander stood next to me. His shoulder was almost touching me, and it shot him through the head from the rear and he went down, killed by his own tank. I called over a couple of stretcher-bearers and I said, "Mr White's been hit." I said, "I think he's dead." So they said, "Yeah," and with that we carried on. We didn't stop the advance because of that. We just stopped because we were catching up with the creeping barrage. That's the reason we stopped. And then we just carried on.'

Lieutenant Arthur White was twenty-two years old.[5]

'Then we got into the two houses our platoon had to capture. And we got round the back of the Germans and it was a bit chaotic for our side, because it was pitch dark and there was Germans and you didn't know who was who. You didn't know who was Germans. And I think one of our men were killed because of that. He went up to somebody who he thought was one of us but it wasn't, it was a German. And the Germans shot first. I think we had three killed (on that attack). That wasn't too bad. Well, it's bad having anyone killed. It could have been worse. That's what I meant. Yeah.'

Twenty-one-year-old Charles White served in the 5th Cameron Highlanders, with whom he had fought since Normandy. His stories of the Reichswald are illustrative of the chaos that reigned during the battle.

'They were behind ya, they were in front of ya, they were at the side of ya. You didn't know where they were. It was a little bit dicey.

'(One night) I got me mess tin of food, walking back up this track, and coming in the opposite direction were three other people. Two were carrying a big dixie between them, and the other was carrying one for tea. So we got close to one another, and we actually passed one another, and they had Airborne helmets on. I thought, *We've got no Airborne up here with us.*

Just as I thought, *Jerries*, he must have thought, *British*. I dropped me mess tins and grabbed me Sten gun, and one of these grabbed his revolver. I had him, and I took the other two as prisoners.'

Charles and his comrades came out on top in that instance, but the tables were often turned.

'At about the second or third day, we'd taken our objective and we were told to dig in.'

The men were then ordered to drop their equipment, taking only weapons and ammunition to 'go look for snipers. We had to leave one fella looking after our kit. I think it was Whiteoak.'

Charles and the others went out on the patrol and 'rounded up a few' snipers. 'They were dealt with,' he said nonchalantly.

When they returned to their kit they found twenty-nine-year-old Frank Whiteoak sitting on the edge of the trench.[6]

'Now, I don't know if you've seen anyone shot, but when they're shot they go white, and then they go a creamy colour, then everything goes dull about them. (Whiteoak's) face was glowing, and his eyes were sparkling, but he didn't move. They'd hit him right in the back of the neck, and I'd never seen a feller like it. He was sitting there at peace with the world, stone dead.'

The Other Side

Twenty-seven-year-old Victor Burton had been called up in 1939 and served in the East Lancs. As an old soldier and a Dunkirk man, he must have been held in awe by the fresh-faced replacements who were arriving to replace the battalion's many losses.

'I used to be running backwards and forwards (to the battalion) on me Bren carrier, and we were getting reinforcements because we'd lost a lot of infantry, and I always remember going back to pick these reinforcements up, and when I saw them, there was about six or eight of them, and I thought, *Ooo, these are young*, so I said, 'How old are ya?' And some were eighteen and a half. Some were nineteen. They'd come straight out from England, and I thought, *There's thousands and thousands of soldiers all the way back to Normandy, and these lads are coming straight from England. (They're) in for a rough time in this forest.*

'Anyway, I hung on at the outskirts of the forest until it got dusk, and then I had to take 'em up. And I took 'um up, and I said, "I'm gonna drop you in this ditch. Jump out in this ditch. But I'm not going t' turn the carrier until you've got away from here. To turn the carrier I've got to lock one track, and rev up like hell and spin around, but as soon as Jerry hears that, he won't half drop some clatter here, so get away from here. Good luck, lads."'

Victor returned to the forest the next day, bringing up food and ammunition. He then returned to Nijmegen, his carrier again fully laden with men.

'I was bringing six bodies back. Not saying they were the lads I took up. Could've been. Could've been anybody, cause they were wrapped in blankets like, with just their boots showing. And I thought, *Oh, hell, have they only had one night of war?* And it might not have been them, but it was somebody.'

Hundreds of 'somebodies' were dying in the Reichswald, and thousands more were injured. Those that remained lived in melting snow, rain and mud. They were constantly shelled, sniped and called into action. Joe Abbot, of the 53rd Reconnaissance Regiment, was asked how the soldiers coped with it all.

'I'll be quite honest with you, I don't know. I mean, when I think about it now, and I think of what you did, and how you went on and on, and the state you got in, and what you must have been like, I don't know.'

Towards the end of the battle Joe saw a sight that would stay with him for the rest of his life – the thousand-yard stares of soldiers coming out of the line.

'I saw HLI lads coming back, just oblivious of whatever was around them, just staring straight ahead. They'd been without food, and tea, or anything. Just, as I say, completely oblivious of anything, because it was a shocking place, and the German firepower was terrific. I'll never forget those infantry coming back, just staring straight ahead.'

But the British soldiers – many of them younger than twenty and facing battle for the first time – did achieve their mission of pushing through the Reichswald after ten days of fierce fighting.

'The Germans didn't think we'd get through (the forest),' said Bruce Coombs, '(but) the Welsh Division went through the middle of it.'

On 18 February the 53rd Division – less its artillery – were pulled back for a couple of days to re-fit and receive replacements. The number of replacements required by each battalion, which should number around 800 men at full strength, gives a clear indication as to the attrition that they suffered in the forest:

The 4th Battalion, Royal Welch Fusiliers received 365 replacements, the 6th Battalion 276, and the 7th Battalion 359. 4 Welch required 281 new men, and the Highland Light Infantry 239. The 2nd Battalion, Monmouthshire Regiment needed 242 replacements, while 148 went to the East Lancs, 137 to 1/5th Welch and 203 to 1 Ox and Bucks.[7]

Bruce Coombs, who had fought through the forest with 6 RWF, was left with a question that was never answered.

'7th Battalion was on the end of the woods, and they'd captured that, and we had to go through 'em. We came down on these Churchill tanks, and as we got near the forest they started shelling us, so we jumped off the tanks, and we're walking along forward. And as we're walking forward we got into the forest, and with that there come down a barrage. They had more gunfire on us there than what they did in Normandy.'

Along with two of his comrades, Bruce rushed for cover beneath the nearest tank.

'We laid low, Wagstaff in front of me, I was in the middle, and Ryan was behind me. It suddenly dawned on me, if that tank started moving, the back one, he wouldn't see us, so I said to Wagstaff, "Let's get out of here."

'I shouted to Ryan, and with that, down comes the barrage again. We were hiding down behind the tree, and all of a sudden I looked over, and the tank had started moving. All I could see was an arm (sticking up) out of the mud. The tank had gone over him.'

Still under shellfire, Wagstaff ran to the front of the tank to get the driver's attention, while Bruce tried the back. He looked for the phone that connected with the crew's intercom, but found that it had been shot away.

'There was nothing we could do. The tank had gone over him and he was buried.'

The two men had put themselves at great risk to come to the aid of their comrade, and now paid the price.

'A shell landed between me and Wagstaff. It blew us off our feet, and it turned my eyelids in. I had a job to get them out. I thought I'd lost my sight for a minute.

'I heard Wagstaff moaning, and he said, "I've been hit." All I could see was a blur. It took a while for my eyes to come back. Wagstaff gets up and he starts going back down the road, and I heard him shouting as he's going back, "Stretcher-bearers!" As it happened he walked back into RHQ (Regimental Headquarters), and the RSM seen him and they took him back.'[8]

When Bruce's eyesight returned he caught up with his platoon and reported to his sergeant.

'I said, "Wagstaff's been wounded, and Ryan's been run over by a tank." He said, "Come back with me, we'll go and look where Ryan is."'

But before this could happen, the two men were approached by one of their officers.

'(He) said, "We've got to go on again."'

The battle continued. The army marched on. Then, in times of peace, came the chance for men to search for the answers that war had denied them.

'I have been back in the forest, looking for that place,' said Bruce. 'It's strange to me. I often wonder if he was found, you know?'

CHAPTER 5

Moyland

15th (Scottish) Division on the road to Kalkar
12–17 February 1945

'What they used to do with the dead comrades, they'd leave them in the road and put a gas cape over them, with their boots sticking out of the bottom. And I thought, that's the way I'm going to end up.'

Tom Gore, 9th Battalion,
The Cameronians (Scottish Rifles)

12 February

Kenneth 'Ken' Ohlson was an artillery Forward Observation Officer of 531 Battery, 190th Field Regiment, and part of the 15th (Scottish) Division. In later months he would become aide-de-camp to General Horrocks, and was at that time given some insight into a particular battle in which he had been involved – it took place on 12 February, on the road from Kleve to Xanten.

'(Horrocks) had the idea that perhaps you could burst down this corridor and get a bridge, and he picked what he told me was two crack regiments to do this. One was the Seaforths, and the other was the Coldstream Guards.'

Ken and a fellow FOO – Peter Spafford – would ride ahead with the assault and direct the fire of the artillery. Ken would be with the mounted infantry, and Peter in a Churchill tank of the Guards.

'(We) formed up at dawn on the outskirts of Kleve in a school playground. Peter's with the leading (element), and he came out of his tank and he'd got a steel helmet on. You can't wear a steel helmet in a tank. You can't get a headset on.

'I said, "What's going on, Pete?" And he said, "I don't like the sound of this at all."'

'This' was an advance on a narrow front during daylight, made along an important road that would no doubt be heavily defended. Any doubts Peter had about the plan were entirely understandable, but his behaviour was out of character enough for Ken to notice it – Peter had won a Military Cross in Normandy for rallying two companies of infantry when all of their officers had been killed or wounded, successfully withdrawing them under heavy fire. Clearly, he was not a man easily worried.

'Anyhow, we moved off, and it was a drizzly day. I was in the Kangaroo, listening to a bit of play on the wireless, and then I suddenly heard a voice say, "My God, I've been killed."

'We hadn't gotten more than a mile, and we obviously weren't making much progress. The leading troops from me were probably another half-mile up the road, and my battery commander, a man called Michael Wingate, came up behind me and said, "I'm terribly sorry, Ken. Peter's been killed."'[1]

It was Peter's voice that Ken had heard on the radio.

'He was a very brave chap. Lovely big ginger-haired Scotsman.'

The push to clear a route to Xanten continued.

'It's a long story, but the short answer is it didn't work, and we had a bloody nose, and the thing was called off the next day.'

Ken was too humble to give more detail, and does not mention that 'the long story' involved actions that earned him a Military Cross. His citation recounts how, following Peter's death, Ken asked for permission to go up with the tanks and replace him. This was refused. He was instead told to go forward with the Officer in Command (OC) of D Company, 7th Seaforths, to report progress and order any artillery tasks required.

D Company had not made it far along the road when the two leading personnel carriers were taken out by Self-Propelled (SP) guns. A total of seven Kangaroos were lost, and a withdrawal was ordered, but some of the infantry had been left behind. Ken remained where he was, directing artillery fire onto the enemy. He then took his vehicle forward under fire to collect the stranded infantry, and recovered them to safety.

A Military Cross was also awarded that day to Lieutenant John McCracken McNair, an officer of the Queen's Own Royal West Kent Regiment, serving as a platoon commander in C Company of the 7th Seaforths. John was a conscientious objector at the outset of the war, but later changed his mind about its justification. His actions, and those of many others, are proof that the act of objecting to the use of violence was not born out of fear for one's own safety.

During the clearing of the village of Hasselt, McNair's company were forced to withdraw by an enemy counter-attack. His platoon was at that time under heavy machine-gun fire, and McNair extracted the first two sections, then returned under fire to get the third, eliminating the machine-gun post in the process. He then learned that his platoon sergeant had been wounded and left behind.

'Lt McNair without hesitation returned to the village to find him, although the enemy by this time was shelling it very heavily and Spandau fire was sweeping the streets. He found and remained with the sergeant until he was able to direct an armoured car to the spot and thereby evacuate the wounded man. It was not until he was certain that all of his men of his platoon and company were clear of the village that Lt McNair himself finally left.'[2]

A second attempt was made by the Seaforths and Guards on the 13th, but this also met with strong resistance and failure, Ken Ohlson barely escaping with his life when the building he was in was blown to pieces. By a stroke of luck he was in the basement at the time, and escaped without injury.

That same day, the 9th Cameronians received their orders for their own attack. For Tom Gore, who had already been wounded in Normandy, it would prove to be one battle too many.

Moyland Wood

On 15 February, as the rain beat down, attempts to force a road to Xanten resumed. The 9th Cameronians were to leave Kleve and follow the road to the village of Moyland, some five miles east.

'Some of us had found umbrellas in the cellars,' said Tom Gore. 'Sergeant Major Smith come down the line and made us throw them away. He said "You look like a lot of Chinese coolies."'

'Our section was leading what they call an "advance to contact". Now this is not a very nice place to be out in front in an advance to contact, in case the enemy contact you first.'

After taking some shelling, and hearing the 'usual cry' of stretcher-bearers, the column moved on. At a cluster of houses they came across 'two Germans, just coming out to get on their bicycles, so we all fired at 'em, and they moved back in the house'.

The patrol got into the building but the two enemy soldiers had escaped out of the back.

'But in the cellar there was about eight Germans, badly wounded, with their legs off. The stink was terrific down there. Their bandages looked filthy. It was nothing to do with us, we had to keep moving. So we just left them.'

Around the next corner was a British reconnaissance car ablaze.

'That was the last thing that hit the enemy before us, apparently.'

Looking down the long straight road, Tom could make out the edge of a forest known as Moyland Wood. Unbeknown to him, the enemy had decided that Moyland was to be held at all costs to stop the Allies reaching Xanten, and had made it one of their strongpoints in the Rhineland. The wood was held by paratroopers and armour, and 'supported by immense artillery and mortar fire'.[3]

'It was to be a sad place for A Company,' said Tom.

The push forward continued, a German vehicle in the distance managing to escape the fire of a British tank.

'We moved up the side of the woods. Dug in, in case the fireworks started. You always dug in. We were there for a couple of hours. Our section was ordered to move up through the woods to see what was there.

'We went up through, and there was a bunker there. We opened the window, and Corporal Grant fired a burst of Sten gun in there, and there must have been sixteen to eighteen fully armed Germans come out of there. There was only six of us.'

The enemy were taken prisoner and sent to the rear. The section then took up position and observed the wooded area in front of them.

'All of a sudden a German soldier come walking out through the (fire) gap. Corporal Grant says one man fire at him, and it turned out to be me. I had to fire at him. So I took aim, put all me training into practice. He must have been about two hundred yards. I set me sights, and fired.'

The German 'dropped like a sack of spuds'.

'"Good shot," they said. And then it suddenly dawned on me, that was my first real kill. And good thoughts never went through me mind. He was somebody's relation, after all. So I weren't proud of me kill.'

Tom dwelled on this as he continued watching for enemy movement. It came from an unlikely place: the man that he'd 'killed'.

'After about ten minutes this German soldier got up, bent forward, 'olding his arm, and he run down through the gap. We all fired at him and he sort of zig-zagged. There was a German position further up the road and he got to that, so I was grateful, really, that he got up and run away.'

The patrol reported back to the battalion and settled in for the night.

'There was a cottage up in front. A thatched cottage, and there was a white flag had come out of there earlier in the day. The whole family had moved out and went through our lines.'

With the building now unoccupied by civilians, Tom's platoon sergeant, Sergeant Rose, fired tracer bullets into the thatch so that it would light up the night, and allow them to see any enemy counter-attacks that might come from the woods.

Tom had hoped for a quiet night, but not long after dark A Company was ordered into the trees.

'It was black as ink in there,' said Tom. 'We kept as close as we could, but we did lose contact with the leading platoon, so we stopped, and all of a sudden somebody shouted, "Grenade! Grenade! Throw a grenade!" up in front of us.'

The wood seemed suddenly full of the clatter of gunfire, the flashes of explosions lighting up the trees.

'There was a hell of a lot of firing up there.'

The other two platoons of A Company pushed up and joined the leading platoon on the high ground, but they were disorganized due to the darkness and the thickness of the woods. The CO gave the company permission to remain where it was and consolidate. They were also ordered to reach their objective by first light, in order to support an attack being made by Canadian soldiers. This objective would need to be reconnoitred in the darkness, and three men were chosen for the dangerous task.

'A sergeant, meself, and Rifleman Baker,' said Tom, adding that Baker was 'the one who told the jokes back in Nijmegen', on the eve of Operation Veritable.

'We crawled out to the woods, and much to my relief, the sergeant thought the same as me – that it would be fatal to go into them woods. Survival's the name of the game, remember. So we laid up for probably about half 'our, which was the longest half 'our of me life, then he told us what he was going to report when we went back, in case we were asked.'

The attack continued in the morning. Tom's platoon was second in the line of A Company's advance as they pushed off to clear more of the woods.

'And all of a sudden, all hell was let loose. We all hit the ground. Several men dashed back through the woods, and took up positions beside us.'

These men belonged to the leading platoon, the highest rank among them a lance-corporal. Tom remembers an officer shouting over the gunfire: '"Corporal, why aren't you with your section?" and the corporal answered him in very strong words. "I ain't got no 'effin section," he said. "They're all taken prisoner or killed!"'

Bullets were whipping through the trees, snapping branches and throwing up dirt. The enemy seemed to be all around.

'Germans were shouting to us, "Come in, Tommy, put your hands up. We can see you. Hands up, Tommy. Come in."'

Something needed to be done before the entire company was cut off and destroyed. Tom recalled his OC, Major Shearer, shouting for one of his NCOs, Corporal Jackman.

'Corporal Jackman had been with us since Normandy, and his leave was due in two days' time. He said he shouldn't have been in this attack cause of his leave,' said Tom, who had spent the battalion's last night in Holland sleeping on the floor beside Jackman. Now they were lying in the dirt together as the enemy's bullets cracked inches above their heads.

'He was on my left. I could have put my 'and back and touched him. And the major was shouting for him, so (Jackman) got up onto his arms, pushed his arms to get up, and *bang*!'

Jackman slumped down, his head turned towards Tom.

'There was a look of dismay on his face, and he must have been shot right through the head I should think. I never looked again, cause these sort of things you don't look. You get the picture and you don't look again.'[4]

A runner then arrived from another platoon, who were fighting their own desperate battle, and reported to the OC.

'He said, "8 Platoon's being counter-attacked, sir!" And Shearer said, "So am I!"'

All momentum in the attack had been lost, and the company was in danger of being picked apart. The only option remaining was to pull back.

'The only casualty we had in our section was a man shot in the bum when we retreated,' said Tom.

And though they were now out of the worst of it, battles continued to rage inside the woods, Tom's company providing fire support. WASP flamethrowers then raced up to shoot long tongues of fire over the enemy positions.

'They burnt the Jerries out. Just burnt them. You could see them running from the trenches on fire and being shot down.'

A few of the enemy had survived to be captured.

'Somebody had took three prisoners,' said Tom. 'I don't know who took 'em because we weren't taking prisoners really, in this close fighting.'

They were quite possibly taken by Sergeant Rose, who had led Tom's platoon through a minefield on 8 February. Rose had not received an award for his bravery that day, but his actions at Moyland were recognized with the Military Medal. The citation recorded that:

'Serjeant Rose, having arranged for covering fire from one section of his platoon, himself made his way forward, attacked and silenced one of the enemy positions. He returned to his platoon, bringing in two prisoners after having killed the other two members of the Spandau team.

'Shortly afterwards, an exactly similar situation developed and Sergeant Rose again went forward single-handed, and having successfully and effectively liquidated the enemy position from which heavy fire from automatic weapons had been directed at his platoon, he returned bringing with him another prisoner.'[5]

'One of them was wounded in the leg,' said Tom, 'and his leg was so swollen that all the stitches had come out of the seam of his trousers.'

After sharing a cigarette with the captured Germans, Tom was ordered to take them back to Brigade Headquarters. Considering what was to follow, perhaps there was a recognition by Tom's NCOs that he was coming to the end of his tether, and in need of a break from the action.

'Further back we picked up another stretcher with a wounded rifleman and some more Germans carrying him. We went back through the woods, and there was a battalion of Canadians.'

Until this point Tom had been unaware that both his battalion, and corps, were 'on loan' to the First Canadian Army. He watched as the wounded were taken away – 'The rifleman and his enemy on the same jeep' – then added his three POWs to a group of 'twenty to thirty' others.

'And the thing to do then was to take the watches off the prisoners,' said Tom, meaning that the soldiers took the watches for themselves. 'I'd already had two off the three prisoners I took back. I asked the other Germans for their watches, and one of them said to me, in plain English, "I've only one watch." They'd all been taken off them.'

Tom then marshalled this larger group of POWs back to Brigade HQ. He was about to return to his company when he saw a line of men waiting for food.

'I soon joined them, and I remember the meal was pork chops, peas, mashed potatoes, and a peach in custard. Now this was nothing like the grub we were getting.' With a full belly, and thoughts of breakfast, 'I decided to stay the night.'

Tom found a room with an unoccupied bed. 'Next morning I went down to breakfast, and a sergeant started asking questions. I set off out the door, intending to go back to the company, and it suddenly dawned on me: *I'm not going back in them woods.*'

The proximity of death, always present, now fell heavily upon him, and Tom pictured himself lying dead, his boots sticking out from a gas cape laid over him.

'Something told me not to go back in that woods again. So instead of turning left I turned right, and walked away from it.'

AWOL

After removing his ammunition and insignia, Tom thumbed a lift on a DUKW heading to the rear, and Nijmegen.

'I went down the NAAFI. All they had to eat was rock buns and tea.'

He then walked into the town and knocked on the front door of a home belonging to a Dutch family, asking to sleep in their garage. They did not find this strange, as billeting in civilian property was common at the time.

'She showed me to a first-class bedroom with white sheets. Next morning there was hot water for a shave. I didn't shave much because you must remember, I was only nineteen.'

In leaving his unit, Tom was far from alone. The British and Commonwealth forces lost 100,000 men to desertion during the war, and this did not include the number of men who returned within thirty-one days, during which time they were deemed 'Absent

Without Leave' (AWOL), rather than 'Dropped From Rolls' (DFR), as deserters were termed. Thousands of men who were both AWOL and DFR were behind the lines at any one time, some with the intention of returning to their units after a break, others doing everything that they could to get home.

After spending some time in Nijmegen, Tom fell in with a group of men who had all made the choice to go AWOL from their units. Their destination was Brussels by way of Eindhoven, and along the way they slept in farm buildings and bartered for food with the owners. One day, 'Breakfast time, the corporal that was with us, made a deal with a farmer for breakfast. We had a fried egg on a bit of black bread, with a cup of acorn coffee I suppose it was.'

The group then left the farm and continued on their way, but it wasn't long until they saw a motorbike coming down the road towards them – the rider was a military policeman. Tom believed that the farmer must have placed a phone call after they'd left his home, and for a time a game of cat and mouse ensued before the group decided that it was better to just face the music.

'We were really thankful, really, that something had happened, cause I don't know what would have happened if we'd got back to Brussels.'

A lorry was called for, and the men taken back and put in 'a great big schoolroom of Absent Without Leave personnel'. After sharing a bucket as a toilet for two days, Tom's escort arrived to take him back to his battalion. The escort – 'a couple of me mates and a lance-corporal, filled me in with all the details.'

These details included what had happened to the battalion in Tom's absence. Attacks on the woods had continued during the 18th and 19th, but despite support from Army Group Artillery and rocket-firing Typhoons, 'the bravery shown by the infantry was not enough',[6] and casualties had been heavy.

'There'd been an Irish section in our platoon,' said Tom. 'They were all gone.'

Moyland Woods was also a place of tragedy for the Canadian Army. Counter-attacks made by elements of 116th Panzer Division caused many casualties on both sides. It wasn't until 22 February, a week after Tom's battalion had gone in on the attack, that Moyland Woods was finally captured by Canadian troops, the enemy forced to withdraw due to events occurring further south – this included another large action in which the 9th Cameronians took part, at Goch. On 26 February they were withdrawn to Tilburg, Holland, to re-fit and receive replacements. It was here that Tom rejoined his comrades.

'There were sixty-four of us there, Absent Without Leave. This is a sad part of this tale, but it's gotta be told with the other. There was so many of us that the 'eadquarter company couldn't feed us, so every mealtime an escort arrived from our own company, and took us back to our own company lines for feeding.'

Tom did not say explicitly that he felt guilt for leaving his platoon, but perhaps the following statement is an indication that he did.

'All our mates were there, all me comrades, and this camaraderie in the section during the war was terrific.'

Tom was eventually marched in front of the commanding officer, Lieutenant-Colonel Remington-Hobbs. 'He read the riot act to me. Told me I'd been a bad boy, and all that business, and he said, "I'll leave this to your company commander."'

This was a temporary commander, Major MacNeil, who later took over A Company from Major Shearer on a permanent basis.

'(MacNeil) in turn said, "I don't know much about this rifleman myself, but I've spoken to his platoon commander, and he gives him a glowing character"' and said how unlike me it was, because I'd done so well in previous actions.

'Remington-Hobbs looked at me, said, "There you are. You *can* do it. Don't come in front of me again."'

Tom was given twenty-eight days' field punishment, which amounted to cleaning pots and pans for the battalion's kitchen, but after five days 'I was kitted out again with me rifle, sixty rounds of ammunition, two hand grenades.'

The battalion was going back into the line.

Tom rejoined his platoon but didn't recognize many of the faces. Twenty-nine men of the 9th Cameronians were killed in the few days of fighting around Moyland, and many more were wounded. Others had fallen in the battle for Goch, and replacements had been sent to fill their shoes.

'All the platoon was full up with all youngsters then,' said Tom. 'They were all eighteen-year-old boys. I was an old one at nineteen.'

CHAPTER 6

Goch

12–22 February 1945

'There was hatred. Hatred for the Germans for what they'd done. For all the boys that had been killed. Some of the infantry regiments had lost 120 per cent since Normandy. They were new people that were there. Everyone was young. They were scraping the barrel.'

Ronald 'Ronnie' Henderson, 13/18th Royal Hussars

The advance of the 43rd (Wessex) to the Goch Escarpment

Twenty-four-year-old Eric Wheeler was an old hand in the 4th Wiltshires, but by February 1945 he knew few of the men that he was fighting beside.

'Virtually the whole battalion had changed. The men I knew best of course were in C Company, but then we lost a lot of those, and with the reinforcements you just didn't know anyone. As in Normandy, you'd have reinforcements one day, and a couple of days later they were gone.'

After the battle for Kleve the 43rd (Wessex) Division had seized Bedburg to the south of the city, where they were counter-attacked by the 116th Panzer Division on 12 February. The stout defence of the 43rd, combined with that of the 53rd Division's repulsion of their own German counter-attacks at the eastern edge of the Reichswald Forest, convinced the enemy that Kleve could not be retaken. Instead, they pulled their forces back to consolidate a new line of defences running from Hasselt on the Kalkar road, along the Esberg ridge just south of Bedburg to the edge of the north-west corner of the Forest of Kleve.[1]

This line would be defended by remnants of the 84th Division on the right, the 15th Panzer Grenadiers on the left and elements of 116th Panzers supporting them both. The newly arrived 364th Division also joined the battle.[2]

Against this enemy, the 43rd (Wessex) Division and 8th Armoured Brigade attacked – their objective was the Goch Escarpment, some six miles south of Kleve.

Their advance began on 13 February, when the 5th Wiltshires pushed south-east of Bedburg. They came under intense shelling, suffering high casualties, but the battalion pressed on and seized the ridge that was their objective. The 4th Wiltshires now pushed through their sister battalion to seize the hamlet of Trippenburg, and its vital crossroads.

'We were at the rear of the company,' said Eric Wheeler, A Company, 4 Wilts, 'and we looked round, and we saw a German half-track full of troops coming about a hundred and fifty yards behind us. We took them on, of course. When we caught up with the company we were told off for not keeping up with the main advance. And that's the sort of thing that's going on all the time, you see.'

Battling against both the winter elements and the enemy, 4 Wilts secured Trippenburg by midnight, the German line now pierced. It was not a situation that the enemy could allow to stand, and at dawn the Wiltshiremen received the worst shelling they'd experienced since Normandy, with Battalion Headquarters receiving 200 shells in a mere fifteen minutes.[3] The enemy then launched a powerful counter-attack of infantry and armour.

'At one time the German tanks broke into our position,' said Eric Wheeler. 'We had to withdraw.'

Frederick Ridout, 4 Wilts, recalled the moment that the panzers broke through.

'We had a 17-pounder anti-tank gun with us and it poked its gun round a corner to engage the tank. He was knocked out straight away. Our anti-tank PIAT was with the forward platoon that had just got overrun. The sergeant said everybody get back to HQ down the road because we had no chance of stopping that. So we all done a quick run down the road, and outside our HQ was some trenches. We all got in there and the tank continued on down behind us.'

The position of 4 Wilts – and with it, the advance of the 43rd Division – hung in the balance, but Sergeant Sidney Curtis was undaunted.

Alone he manned a 6-pounder anti-tank gun, which was the last remaining in action. As the enemy broke through the lines, Sergeant Curtis engaged the leading tank. It was a difficult target to hit, obscured by smoke from burning houses, but the first shot from the gun did not escape the tank's attention.

The turret turned, and the gun laid onto Sergeant Curtis. The tank's first shot missed. The second hit close enough to wound him, but not enough to stop him. Sergeant Curtis stood his ground in the face of the panzer, and fired again. The anti-tank gun then jammed, and Sergeant Curtis, still under fire, worked to clear it. But the tank's crew had had enough, and retreated.

The battalion's war diarist noted that 'Sergeant Curtis particularly distinguished himself in A Coy area by continually firing his 6 pdr single handed.'[4] He was recommended for a Distinguished Conduct Medal (DCM) – an award one grade lower than a Victoria Cross (VC) – but instead received the Military Medal, one grade lower than that for which he was recommended. The author of his citation wrote that 'by his coolness and devotion to duty, Sergeant Curtis undoubtedly saved the situation and is largely responsible for the failure of the enemy counter-attack.'[5]

'He managed to make the Germans withdraw,' said Eric Wheeler, 'so we went back to our original positions, but for a couple of hours there it was very, very dicey indeed.'

And yet Sergeant Curtis was not mentioned by name or deed in the 43rd's Divisional History, the author of which was a brigadier in the division at the time, and later its commander. In the nine pages dedicated to the 43rd's advance to the Goch escarpment, there is not a single mention of the brave actions of any man who did not hold a commission, a reminder of the 'classism' that often exists in such histories.

One of those officers who was, quite rightly, mentioned by name is Captain Anthony Townsend, 94th Field Regiment, Royal Artillery, who was also instrumental in breaking up the counter-attack on Trippenburg. The house in which he'd placed his observation post (OP) was struck three times by enemy shelling, but Captain Townsend continued to observe and call for fire. When the two forward platoons were overrun, he rallied the rear platoon and succeeded in halting the attack. Captain Townsend then went forward alone under heavy fire to see if the two forward platoons could be reorganized, but found only the enemy, onto whom he then directed further fire.

The citation of his Military Cross finishes:

'Undoubtedly by his initiative and example, he was responsible for preventing the enemy from regaining ground at a critical stage of the battle and for inflicting heavy punishment on the enemy.'[6]

'Thanks to the courage of Captain Townsend the enemy were brought to a halt,' recorded the Divisional History. It also noted that shelling at this time 'reached fantastic proportions'.[7]

'I didn't realize it was a major counter-attack at the time,' said John Corbyn, the commanding officer of 4 Wilts, 'but according to the history books, it was a major counter-attack to try and stop the advance into that part of Germany. Thanks to the artillery, we beat that off, and at one place where a large number of Germans were seen in a wooded area to the right-hand side of the road to where I was, they put down a thing called a mattress – something like 480 rockets.

'I can't think if anything managed to survive after that, it was really a tremendously impressive sight. The whole forest seemed to erupt. It was our first experience with rockets. The devastation they could do was enormous.'

Now in the late morning, 4 Wilts were passed through by 5 Wilts, who came in for heavy machine-gun fire, shelling and hand-to-hand fighting. With the exception of one major, all senior officers in the battalion became casualties. Fighting continued into the night, the battalion securing a crossroads 400 yards east of the Forest of Kleve, from which they were taking heavy fire. All told, casualties in the 5th Wiltshires numbered more than 200. To give some context to this figure, it is comparable to the casualties sustained by the first battalions to land on D-Day.

The author of the 43rd's Divisional History recorded that '5 Wiltshire had done all, indeed, almost more than all that was humanly possible and were now exhausted.'[8]

The 4th Dorsets were fed forward to continue the attack, but the enemy had brought up their own fresh reserves, Battle Group Hutze, and the two forces met head on. Douglas Old, 4th Dorsets, was badly wounded around this time.

'I was on the line party, telephone line. I was kneeling down on the side of a slit trench connecting a phone and this shell burst about ten yards in front of me. Luckily only one piece hit me. Smashed my arm up to bits.

'There was two of us there and this other chap got a bit of shrapnel in his head, but he was alright. He went back to D Company and they got stretcher-bearers and they got me back. I can't remember a lot about it. The doctor that attended me (was) Captain Jacobs, wonderful bloke. A few days after, he was killed.'

Captain Kirkwood, 4th Dorsets, assumed command of his company when his major was wounded, and 'despite short-range German automatic fire, mortaring, and shelling of his area, the company gained its objectives, which were held by resolute elite German troops.'[9]

After more than four hours of fighting, the Dorsets were passed through by the 7th Hampshires, and the battle continued into the night. Each of the battalions lost a soldier who was only seventeen years old. Thomas Smith, 7th Hampshires, was from Lambeth. John Hutchinson, 4th Dorsets, was from Much Hadham. His parents, Norman and Elizabeth, prayed that his sacrifice be not in vain.[10]

The 43rd Division had now been in the attack for more than twenty-four hours. The commander of 214th Brigade wrote that

'In a prolonged battle such as this between troops of equally high morale and armament, there comes a crisis when those directly engaged reach the limit of endurance. The commander who can time his final stroke with his reserve for this critical moment wins the victory.'[11]

Major-General Thomas, General Officer Commanding the 43rd Division, decided that the Forest of Kleve would be best left to the RAF's Typhoons and the army's artillery. Instead, he instructed 214th Brigade, augmented by the 4th Battalion, Somerset Light Infantry, to press on in the direction of the Goch Escarpment.

130th Brigade were given the task of securing a start line for the 214th, which would require an attack by the 5th Dorsets on the night of the 15th/16th. This was then delayed because of another enemy counter-attack on the positions of the 7th Hampshires, and the Dorset's attack instead launched the next morning, and with the support of tanks from 13th/18th Royal Hussars.

Weather conditions were so bad that visibility was almost down to nothing. The nerves of the tank crews were taut as they searched for the shapes of enemy armour in the driving rain and sleet, one crew of the Hussars scoring a kill on an enemy SP gun at a range of thirty yards.[12]

Throughout this time the enemy shelled with an intensity that old soldiers said they hadn't seen since Normandy. Ronnie Henderson, a twenty-year-old tank driver in the regiment, was 'frightened to death', and recalled having to drive over the many dead.

'You just couldn't get away from bodies. It didn't stink like it did in Normandy, but some of the sights were dreadful. It wasn't the sights – we'd got hardened to that long ago – it was the fear of the mines, and the bitterness, and the cold, the lack of sleep as well. We didn't expect to live. We'd seen so many go, and so many new ones come. It was going to be our turn soon. It was the inevitability of it all. It was just a matter of time until you got yours.'

With the aid of the Hussars, 130th Brigade secured their objectives by 1520 hrs on the 16th, just as the leading battalions of 214th Brigade arrived to push through them. This was the 1st Battalion of the Worcestershire Regiment and 7 SLI, supported by the 4th/7th

Dragoon Guards. Together they advanced behind a massive, rolling artillery bombardment. Suddenly the advance was moving at pace and by nightfall – which came early at that time of the year – 214th Brigade had covered more than 3,000 yards.

'Attacks went well although the Bosch fought hard,' recorded the war diarist of 4th/7th Dragoons, 'but (the) sheer weight of metal and determination beat him.'[13]

The enemy's line had been broken, and Major-General Thomas played his masterstroke. 'The 5th Duke of Cornwall's Light Infantry, its men mounted in Kangaroos and supported by B Squadron of the 4th/7th Dragoon Guards (. . .) deployed into five columns and headed due south.'[14]

'This armoured column was an impressive sight as it went by us in the twilight,' recorded the Dragoons' diarist.

Arthur Jones, 5 DCLI, remembered the moment when they arrived on their objective.

'A lorry started to start up just down the road in the village, and one of our chaps opened up with a PIAT. It was awfully quiet. We moved down the road, goes into the cellar of this house, and there was all the family and all their foreign workers.'

These 'foreign workers' were some of the millions who had been taken from their homes and put to work in the Reich, and would become a common sight for the British soldiers as they advanced across Germany. With the village seemingly quiet and secure, Arthur was then sent back to see if the company's anti-tank guns had arrived.

'There up in front of me was about eight or nine (men) moving up the road. As they were moving up towards this lorry that was burning I could see they had different helmets than we had, and I thought they were Americans, to tell you the truth.'

Other British soldiers in the village thought differently.

'(They) opened up with a Bren gun,' said Arthur. 'How they missed me I don't know.'

He then ran back to his sergeant and told him that 'Jerry'd retaken the village. Anyway, it turned out that (it) was a German patrol. If I'd have come out just a minute or two before, I'd have walked right into them. At the time everybody's pulling me leg about it, but it wasn't funny, really.'

The village taken, the platoon got what sleep they could as one man stood sentry. Arthur recalled the soldier who took over the duty from him.

'He was a lovely bloke, but you couldn't rely on him for anything. I woke him up and tell him he was on guard. Anyway, we all woke up in the morning, broad daylight, and we'd been asleep all night. I goes to dash upstairs, and I run right into a Jerry coming down the stairs. He just fell into my arms, and we finished up in a heap at the bottom of the stairs.'

Arthur took the man prisoner, but it was a short reprieve.

'By the morning, Jerry knew we were there. He shelled us until there weren't hardly one brick on top of another.'

But the DCLI had cut the road from Goch to Kalkar, and, more importantly, the enemy's defence line.

Major-General Thomas now played his final 'card' and sent the 4 SLI to capture the Goch Escarpment. They attacked at night, taking the Germans by surprise, and by dawn the escarpment was firmly in their possession,

General Brian Horrocks called this 'the turning point' in the battle for the Rhineland. It was, of course, a turning point bought with lives and limbs. Fought between 13 and 16 February, the 43rd Division's brilliant but bloody advance had brought the army to within a thousand yards of the fortified town of Goch.

Now they had to take it.

The capture of Goch

The task of capturing Goch would fall on two 'Jock' divisions.

To the west of the town, 51st Highland Division was advancing along the road from Hekkens. Having been pulled back from Moyland, and given a few days to reinforce and reorganize in Kleve, the 15th (Scottish) Division now came down to push through the 43rd. Opposing the Jocks were elements of the German 180th and 190th Infantry Divisions, and the 2nd Parachute Regiment.

On 17 February, Alfred Leigh and the 2nd Seaforths went into the attack. Monty's Moonlight lit up the clouds, and arcs of tracer fire streamed overhead as Vickers machine guns fired them in. Neither was of comfort to Alfred, who was sweating with fear.

'Believe me, I've never sweated so much in all my life. (It was) pouring off me.'

It wasn't until the platoon reorganized at a farmhouse that they realized that their section commander, 'a young lance-corporal called Vic Day, just come back off leave', was missing.

Alfred asked permission to go back to look for him. 'The reply was no. As we advanced he must have been hit by a Middlesex bullet, because the buggers were firing low. You could hear them coming over. We heard later on that he'd been picked up by a tank. He died.'[15]

The town that the men were approaching was an important communications hub for the Wehrmacht, and had received the attention of the RAF's Bomber Command. To Ronnie Henderson, 13th/18th Hussars, both Kleve and Goch were 'unrecognizable towns. They were just a pile of rubble. There was no need for that,' he added.

Harry Simpson, 7th Black Watch, recalled coming under shellfire on 17 February.

'I lost a very old chap, a very good chap. Had him in the carriers all through the war, from the time I joined battalion. He was a wonderful man. Never said nothing to anything. Whenever he was given a job to do, he did it. He was in B Company with me. We found him dead on the side of the road.'

The 7th Battalion then made its entry into Goch on the 20th. Harry recalled that upon reaching the outskirts, the leading platoon went forwards without opposition.

'(The Germans) let them through. That was one of their favourite jobs if they could do it. When the platoon got within close distance, the Germans opened up on them. (The platoon) took refuge in this factory, and the Germans were pushing tanks within this factory from their side, knocking down the walls and poking their guns through.

'Oh, God. That was terrific. 10 Platoon, we were laid there waiting to move forward. The Company Sergeant Major, Sergeant Major Rob Roy, he was the man that piped the 2nd Battalion out of Tobruk. He was severely wounded, and I took over, being the senior sergeant in the company. I took over as sergeant major.

'11 Platoon, which was on my right, they were in a field, pinned down by the enemy. We were stood there waiting for orders and wondering what to do when a big corporal, an ex 2nd Battalion man, rolled up. I said, "You're not by any chance deserting your platoon, are you? Because you're the only one that's come back."

'You could see the panic had set in,' said Harry, who then went forward with B Company's OC, Major Peck, to see what could be done about the situation. They soon came under fire from the tanks themselves, and Major Peck was badly wounded.

'He had a foot blown off,' said Harry. 'Stretcher-bearers picked him up.'

Harry continued to go forwards and reached 'Big Jim', the stricken sergeant of 12 Platoon. 'I carried Big Jim back to the Gordon's RAP, and I had to have a rest because he's a very big man.'

After leaving his comrade at the Regimental Aid Post of the Gordon Highlanders, Harry chanced upon a butcher's shop and found a side of bacon that he picked up for his troops.

'On coming out I saw two or three Gordon men. I said, "Are you having a look 'round for food?" He said, 'No, are we hell, there's a bloody bank around here. We're going to see if it's got any money in it."'

Harry chuckled. 'And they had the PIAT!'

He was heading back to his company when there was a loud explosion behind him.

'They'd blown the front door off the safe inside the bank. Unfortunately, the blast from the PIAT damaged all the notes.'

Harry returned to his company with his bacon, and began cutting it into rations for his men. He also shared it with a German family whose home they'd occupied. 'They were bedraggled, clothes were hanging off of them. The house was more or less demolished, and they were really terrified. So, naturally, the British soldier, he thought of the children and the woman, and we divided the food up between them, and fed them. They really appreciated it. And then when we opened our (ration) packs later in the day – sweets and biscuits – we gave it to the people round about.'

It wasn't until 0700 on the 21st that the factory – described in the war diary as a large building – was cleared with the use of Crocodile flamethrowers.

That same day, as the 7th Argylls were passing through 7th Black Watch's positions, both battalions were bombed by a Dutch squadron of RAF medium bombers, and suffered casualties. The 7th Black Watch's losses for their first twenty-four hours in Goch were: six killed, thirty-two wounded and six missing.

Harry was himself injured by friendly fire while in Goch.

'We had to wade across this stream, and it came across our chests. Hell, it was cold! And when we got over, the same thing happened again – under our own shell fire. They were dropping short, but until the FOO (Forward Observation Officer) radioed back to lift his barrage, some of us got wounded. I was on the right shoulder. It was only a very small piece of shrapnel. Went in my right shoulder, but by God it was painful. I finished up at the RAP and the medical sergeant doctored me up and I went back.'

Fighting with the 5th Black Watch at Goch was Tom Renouf, a nineteen-year-old conscript from Musselburgh, on the East Lothian Coast.

'At the time, going to war seemed like a normal part of life. I was far from scared; in fact, I relished the prospect of adventure, not knowing it was going to be purgatory.'[16]

During the battle of Goch, Tom's battalion were to give fire support for the 5/7th Gordon Highlanders as they rushed across a square to seize a hospital on the other side. It was a day he would never forget.

'Watching them cross the square was like a horror film you could not turn off. Despite our fierce covering fire, the bell-tower erupted with machine-gun and sniper fire. The young Gordons dropped like flies, one after the other.'[17]

D Company, 5 BW, also crossed the square, and persuaded a

dozen German soldiers and their colonel to give up by throwing grenades into the basements from where they'd been firing. Tom recalled that several Gordons then had to be dragged away from the German officer. 'Otherwise, he would have suffered the same fate as the corpses in the square.'[18]

Private Bill Robertson of A Company, 5/7 Gordons was one of those to rush through the murderous hail of fire.

'Crossing the square at Goch might well be a story worth telling but for me it was all a bad dream, a memory I want to forget.'[19]

Ian Nelson, a nineteen-year-old draftee from Edinburgh, was also at Goch with 5 Black Watch. He was in the upstairs of a house when his sergeant pointed across the street.

'He says, "That house across there, there's somebody over there." And he showed me the window.'

Ian set up his weapon and fired.

'I got the PIAT right through the window. I thought, *Oh well, that will sort that one out, eh?*'

But the fortunes of war can change in an instant.

'The Germans must have spotted where it had come from, and I got it.'

A German bazooka round came flying back towards Ian, through his own window.

'Luckily, with me being a small fellow, it went over my head and exploded on the other side of the room.'

The blast knocked him unconscious.

'I come to and it was pitch black. I heard my mate moaning. I'm groping about, trying to find the stairs to get down.'

These he found, but they were now blocked with debris. '(So) I done the only thing I could think of at the time.'

Ian pulled himself over the windowsill and dropped down into the street below.

'I got back to HQ. I got taken back to hospital.'

The back of Ian's body had been peppered with shrapnel from top to bottom. 'That was me, finished for the war.'

James Wilkinson, 6 KOSB, was also injured in the town.

'They were firing at us all night. We was in German trenches.

I crawled round this trench, and as I crawled up to where it turns round the corner, something – *BAAAANG* – something hit me on the 'ead. One of our blokes (had) panicked, threw his 36 grenade. Never pulled the pin, fortunately.'

The next morning his platoon captured the house where the enemy fire had been coming from.

'The blokes that had been firing at us all night, they put their 'ands up. And funny enough, they were just like us. We gave them cigarettes, and we was all talking in there, you know, just like old comrades. Funny. What treatment they got further back I don't know. They talked to us, and we talked to them about their families and all that. Probably when they got back to the base-wallahs they probably got grilled.'

That night James and his comrades boiled up margarine that they'd found in a cellar.

'I went to put me bread in, the other chap hit the bloody tin and the lot went over my hands. Boiling hot fat. I yelled like hell and they were laughing their heads off. They thought it was funny. Being it was so badly burned, I lost sense of feeling. It went numb.'

James protested about going back to the RAP, as it would involve moving along a road under shell fire, but he would be a hindrance at the front now that he couldn't use his weapon.

'I got to the RAP. Doctor looked at it – he said, "You'll have to go back to the next point."'

James was transported back to a hospital in Nijmegen, where his hands were treated for burns. He was then moved by train to another hospital in France, where the cause of his injuries drew suspicion.

'I had to make a statement. (They) grilled me. Asked me how it was done. Who was there, and what was happening, everything under the sun.'

After being cleared of suspicion of causing a self-inflicted wound, James was sent to a convalescence camp, where he received treatment for battle fatigue.

'You had what they called therapy. If your nerves was shot to pieces, they gave you therapy. They gave more counselling more or less.'

James was asked if this treatment was necessary, and if he had 'lost his nerve'.

'Yes, I did actually. Towards the end, yeah. It showed itself. You shook. Your nerves were shot to pieces. I'll tell you what it felt like. Three years ago, I had depression. And it felt like that. You felt absolutely down. Everything was black-looking, and I had these shakes. I think they sent me there as a good rest. I was always on the nervous side, you know?'

Out of the line

On 20 February, 227th (Highland) Brigade, 15th (Scottish) put in an attack a few miles east of Goch. The target was a large castle – which one soldier described more like a chateau – that dominated the views of the surrounding land. The attack on Schloss Kalbeck was launched by Glasgow Highlanders mounted in Kangaroos, and the Argylls on the back of the Guards Armoured's Churchills.

Ray Ashton and the Middlesex Regiment were there to provide fire support.

'On the way there, I'd been on the radio maintaining contact with our Company HQ, and I had a strange feeling. I was interrupted on two occasions by a voice I didn't recognize, and I reckon it was Germans monitoring our (communications). I told Jerry, "Get off the air, Jerry", and I didn't have any more from them.'

Ray assumed that the enemy had been monitoring his communications in order to locate their position via VHF (very high frequency) triangulation.

'My particular pal on the carrier was a Corporal (Bill) Emery, who was in charge of the platoon signals. Bill and I, we got on well. He'd actually dropped a rank from sergeant to corporal to join a platoon, and he was a good bit older than me, and he used to sort of look after me. (He was) a bit of a father figure to me, and yet he would ask my advice about his married life, which was a bit rocky.'

Bill and Ray were digging in a half-mile from the Schloss, under the cover of trees. They were only about a foot down when they came under mortar fire.

'This mortar struck. I never heard it. All I remember is a flash, and feeling somebody punching you in the arm with a knuckle. It's sort of a bruisy feeling. Not any real pain. I must have passed out in the slit trench, I suppose, and I lifted me arm, and my head felt as though it was in two halves. I was convinced I was dead. My arm was sort of folded in half. And then I had an out-of-body experience.

'I was then up in the air, maybe a hundred feet, I don't know, and looking down on the mortar position. I could see all the mortar pits, all dug out in the field. All our vehicles, parked and camouflaged underneath the trees. For a long while I just thought I'd been blown (upwards), but it never happened obviously. I'd have come up through the trees and I'd have been knocked to flipping pieces if I had been blown (upwards). Next thing, I'm back in the slit trench, and Bill's (bandaging) up my arm.'

As the mortars continued to explode around them, 'Bill made three attempts to get me out under fire, and in the meantime put out a fire on a trailer load of mortar bombs with shovelfuls of earth.'

On the fourth attempt, and with Ray on his back, Bill Emery reached a stretcher carrier and loaded Ray aboard.

'He certainly should have had a decoration,' said Ray, acknowledging that not all worthy acts were officially recognized. 'There was lots of decorations deserved. Bill Emery subsequently died, but I did manage to get a record of his act put in the battalion memoirs. So, you know, it's on record. He was a great lad.'

By 22 February Goch was firmly in British hands, but still under regular shelling. Tom Renouf's unit, 5 BW, were withdrawn from the town for a few days of rest in a nearby village. When Tom went in search of his much-admired platoon sergeant, he found him in a house occupied by a German woman and her two daughters.

'It was like entering a brothel, or at least a very liberal public house. I was astounded by the extent of the fraternization. Bob had the woman, a buxom brunette, on his knee. They were canoodling, having a merry old time, and several other soldiers were also in very high spirits.

'As a regular churchgoer, coming from a sheltered upbringing,

I was disappointed to see Bob in this new and less than wholesome light. The other lads were trying to latch onto the woman's daughters, who were only about fifteen or sixteen. The woman kept shouting in German, "No, not my girls – they're only young," but she was laughing as she said it.'[20]

Goch marked the end of 15th (Scottish) and 51st (Highland)'s direct role in Operation Veritable. Not only had they been earmarked by Montgomery as the assault divisions for the crossing of the Rhine, but both had suffered heavy casualties. When passing through the Gordons at Goch, Stanley Whitehouse, 1st Black Watch, saw a four-foot pile of bodies still being built. One of his platoon approved of the number of dead.

'"That's how I like to see the Jerries – piled high," said Beachy to the Gordons, who were standing about, looking sullen.

'"Trouble is," said one of them, "they're our lads."'[21]

In the operations in the Reichswald, Gennep, Heyen and Goch, the 1st Battalion, Gordon Highlanders had suffered four officers and twenty-nine other ranks killed, fourteen and 106 wounded, and two and forty-eight missing.[22]

Martin Lindsay, the regiment's second in command, described the 'dramatic burial' of those killed near Thomashof, during the battle to capture Goch.

'There were two long graves, one full of Gordons and the other full of Germans, and Ewen stood on the mound of earth, silhouetted against a burning farmhouse, in battledress with a white padre's collar, and a steel helmet in his hand.

'A small group of us stood in front, listening for the whistle of shells and ready to dart back inside the building at any moment. I was very upset that little Chamberlain, who had so long been my signaller, was amongst those we buried. He had always had a ready smile for me.'[23]

CHAPTER 7

Iron Sides

3rd Division enter the battle
26 February – 1 March 1945

'This was the main thing that always sticks in my mind. We started coming across the first aid (posts), with all the casualties. I think we lost thirty-five killed, two missing, and 127 wounded, and the track was just lined with stretchers with wounded on them.

We had some Old Sweats in the regiment. Territorials what had served in India in the late 30s. And they was two of them. They was really not brothers, but brothers in comradeship. They was the older lads. Let's face it, I was eighteen, Harry was eighteen. These must have been in their thirties, and one of them, ginger-haired lad, he was an Irish kid. He was laid there, swathed in bandages around his chest. Blood. And his friend was a little chap, real thin-faced, five foot nothing, thin as a rake, crying his eyes out, calling his name. Yeah, it's getting to me now.'

Raymond Robinson, 2nd Battalion,
East Yorkshire Regiment

Yorkshire Bridge

The 3rd Infantry Division had earned their reputation of being as tough as iron in the First World War, and cemented it in the Second, when they landed on Sword Beach. When the division was committed to Operation Veritable at the end of February many veterans of D-Day remained within its ranks, but they were far outnumbered by the battle-casualty replacements that had flooded in since June.

One such replacement was Raymond Robinson, from Kingston upon Hull. Ray was thirteen years old when war was declared, and during the Blitz his hometown was a frequent target for the Luftwaffe. Ray would spend the nights with his aunt on the outskirts of town, and recalled one morning when he emerged from the bomb shelter.

'Stoneferry, along the river, was just ablaze. All the oil mills that were situated along there was all in flames. And looking towards the centre of the city, the whole city was ablaze with fire, and smoke.'

Ray's own home had suffered damage, and his family were forced to move. He was called up for service four years later, in June 1944, and one can only imagine the worry of his mother, with all three of her boys now at war. After four months of training, at eighteen years old, Ray was sent to Europe.

After moving through a series of transit camps, he arrived at his 'new home' on New Year's Eve 1944. The 2nd Battalion, East Yorkshire Regiment were out of the line, refitting and resting in Holland, and Ray might have reckoned that it would be some time before he saw his first casualty.

'A girl stopped (one of our soldiers). She'd only be about nine or ten. This little girl handed him one of these grenades she must have found. As he'd taken it off her, it went off. The young girl, she was alright. He was laid on the floor, both his hands blown off, his stomach, and his face. Blinded him.'

The wounded soldier was taken to hospital but died three days later.

'That was an introduction to war, for us, cause all us reinforcements had never seen anything like that at the time, you see.'

Whatever innocence the soldiers retained after that night would soon be lost. At the end of February, the East Yorkshires and the rest of 3rd Division were released into the battle, fed forwards to play their part in the closing stages of the Rhineland campaign.

'We was going through the main battle areas, and just seeing all the villages and the towns all bombed and shelled,' said Ray. 'Nothing but ruin. Fields full of dead horses, and cattle, there with their legs in the air. That was the thing, was animals. Poor animals been killed. Seeing where tank battles (had happened), and passing those tanks with their turrets blown off, and their tracks blown off. Passing areas where the Germans had blown the dams of the dykes, and rivers, and going through mud where they'd had to lay these metal plates to let the transport get through.

'We passed the place called Goch, where there had been a big battle, and it was still going on, actually. You could see Goch alight, and hear all the sounds of battle. The artillery and machine guns. And that was when we knew we were getting near the front, because going there, you know the NCOs in the trucks are saying, "Let's have a song, lads," and we're all singing these war songs like "Roll up the Barrel", and as you got nearer the front, the singing had died off. You knew you was heading for it.'

The Yorkshiremen finally disembarked their lorries into hail and sleet, and were given a meal of corned-beef stew and veg.

'We relieved the 51st Highland Division then, and they come to lead us in to their positions. Well, it was pitch black. Going through the forest, holding the bayonet (scabbard) of the man in front, going down the ditches, you was slipping in the mud. It was terrible, actually,' Ray laughed, able to see the funny side of such things.

Once at the frontline, the men took over the trenches of the unit they were relieving.

'I was with me mate Harry McGarr. Everything was quiet in the area at that time, although you could hear explosions and artillery in the distance. Very scary time for me at that time, you know.'

Ray spent the next day in the trench, keeping low to avoid snipers.

'You couldn't move around. (The next) morning, we had an O Group where (the platoon) gathered around in a little dip. The officer, he was telling us what our duties was for that day. He explained that we had five positions to take. We were supposed to come to the bridge, which was the main objective.'

The bridge was situated on a tributary of the River Niers, its capture essential so that attacks could continue south-east, to Weeze.

On 27 February the East Yorks soldiers moved to their start lines. Ray's platoon would be going into action from the edge of the woods, with farm land ahead of them.

'It was a big area, all fields. Woods on the left, woods on the right, a row of trees leading up to this farmyard in the middle of this area. Possibly about half a mile away, woods again. Our section were the first section to get across to this farmhouse. We started off when the whistle went while the other two sections was giving covering fire. You always want to be close (to each other) until you get the orders from the NCOs, "Spread out, lads, you've got to spread out."

'We were getting fired at from the house. Everybody was firing from the hip, or trying to fire from the hip. You was slipping. It was a ploughed field with about 18-inch furrows. Frosty. Been freezing during the night. You couldn't keep your feet. You was falling down all over the place, which I imagine was pretty good, cause you weren't giving no target for snipers.

'By that time we were getting nearer the house. We did have a casualty there, who was our Bren gunner. He got shot in the groin. Snipers always go for NCOs, officers, or the men with a machine gun.

'Our corporal then, I believe his name was Danny Moat, he was a Hull lad. He was setting you out. "You go there, you give covering fire, you go there." He dropped me on top of this raise. "Give covering fire there." My mate Harry, he was lucky, he got dropped behind a big tree. The other lads was just spread out in an arc.

'I proceeded to start firing at the house. Windows. The doors. The eaves. I'd been taught that the enemy had a habit of going into the false roof, knocking a tile out, and firing from there.'

Ray wasn't sure how long this firing went on for.

'A white flag came out of the front door, which stopped all of the firing, and a lot of civilians started coming out. They disappeared. They must have had a big dugout in the front garden. So that happened, (and then) the war started again.'

The civilians out of the way, both sides resumed firing.

'By that time one of the other sections was coming over, ready for the assault section. As I was putting my clip of five in, I happened to look to my left, and I just saw a few of the lads in the assault section coming around. Their job was to get into that house, and at that time I saw an explosion. It must have been a mortar shell just land near the assault section, and I saw one or two of them go down.'

Ray was also struck.

'All I remember was a big smack in the mouth. It must have been a clod of rock-hard, frozen earth.'

Ray saw his officer heading for a small gate in a fence in front of the farmhouse, then he looked away to fire.

'As I looked (again), I saw our platoon officer slumped over the gate, leaned up. Dead. As I'd been firing he must have been leading the rest of what was left of the (assault) group. He'd got to the front of the house and he'd been shot.

'After that, everything quietened off. And then the door opened again and a white flag came out, and who appeared but a young lad, dressed in paratroopers' uniform. He had a satchel over his shoulder with a red cross on. I would say he'd be no older than thirteen or fourteen.'

Some of the experienced NCOs in the platoon, who perhaps knew some words of German after fighting them for so long, instructed the young soldier to bring out his comrades.

'After about ten minutes seven Jerries come out. Paratroopers – big tall lads, young, in their early twenties – come out with their hands up. After a few minutes our corporal, I'm sure he said to me and Harry, "Right, take these back."'

It was the last time that Ray would see his section commander alive. Corporal Albert Daniel Moat was killed later that day, at the age of twenty-one.[1]

The two East Yorks replacements, who had just received their baptism of fire, escorted the prisoners back across the ground that they'd just assaulted.

Close by, D-Day veteran Peter Brown's company had been tasked with seizing and holding the bridge on the Üdem–Weeze road.

'(It was) only a narrow sort of river but it was quite important that we captured this bridge. I remember we set off from the forest, and we had to cross this ploughed field and came under machine-gun fire, and for the second time I was lucky. I got down in this sort of mortar hole.

'We carried a spade down the back of (our) pack for digging trenches. A couple of bullets hit that spade and pinged off the blade. That was a bit hairy, there. We were getting quite a lot of casualties from shell and mortar fire.

'We got across this ploughed field and over this bridge. There was a 500lb bomb strapped under the bridge, ready to be blown, but we'd moved quickly enough to get over it before they were able to blow it. On the other side of the bridge was this farmhouse, and we dug in around the paddock. We got dug in as dusk was falling. We're getting shelled, and the next thing, we got counter-attacked.'

This counter-attack was made by infantry and armour, the enemy tanks running over slit trenches to crush the men inside, their commanders calling upon the Yorkshiremen to surrender.

'We could see these Jerries coming through the woods towards us,' continued Peter Brown. 'Our platoon commander then was a fella called Second Lieutenant Glue. Sticky Glue, we called him. He was sort of knelt behind my trench.'

Low on ammunition, Glue gave the word for the men to fall back to the farmhouse.

'Fella called Penrice, who was on the Bren gun, he hopped out and made a grab for the carrying handle of the Bren and missed it and got hold of the barrel, which was red hot, so he's doing a little dance on the edge of his trench,' said Peter, chuckling at the memory.

He joined the others racing back towards the buildings, but collided with a runner who was bringing ammunition forward.

'I flattened him.'

The man that Peter collided with was quite possibly Private James Russell, who was later awarded the Military Medal.

'During one counter-attack, when a forward section had been overrun, Private Russell volunteered to go out in the face of fierce Spandau and Schmeisser fire to bring in casualties and actually succeeded in doing so. When ammunition was running out this soldier collected a further supply from another platoon, which involved crossing the bridge under heavy fire . . .

Later, hearing cries for help from the trees just forward of his position, Private Russell went out alone to see who was there and brought in a wounded German. Throughout the entire action this soldier showed a complete disregard of his own personal safety.'[2]

Peter Brown and others pulled back and consolidated on the farmhouse, and the enemy counter-attacks continued with relentless ferocity. The farm was in danger of being overrun, and with it the bridge, which could then be destroyed by the enemy. It was a desperate situation that called for desperate measures.

'The company commander called down the corps artillery on the farm,' said Peter. 'Practically every gun in the corps fired on that area.'

Peter and his comrades took what cover they could as their own artillery smashed into the paddocks, fields and forests around them.

'Only one shell hit the farmhouse,' said Peter, who caught a piece of shrapnel in the area that soldiers fear most – the groin. Rather than look at the damage, Peter kept himself busy by patching up a soldier with wounds to the face. Then, at last, he checked himself over.

'I was always in the habit of carrying letters from home in my map pocket, and when I looked, I had a bundle of letters, and this shrapnel had hit that packet of letters, and it was jammed in there. I'd got a bruise in my groin but nothing worse.'

It was a narrow escape, but the company was not out of danger – enemy soldiers began to break into the building.

'We had a lance sergeant, he came out of the kitchen and there was a corridor came down to the door of the farmhouse, and as he came out of the kitchen there was a Jerry coming into the door. Well, as I say, we had no ammunition. He picked a potato up and threw it at this Jerry, who turned tail and ran.'

The company was finally resupplied around midnight by Major Charles Kenneth King, better known to the battalion's soldiers as 'Banger King'.

'If you go to a John Wayne film, he was the chap who all the battalion would have followed through hell,' said Ray Robinson.

Major Charles King would be awarded the Distinguished Service Order for his actions in the battle – his second of the war – and his driver – Ripley – received a Mention in Despatches. With ammunition and rations in his carrier, the major went forward under heavy artillery and mortar fire, and delivered a meal to all forward companies. He also took the ammunition carrier straight past the enemy position in the wood, under machine-gun fire the entire time, and delivered ammunition, radio batteries and food to the men holding the bridge.

King then ran the gauntlet a second time, returning to the commanding officer with invaluable first-hand information about the situation at the bridge. The CO put this to good use, committing his companies accordingly, and the East Yorks were able to hold their small but vital bridgehead.

The next day the 53rd (Welsh) Division pushed through and crossed 'Yorkshire Bridge', newly rechristened in honour of the soldiers who took it.

Peter Brown recalled the moment.

'It was Welshmen who relieved us, because it was St David's Day, (and) they all had daffodils in their helmets.'

It must have been a strange sight to Peter, but a welcome one.

'In our platoon I think there was about five of us left.'

Casualties across the entire battalion had been heavy, the success of attacks often falling on junior NCOs who had to step up and fill the positions of their killed and wounded leaders.

When Corporal Noel Cox's platoon commander was killed and all other NCOs in the platoon wounded, he rallied the remainder of his men in the face of heavy artillery and small-arms fire and led them in a successful attack on their objective, which was a strongly held farm building.[3] He was later awarded a Military Medal, as was Corporal Thomas McGarrell, who led his section under heavy fire to attack the positions that were pinning down his platoon, repeating this action when the company came under heavy fire on his objective. [4]

After his own platoon's successful but costly attack on a farmhouse, Ray Robinson and his friend Harry had been sent to the rear as a prisoner escort. They came across the battalion's first aid posts, wounded men everywhere they looked. One sight in particular remained with Ray. A couple of 'Old Sweats' from his regiment who had served together since the 1930s and were as close as brothers. One of these men was lying on a stretcher on the track, his chest swathed in bloody bandages. His friend 'was crying his eyes out, calling his name. Yeah . . .' Ray faltered. 'It's getting to me now.' He gathered himself for a moment, then continued with his story.

'There was about four of five tents there, where they was taking the casualties. And there was a little area where they was keeping the prisoners. I think there was a Canadian war correspondent there with a camera. He took our photograph. Of course, you can imagine, there was Harry McGarr, five foot nothing, with seven paratroopers all over six foot.'

Ray and Harry were then told to take their prisoners further back down the line. After handing them over, Ray had the blood on his face cleaned up by a medical orderly, and then he and Harry joined a composite section formed of other soldiers who had also been sent back on the same task. Together they moved up to the front, coming to 'a very big house. Like a mansion. This house was on fire, blazing. In front of the house was about eight bodies, covered over with groundsheets. It was a mixture of our lads and Germans. We went over, and I lifted a groundsheet up to see if I recognized any of our lads, and it was our sergeant major (Christopher Loughran). That put me down a bit.'[5]

The battalion sustained 156 casualties to secure the narrow bridgehead, with forty-four men killed.

'We lost four killed (from our platoon), and I don't know how many wounded,' said Ray. 'We lost the Bren gunner, we lost the platoon officer, we lost our corporal, and we'd lost one of the lads who, like me, was the first time he'd been in action.'

Kervenheim

Lieutenant Vic Sayer was a twenty-year-old platoon commander in the 2nd Battalion, King's Shropshire Light Infantry (KSLI). On 28 February 1945, he waited to go into action near the small town of Kervenheim, an important road junction and what looked like the linchpin of the last line of the enemy's defence west of the Hochwald Layback.[6] It was not terrain that suited the attacker.

'It's pretty open,' recalled Vic. 'Muddy. And all the roads ran across. There wasn't a road running direct (to the town).'

The KSLI, along with the Warwicks, were to seize the ground left and right of Kervenheim respectively. The Norfolks would then push up between them to seize the town itself. They would be supported by Guards Armoured tanks, specialist armour of the 79th Armoured Division, a mass of artillery, and fighter bombers.

'We had twelve field regiments (of artillery) and three medium regiments supporting this attack,' said Vic. 'That's 300-and-odd 25-pounders, and the divisional Pepperpot – all the Bofors and the 4.2-inch mortars, and the noise is indescribable. The barrage started at two o'clock and we set off. We were one of the reserve companies.'

The two flanking battalions began to fight their way forwards. At 1445 the Warwicks reported that one of their companies was across the river, and the Norfolks were told to begin their own attack, the infantry following on behind flail tanks and other specialized armour, while Churchill tanks of the Guards Division covered the infantry with their fire.

Going was slow, and it soon became clear that the flanks were still being hotly contested, and the battles of those battalions was spilling over into the centre. Former soldier and correspondent Reginald W. Thompson was present, and his description of the war-like scene borders on the poetic:

'A hare sat motionless, ears flat, and small birds flew madly in zig-zags, hemmed within the invisible cage of battle . . .

'. . . machine gun fire pressed the waiting Norfolks close against the wet earth, urgently to dig narrow slots for shelter.

'The sun was almost down, and a slender rift of gold showed in the western sky . . .

'"We ought to be moving," said a tank commander. "If we're going to move."

'The barrage in support of the attack of the Norfolks was due. The Typhoons and Spitfires dive bombed within four hundred yards on the right in the last flight before night.

'Out of the crimson murk of smoke and flame, hedged in by spouting columns of earth, a pitiful cavalcade stumbled from the farmstead, the old and the young, a man with a dog in the lead, a woman, children, goats, geese, bewildered, overtaken by war. In this alone war had not changed. In this fashion, in all the long history of warfare, peasants had stumbled from their homes.'[7]

Held up by mud and the enemy, the attack was given up for the night.

'We had to stop,' said Vic Sayer. 'Partly I think through darkness, but partly because the battalion was exposed, and we dug in.'

On 1 March the attack was resumed, with the Norfolks on the right to go to Kervenheim, and 2 KSLI to clear positions on the left.

'We set off and got our objective.' said Vic. 'On the advance, the platoon commander (of 14 Platoon) was very seriously wounded and the platoon sergeant had his foot blown off by a Schu mine. The platoon stopped and were picked up by the reserve company coming up behind, so there were only two platoons on our objective.

'We had some Coldstream tanks with us. They sat a little behind us on this objective, and then a complete Moaning Minnie stonk landed just a few yards from where we were. Sergeant Fox in my platoon was killed.[8] There must have been other casualties, and we were feverishly digging in.

'I suppose it was about three o'clock in the afternoon. We got orders to move to our right across the front to take out a pocket that Z Company was having trouble with on their left.'

One of Z Company's soldiers was thirty-year-old Glaswegian Private James Stokes. Stokes had originally enlisted in the Royal Artillery after his call-up, but was imprisoned in 1944 for his part in a brawl. He was then given a reprieve to take part in the Normandy landings with the KSLI, and at Kervenheim he was a member of the leading section.

During the advance, Private Stokes's platoon came under intense fire from a farm building and was pinned down. Without waiting for orders he rushed towards the building, firing from the hip, and emerged soon after with twelve prisoners, and a wound to his neck.

Stokes was ordered back to the Regimental Aid Post but refused to go. He carried on with the platoon towards their next objective, and they again came under heavy fire. Once again, without orders, Stokes rushed forwards to the house from where the enemy was shooting, firing from the hip. He was seen to drop his rifle and fall to the ground, apparently wounded a second time, but Stokes then regained his footing and his weapon, and continued to charge.

He entered the building, and all fire from within ceased. Stokes then rejoined his platoon, bringing another five prisoners with him.

His company now formed up for an attack on its final objective, which was a group of buildings that comprised an enemy strongpoint. Already severely wounded and suffering from loss of blood, Private Stokes – without orders – ran across sixty yards of open ground while under intense fire, again firing from the hip. Twenty yards from this final objective, he fell to the ground. His company, inspired by his actions, were following behind. Stokes's final action was to raise his hand and shout goodbye to his comrades. He died on the battlefield, having suffered eight wounds to his upper body.[9]

'Private Stokes was awarded a posthumous VC,' said Vic Sayer, whose own company was taking heavy casualties. The Norfolks, in Kervenheim itself, were also embroiled in bloody battle.

'The Norfolks were suffering terrible casualties. It was the worst day of the war, actually, getting into Kervenheim.'

After a night spent under shelling in a wood, the Norfolks were dismayed to discover that the ground over which they were attacking offered about as much cover as a cricket pitch. The situation deteriorated as the Coldstream tanks supporting them bogged down and could offer little support. Reginal W. Thompson recalled that, over the radio, the Forward Observation Officer with the tanks said that: '"It's awfully bare . . ." A direct hit on the tank ripped off the end of the sentence.'[10]

Trapped in this open ground, A Company of the Norfolks came under withering fire from farm buildings on their right.

'The friends I had made over the winter were just cut to ribbons,' recalled one soldier. 'Over 100 lay dead or wounded within a few mind-blowing minutes.'[11]

Lieutenant Robert Lincoln, who was doing double duty as both platoon commander and company second in command, was wounded while leading his platoon in the first wave of the assault. The citation of his Military Cross stated that 'It was entirely due to the successful capture of the first objective and penetration beyond effected by this officer that the subsequent capture of the town was possible.'[12]

Lieutenant George Dicks, commanding a platoon of B Company, was hit in the groin when he was fifty yards short of his objective, but in spite of his wound he was the first man to reach the fortified building. He was then wounded a second time, in the chest, but continued to issue orders and encouragement to his men and directed their assault. He was also awarded the Military Cross.[13]

One of the few men who had made it through the murderous fire with Lieutenant Dicks was D-Day man Corporal Mason, who had seen his Bren gunner killed and PIAT man wounded. Mason and his platoon sergeant went ahead to scout but soon came under more heavy fire. They rushed back, the sergeant with a bullet in his leg, but then Mason was thrown into the air by an exploding shell. He suffered shrapnel wounds to his back and buttocks, but his life had likely been saved by the pack on his back, which was torn to shreds.

Gil Attwood, from Hemel Hempstead, was serving in D Company. His platoon had secured a farmhouse and barn on the outskirts of Kervenheim, but they came under heavy fire from a large building nearby while attempting to push further into the town. While their machine-gunner Paddy provided covering fire, two sections of his platoon ran into the next building.

Hearing an eruption of gunfire coming from within the house, Gil positioned himself to cut off any retreating enemy, but this left him exposed and out of cover, and almost cost him his life.

'I heard a crack and something burned a strip across the strap of my helmet.'

The bullet had missed him by a hair, and Gil quickly dashed back into what shelter he could find in the barn.

'Things were going badly in the second house and we all had

to withdraw back into the first one, but as we did a missile from a bazooka hit the outbuilding, killing Paddy and injuring others, and also setting fire to the straw so the outbuilding too became untenable.'

Private K. Wilby was serving in the same platoon, and recalled what happened next.

'The rest of the platoon withdrew to the farmhouse and I was left in the barn with two friends of mine. One had been killed outright, the other badly wounded – I stayed with him; after five or ten minutes he died.

'After that, I was still stuck fast in that barn. The Germans were still counter-attacking the barn with only me in it. There was hardly any roof to that barn, but the Germans must have seen me through some hole or something, and they kept throwing grenades over into the barn . . . This carried on for five or ten minutes, me dodging from one end of the barn to the other – it wasn't funny at the time.

'When that finished I managed to get through into the farmhouse with the rest of the platoon – I got settled with them and put my Bren gun through the window. After about ten minutes the Germans with a Bazooka team came round the buildings into the barn where I had been; they must have been looking for me. I saw this Bazooka team, switched from safety and lined up my Bren on the Bazooka man as silently as possible so that he couldn't hear me, but he turned round and I fired straight away and killed him and wounded his number two.'[14]

From an upstairs window Gil Attwood saw the Bazooka team go down, but more of the enemy stormed through the front door of the house.

'My natural reaction was to turn round and run back into the hall and return the fire but Lance-Corporal Allan told me to stay put and he rushed back into the hallway to tackle them.

'This resulted in a massive exchange of fire, at the end of which, most if not all those in it were killed.'[15]

During the night the enemy slipped away from Kervenheim to live to fight another day – they left behind them a town and fields strewn with bodies. Forty-two soldiers of the Royal Norfolk

Regiment were killed. Among them was Harold Miles, from Brighton, who was seventeen years old.[16] The battalion also suffered more than 120 men wounded.

The 2nd Battalion, the King's Shropshire Light Infantry, also suffered great loss, with twenty-seven men killed.

'We came under a lot of fire,' said Vic Sayer. 'Adrian Wilson, commanding 15 Platoon, and his batman were both killed by machine-gun fire.'[17]

Vic was the only platoon commander in his company to not be killed or seriously wounded. Decades later, he attended a reunion with comrades of 2 KSLI. One of the veterans, who had been wounded on D-Day, told Vic that 'Kervenheim was the worst day of the war.'

It was not an isolated opinion.

'One or two of the old boys from Normandy said it was the worst they'd experienced,' said Vic. 'I know at the end of the day I finished up with sixteen men in my platoon. (We had) one killed, and eleven wounded.

'When you hear people talk about Dresden – "Oh, they shouldn't have bombed it because the war was good as won", well I can say for certainty that it wasn't as good as won down where we were.

'Another fiction is that by the end of the war the German army was full of (second-rate) battalions. Well, when you've got a para division of young men, on the west bank of (the) Rhine, they're not going to give in. They were as good a soldier as you could find anywhere.'

Three miles east of Kervenheim, soldiers of the 53rd Division were advancing into a killing ground of their own.

CHAPTER 8

Another Taste of Hell

The 53rd Division's push from Goch to Alpen
26 February – 8 March 1945

'We had quite a few casualties. And the sad thing was, when we were being reinforced by new infantry trainees, we experienced quite a few casualties of trainees who really had just joined us out of training, and that was a great sadness. When you realize that they'd only been in the army a matter of a few months, and had been either wounded or killed in the latter stages of the war.'

Norman Griffin, 7th Battalion, Royal Welch Fusiliers

On 24 February, to the south of Goch, the 53rd (Welsh) launched Operation Leek with the aim of capturing Weeze. Following the success of this operation the division was to push south-east to Kevelear before seizing the towns of Geldern, Issum and Alpen.

'It was a killing ground,' tank driver Ronnie Henderson said of the battlefield. 'An absolute killing ground.'

Ronnie's regiment, the 13th/18th Royal Hussars, were part of 8th Armoured Brigade, which was operating in support of 53rd (Welsh).

'The infantry were dropping all around. And I thought how brave some of these infantry lads were. How boys can give their lives like that. Tremendous admiration for the infantry. That's what we had. Tremendous admiration. It was unbelievable what those infantry lads went through. Dreadful. They had a terrible time of it.'

The Hussars had a terrible time of their own. On the first day of Operation Leek, A Squadron had four tanks 'brewed up' by SP guns and a further three hit mines. One officer and four other ranks were wounded, and three killed. C Squadron lost one tank, with one officer wounded, and B Squadron five tanks, with three men wounded.

It was not clear from his interview or memoir which squadron Ronnie was serving with at the time, but he mentioned that he was in support of 4 Welch at one point, which likely made him a member of C. On the 28th this squadron and two companies of 6 RWF moved towards Yorkshire Bridge to support the East Yorks, engaging SP guns, anti-tank guns, and infantry. During their recce to the bridge, five of 6 RWF's key officers were killed or wounded during an enemy counter-attack.

The next day, 1 March, 7 RWF and 4 Welch, supported by tanks of the Sherwood Rangers, pushed south across the bridge that had been captured with the blood of Yorkshiremen. A soldier of the 53rd's Recce Regiment recalled that 'The bodies of the men felled in previous action were still lying where they had fallen.'[1]

The Welsh soldiers were celebrating St David's Day, and while Peter Brown of the East Yorks remembered them wearing daffodils on their helmets, Captain J. D. Cuthbertson, 7 RWF, recorded that 'forward companies on St David's Day with leeks being bravely worn on every helmet, now in exposed positions, were heavily shelled and mortared.'[2]

The artillery and mortars of the 53rd Division gave as good as they got. That day, Lieutenant-Colonel Crozier, Commanding Officer of the 1st Battalion, Manchester Regiment, recorded that: 'I put a thousand phosphorous bombs into Weeze today. I hope the Bosch found it hot.'[3]

'All through the week we threw some ammunition down over there,' said William Tichard, 83rd Field Regiment, Royal Artillery. 'Really threw, because the panzers was in there and the Welch Fusiliers went up against them. They did a really good job but they lost a lot of men.'

'I don't know how the Germans used to stick it,' Bruce Coombs, 6 RWF, said of the artillery fire. 'It was terrible.'

The Royal Artillery were one invaluable resource for the Infantry Division. The Royal Engineers were another.

Robert Smith was a sapper in the 282nd Field Company.

'We resumed our normal role of road maintenance and clearance of the rubble. It was open country until a number of craters were found on the road. Some of which had been made by British shelling, some by the bombers, and some deliberately made by the retreating Germans.

'These caused great problems, as the enemy had filled some of them with literally tons of TNT explosives, put mines and booby traps on top of them, and then covered them. The lads had great difficulty in dealing with these, quite often suffering minor injuries. All we could do was to see if they were booby-trapped. Secondly, remove the mines off the top, and then fill them in with whatever was available. During these operations, one of the lads of my platoon was awarded the Military Medal.'

While under heavy shelling, Lance-Corporal Rees Morgan stood exposed for over an hour as he directed an armoured bulldozer to fill in two craters on the Goch–Weeze road. Later, and still under heavy fire, he dug down to remove a charge of TNT and mines. The enemy had partially detonated the charge, making it extremely sensitive to remove.[4]

Travers Cosgrove, 244th Field Company, had been on leave at the beginning of Veritable, but returned to the 53rd Division in time for the push on Weeze. 'The most notable thing I was involved in was the Skid Bailey bridge over the anti-tank ditch north of Weeze. This was built four or five miles north, up the road, and built onto wooden skids.'

It would be the work of 4 RWF to seize the anti-tank ditches and take the town. With them was William Crawshay, whose family had a long connection with the army, and war. They had owned the most successful iron works in the world, manufacturing, among many things, the canons for Admiral Nelson's fleet. One of William's relatives, J.E.C. Partridge, was the founder of the Army Rugby Union. William himself was commissioned into the Royal Welch Fusiliers and saw service behind enemy lines with the Special

Operations Executive (SOE). He then returned to the RWF, taking over a company of the 4th Battalion just in time for the battle of Weeze.

They began their attack at 0100 hrs on 1 March.

'(The Germans fought) pretty well. They were mainly boys. As I remember they didn't all throw up their hands. They tried hard. They fought quite well. They still had a nasty element of 88 guns. They were able to give us quite a tough time.'

At 0450 the second anti-tank ditch was reached. B Company slid down and clambered out the other side to form a defence, while the sappers began to span the bridge so that armour could cross. Some two hours later, B Company reported that the enemy was preparing to counter-attack. This was broken up with a heavy artillery barrage, but a second counter-attack was made at 0715, and included three panzers of the King Tiger model – a 68-ton behemoth with an 88mm gun, and armour as thick as seven inches.

'I saw a tank coming straight for our cottage HQ, infantry with them,' recorded Major Tim Dumas. 'We called for SOS fire. At that point our cottage was full of Germans.'[5]

Major Dumas and around ten other men were taken prisoner, but the situation for the battalion was saved by the rapid and accurate fire of the artillery, coupled with the gallant defence of the soldiers at the sharp end. Twenty-eight soldiers of 4 RWF were killed in the action at Weeze, ninety-three were wounded and a further thirty-three were missing – many of them taken prisoner.

By 1100, 4 RWF were firmly entrenched in town, and the enemy were heading in the opposite direction.

This had a lot to do with events unfolding outside of Weeze. At the same time as 4 RWF were seizing the town, the East Lancashires, Divisional Recce Force and Sherwood Rangers were engaged in action on the south-eastern outskirts along the River Niers, creating a noose around the enemy's neck that they chose to pull out of before they were surrounded and captured. This undoubtedly saved many lives in Weeze, but it came at its own cost.

Sherman tanks of 8th Armoured Brigade add their fire to the opening barrage of Operation Veritable, 8 February 1945.

Vickers machine guns of the 8th Battalion, Middlesex Regiment support the advance of the 51st (Highland) Division, 8 February 1945.

Churchill tanks (likely belonging to 107th Regiment RAC) and soldiers of the Highland Division advance on the Reichswald, 8 February 1945.

Gordon Highlanders in the Reichswald Forest, where fighting was often from one tree to the next, 9 February 1945.

A Sherman Firefly engages targets in Kleve as soldiers seek cover in the rubble (foreground), 11 February 1945.

2nd Battalion, Seaforth Highlanders pushing along one of the few tracks in the Reichswald, the day after their bloody battle at the Hekkens crossroads, 11 February 1945.

A universal carrier of 51st (Highland) Division struggles with the deep mud of the Rhineland, 10 February 1945.

A Weasel tracked cargo carrier leads a DUKW along the flooded road from Kranenburg to Kleve, 15 February 1945.

Shermans of 4th/7th Dragoon Guards shortly after the advance to seize the Goch escarpment, 17 February 1945. The tank in the foreground is Austin Baker's 'Shaggy Dog'.

Soldiers of the 53rd (Welsh) Division passing through the ruins of Goch on their way to Weeze, and eventually Alpen, during which time they would experience 'another taste of hell', 25 February 1945.

The youth of their nations. *Left:* Corporal Bennett of the King's Own Yorkshire Light Infantry, 2 March 1945. *Right:* German POW captured during Operation Veritable, 11 February 1945.

Infantry of the 3rd Division climbing aboard their Kangaroos after the attack on Kervenheim, 3 March 1945.

Sherwood Foresters meet US soldiers at Issum after the long-awaited link up of the two armies in the Rhineland, 6 March 1945.

A battery of rockets fire across the Rhine during the opening bombardment of Operation Plunder, which involved more than 4,000 Allied guns, 23 March 1945.

Top left: Buffalos continue to ferry soldiers across the Rhine after bridgeheads were secured during the night. *Top right:* 'Jocks' of 15th (Scottish) Division disembark from a storm boat – days of heavy fighting lie ahead, 24 March 1945.

Above and right: Mortarmen of 8th Battalion, Royal Scots come under enemy shell fire, then race to get their wounded comrade to safety, 24 March 1945.

Tank Action

On 1 March, Bob Atkinson and the 1st East Lancashires were advancing through woodland broken with small pastures and farm buildings.

'We were supported by tanks, and the first thing that happened, one of the tanks got hit. They all bailed out. They tried to join us, and when a couple of shells dropped near us they buggered off,' he chuckled.

'We come to the next (clearing), and there was a farmhouse. Just a farmhouse on its own, with the buildings round, and we got a lot of fire from there. They fought right up to when we got to the stone wall 'round (the) house, then they come out with their hands up.'

Though the fight was over, the prisoners were not out of harm's way. An old soldier in the company had been killed, and his friend – who had known him since before the war – was mad with rage.

'They had a job to stop him shooting (the prisoners). His mate had been shot. They had to take t' gun off him or he'd have killed (the) lot. They'd been together all the time, and they were regulars. Must have joined up together, and came from (the) same spot.'

Bob's friend, Johnny Baldwin, had been injured in the action, but didn't seem too upset about it.

'He got wounded in t' leg. Well, ankle really. "I've got a Blighty!" he said to me, did Johnny.'

A 'Blighty' was the common term for a wound that would necessitate evacuation to Britain. Bob had also been struck by 'a bit of shrapnel' in his back, but he was going nowhere.

'The MO, because he couldn't find a big hole, he said there was nothing there, but there was a patch of blood as big as a pancake on me vest and me shirt, so there must have been something gone in somewhere.'

Eleven soldiers of the East Lancs died that day. Some were veterans of Dunkirk. Others, eighteen-year-old replacements.

Frank Brodie, of the same battalion, was towing his anti-tank gun with his Bren carrier when he came up against the enemy's armour.

'We moved off from there down this main road, and we came to a point where we split up, and Johnny went t' right, and I went t' left. And at that point in time we had a Tiger tank in front of us what opened up. As I struck off down t' left, this tank must have been following us. It was firing at us as we were going, but somehow it couldn't get (the) gun down low enough on us. It were just going over (the) top of us wit' shells.

'We got to the farm, dropped the gun, and got into action, and opened up on this tank. All we could see was the left-hand side of the turret, and a bit of track. And when we were firing at him it just seemed to be bouncing off.'

Frank estimates that the range was 800 yards.

'I were directing fire on it, and I were watching it through binoculars, and it hit, and the tracer flew off. (After) about six or seven rounds he backed off.'

Ernie Leppard, Sherwood Rangers, also met enemy armour along the Niers. There was no good time for such encounters, but things were made worse by the fact that his Sherman Firefly tank – a replacement for the one he'd lost to enemy action at Kleve – was giving his crew plenty of problems.

'My gunner was complaining that the gun wasn't firing properly. The driver was complaining that the battery was running short on it, so there was something wrong with it.

'This area, it was in a wooded area. The Germans shelled us when we was forming up and the Germans were holding this farmhouse. It was urgent that we got pushed on so we were all lined up and we were to go over the brow of this hill and down towards this farmhouse. Whoever gave this cock-eyed order needs shooting himself, I think. The Sherman couldn't fire on the move, so you go over the brow of the hill, the infantry got over the brow of the hill and three or four Spandau machine guns opened up on them, so they laid flat and we were to go over in one charge, top speed, to go at this farmhouse. We reached the brow and there's a German Panther tank in the corner.'

Later in the interview, Ernie corrects himself to say that the enemy tanks were in fact Jagdpanthers – tank destroyers with an

88mm gun – but during the battle he was under the belief that it was Panthers he was facing.

'He's firing along the line. We could see the shells whipping up and the chap on the left, he got to the farmhouse but they come out with bazookas and hit his tank with a bazooka. The next tank, the Panther tank in the corner, shell straight on through him, buried in his engine. They bailed out but the tank didn't catch fire. Two or three of ours got hit, and we were more or less on the right and our driver was in a panic, he charged into some woods, on the right-hand side, and he didn't take his bloody foot off the accelerator.

'We charged into the wood, hit a tree, everything come down with a clatter. He had knocked himself out, the gun skewed round and everything went dead. The tank went completely dead. A load of acrid smoke came inside it so we all bailed out, thought we'd been hit. Outside it was a bloody sight worse than it was inside – they was mortaring and machine-gunning us – so we jumped back in.

'We had to chop a tree down to hand-crank the gun round to the farmhouse. We fired the gun a bit and they put in another attack, took the farmhouse, then it was about evening. Again, everyone had just disappeared, left us. We was completely dead, no radio, and it was getting dark. We didn't want to go wandering about in the dark so we slept in the tank that night.

'About two o'clock our driver said, "There's bloody Germans outside knocking on the tank." We heard the words 'surrender' and I think we were that low morale that if they were asking us to surrender, we would have done, but *they* was wishing to surrender. So we, bloody annoyed getting woken up that time of morning, made a cup of tea. We was running short of rations and we didn't want to feed them so we took their arms off them and sent them across the field to find some infantry. We didn't want them at all.

'After they'd gone, Johnny said to me, "Did you see their uniforms?"

'"No, why?"

'He said: "They're bloody tank uniforms they was wearing." The black wrapover tunics the tank crews wore. He said, "I bet they was from that bloody tank that knocked us out. I'm glad we got rid of them."'

A recovery vehicle was eventually sent out to Ernie's crew, and a new battery got the tank back into action.

'We go down this lane about 100 yards and there's this (Jagdpanther) that had hit us the night before. Behind it there was another one – completely intact, nothing wrong with it. We spent half an hour or so looking over it. They must have run out of petrol. It was a marvellous tank. There was eleven of us that went over the hill (the previous day) and it was picking us off and we had no answer to them.'

B Squadron, Sherwood Rangers lost six tanks in that attack. Only one had been destroyed by a Jagdpanther. Panzerfausts, and the collision with the tree, had caused much of the damage to the others. Two of the tanks, including Ernie's, were able to be recovered. This was conducted by the regiment's Light Aid Detachment (LAD). Their padre, meanwhile, concerned himself with recovering bodies, his actions recorded by historian James Holland:

'Of the two men killed, Corporal Ken Turner was discovered a short distance away from the fighting. He'd been horrifically wounded in the legs when his tank had been hit by a Panzerfaust. The Germans had picked him up and taken him to their own RAP where his shattered leg had been amputated. He'd not survived, however, and he'd been left, abandoned by the Germans when they fled the RAP. It took the padre a while to find him, but when he did, he carefully buried him and marked his grave.'[6]

This padre was Reverend Leslie Skinner, the first British chaplain ashore on D-Day. He was a pillar of strength for soldiers, and their bereaved families, writing letters to the family of every man lost, and continuing this correspondence with many after the war. The reverend also insisted that he be the one to recover the regiment's dead from knocked-out tanks, sparing the men's comrades from the horror.

His compassion, and his courage, knew no bounds.

The end of the beginning

After a night where they were held up by SPs and an 88mm gun, 1 Ox and Bucks entered Kevelaer on 2 March with little opposition.

The enemy had pulled back, leaving mines and booby traps in their wake, which caused several casualties.

'I pushed the door open with my left hand,' said Corporal Jim Wilsdon. 'There was a blinding flash and explosion. I was thrown back into the street, unable to see or hear.'[7]

Jim lost several fingers, and two other men were injured. There were further casualties that day when a German SP gun knocked out four Kangaroos carrying men of 1 HLI.

There was, however, good news to be had when the 53rd Recce Regiment pushed south to Geldern, where they linked up outside of the town with the US 35th Infantry Division, who were pushing up as part of Operation Grenade. It may have been weeks behind schedule, but the British and US forces could now finish the battle side by side.

Ronnie Henderson's part in the campaign came to an end soon after. On what he believed was 4 March, Ronnie was alone in a cellar when 'suddenly the whole place was smoke, fumes and flames. I couldn't get out. I had a hell of a job getting out. And when I did get out into the street me shirt was on fire down the front. I felt me hot face and hands, and I realized that I'd been burnt.'

Ronnie may have become a victim of a booby trap, or shell. Either way, he needed help. Out on the road he flagged down a truck and caught a lift to an aid post belonging to the Sherwood Rangers. From there Ronnie was evacuated down the line, and eventually to Britain. There's no mention of the incident in the unit's war diary, but this tallies with Ronnie's story that he left without telling anyone, his first priority being treatment. He worried that this would lead to him being labelled as a deserter, and that his family would receive a telegram telling them such, but this did not come to pass.

With his hands burned and bandaged, Ronnie required the help of the hospital padre to keep up with his correspondence.

'I was writing to two girls at the time. I knew that I was going to go home on leave and I had to pack one of them up, I couldn't visit them both.'

Ronnie's decision was made when one of the girls sent him a parcel of fruit.

'I wrote and packed the other one up. And then the following day fruit arrived from her as well. So I wrote and packed the other one up (as well).'

After a month in hospital Ronnie was given a week of leave in Britain, visiting a girl that he'd met during his training. All was well that ended well, and she eventually became his wife.

On the same day that Ronnie was injured, and in an echo of medieval times, Travers Cosgrove and his troop of sappers were required to bridge a moat at Geldern. This also necessitated repairing the cratered road that approached it. Travers spied a nearby builders' yard full of materials, but decided that it would be better to hold on to this for other engineering tasks.

'We didn't want to just bulldoze that into the holes, so we pulled the builders' house down instead, and pushed that into a hole. That wasn't enough, so we pulled down houses on the other bank with an armoured dozer.'

A bridge was built and the moat at Geldern was crossed. The Sherwood Rangers and 1 Ox and Bucks, who were mounted in Kangaroos, then pushed through. Their destination was Issum, a small town bisected by the Issumer Fleuth river. One of the first to arrive in the western side of the town was Stuart Hills, who was leading a recce troop of the Sherwood Rangers.

'I wanted to get into Issum first and ordered Sergeant Pothecary to come with me, so we entered the town at top speed. No Germans were there but the place was under shellfire and I found that the bridges out of town on the far side had been destroyed. Accordingly I halted my troop and set up a forward HQ. There was still a lot of shelling, which made things uncomfortable, and once a shell narrowly missed me when I was standing at the window of a house. Both window and wall were shattered and, covered with dust and fragments of glass and brickwork, I dived under an adjacent infantry troop carrier for protection. There was another body beside me seeking similar shelter and, as the smoke cleared, I recognized a familiar face from my school-days, that of Ernie Delevigne, the driver of the vehicle concerned. I was so surprised that all I could say was, "What the hell are you doing here?"'[8]

An armoured bulldozer of the Sherwood Rangers then knocked down a house and pushed the rubble into the river to make a base for a bridge that would need to be laid across it. The work of the bulldozer was directed by Travers Cosgrove, who had been sent up to recce the site after completing his bridge at Geldern.

Travers handed over command when the bridging unit arrived, but moments later his fellow sapper officer was struck in the knee by shrapnel. Travers then reassumed command himself and supervised construction of a Scissors bridge – a moveable bridging unit attached to a tracked vehicle chassis. During his interview with the Imperial War Museum, Travers had not once mentioned that the bridge was under any kind of fire, let alone prolonged and accurate shelling. The citation for his award of the Military Cross is rather more forthcoming:

'. . . exposing himself to shell and mortar fire, now much intensified . . . for three hours he remained until the Scissors bridge was launched. The success of the operation, which played a vital part in the continued advance of the armour, was almost entirely due to Lieutenant Cosgrove's initiative, courage, and resource.'[9]

When infantry patrols reported that the enemy were gathering on the other side of the river, Stuart Hills was ordered to place a tank close by the sappers to offer them some protection.

At 0700 the next morning, 5 March, 4 RWF and the Sherwood Rangers were tasked with crossing the bridge, clearing the other side of Issum and creating a bridgehead that would allow 53rd Division to push on to Alpen, some five miles to the north-east. Ernie Leppard, of the Sherwood Rangers, was there as the loader/wireless operator in his Sherman Firefly.

'My tank commander fell out with his friend, the tank sergeant, because we were pushed in the lead over the bridge.'

Ernie's tank went over the bridge at first light with 'about six' tanks following.

'We're just about 100 yards up the road, and one road leads right of this small town. There's a clump of trees right on the top about 1,000 yards in front, and suddenly we're hit. The first shot knocked our track off.'

The moment was witnessed by Stuart Hills, who saw a second

armour-piercing round zip over the top of Ernie's turret. Under mortar and machine-gun fire, the crew bailed out.

'All our bloody tanks were disappearing,' said Ernie. 'The infantry said there's a shelter over in the corner which is HQ, which was a German bunker just by the bridge. So we dashed over to it and they started mortaring and shelling. We was standing outside and a mortar killed some of the infantry standing outside.'

Ernie and his crew helped to recover the dead and wounded.

'Very disturbing to carry a body down in this bunker and his bloody head comes off in your hands. Anyway we took him down but we could see he was dead because his head had come off so we took him back up again and put him outside.

'When we get in this bunker, it was the Welsh Division. There was something wrong with that (company). There was a major inside at this command post and we were stuck in his bunker most of the day. All he did was scream over the radio for reinforcements. There was about thirty people in this bunker, from officers and sergeants, and everybody was giving everybody else orders to go outside and take part in the actions outside. There was about a hundred Germans defending this small town and there was only about forty in the company of infantry outside against them. There was more down in this bloody bunker than there was outside fighting them. He had about eight runners that were running out with information backwards and forwards. The runners were disappearing, and gradually it was down to the last runner. This was about three o'clock in the afternoon and we'd been down in this bunker since seven. They was shelling this bridge, which no reinforcements ever come over. Every two or three minutes we had a shell burst around or even on top of the bunker.

'(By) about three o'clock their runners were getting a bit low and the wounded were coming in and they turned to us. "About time you bloody tank boys went out and acted as infantry!" And we looked at each other and thought, *It's about time we left*. About three o'clock and we hadn't had anything to eat all day, had no breakfast, so thought we'd try and make our way back to our tank and see if there's any rations we could have on it.

'So we made a beeline and got back to the tank by about four o'clock, and the reason nobody had come over the bridge (was) because just down the road on the right a Spandau had got the bridge targeted, so we fired a shot (at it). There was nothing wrong with the tank, (it just had) the track off, a gouge in the turret, so we put the Spandau out of action and got ourselves a meal in the tank and let them carry on with their bloody battle.'

At the time the 53rd (Welsh) Division had been in almost-continuous action and field conditions for four weeks, and the loss of experienced officers and NCOs was beginning to tell.

That same day, 7 RWF passed through the Issum bridgehead to continue the attack. They were without a second in command, and two of the company commanders were new to the job. The battalion's adjutant had only taken his position a few days earlier, filling 'dead men's shoes' in the middle of a battle.

Things got worse an hour before the battalion were due to launch their attack.

'We lost our CO, Colonel Dickson,' said Norman Griffin. 'We lost him to a sniper. He was a very brave man.'

Lieutenant-Colonel George Dickson, who had been responsible for the lives of more than 800 men, was thirty years old when he was mortally wounded.[10]

There was no second in command to take over when Colonel Dickson was shot, so Major Mervyn Saunders, a battery commander of the 83rd Field Regiment, who were supporting 7 RWF, stepped into the role. It must have been a daunting task, given that he had no experience of handling an infantry battalion, let alone directing an operation that combined tanks and artillery. However, the citation of his DSO records that 'he skillfully and bravely led 7 RWF through the attack, which lasted for twelve hours, and took 200 prisoners'. Major Saunders was also given the distinction of wearing the treasured 'flash' of the Royal Welch Fusiliers – a tradition that dates back to the early eighteenth century, and an honour in the army that is only accorded to the RWF.

Fellow battery commander Major Richard Hughes MC, attached to the 2nd Monmouthshires, supported an attack on the outskirts of Alpen the next day, 6 March.

'This whole business was another taste of hell. We were all so tired that keeping our eyes open was difficult. Our objective was to clear the main road to the end of the thick wood (Die Leucht forest) before Alpen, where we should meet the Americans on our right and the Guards on our left.

'We succeeded in reaching our objective, but neither Americans nor Guards turned up. We were heavily shelled all day trying to get up the road, then found a farmhouse for Battalion HQ. This was continuously shelled, then an SP gun came up and fired several rounds right through it. The Boche came around us during the night. It can readily be understood that – weary as we were – nobody slept.'[11]

This attack by 2 Mons and 4 Welch was supported by A Squadron of the 13th/18th Hussars, who lost three tanks to SP guns. Their losses for the day were three killed and eight wounded.

The infantry that A Squadron were supporting were badly mauled, and by the end of the attack they could only muster eight men on the objective – what should have been a company was reduced to less than a section. Fourteen men from 2 Mons were killed that day, and fifty-seven wounded. 4 Welch lost seven men killed on 7 March, and twenty on the 8th.

The end of the war must have seemed incredibly distant to the young replacements who had slogged through the Reichswald, and fought through the towns and woods of the Eastern Rhineland. Other, old soldiers, had been fighting since 1940. James Eves, East Lancashires, recalled the death of a long-standing friend who had been with him at Dunkirk.

'We were going up this road. We came to a road block. The CO, in his Bren gun carrier, was in the front of me. I was behind, and then behind me was the Royal Artillery half-track for the artillery observer. When we got to this roadblock, we stopped, and the CO said to his driver, "Come on, go around the side." He said, "No, sir, they haven't blocked this road and not mined there, we need the pioneers."

'The next thing, the battery commander, who I think was someone called McKindel, Major McKindel, he said to the CO, "Oh, if your men are afraid to go around there, my man isn't."

'This armoured half-track pulled off. It was going up the grass bank at the side when the dismounted carrier platoon, with Sergeant Lee at the front, came marching up the road. And he was right on the level with the front wheel of this half-track when it hit a mine, and blew (Lee's) legs off.'

Sergeant Albert Lee died of his wounds a few days later, and was greatly missed by James.

'He was a Blackburn lad, and he were a good pal of mine.'[12]

General Horrocks put the 53rd Division's casualties at 5,000, and wrote that it was the 53rd who, 'in my opinion, suffered most' during Operation Veritable.[13]

2 Mons alone suffered 300 casualties in the Rhineland. Major Richard Hughes MC had fought with them all the way.

'On the morning of 6 March a round cheerful red face that I knew from another regiment in the early days appeared saying, "Hello, Old Man! We have heard about the bloody time you have had." I was so utterly weary that I gazed at him and said, "Who are you?" Back came the answer: "52nd Division. We are relieving you!"

'It did not seem possible that it could be true! For twenty-eight continuous days we had fought, and been out of contact with the enemy for only one night. Only once had I had my clothes off, and for only one night had I not been always on alert in case of a call for fire. I could hardly believe it!'[14]

To the north of the bloodied but unbowed Welsh Division, Guards, Yellow Devils, Black Bulls and Black Rats were making their own final push on the Rhine.

CHAPTER 9

Reaching the Rhine

Operation Blockbuster
26 February – 12 March 1945

'The Germans of course were defending their homeland, and they were defending it very, very strongly. Most of the battles were very, very hard-fought, lots of artillery. There was no respite until the Germans had been pushed back to the Rhine itself. It was really hard-going, and hard fighting. The infantry in particular, they did a damn good job.'

Sidney England, 3/4th County of
London Yeomanry (Sharpshooters)

Black Bulls and Black Rats

Fred Cooper, who was commanding a section in the 2nd Battalion, King's Royal Rifle Corps, was finally on the enemy's home soil after fighting them in North Africa, Italy, France and the Low Countries. Now in Germany, he found that the attitude of his fellow soldiers was hardening.

'Our people seemed then to adopt a scorched-earth policy. Whereas in France, Belgium and 'olland, you never got it. In Germany, almost as soon as we got there, 'ouses were ablaze. (They were) putting incendiary shells and incendiary bullets into the 'ouses and settin' fire to 'em, you know. Our people were not afraid to knock 'ouses down, set fire to 'em. We were in the enemy's country, and anythin' goes. That seemed to be the attitude.'

On 23 February the waters of the flooded Roer had finally receded to the point where the Ninth US Army could launch Operation Grenade. At last, as had always been the plan, the German defenders of the Rhineland would now face a battle on two fronts, and on 26 February the British and Canadian forces launched Operation Blockbuster, a renewed effort to overcome the last German line of defence before the Rhine.

The British 11th Armoured Division – known as the Black Bulls – were released from reserve to take part. Their objectives were to take the town of Üdem and then to push east and seize the southern edge of the Hochwald Layback – a wooded ridge a few miles west of the Rhine. The 11th would also be augmented by the attachment of 4th Armoured Brigade – the Black Rats. It was a powerful force, but one that would be constricted by the mud and terrain of the sodden Rhineland. Still, the moment of entering onto the enemy's home soil was one to remember, and a twenty-one-year-old officer of the Scots Greys recorded his feelings.

'It is difficult to find the words to express my emotions as I saw the crudely sign-written board saying, "YOU ARE NOW ENTERING GERMANY". Since 1939 Britain had been subjected to defeat after defeat in Europe, Africa and the Far East. Our towns and cities had been bombed and torched with incendiaries. Countless thousands of men and women had been killed, maimed and injured on land, sea and in the air and Hitler's U-boats had done their best to starve us out. Standing alone, Britain had been on its knees but it had fought back and now, with the might of America at its side, it was winning.'[1]

The name of this officer was Murray Walker. In later years, he would be known across the world as the voice of Formula One Racing.

Serving in the same brigade as Murray, the newly promoted Sergeant Fred Cooper came under heavy shellfire while in scrubland outside of Üdem.

'We'd been doing a daylight attack, and we had one or two

casualties. It was not very nice, you know. You were concealed from view, but he knew you were there and he was putting shells down. We had this from about eight o'clock in the morning, and we finished up at about six o'clock at night at a crossroads.'

The crossroads had been held by Germans in zig-zag trenches, who had since pulled out. There was a house on the crossroads, and beyond it a 'mansion' on high ground. Fred was picked to go on a three-man patrol to check both buildings.

'I had a good section. Officers used to come to me and say, "Now I want your section to patrol tonight", and when I went back and told the lads they used to say to me, "But we was out last night and the night before. What about the others?", and I used to go back to the officer and say, "The lads are not happy about this, sir."'

Such protests tended to fall on deaf ears.

'We had a young officer who'd just joined us, and his name was Hugh Elgar. He was the son of the Bishop of Bournemouth. His brother was also an officer in the regiment.'

As the three-man patrol went out, the rest of the platoon would be prepared to provide covering fire if needed. One of the men remaining behind had joined them about a month earlier, and was known to Fred.

'He had met my wife's sister, and he was courting her at the time. I had some sort of relationship with him. We were both courting two sisters. He was only a youngster, he was about nineteen. Barely nineteen. We were waiting for the off, and he come up to me crying. Crying his eyes out.'

Fred asked him what the matter was.

'He said, "We've had all this (shelling) today, now I'm out on patrol tonight." Tears were streaming down his face. So, you know, what can you say? I wasn't in a very happy mood, you know. I'd been suffering the same as him during the course of the day. And I had to be quite blunt with him. I said, "What's the matter with you, you silly bastard, you're not out on patrol." I said, "Me and Davies are out on patrol, you'll just give us covering fire." I left it at that.'

Fred's patrol found six German soldiers in the cellar of the house on the crossroads, one of them badly wounded. He asked Fred for a cigarette, who handed him a few before going back outside.

'Then we got fired at. (We) lobbed a couple of grenades, waited there for about half an hour, nothing happened, so the officer said, "Well, we better go do this mansion."'

'I think we got within fifty yards of the place,' said Fred, who assumed that it was clear because they'd been able to approach up to a short distance, and under moonlight. They then returned to the crossroads where the company had taken over the zig-zag trenches. Soldiers from the 53rd Division were up top, waiting to put in an attack on the mansion.

'What a night we had,' said Fred, who had Welsh Division soldiers jumping down on him whenever the crossroads was shelled. 'I was black and blue.'

The shelling reached such a height that the company was pulled back to a barn a few hundred yards to their rear.

'I stopped by the barn door to watch the others come in. Well, when they came in they were in single file, and (Jerry) must have watched us coming in, and took a point on that, and as soon as they'd got about ten yards (Jerry) put a salvo of shells down. And I can remember looking at the bloke at the front of the section, and a shell landed right in front of his foot, and he looked for all the world to me as if he'd kicked it.'

By some miracle the soldier was 'completely unhurt'.

Others had not been so fortunate. Fred ran out to help the casualties, who included 'Dusty' Miller, the young soldier who was courting Fred's sister-in-law.

'The chap in the ambulance, I knew. Corporal Burge. And he loaded the casualties in, so I said to him, "How's young Dusty Miller?" "Fred," he said, "he's got a bit through the 'ead, and a bit through the lung." He said, "He won't see it back." And sure enough, about twenty minutes later, message come through, "Rifleman Miller, dead".[2]

'I had to write quite a lengthy letter back to the family explaining the situation.'

One can only imagine the worry of Fred's wife, knowing that

she too might suffer the same grief as her sister. A couple of days later, 2 March, Fred's company was again in action in the farmland outside of Üdem.

'The tanks were coming across the field and they got fired on by the 88mm guns, and they got machine-gun fire as well.'

The infantry were sent to root the guns out, and made for a wooded embankment close to the farm that was their objective.

'They filtered us through the woods, and we started moving along the top of the ridge, and he fired at us and we all went to ground. We got pinned down. We were pinned down for about 'alf an 'our. Every time we moved (there was) a burst of machine-gun fire. The officer said to me, "I'm going back to contact the company commander."'

Fred remained in position for some time before deciding that the men were being exposed for no good reason.

'I thought to myself in the end, *Well, what's the point in staying 'ere?*, so I pulled them all back into the woods. We had to leave one there, a chap named Dossett. He got a bullet right through (the forehead). He's laying dead.'

One of the other men in the platoon caught Fred's attention – Rudkins, an illiterate soldier who used to carry several fountain pens in his pocket.

'Well, when we pulled out of this wood, we left Dossett there, dead, and I see two blokes helping this Rudkins along. And I went over – you're not in a very bright mood after being pinned down for 'alf an 'our – I said, "What the bloody 'ell's the matter with you then?" He's got tears runnin' down his face, and he says, "I can't help it, I can't stop shakin'."'

Fred took the man back to the company. 'The first person I (then) bumped into was Roly Gibbs, the company commander. So I said to him, "Excuse me, sir, have you seen Rudkins?"

'"Sergeant Cooper," he said, "it's distressing. Do you know that's going to take him two or three years to get over that? When a man just snaps like that," he said, "it takes a long time."

'"A snap like that," he said, "it's sad."'

Having failed to get onto their objective on the first attempt, a new plan was devised – one that would involve mounting in Kangaroos and driving straight down the throat of the enemy.

'You can understand the lads were a bit dejected, you know, having been pinned down, and left somebody dead there, and seen somebody go bomb-happy. So they were rather reluctant to get into these things.'

Fred knew that it was a moment that called for leadership by example.

'I got in first, and I've made the biggest mistake of me life, there.'

The platoon finally loaded, the Kangaroos drivers went hell for leather across the open field.

'These blokes wasn't fussy,' said Fred. 'They just banged into the farmhouse wall.'

The troops were thrown forward into a heap. They then began to quickly scramble out before the enemy could put a Panzerfaust into the armour.

'My lot got out before me,' said Fred, 'and when I got out they'd all disappeared.'

The plan had called for half of the men to take the farmhouse while the other half, with Fred, took the barn.

'I'm hitting the barn. They're all in the farmhouse! I'm on me own in the barn.

'It was a long barn. At the far end, there was a wide door and there was about six Germans there. There was no indication that they were prepared to surrender. If they'd have put their hands up, we'd have respected that and I'd have just ushered them along. But they stood at the door, and I started firing.

'I must have fired off at least six magazines, and these Germans are still there. All of a sudden there was a loud shot behind me, and it was the platoon sergeant. One shot from a rifle and a German dropped down, and I'd fired 180 bullets and never hit a thing. That's how I evaluated the Sten gun. Absolute rubbish.'

With one of their comrades dead beside them, the remaining enemy in the barn decided that the time had come to surrender.

'Once they put their hand up, they're on your side virtually.

You always respect that. I've always said it takes ten men to keep one in the line,' said Fred, referring to the fact that for every soldier on the frontline, many more were in the rear echelons. 'I'm just the unlucky bugger who's in the line, and he's in the same position, and you respect him, you know. He's done his bit and that's it.'

A familiar pattern was now repeated – once the enemy lost a position on the frontline it came under heavy shellfire from guns in the rear.

'It landed bang on. One of our lads, Tom Marshall, he had a family of about four – devoted family man – he went down.'

Fred ordered the POWs to pull down a door that could be used as a makeshift stretcher.

'Someone said, "Alright, Tom?" He said, "Yeah, I'm alright."'

But when the wounded soldier was lifted onto the 'stretcher', the extent of the damage to his leg became clear.

'It was 'olding on by the back tendon. When I realized that, I put him down and lifted him by the high part of the leg, by the knee, and put him on the door.

'I said, "You alright, Tommy?"

'And he said, "No, Fred, me leg, me leg!"

'And I picked up his leg and just twisted it around. "Alright now, Tom?"

'"Yeah, that's alright, Fred."

'A Bren gun carrier came up to take him back, and by this time it's evening. On the way back it got stuck, and he died.'[3]

The enemy continued to shell the farmhouse, which was now occupied by British soldiers, German POWs, and the family who lived there.

'A grandmother, a daughter, her husband and a small child, and they'd packed all their belongings on a cart. And about ten o'clock, they went out to get on the cart, and the Germans see a bit of movement and put shells down.'

The younger woman lost a large chunk of her thigh and was screaming in pain. Her child cried with worry.

'The older woman, I've never seen a sight like it. She'd had her nose sliced off. I don't understand the make-up of the human face, too much. I know what I've got, and I know how to shave it. She had like two white balloons hanging down (from her nostrils).'

Fred's platoon tried to get an ambulance to take the woman back for treatment, but they were too busy dealing with casualties all up and down the line.

'All the time you could hear this lady trying to breathe,' said Fred, making choking sounds. 'The noise, you know, it haunted you, really.'

The platoon's fatal casualty of the previous day, Private Dossett, was still lying where he was killed on the ridge.

'The next day, this officer, he said, "Look, we've got this body out there, and I don't like to see any of my men laying there unattended. I want two volunteers to get him back and get him properly buried." So he called for volunteers, and nobody volunteered.

'I put me hand up and said, "Well, I'll go." Didn't fancy it much, you know, because of the amount of shelling. So Mickey Butler, he was another section leader, he said, "I'll go with Fred." So the officer said to the rest of the platoon, "I'm taking a grave risk here with two of my section leaders, putting them both at risk. You ought to be ashamed of yourself." This was how he spoke to 'em.'

Fred and Mickey put a door into the back of a Bren carrier that had come up with B Company, who were now pushing through Fred's company. Then they returned to the site where Dossett had been killed, and came under shelling while placing his body on the door, and the door onto the carrier. The shellfire spooked the carrier's driver, who quickly pulled away.

'The body and the door fell off. Me and Mick Butler had to put the body back on the door, lift it up, and put it back on the carrier, and we had to run behind the carrier holding it.'

Back at the farm, Fred ran into his regimental sergeant major, George Slater, who Fred recalled would often shout at Dossett for not having his buttons done up.

'I've just brought a body back for burial, George,' Fred told the RSM.

'"Who's going to be buried, then?" And I said, "Young Dossett."

Tears immediately welled down his face, and he came out, and he looked at him. He said, "Leave this to me."

'I went back in about an hour's time and he'd just about finished the hole. "Give me a hand," he said, and we lifted him in.'

RSM Slater then stood over the grave and saluted the fallen soldier.

'We left him with a shovel in his hand, tears still streaming down his face. I'll never forget that.'

Private Frank Dossett, of Tottenham, was later reburied in the Reichswald War Cemetery.[4]

The battalion was relieved after several days of action, and Fred closed his eyes.

'I slept for eighteen hours. And when I woke up, like a lot of other people, I was in the most distressed state possible. Couldn't be more depressed, you know. I thought, you know, *You can't go on like this, you're gonna get killed tomorrow.* It's in you. You feel it. So depressed it's unbelievable.'

Guards and Yellow Devils

As Canadian divisions fought a bloody battle to secure the northern end of the Hochwald Layback, the Guards Armoured and 43rd (Wessex) Divisions pushed down the Kleve–Xanten road in a last-ditch attempt to seize a bridge over the Rhine.

Robert Keenan and his tank crew in the 4th (Armoured) Coldstreams had cheered when they'd entered Germany – 'Loud hoorays from everybody, we're in Germany at last!' – but weeks of bitter fighting had followed. Robert recalled one action on 5 March, at Kalkar.

'Being in the troop leader's tank, you were in the front. We went to the starting line, went up the road, turned right up this road. Lo and behold, we got round a corner and the ditch was full of German soldiers. They were as surprised as we were, and they scarpered on their hands and knees trying to get away up this ditch. And of course we were just firing at them as we went up.'

A shell jammed in the tank's main armament, and the crew now had to rely on their machine guns.

'Lieutenant Rob (Brand) was in command, he was in the top. Then, at the same time, on a tank behind us, a mortar bomb had landed on the back of the tank. And I think it was either that, a bullet, or a splinter from the mortar went through (Lieutenant Rob's) cheek, through his mouth. He wasn't seriously wounded, he was alright.'

Robert continued to engage the enemy.

'There were Germans coming across the road from the other flank, and I was firing the machine gun as much as I could at them. They were assembling in the farmhouse on the left flank, and the farmyard was full of Germans. But I couldn't do anything about it because the main gun was jammed. I was firing the machine gun as best I could. There was a pause then, there was nobody coming. I was looking through the telescope, and a German soldier just stepped out, and he was like in one of the magazines, with the helmet, the leather, the submachine gun, the metal canister with his respirator, jackboots. He stood there in front of the tank, and I was so astounded, I looked. By the time the front machine gunner had seen him, I had gotten a clearance round and cleared the jammed round and loaded the gun up. He looked at the tank and just then I gave a quick burst – I missed him – he stepped back. I knew he had been after a bazooka somebody discarded, so I fired a round into the ditch to blow the bazooka up so it was no good to him again.'

It was a memory so vivid that it stayed with Robert for the rest of his life.

'I still see him. I see him regularly, in that ditch, looking up at that tank. He don't know how lucky he was,' he chuckled.

After the action, Lieutenant Rob was taken away to have his wound treated. He wasn't the only casualty.

'Ronnie Horn had been hit, and they got him out, but poor Ronnie died in the hospital.'[5]

Alan Brooke Pemberton was a junior officer in the same regiment. Though aged only twenty-one, Alan had already served in

North Africa and Italy, where he had been wounded. Following his recuperation, he took command of 8 Platoon, 1 Company, 5th Coldstream Guards in November 1944. Towards the end of Operation Blockbuster, his division was involved in the final attempt to seize a bridge on the Rhine.

'We had one rather memorable battle in which we had to attack towards Wesel. It was across flat farmland, with isolated farms and not much cover.'

The Guards achieved their objectives, 'but then we had to endure the most horrific bombardment, which turned out to be the Germans' last effort to keep us back while they evacuated and crossed the Rhine.'

Arthur Jones, 5 DCLI, recalled this massive barrage.

'We suddenly come under some very heavy shellfire from the other side of the Rhine. The officer in charge of this platoon, he said to our sergeant, "You're under observation from that tower (in Wesel), I want you to engage it."

'The shellfire was so intense it was suicide to run out there. So what we done, there was a bit of a bunker by the gun. One would dash out, put a round up the spout, dash back into the bunker again. The other would dash out and fire it. And that's how we fired six rounds of ammunition at Wesel's church tower. Miles out of range. Just a waste of time, really. But the effort was there, the thought was there, and nothing else.'

The job of taking Xanten, once a Roman town on the border of the Empire, had been given to Canadian divisions. After days of heavy fighting, with casualties numbering around 1,000, the town fell on 9 March.

The following day, David Baines, 7 Medium Regiment, was looking for a place to get his battery's guns into action.

'I saw what looked like a suitable place and walked in. Told my truck to stop and walked into the field, and was setting out where the guns should go, and I suddenly heard a hell of a bang behind me, and my truck had gone up on a mine that had been in the gateway, which obviously had not gone off when I'd walked through. It blew the truck apart, killed my signaller who was in the back, slightly damaged the driver, and I always felt very guilty about that. If I'd taken a bit longer, and gone rather slowly, no doubt I might have picked up the fact that there was a mine in the gateway. I was very upset.'

David had been living and fighting alongside his signaller, twenty-year-old Leslie Smith, for several months.[6]

He was one of the last British soldiers to be killed during Operation Veritable. 'During the evening we heard the big explosion when they blew the last bridge going over the Rhine,' said Ernie Leppard, who had to bail out of his tank three times during the campaign.

The remaining enemy in the Rhineland had retreated on the night of 10/11 March, and blew the bridges at Xanten behind them. The rail bridge at Wesel was also destroyed, leaving no intact bridge in the British sector.

Operation Veritable was now at an end, with both the British and US armies in total possession of the western side of the Rhine. A week earlier, some of the soldiers who had fought to clear the Rhineland received an unexpected visitor.

'Churchill came along in a scout car,' said Laurence Symes, 7th Royal Hampshire. 'He was rather a rotund gentleman so he couldn't get down in the scout car, but he was sat on the entrance at the top and he came along with a cigar in his hand, waving to us all. There was a little bit of shelling going on but it certainly gave us a lift to see this dear old gentleman showing himself like that.'

Roland Dane, 7th Black Watch, had a different opinion of the visit.

'We were ordered to stand at the side of the road, which I didn't. I think it was the ordering. (The rifle companies) had just come out the battle at Goch, and they'd lost quite a few casualties fighting in Goch, and I don't think they were very appreciative that somebody wanted a cheer. I didn't feel like cheering to be honest.'

It had taken a month of bitter fighting to clear the enemy from the Rhineland, and losses on both sides had been heavy. The German army lost 40,000 men killed or wounded and 50,000 taken prisoner,[7] and General Horrocks put the Anglo-Canadian cost at 15,634 casualties, around two thirds of them British.⁸ Some 3,600 of the Canadian Army's casualties were sustained in the final two weeks of fighting, testament to the ferocity of the defence that continued to the end.

The casualty rates of several battalions in the Reichswald and Rhineland were comparable to those that landed on D-Day. The 2nd East Yorkshires, who went ashore at Sword Beach, took 209 casualties in the first twenty-four hours of the invasion of France, and 156 in the little-known battle around Yorkshire Bridge. The 5th Wiltshires, during the push on the Goch Escarpment, suffered more than 200 casualties in a day.

For whatever reason, neither the Rhineland campaign nor the men who fought it receive the same deserved attention as is given to the Battle of Normandy, or Market Garden, and in that we as a nation have been remiss. In the face of a determined foe, brutal casualties and gruelling conditions, British soldiers had won a crucial victory, and brought the end of the war one bloody step closer.

To take the next, they would have to cross the Rhine.

PART 2

Crossing the Rhine

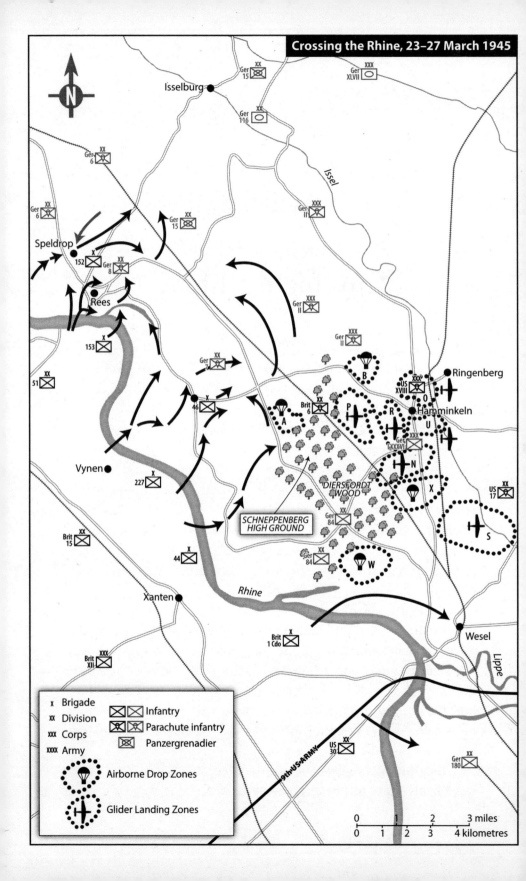

CHAPTER 10

Operation Plunder

British plans and preparation for the crossing of the Rhine

Standing in a farmer's field in the middle of the night, I look through high arches that frame bright lights in the distance. This rail bridge, at Wesel, has not served its intended purpose for eighty years. Instead, as the final bridge blown by the German army as it pulled back behind the Rhine, it stands sentinel over one of the last great battlegrounds in the west.

The operation that took place here was the largest mounted by the British army since D-Day. Looking out across the water, it's easy to understand why. At night the Rhine appears more lake than river, a black mass that oozes danger and strength. One can understand why its waters were once revered as a god, and how they formed the barrier that had defended Germanic lands for thousands of years.

I look across to Wesel, try to picture the sky full of the silhouettes of aircraft, flak exploding in the air as the bombers turned the town to rubble and flame. I imagine fields full of war-worn men, old soldiers preparing themselves for one more rendezvous with death. Eighteen-year-old replacements, wide-eyed, feeling 'that horrible steel' in their stomachs for the first time. The black shapes of assault vehicles creeping forward, tracers zipping and skipping both ways over the dark waters of the Rhine.

'They just didn't give up,' said commando Peter Fussell, who was on his third major amphibious assault of the war. 'We were being fired on by machine-gun fire, mortar fire and sniper fire all the time we were crossing the Rhine.'

On the night of 23 March, close to where I am standing, No. 1 Commando Brigade launched their attack on Wesel. Downriver, a little west, 15th (Scottish) and 51st (Highland) Divisions made their own crossings, clashing with their old enemy from the Rhineland – the elite German paratroopers. Then, a few hours after daylight on the 24th, the sky filled with more than 3,000 aircraft, as the Allies' own Airborne soldiers dropped a few miles from the bridgeheads. This combined assault was a colossal undertaking involving many hundreds of thousands of men from Britain, Canada and the United States.

Every branch of Britain's armed forces was represented on the Rhine. Opposing them were the depleted formations of II Fallschirmjäger Korps and the 84th Infantry Division, both supported by their own armour, as well as reserves of panzers and panzer grenadiers from XLVII Panzer Korps. Allied intelligence assessed that 116th Panzer Division had up to seventy tanks, while 15th Panzer Grenadier Division had fifteen, with as many as thirty SP guns. All told, the British expected to face some 58,000 German troops, 16,000 of them occupying positions on the river line. More than 800 anti-aircraft guns were also in the area.

To conceal the British army's build-up and intention in the weeks preceding the assault, artillery officers went forward alone to recce the sites that their guns would occupy at the final moment. Masses of supplies were lined along roads and placed in towns and villages, camouflaged as hedgerows and buildings respectively. A thick, continuous smoke screen was laid along the west bank to hide movements and men from the eyes of German observers. It was a measure that saved lives, but ruined meals.

'Everything we ate smelled of paraffin,' complained Sidney England, an experienced soldier who saw his first action in Italy. Sidney's regiment, the County of London Yeomanry, had suffered greatly in Normandy at the hands of Tigers led by tank ace Michael Pittman, who was himself killed in an Anglo-Canadian ambush later in the campaign.

Captain Tom Boardman, an officer in the 1st Northamptonshire Yeomanry, was awarded the Military Cross for his part in that action. His regiment had since been re-equipped and re-trained on Buffalo amphibious armoured carriers and would be responsible for getting their 'old friends', the Highland Division, across the great German river.

'I remember reconnoitring the banks of the Rhine. To our horror, the (current) was much stronger than one imagined it to be. The banks seemed a good deal steeper. One had considerable concern (over) how we would fare in those conditions.'

The Rhine, flooded in places due to the destruction of dykes, was 200–400 yards wide. Martin Lindsay was one of those who would be taken across its waters by the Northants. His battalion, the 1st Gordon Highlanders, had sustained 200 casualties during Operation Veritable, and were pulled back to Holland on 6 March to re-fit. It was a frustrating time for Martin and his fellow officers, who wanted to cross the Rhine straight away rather than give the enemy the chance to strengthen their defences. But he acknowledged that Britain also needed to prepare for such a big undertaking, not least in building up ammunition supplies.[1]

'With the shortage of experienced platoon commanders and NCOs our minor tactics were by now so minor as to be almost non-existent, so we had to have something to compensate, which, as usual, was overwhelming artillery support.'[2]

Around a million shells were being stockpiled for the British guns, and more than 30,000 tons of engineering material piled along the road north from Goch. Atop of this were tens of thousands of tons of combat supplies and rations.[3] And then, of course, there was the issue of assembling the soldiers.

Robert 'Bob' Summers, Royal Engineers, was a twenty-one-year-old replacement officer who joined his unit, 555th Field Company, in late February. Bob took over 2 Platoon, which was sixty-four men strong. No mention was made of who he was replacing. 'His books and things were still there, and I began to wonder a bit. The impression I got (was), *Oh, he's probably been posted somewhere,* you know. It wasn't until quite a bit after I realized

I was stepping in dead man's shoes. Looking back on it, I suppose it's a good thing you were so ignorant at the time.'

Bob's first task was to find assembly areas for thousands of troops coming up to make the crossing. 'I was finding suitable fields, and places, where certain units could be housed.'

While the assault and reserve divisions were held back in assembly areas, the front needed to be secured against enemy incursion. William Snell had landed at Sword Beach with 3rd Division, and served in 1 KOSB. 'We were in this smoke screen for must've been three weeks, and we had to patrol the riverbank. We got a British secret service man, he'd come across, and he'd been in the German lines and he had these two Germans with him. He was lucky that he didn't get shot.'

The 'spy', like his prisoners, had been dressed in German uniform.

'He shouted that he was British so they didn't open fire. So we took him, disarmed them and took them to HQ, Company HQ, where they were interrogated and eventually went back to Battalion HQ, and we got the report back that he was British secret service, who had been behind the German lines in Rees. These two Germans who had been with him had helped him and brought him to comparative safety.'

Comparative safety was right – the British forces building up for the attack were still under the range of powerful German guns, and more. Ronnie Henderson, 13th/18th Hussars, recalled an incident that befell his regiment on 12 March. At this time Ronnie was himself in hospital, recovering from wounds.

'Regimental Headquarters suffered an attack from a Messerschmitt Me 262, one of the new jet aircraft being introduced by the Luftwaffe. A cluster of bombs was dropped and caught a number of troops as they were returning from tea, killing seven and wounding twenty-eight. Together with some heavy shelling that evening and further casualties, including another trooper killed, that day was one of the worst for casualties experienced by the regiment.'[4]

The Allies' own bombers and fighter-bombers were engaged in hitting targets on the other side of the Rhine. Operations to isolate the battlefield began on 10 March, striking rail yards, bridges and anything else that could be used for bringing in German reinforcements. Three days before the river assault, the RAF began a programme of harassment bombing, the aim of which was to lower the enemy's morale, hinder the preparations of their defences, and to disrupt their communications.

For the most part of mid- to late March, the Allied guns were kept quiet and camouflaged to avoid giving away their positions and, with that, the likely crossing points that would be used. Then, at 1800 hrs on 23 March, a colossal barrage began on the heels of a Bomber Command raid on Wesel, with 1,300 British guns and several thousand American opening fire onto the enemy's own known artillery positions, headquarters and defences. Over the next twelve hours the British gunners would expend some 125,000 shells.[5]

'It made a lot of our chaps a little bit bomb-happy,' said William Snell. 'You could hear the shells coming, machine guns were going, mortars were going. Someone said it was a bigger barrage than the one at El Alamein.'

William and his comrades were sent forwards under cover of darkness to mark marshalling lanes for the incoming assault troops.

'I got wounded. It wasn't a very bad wound, I managed to stay with them until daybreak. It was a shell that dropped and I got a small bit of shrapnel in me leg. When we got back I was ordered to go to the field service station, and from there they sent me back up through the casualty clearing station.'

Sergeant Fred Cooper, who was commanding a section of soldiers in 2 KRRC, lost one of his men in the barrage. 'He was an ex Rifle Brigade man, and he'd been court martialled for desertion. I think he'd done about fifty-six days or something. When he come (to the platoon), he was very, very helpful.' Pleased and perhaps surprised, Fred praised the man's behaviour. 'He said, "Fred, I don't care what I do, but when that banging starts," he said, "believe me, I'm away." And he made no bones about it.

'When the initial barrage for the Rhine took place, he was gone, true to his word.'

Many soldiers who had stretched their luck from Normandy, or before, felt that it would give out before war's end. David Render, Sherwood Rangers, was convinced of it.

'Although their defeat was imminent, the enemy showed no signs of giving up and gave every indication that they would make us pay dearly for every yard of ground we gained once across the Rhine. My fatalism remained and I believed that the odds dictated that I would probably get killed. But the end was in sight and there was a chance that one might make it through. In many ways the prospect of becoming one of the last casualties of the war made things worse.'[6]

'Everyone was a little bit in trepidation about what was to come,' agreed Sidney England, 'because if we could get across the Rhine, well, it could be the end.'

CHAPTER 11

Operation Turnscrew

*The 51st (Highland) Division's battle on the Rhine
23 March – 1st April 1945*

'All of a sudden this German came (down the road) in an American jeep, took from the Ardennes. And he stopped, and he got off that jeep so fast I never saw a bloke move so fast in all my life. Anyway, he didn't get far. Then we had a jeep.'

Alfred Leigh, 2nd Battalion, The Seaforth Highlanders

Martin Lindsay, second in command of the 1st Battalion, Gordon Highlanders, had once looked forward to the thrill of battle.

'Now, though I had not yet got to the stage of dreading an action, I got no pleasure from it and looked forward only to the end of the war.'[1]

As shells pummelled the towns and villages across the river, and the tracer of machine guns seemed to dance lazily through the air, the Highlanders loaded into the rectangular hulls of the Buffalos. Tom Boardman, of the Northamptonshire Yeomanry, described the difficulties of the crossing for the drivers.

'You've got to go into the water pointing upstream, go across pointing upstream, which obviously brings you over considerably downstream. The critical thing is to get your Buffalo turned at the right moment, so you were square onto the bank the moment your tracks hit it, and you're in bottom gear. Considerable skill on the part of the drivers. Split-second (timing).

'It was disaster to miss your landing. You couldn't just put out back into the river, be clear and have another go. It wasn't an easy thing. Crossing that stretch of water in not easy conditions, and in a vehicle which is alright but wasn't ideal. It wouldn't have passed many safety regulations, I'm sure.'

Much rested on the skill of the Buffalos' young drivers, and they did not fail.

'The drivers, they were bloody good,' said Tom.

At 2030hrs, Sergeant Harry Simpson, 7th Black Watch, went across the Rhine. The noise of the barrage was so mighty that it drowned out the sound of the Buffalo's engine, and as it climbed up onto the eastern bank of the river and came to a shuddering halt, B Company's men began to clamber up over the sides and jump down onto the enemy-held soil. Immediately there were explosions, and screams.

'We landed in anti-personnel mines,' said Harry. 'I well remember Corporal Thomas, a Welshman, he lost his legs, and one or two other men with him were killed.'

B Company lost two section commanders and two Bren gunners to the mines. There was no knowing how many more were buried, or where, but the men of the Black Watch pressed on regardless.

'When we jumped we were terrified, because we'd seen them go down. We gritted our teeth, closed our eyes, and hoped that when we did land we'd be alright.'

They pressed on from the river's bank and captured the farm of Pottdeckel, little more than smouldering ruins, then pushed on and dug in at the farm of Kivitt. Things were going about as well as could be expected, but Harry was not at ease.

'Through the night I was a bit doubtful.'

One of the things that worried him was an area of dead ground near the buildings.

'If any of the enemy got in this ditch, they could approach the house without being seen by the platoon.'

Meanwhile, the 7th Argyll and Sutherland Highlanders had crossed the Rhine at the same time as the 7th Black Watch, and made similarly good progress. The 1st Black Watch followed behind in storm boats as a second wave, and went into the attack at the village of Klein Esserden, where they hit the strongest resistance yet met by the division. It was deep into the night before they secured this first village and went on to a second, Speldrop, where the battle was no less vicious. The battalion was barely gaining a foothold when the enemy paratroopers launched a fierce counter-attack supported by self-propelled guns.

Lieutenant Henderson, 1st Black Watch, understood that this was a critical moment in the operation. He ordered the rest of his patrol to take cover while he and a Bren gunner went forward to scout the enemy's strength and positions. Within seconds an enemy machine gun opened up at very close range. The Bren gunner was killed and Lieutenant Henderson's revolver was shot out of his hand. Armed with nothing but a shovel, he charged the machine-gun position alone and killed the gunner.

He then returned to the rest of the patrol, who were still under heavy fire. The only nearby building was already in flames, but it was a case of any port in a storm, and this a storm of steel. Henderson led his men inside the smoke and flame and set them out in defence. Realizing that they were now without a Bren gun, Henderson crawled the sixty yards to recover the machine gun of his fallen gunner, then returned to his men, who were not only completely cut off, but without any means of communication to the rest of the battalion.

Henderson's small group held out for over twelve hours, despite many attempts to overrun them. They were under fire the entire time, including from several bazookas firing from close range. It would take a fresh Canadian battalion supported by tanks to finally capture the tiny village, but by holding out as long as he did, Lieutenant Henderson had greatly influenced the course of the battle, the bodies of thirty-five German dead later found around his position.[2] 1st Black Watch also suffered greatly, with eighty-one casualties in their first twenty-four hours of battle.

Lieutenant Henderson was himself wounded during fighting in the bridgehead, and was evacuated to England. It was in hospital that John 'Tug' Wilson, 7th Black Watch, got to know the brave lieutenant who had charged a machine gun armed with nothing but a shovel.

'He was training to be a Church of Scotland padre!' John said, amused. 'Awfully nice chap, he was. He'd been wounded rather badly. We were both in the same ward, and while we were there he had been awarded a DSO.'

'I had hoped that he might be given the Victoria Cross,' wrote General Brian Horrocks.[3]

5th Black Watch were carried across the Rhine that night by 4 RTR, the moment recalled by Major JD McGregor: 'The noise was deafening. The dark overcast sky was lit by searchlights, red tracer bullets. Morale was high and excitement was at a fever pitch. Someone started to sing and the singing spread from group to group. The padre led with "Onward Christian Soldiers" but the unmistakable "Ball of Kirriemuir" was heard despite the frightful din.'[4]

The boisterous 'Ball of Kirriemuir' is also known as 'Four-and-Twenty Virgins', which gives a rather more accurate indication of its lyrics.

'Then the pipers took over and "Scotland the Brave" echoed across the scene.'[5]

Tom Renouf was a section commander in the battalion, and recalled the crossing.

'David Reid started to play his mouth organ. We all started singing as if we didn't have a care in the world.'[6]

Tom's platoon commander, twenty-five-year-old Sergeant Bob Fowler, had been fighting since 1940. He took a turn on the mouth organ, then slipped a piece of paper into Tom's breast pocket, telling him that:

'"If anything happens to me, write and tell my mother." I told him he was indestructible and he laughed wistfully.'[7]

The Buffalos reached the east bank after a few minutes on the water, and the battalion disembarked, its destination the town of Rees. Tom's company were crossing open, flat farmland when they came under machine-gun fire. Sergeant Fowler ordered Tom to take his section and silence the enemy position. Taking the Bren from his gunner, Tom led a charge as he fired from the hip. Grenades were thrown into the bunker, and the enemy surrendered. For these actions Tom would later be awarded the Military Medal, but at the time his congratulation was to be offered a well done and a cup of tea from Sergeant Fowler.

Further west along the river, and as dawn crept closer on the 24th, Harry Simpson and B Company, 7th Black Watch were about to have their own close-quarter battle. Although B Company had occupied the farmhouses and outbuildings with ease the night before, Harry, an old hand at war, knew that first light was likely to bring with it a strong counter-attack. He also expected that a mist would come off the river and hide the enemy's movements.

'So I went upstairs, and I climbed through the rafters (and) knocked some tiles off so that I could see out. Dawn was about breaking, and I was very fortunate.'

From his vantage in the loft, Harry was able to see above the mist that was rolling off the Rhine. What appeared before him was not a welcome sight.

'About five or six hundred yards (away), I saw groups of men assembling and taking cover.'

Harry was looking at the enemy's start line as they prepared to launch an attack. He quickly called for B Company to stand to, then told his light mortars to prepare to fire onto the enemy.

'The mist was gradually lowering, and I could see the masses of them coming towards us.'

Harry told his mortars to fire, the first round hitting exactly on the start line. He then ordered his mortarmen to decrease their range by fifty yards after every two bombs so that they remained on the backs of the advancing enemy.

'The enemy was converging on our left. We kept on firing away, and then all of a sudden, approaching the gap was a number of personnel.'

A Bren gun had been placed to cover this likely avenue of attack. 'He was firing at an angle across it, so that anybody coming through it would be hit by an angle of fire.'

Harry left the loft and looked out of a bedroom window, seeing two Germans in the lee of the wall.

'So me, like a fool, I did a thing that you should never do: I exposed myself to shoot them from above, because I knew that if they got up the wall, they'd hit the defenders. So I shot them, and when I looked up to see where they'd come from, I saw this bloody thing flying through the air. It looked like a great big football. I thought, *Oh hell, it's a Panzerfaust.*

'I dropped below the window ledge, and fortunately it was a very old house, it must have been a thick wall. It hit below the window, and all I felt was the explosion and the blast, and it picked me up, threw me across the room, and through the door on the top of the steps.'

Harry, covered in debris, tumbled down and came to a stop on the kitchen floor. 'And all I saw was six jackboots!'

He'd landed at the feet of three Volkssturm soldiers.

'But the element of surprise is a great thing when people are confronted by it, if they don't have their wits about them, which they didn't. I just jumped up and lashed out with the only thing I had, which was my legs and my fists. And I hit this little chap – he was about sixty – I hit him across the bloody jaw. Down he went and started crying. The other two, I knocked the bloody weapons out of their hands and give them a belting or two.'

Harry's weapon had been bent in two by the blast upstairs, but he'd miraculously escaped both the Panzerfaust and the fall without injury. He took the three Germans prisoner, sent them down into the cellar, then collected grenades that he began to throw over the farmhouse. 'We created a hell of a chaos, there. Anyway, to cut a long story short, it quietened down eventually.'

'Fifteen to twenty' Germans lay dead in the gap that they'd tried to storm. 'I assume that some of them crawled back to the ditch,' said Harry, who was later relieved at the position by Canadian Scottish soldiers attached to 154th Brigade for the operation.

The war diary of 7th Black Watch recorded that the enemy had attacked in company strength, with at least twelve of them killed, sixteen wounded and twenty taken prisoner. B Company lost two men killed on a day of great loss for both the Black Watch, and the Highland Division.

Major-General Tom Rennie, forty-five years old, had first fought the enemy in France, 1940, where he had been taken prisoner at St Valery but escaped some days later. Rennie had commanded the 5th Black Watch at El Alamein, and 154th Brigade at Sicily. He then took command of the untested 3rd Division and got them battle-ready for Normandy, where he was wounded a few days after they landed on Sword Beach. Rennie was then appointed to command of 51st Division in August of 1944 and had led them with distinction ever since. He was beloved of his Highlanders, eschewing the red banded hat of his rank for a tam o'shanter of the Black Watch, and setting great store by personal example and bravery.

Captain Angus Stewart, 7th Argylls, had just been wished good luck by the general when he saw him killed on the east side of the Rhine.

'As he was passing us the mortar bombs came down and he was caught by an unlucky splinter. His death really shattered us. He was known so intimately and was held in such regard by everybody.'[8]

'(It) was a terrible blow,' said Martin Lindsay, Gordon Highlanders. 'It was especially sad as he had gone so far with us and had now been killed on the last lap.'[9]

Like General Rennie, Berkeley Meredith, Staffordshire Yeomanry, had also come ashore on D-Day at Sword Beach. The night before the Rhine crossing Berkeley had run into a friend of his from civilian life, now an officer in the Black Watch, who the Staffordshires would be supporting.

Their amphibious tanks launched into the river in the early morning of the 24th, and under shellfire.

'A DD tank, with its skirting raised, with the thing inflated, is a highly vulnerable target. Shrapnel will rip the sides of the apron, and obviously, you're a dead duck if you're holed.'

Three of the leading squadron's tanks were struck and sunk. A further three became bogged down.[10] Berkeley's tank was one of them.

'We just could not get up the bank. It was so slippery and muddy. Perhaps it would have been better if we'd just stayed stuck where we were, because we hadn't gone very far when our tank was hit by a shell. I think it must have been a high-explosive shell. I was sitting down operating the radio, and the tank commander suddenly slumped down into the lower seat, and I looked around. He'd been hit by the blast. I'm sure it was a high-explosive shell because his face was missing, and he'd been killed outright.

'It was the only crew member I'd lost up till then. And I suppose it was probably one of the most traumatic feelings I could have had at that time. Silly things come to my mind. We didn't know what had hit us. Your first instinct as a tank man is to bail out first and to sort it out afterwards.'

When it was obvious that the tank was not going to brew up, the crew returned to their commander's body.

'The blast had obviously hit his face, or his head. And his brain was lying on top of the tank turret, just as though it had been removed surgically. It's just a picture that sticks in your mind.

'Our gunner (Taffy), it transpired, had been hit by a piece of shrapnel, so he was bleeding a bit. He thought that I had been hit because my overalls were covered in blood, but it wasn't my blood, it was the blood of (Captain) Thompson, our tank commander.'[11]

Seven men from the Staffordshire Yeomanry died on the Rhine that day. Berkeley recalled the temperament of Captain Thompson, and how it did not seem fit for a man who was asked to wage war.

'He wasn't an aggressive sort of person. He just seemed to me that he shouldn't have been there. There you go. It was a pretty devastating day for us.'

The death had a 'psychological effect' on Berkeley. 'I couldn't go anywhere near that particular tank again. That was a bad day,' he said softly. 'A bad day.'

Soldiers deal with death in different ways. Where some are deeply moved, and reflective, others might joke away a tale. Whether this is out of callousness, or as a way of easing the pain, is known only to them.

Alfred Leigh, 2nd Seaforths, had crossed the Rhine by boat during the night. His battalion had attacked northwards to Rees and came up against strong opposition in the factory area.

'Three Germans came around the corner, and we'd been trained to say, "*'Ande hoch.*" ("Hands up.") I said, "*'Ande hoch, 'ande hoch!*"'

The Germans raised their weapons instead.

'So I fired from the hip, and I caught the centre one. He went down. The other two Jerries took to their heels, and I took to me heels.'

Alfred caught up with the rest of his section, where they were held up by an anti-tank ditch and heavy fire. The front became stagnant, both sides firing automatic bursts and sniping at anything that moved along this new frontline. Alfred found himself sharing a trench with a man that had been sent to the battalion from mess duties in Scotland.

'They were scraping the barrel for blokes now. We were getting short of infantrymen. He was a regular. He had a wife, and a child. So he dug in the back garden with us. The Germans were in a house down the road, (we're) having a bit of a barney with them, one or two things happened. One of the lads fired a PIAT at the house. Jerry fired back with a Spandau. He blew the cheek out of one of the corporal's faces. He had a ghastly wound. And things went quiet. I found these pickled eggs in the cellar.'

Alfred was cooking a few up when he was joined by the replacement. 'I fried him four eggs in his mess tin. (I said,) "Eat 'em in here, in the cellar." He said, "No, I'm going back to the slit trench."'

It was a fatal decision.

'Old Jerry must have seen him. He got a burst of Spandau through the back of his head. Blew half his head away. He still had his tin hat on. He was not at the bottom of the trench. He was like wedged in his trench, but he still had the mess tin with the four eggs in it. That was in his right hand. He was dead, like, you know. Unfortunately the eggs were cold by then. Anyway, that was his lot.'

Martin Lindsay and the 1st Gordon Highlanders had passed through the 5th Black Watch and were in the thick of the fighting for Rees, battling their way towards the enemy's strongpoint situated in ruins of the town's large church.[12] After his colonel was hit, and had to be evacuated, Martin assumed command of the battalion.

'The clearing of every single house was a separate little military operation requiring a special reconnaissance, plan and execution. And the enemy was resisting fiercely all the time with Spandaus, bazookas and snipers, and only withdrawing a little further back at the last moment when their position became untenable.'[13]

The Gordons were given welcome assistance by Captain McNair and his three-gun crews from 454th Mountain Battery, Royal Artillery. They were equipped with archaic 3.7in howitzers of the kind that was usually seen being disassembled and carried at a military tattoo rather than on a modern battlefield, but someone had possessed the foresight to realize that these guns could be broken down to fit in a Buffalo, and would provide much-needed fire support on the east bank.

McNair himself was something of a character.

'Exactly which window is the sniper in?' he asked the Gordons, seconds before a single shot cracked by his head. 'Oh, that one!'

McNair and his crew even set up the gun in the upstairs of a building, from where they blasted nearby enemy positions, as recalled by Martin Lindsay:

'It set houses on fire as well as any Crocodile, and the effect on the enemy was devastating.

'This very brave officer took incredible risks; finally he ran out into a street which was under fire and pulled in a wounded officer. He and his gun became the talk of the companies, and already, in a few hours, he had become an almost legendary character!'[14]

And while McNair's gunfire was aiding the advance of the Gordons, the toll taken on them by the enemy defenders was grim. One after another, Martin's officers were killed or wounded. Particularly the young subalterns who were leading from the front, and by courageous example.

During the fighting at Rees, Tom Renouf, 5th Black Watch, noticed that his own platoon commander 'had lost his nerve'. Sergeant Fowler, long a tower of strength for his men, tried desperately to hide his fear, but continually scurried for cover in a state of terror.

The antidote for his fear came from an unlikely place.

A burst of shrapnel cut through the air. Fowler let out a yell, then called out that he'd been hit. Tom Renouf rushed to his side, finding his sergeant's trousers wet with blood.

'When I urged him to go back to the regimental aid post, he said with great conviction, "No, not until we finish this attack." The real Bob Fowler was back. The fear and the terror had left him and he regained his courage.'[15]

Sergeant Fowler had regained his courage and then some. First he led his platoon in a series of attacks, which he led from the front. Then, when they became pinned down by an enemy strongpoint, Fowler picked three men and set off to silence the enemy positions.

'He was away for well over an hour. When he returned, he looked tired – as if his wound was beginning to trouble him – but his first concern was for his boys in 7 Platoon. He checked on all of us, and then casually mentioned that the Spandaus would not be bothering us again.'[16]

Sergeant Fowler had silenced several enemy positions, and only left for the aid post when ordered to do so by the company commander, Major Mathew. The man who 'had lost his nerve' was later awarded the Distinguished Conduct Medal, and was credited with saving many British lives. These actions, however, almost cost him his own. Bob Fowler developed blood poisoning from his wounds, and slipped into a coma that lasted six days. It was almost twenty years later that Tom Renouf saw his beloved sergeant again, the two men coming face to face at a Highland Division reunion in Perth.

Many of those who attended that day were involved in the bitter fighting at Rees, which had to be cleared house by house, and street by street. Sensing the inevitable conclusion, many of the enemy slipped away. The town was declared clear by 1030 hrs on the 25th, but fighting would continue to rage around Rees for several more days.

Martin Lindsay walked the ruined streets, finding fifteen silenced machine-gun positions in a 100-yard area – combined, these guns were capable of firing some 15,000 rounds a minute. Little wonder the town had been such hell to take. He then came across Blackman, a Highlander who was known for keeping his cool, and learned that the soldier had been clipped in the face by shrapnel from a bazooka round. Blackman had disappeared alone for half an hour on a private vendetta to find the man who'd fired it. Martin had two leave passes to give out that day, and offered one to Blackman.

'He turned it down, saying he wasn't going to take any leave until he had caught up with the man with the bazooka.'[17]

CHAPTER 12

Operation Widgeon

No. 1 Commando Brigade at Wesel
23–25 March 1945

'If you volunteer for the commandos, you should have known what you was going into. And like I said at the time, when I went into action, I went in ready. I knew what could have happened, right? But I also knew that if you was gonna kill me, mate, I was gonna kill some of you first. I knew that. I was determined about that. That was sure.'

Stan Scott, No. 3 Commando

The Crossing

Growing up in Tottenham, Stan Scott had heard a lot about war from his father and uncles, who had all fought in the First. When the Second was declared, young Stan was under no illusions about what lay ahead.

'I just thought, *Christ, here we go again. More bloody misery.*'

Stan's first taste of that bloody misery was the Blitz, where he helped keep a watch for fires and shovelled dirt onto burning incendiary bombs. He enlisted into the Territorial Army in 1940, but this service soon came to an end when his mother found out – he had lied about his age, and was three years too young. It had been a winding road for Stan ever since, taking him to the desert, Sword Beach, and across North West Europe.

Now, with the entirety of No. 1 Commando Brigade, Stan was poised to cross the Rhine and seize the town of Wesel. A little before last light on 23 March, he heard a familiar sound from his childhood. The drone of bombers.

'All of a sudden a plane approached,' said fellow D-Day man Geoff Scottson, No. 6 Commando. 'It was a Mosquito, you could see it. It went right over Wesel and dropped a flare. And as the flare come down there was a groan in the sky, and there was twenty Lancasters, one after the other, came across one at a time and dropped their bombs right on the centre of Wesel. It was the most spectacular event that I'd seen in the war.'

The raid was made by eighty Lancasters of No. 3 Group, RAF and set Wesel aflame.[1]

'They were flying at a height of no more than 1,000 feet,' said Peter Fussell, a veteran of the Dieppe Raid and Sword Beach. 'As soon as the pathfinder had got over the town of Wesel, he dropped chandelier flares and the remainder came over and dropped their bombs. They were huge.'

Lieutenant Alan Tate served in No. 45 (Royal Marine) Commando. Nineteen years old, from Sunderland, he had already won the Military Cross for his actions in Holland.

'We went to a huge flat marshalling area in a meadow. The engineers had placed some sort of tins in rows. Each tin had a candle inside it, and each tin had a triangle, a circular hole, a cross, or a square. And we were told to follow one of those. We marched in lines down the tins that lay on the ground.'

They did this as the thunder of guns rumbled along the Rhine, the barrage opening on the heels of the Lancasters. Shells whined overhead, causing a constant overlapping crash and flash of explosions on the far shore.

'It was heavy stuff firing from the back, including Americans,' said Alan. 'Their artillery was very good. And then 25-pounders a bit closer. And 3-inch mortars, and rocket-firing vehicles launching rockets. With one thing and another the ground was actually shaking. I remember somebody saying, "I hope the artillery barrage has done its work." And I remembered reading about Monte Cassino, where the bombers reduced the monastery to rubble, and the Germans turned the rubble into a fort.'

Alan served in one of the two Royal Marine Commandos in the brigade, the other being No. 46 (Royal Marine) Commando. In 1942, the Royal Marines had been reorganized into Commando units and were incorporated into the same Special Service brigades as army commandos. No doubt there were rivalries between the marines and soldiers, no different to battalions in any other brigade, but when it came down to it the commandos relied on each other for their lives, and all had earned the green beret, which they often wore into battle in favour of their steel helmets.

The rest of No. 1 Commando Brigade was made up of Brigade HQ and No. 3 and No. 6 Commando. At full strength, each Commando numbered around 450 men divided into 75-man troops. Brigadier Derek Mills-Roberts, who had taken over command of the brigade from the wounded Lord Lovat in Normandy, recalled that he had 1,600 commandos under his command for the attack on Wesel.

The commandos, who had last seen major action in January during Operation Blackcock, formed up a kilometre or so north of where the destroyed Wesel rail bridge lay sagging in the river.

'It was fantastic,' said Peter Fussell, who was with Brigade HQ. 'The whole brigade put on one bank of the Rhine. There was very heavy, dense smoke screens right down the Rhine to deny the Germans observation of our movements, because by this time a lot of bridging equipment and power boats, storm boats, Buffalos, DUKWs had been brought up.'

Andy Brown was a veteran of D-Day and knew first hand the perils of amphibious assault. He would be part of the first crossing, made by No. 6 Commando at 2130 in soft-skinned storm boats.

'On the night of crossing the old RSM came up, Woody Woodcock, and give us a good old drink of rum. I had my fair share. There was a little reinforcement kiddie we had (Ward). He was only eighteen. Little baby face, he was.'

Andy, twenty-two years old himself, showed the 'kiddie' how to wear all of his equipment loose so that it could be quickly released should he end up in the water.

'Of course, the rest of the boys were laughing.'

They also mocked Andy and Ward for wearing two 'Mae Wests' – inflatable life vests – instead of one. Andy tried to convince one of his friends to wear the same, but the man assured him that he was a strong swimmer and didn't need it.

'We got into the boats and we started to go across,' said Andy.

They did so beneath the guns of the enemy, arcs of tracer streaking across the river, bullets puncturing both men and boat. Holed and encumbered with the weight of fully armed and equipped commandos, many of the boats began to sink down into the cold black waters of the Rhine.

Andy's boat was one of them. His equipment already loose, he released his buckles and straps and let himself be taken by the river, his equipment sinking away below him.

'I swam around for some time and I came across a mate of mine, Jack Sanderson. He just had his mouth above the water.'

Jack's equipment was still fastened tightly to him, the weight of it pulling him under despite his life vest.

'He was having a tremendous struggle to keep up. I tried to undo his lapels, and couldn't undo 'em, and he started to go under with the weight of the Alpine pack filling up, and taking me with him. I had to do the necessary to get away. He took me down. I nearly drowned myself.'

Jack lost his life in the water,[2] but Andy was able to break the surface, struggling to regain his breath as the current carried him downriver. He might well have died of exposure, but was saved by the forethought of Brigadier Mills-Roberts, who had insisted that reliable power dories accompany the storm boats. They were manned by the Recce Regiment of the 52nd (Lowland) Division, who were also to provide beach control parties and radio links on the east bank of the Rhine. The power dories acted as rescue vessels, pulling stricken commandos out of the water, including Andy.

He had a surprise when he got into the boat.

'Who should be sitting in there but this little kiddie Ward who I'd put the two Mae Wests on. So I said to these (boat crew), "Have you picked any more up?"'

The answer was 'no'. Searching in the darkness, and against time, the rescue crew had not been able to reach the men who had been fighting against the weight of their equipment.

Andy and Ward's night was not over. Andy was given dry clothes and a Bren gun and hurried to catch up with his troop. It was only then that he learned how many of his comrades were missing.

'Seven of the (troop) were drowned. They're all buried in the Reichswald Cemetery. I go over there regular to see them.'

No. 46 (Royal Marine) Commando left their start line at 2200, the Buffalos rumbling across a meadow, dipping down the bank and straining their engines against the current of the Rhine. Brigade HQ crossed with them, Peter Fussell recalling that they were under fire the entire time.

'How the Germans got their heads above the debris and destruction of Wesel, don't ask me. The key to their defences lay in the fanaticism of the younger Nazis and German youth, where they just didn't give up.'

Within five minutes they were across, commandos leaping down and rushing forwards to secure the bridgehead, fierce fighting commencing around two watermen's houses that had been turned into strongpoints. At the same time, the Buffalos returned to collect No. 3 and No. 45 (Royal Marine) Commando.

'We were told not to move any further,' said Peter Fussell. 'We couldn't understand why because here we were sitting ducks. We were in the wide open, we hadn't dug in or anything like that because we were expecting to move into Wesel. So we naturally thought that we were waiting for the dust to settle before we went in, in case there was something in the bombs. It could have been chemicals.'

But the reason for the delay was not the first raid, but a second. As No. 3 and No. 45 Commando began their crossing, 197 Lancasters and 23 Mosquitos of Nos 5 and 8 Groups carried out the final raid of the war on Wesel.

Peter Fussell watched as the Lancasters approached into what must have felt like touching distance.

'We heard the drone of more aircraft and (more) Lancasters

came over, again led by the pathfinder. As soon as he got over what was left of Wesel, he dropped a chandelier of flares.'

This was the marker for the 'heavies'.

'They dropped their bombs and they were again the same type – these huge dustbin-looking types. But this time it was more frightening, the bomb bays were open and when we looked up we were not under cover at all. They began dropping their bombs immediately overhead and the nearest that fell to where I was lying was about fifty yards away, and it was not funny to have a huge bomb drop that close. The crater that was created, how it didn't hurt us or kill us I don't know. I would have thought my ears would have been perforated.'

The RAF sortie dropped more than 1,000 tons of high explosive on Wesel, and at an intended distance of 1,000 yards from the brigade – 97 per cent of the town now lay in ruins.[3]

As the bombers turned for home, No. 6 Commando rose and went into the attack, marking a safe route for the rest of the brigade to follow. One can only imagine how punch-drunk they felt after being so close to the concussion waves of explosions powerful enough to shake the ground beneath their feet. But if the commandos were in bad shape, the enemy under the bombs had fared much worse. Yet still they rose to meet the attack, soldiers of the 180th Division emerging from bunkers and cellars, anti-aircraft batteries training their weapons on the now approaching commandos.

Geoff Scottson, No. 6 Commando, was delayed in joining the attack, having had to return for a second storm boat when the first started going around in circles.

'3 Commando was coming along the bank from further upstream, where they had landed, and meeting us. Germans coming the other side. It was quite a mess for a while.'

Henry Cosgrove, No. 45 (Royal Marine) Commando, crossed the Rhine with an unusual companion.

'I had a pet duck, which I called Hector. Big white duck. We no sooner got near the water than Hector started quacking. I had to tie his beak up. I had him strapped across the top of me pack. He was gonna be a meal. Anyway, we set off, Hector with his beak tied.'

Henry recalled that the commando landed into 'a bit of a shemozzle'.

'We managed alright, and we got ashore and with a little bit of firepower we edged our way in.'

Alan Tate described the moment that his vehicle reached the shore.

'I remember standing on the front of this Buffalo and shouting rude words to everybody – I was just getting excited, I guess – and jumped off. I didn't lose anybody, and we made our way towards the town.'

Of the same commando, Fred Harris was struck by the sight of German prisoners surrendering, their bodies shaking and eyes hollow from the effects of the bombing.

'Poor old Jerries was coming back in, shaking their heads. Really, really took the blast, you know. Bomb-happy to say the least.'

Some hour and a half after the second wave of bombers struck Wesel, the full strength of No. 1 Commando Brigade was involved in fighting for the town. It was a battle that would rage for two days.

The fight for Wesel

No. 45 (Royal Marine) Commando made their entry into Wesel at 0030 hrs on 24 March.

'When we got to the outskirts of the town it was just a mass of rubble,' said Lieutenant Alan Tate. 'Wesel's roughly triangular. The base of the triangle is the River Rhine. The right-hand side of the triangle, and part of the left-hand side is bounded by railways, about five or six tracks across. We ended on the left-hand side of the triangle, and our objective was a factory complex, twenty or thirty quite large buildings, which were at the apex of the triangle.'

'All these directions we got were useless,' said Henry Cosgrove, 'because the roads we were supposed to be travelling on were gone. It was a pile of bricks, the place, but we knew that we had to get (to) the other side of it so we carried on across.'

Francis Burton was the signaller of No. 45 (Royal Marine)

Commando's commanding officer, Lieutenant Colonel Grey. It was a position that necessitated a lot of exposure to the enemy, as both officers and their radio men were favourite targets of snipers and artillery observation officers. Francis had been wounded in the arm during action in Holland, and although in great pain, he had continued to do his job as the vital link between the commando's HQ, troops and support elements. For this he had been awarded the Military Medal. Now he was again in the thick of the fighting.

'Colonel Grey and I were moving up this street. Of course, the buildings were on fire. Even though it was night time it was brilliantly lit. And we saw these three or four Germans further up the road with a Panzerfaust, aiming down the road in our direction.

'There was a big fallen tree across the road, and the colonel and I dropped down behind this tree, and they fired this Panzerfaust, and it hit the tree in front of us.

'Colonel Grey was badly wounded in the arm. I thought I'd been wounded again, because I could feel a trickle of blood down my face. Anyway, it was only a little nick, really. But Colonel Grey, although badly wounded, he carried on.'

Eddie Treacher, from Shoreditch, was also wounded by the Panzerfaust.

'All of a sudden there was such a crash in front of us. Sparks everywhere. I fell back and hit a tree, and I thought, *Oh, God*, and me arm went dead. I lost me rifle, and the colonel got wounded. There was six others wounded.

'They say to me it was two Panzerfausts, but I only heard one. It hit me in the legs. I've got scars there now,' Eddie told his interviewer. 'I mean, I can show you now, look. See them? That's all scars. And I got hit all up the right side. Hit on the chest, hit on the shoulder, and I still got shrapnel in me chest. Me arm was paralysed, completely paralysed, and I was in a terrible state, I was really battered.

'They took me into a barn affair. They give me some tablets. They knocked me out completely.'

By 0100 hrs parts of the brigade had reached the destroyed town centre. Sergeant Frederick John Worthington, No. 6 Commando, was in command of a small defensive position when he noticed an enemy patrol infiltrating back into the city. Realizing that they were heading for a part of the town that was not yet firmly held, he left a few men in the defensive position, took the other eight and immediately set off to lay an ambush, reaching the side road just in time to meet the enemy head on.

Using the houses at the side of the road for cover, the commandos killed and wounded eight of the enemy, took five of them prisoner, and sent the rest running back in the direction from which they'd come. Sergeant Worthington had been injured in the early moments of the firefight but refused to hand over command, or have his wound treated, until he brought the patrol back. He was later awarded the Military Medal for these actions, the five prisoners added to No. 6 Commando's 'bag', which was growing larger by the hour.

The unit's war diary reported that the total number of POWs taken was eight officers and 258 other ranks. 'Many fatal casualties were inflicted on the enemy including General Deutsch, commanding Wesel area.'[4]

Peter Fussell recalled one version of events regarding the general's death. 'A sergeant major, I believe from No. 6 Commando, had gone in with his Tommy gun, and he sprayed the cellar.' Deutsch was one of the officers sheltering there and was killed.

The CO of the unit, Colonel Lewis, said that General Deutsch, trapped in his bunker, 'became very aggressive and quite dangerous. He had to be shot.'[5]

Private Phillip Pritchard, No. 6 Commando, heard a different story, relayed to him from a lance-corporal digging a grave in Wesel.

'This seemed strange to us and we asked him why. It appears that he was one of the party searching through the cellars when he was confronted by a German officer. The Lance-Corporal immediately said "Hands up!", whereupon the German replied, "I am General von Deutsch and I only surrender to an officer of equal rank." The Lance-Corporal is supposed to have said, "Well, this will equalise you," and fired his Thompson at him with fatal results. The story was that the Brigadier (Mills-Roberts) was furious and ordered the Lance-Corporal to bury the General as a punishment. Anyway, this was the gist of the story and the unfortunate Lance-Corporal said, 'That's the last time I kill a general!'[6]

No doubt there are as many variations of the Deutsch story as there were Commandos in Wesel – it wasn't every day that a soldier killed a general.

Brigadier Mills-Roberts mentions the death in his autobiography, writing that the general refused to surrender in his bunker and was shot by a patrol of No. 6 Commando. Of far greater importance to him was the discovery of a map showing all of the enemy's flak positions in the area. This intelligence was relayed back over the radio, the brigadier hoping that it would save lives during the Airborne's assault the next day. Until that moment came, the commandos would be fighting alone.

Henry Cosgrove – along with Hector the duck – dug in at a crossroads with his section. They knocked loopholes through the walls of a ruin to create firing points, as well as reinforcing the cellar with wood taken from bombed-out buildings. This was completed just in time before the enemy launched the first in a series of counter-attacks.

'We were fine,' said Henry. 'We found there was a tremendous power of fire coming from this big building. No. 6 Commando were in there, and they were high up, so they were covering us. Nothing was getting near to us to have a go at on the crossroads.'

Henry then went to check on his pet.

'Well, Hector I'd put in a box in the corner of a cellar, and you'll not believe it, Hector had laid an egg. So I had to rename it Hectorine. I gave (the duck) away to a Romanian girl the next day. They were starving, poor kids. Only about fourteen, fifteen, these kiddies. Bloody starving.'

These Romanians were part of the slave labour force who had been put to work in Wesel's 'wire' factory, which was the main objective of No. 45 (Royal Marine) Commando. It was seized and consolidated upon by 0430 hrs on the 24th.

'We were ordered to get out of the rubble and walk along the railway track, which we did and got away with it,' said Alan Tate.

'We entered the factory, which was supposed to be making important bits and pieces for the war, but was in fact making lavatory pans, which were stacked one inside the other about twelve pans high. So of course, going through the factory, all covered in dust, surrounded by shot and shell, could your average British soldier resist pushing over the heaps of lavatory pans? No, he could not, so there were mysterious crashes going off all over the place.'

Derrick Cakebread, from Tottenham, was a sniper in the same Commando, and used bags of plaster in the factory to create fighting positions. The makeshift defences were soon in use.

'We was getting stonked. They kept on it, attacking us, reinforcements coming in. Very good, they were. Oh, yeah. They kept on coming up. They wouldn't give in, they wouldn't, no.'

The first of these attacks was made by infantry supported by a self-propelled gun. The infantry were driven off, but the SP gun continued to shell the commandos throughout the night.

'We took up positions on the side of this factory on a little railway junction,' said Fred Harris, who was also from Tottenham. 'I was digging in a little position underneath these railway trucks, and one of our officers said, "There's an SP gun coming in the field." He says, "See if you can get onto it, try and get a bead on it."

'Of course I couldn't, low down, so I jumped up and slid open this railway wagon. I jumped in and I got the Bren gun in. I heard another guy come in after me. I didn't know who it was because it was quite dark inside. I pushed the door on the other side of the truck open, and there in the middle of this field is this SP gun sat in there, and there's two or three Jerries running along with canisters, carrying shells, they were. And of course I put a few bursts over there, and I heard this guy behind me, and I said, "Who's that?" And he said, "Scouse." Little Scouse Ord. He said, "What's on, Cabbie?" I said, "Well, we've got an SP gun. I've put a few bursts over there." I fired on it again, and all of a sudden the Old Jerry must have spotted where I was coming from, and he fired back, and he shot right away through the side of this truck, and I heard a thump on this side, and little Scouse Ord had took a bullet.

'I called out, "Medics!" like, and I got the medic, and helped him out the truck, but he was gone by then, Little Scouse. Lovely little bloke. Little Liverpool boy. Scouse Ord. Yeah.

'You know, I suppose that's what you call the fortunes of war. Ordinarily I suppose you wouldn't get up in a railway truck like that, but, you know, we was in that kind of position where there was an SP gun that we couldn't see, and he was doing some damage, so I went into the truck, and it didn't go that good.'

Inside the factory, twenty-year-old Walter Bigland, from Liverpool, was manning a Bren gun position when a corporal told him that his friend Kenny Ord had been killed, and how. 'If he'd have stayed on the ground, he wouldn't have—' Walter stopped abruptly and took a deep breath. He says nothing more about Kenneth Ord, who died at the age of nineteen.[7]

More German armour could be heard forming up in a small wood to the north of Wesel. Unbeknown to the commandos, the few remaining German tanks in the area had been pulled together to launch an attack into the town. But it was an attack that was never allowed to happen. Forward Observation Officers called down fire from the masses of guns on the west of the Rhine, and hundreds of shells turned the copse into splinters, the enemy counter-attack broken up before it could ever begin. The commandos were also supported by tactical fighters of the RAF.

'Our job in the Rhine crossing was to be ground support for the army,' said Christopher 'Kit' North-Lewis, who commanded a wing of Typhoons. 'We were given targets at first light, the other side of Wesel. I led the first attack, and as I pulled out of the attack I was hit, and I realized that I was going to have difficulty in making it back.

'I turned at low level, having told somebody else to take over the squadrons I was leading. Attempted to make my way home. But over the top of Wesel the engine stopped. I had then the choice of trying to glide to the other side of the Rhine, but I was only at two or three hundred feet, and so I realized I wouldn't make it.

'I force-landed in a field, wheels up, in the German lines. I got out of the aircraft. I hadn't hurt myself. I climbed out of the aircraft and was taken prisoner.'

After a period of captivity, during which some of the soldiers wanted to use Kit as a human shield to escape the closing pocket at Wesel, the enemy platoon eventually surrendered to him.

'So there I was, with a German platoon of paratroopers, all armed to the teeth, not knowing what to do.'

Kit considered walking back to Wesel, then realized he had no idea where mines might be laying in wait. A solution was provided by an abandoned canoe belonging to the Wesel Canoe Club.

'So I got the Germans to launch this. I then paddled across the Rhine to the British side where a whole lot of troops were pointing their rifles at me, and I was shouting, "Don't shoot, I'm a British officer!"'

Kit made it ashore and informed the soldiers about the situation on the opposite bank.

'All I was asked was, "Have they any watches?"'

Kit had survived the moment of capture. Others did not. A couple of hours after Kit had been shot down, Alan Tate led his men to a number of houses near to the factory.

'I walked through a large industrial shed with a convenient hole in the wall, and there was a little courtyard between me and the backs of the houses, and in the middle of that courtyard was a German mobile shelter. Whether there was somebody in there we didn't know, so I told my chaps to stay where they were. It was about half past ten in the morning, and I walked across the open space and straight into the back door of the nearest house.

'There was a German walking past the front window, so I moved to the window, and again, for some reason, there wasn't (glass). Whether the glass had been broken by the bombing I can't at this time remember, but the street was about twenty feet wide, no sidewalks. One side had continuous buildings – that's the side I was on, and the other side had a high and impenetrable hedge. And there were eight Germans, walking by the window, pushing bicycles.

'So I leaned out and made "*Hände hoch*"-type noises. Unfortunately, of the eight, one or two put their hands up. But the others began to make war-like gestures, and point rifles at me and things.'

Alan fired first.

'I went down the line with my Thompson submachine gun. They all fell down. I ran upstairs, changing my magazine. Leaned out of the upstairs window and went down the line the other way, just to make sure they were dead, and they all were.'

Around this same time, at his checkpoint on the crossroads, Henry Cosgrove recalled that 'All hell broke loose.'

'Dakotas were coming over, dropping parachutists, and they were ending up in the river and everywhere else bar where they should be. I saw a couple of Dakotas go down from the little aperture where I was.'

What Henry was witnessing was Operation Varsity, the airborne drop over the Rhine that began at 1000 hrs, and the aircraft that he saw lost may have been C-46 Commandos belonging to the United States Army Air Forces (USAAF) – nineteen were shot down and a further thirty-eight damaged, a situation so terrible that many aircrews dropped their US paratroopers out of position.

The British artillery had to cease fire to avoid hitting the aircraft, and for four hours the commandos were without their support. Sensing an opportunity, the enemy pressed an attack against B Troop, No. 45 (Royal Marine) Commando.

Lance-Corporal John Sykes was in charge of the forward Bren group sited outside of their building. Two enemy SP guns approached to a distance of 500 yards and engaged the troop, one of the shells bursting a few feet above Sykes' position, and seriously wounding his assistant gunner. Sykes assisted the medical orderly in removing his wounded comrade, then engaged an enemy machine-gun position. A few minutes later another shell burst in front of him, the blast so close that it blew the Bren gun out of the trench. Sykes broke cover and risked machine-gun fire to retrieve it, returning to the trench and re-engaging the enemy. A third shell now struck the wall to his left, shrapnel hitting the barrel of the Bren with such force that it was bent, and the gun now useless. Undaunted, Sykes ran to the Troop HQ for the spare machine gun, then returned to his position and opened fire.

B Troop fought off the counter-attack, and Lance-Corporal Sykes was awarded the Military Medal. His citation concluded that: 'His aggressive spirit and determination to fight back was a shining example of courage during a most trying period and was an inspiration to all ranks.'[8]

Now that the fighting was easing, some of the marines took the opportunity to 'look around' the factory.

'There was a big safe in the corner of one of these offices,' said Fred Harris. 'They was all trying to open it up with pickaxe handles and that sort of thing. One of the guys said, "Let's put a PIAT bomb into it."

'We barricaded the door up, and got this PIAT up, and fired at this safe from about, oooh, not more than thirty foot. It tore this bloomin' safe to pieces, and thousands and thousands of pay packets came out of it. We found afterwards that all the workers in this factory were slave labour, like, and this was their sort of pittance. Course, we were stuffing it all in our jackets.'

The 1st Battalion, Cheshire Regiment landed at Wesel in the afternoon of the 24th to support the commandos. This allowed for further operations to clear the remaining enemy from the town, as well as the evacuation of the wounded.

The next day, at 1200 hrs, B Troop, under command of Lieutenant John Day, were ordered to patrol the area around Wesel's barracks. Jack Sinclair's section, under Lieutenant MacDonald, were to make contact with the American paratroopers who had landed outside of Wesel.

'We'd just met the Americans and (there was) a single shot, one shot from our right, and it hit the marine who was stood behind me. Elliot.'

The marines scattered in one direction, the US Airborne in another. There was no time to recover the comrade, as B Troop was ordered to withdraw. US Airborne troops, supported by tanks, were pushing through to the river east of the town. By evening all resistance had ceased and the town was reported clear.'[9]

It was now that Jack was able to return for his comrade.

'I said to a young marine there – Dempsey, big lad he was – "We'll go and pick up Elliot." We didn't know whether he was dead or not. I said, "We'll nip round the house, pick him up, bring him back, and take him back with us." So we did that.'

They found Elliot, who had been shot in the head.

'But he was alive, and we took him back with us for medical treatment.'

Elliot survived his wounds, and was one of the ninety-seven casualties sustained by the brigade at Wesel between 23 and 25 March,[10] twenty-six of whom were killed.[11] Hundreds of the enemy had been killed, and 850 taken prisoner.[12]

Colonel Gray, who had remained in command of No. 45 (Royal Marine) Commando despite being badly wounded and in great pain, allowed himself to be evacuated after the final counter-attack had been beaten, and would later be awarded a bar for his Distinguished Service Order. He, Elliot and casualties of both sides were evacuated back across the Rhine, while the dead lay where they had fallen.

Nineteen-year-old Alan Tate was ordered to return to the bodies of the eight men he had killed on the morning of the 24th and to check them for intelligence. 'Which was not a nice job. One lad, I put my hand in his pocket and got his wallet out. He had a photograph of him with his family, and I must say I felt quite sorry for him. One didn't normally feel sorry for anybody, but I was quite sorry for him. He was there with his family.

'I kept this photograph in my wallet, which I subsequently lost, so I was never able to do anything with it, like send it to his family. I don't think they would have liked to have it, actually.

'Anyway, that was the end of Wesel.'

CHAPTER 13

Operation Torchlight

The 15th (Scottish) Division's battle on the Rhine
23–28 March 1945

'I lost one of the Bren gun operators just as we were getting into the Buffalos. He passed out. I never did discover whether that was intentional or not. I have a feeling it was. I think ninety per cent of them didn't want to go across that river, but they had to.
We lost a few people, as you always expect you're going to.'

Sergeant Alfred Wooltorton, 2nd Battalion,
Seaforth Highlanders

The third and final British amphibious attack on the Rhine was carried out by 15th (Scottish) Division. Operation Torchlight called for a two-brigade front, with one held in reserve – this was the 46th, who had been the first into action in the Rhineland.

'It sounds good, the reserve brigade,' said Tom Gore, 9th Cameronians, 'but it's not always the best place to be because the reserve brigade gets pushed in where the opposition is heaviest. If a battalion hits trouble, and they want an extra battalion, the reserve brigade comes in for that, with the three battalions.'

It was a little over a month since Tom had gone Absent Without Leave during the battle at Moyland. Now on the Rhine, he and his comrades dug the slit trenches where they would wait until being called across the river.

Sleep was unlikely, the ground shaking with the concussions of the barrage. At 0100 hrs, on 15th Division's front, the artillery was joined by everything from anti-aircraft guns to Vickers machine guns as 'everything but the kitchen sink' was thrown at the enemy.

Tom Gore watched this 'Pepperpot' from his slit trench.

'Early in the morning there was a terrific display of fireworks just in front of us. They had Bofors firing across, and artillery was firing.'

At 0200 hrs on 24 March, 15th Division launched its first wave – 6th Royal Scots Fusiliers and 8th Royal Scots launched from north-east of Xanten, while 10th Highland Light Infantry and 2nd Argyll and Sutherland Highlanders attacked from the area of Vynen.

The job of carrying the Scotsmen belonged to the East Riding Yeomanry, who had been re-trained and equipped with Buffalos for this task.

Thirty-year-old Albert Adams first saw action during the Battle of France in 1940. He had returned to the country four years later, as the driver of a DD Sherman tank that landed at Sword Beach. At the Rhine, Alfred was once again in the first wave of an amphibious assault, the driver of one of the East Riding's Buffalos.

'Our instructions were to get to the other side, stay in the water, and the infantry had to jump off the front of the Buffalo into the water. We got across, and I said to the commander of the infantry, "Stay aboard, I'll give you a dry landing," and I drove right up.'

The infantry dismounted and ran forwards. The leg of one man caught a tripwire, and a flare burst into bright light.

'Machine guns started firing then, and (the infantry) all dropped down.'

The enemy gunners did not need to pick out individual soldiers, instead firing on fixed lines. With enough lead in the air, some was sure to find flesh. Albert's Buffalo later returned across the river with a cargo of wounded men, and German prisoners. They landed on a bank under shelling.

'Our tank was shelled. It was set on fire. I dropped the tailgate at the back. The wounded were on stretchers. I got one of the other lads: "Come on, give us a hand." We got the stretchers out. Anyway,

I organized the evacuation of all the injured in the Buffalo. Eventually we got them all the way to a first aid post.'

It was a short summary of an eventful action, another view of which was written by one of Alfred's officers, and read to Alfred by his interviewer.

'This NCO was Troop Leader's driver of the leading Buffalo in the night assault on the Rhine. It was through his calm and careful handling of the craft that his troop leader was able to manoeuvre and silence the enemy Spandaus, and so enable the infantry to scramble safely ashore under this offensive protection.

'On a subsequent journey back carrying German prisoners, and wounded, they were very heavily shelled. Three Germans were killed, and ten wounded, and during this shelling he deliberately placed himself over one of our own stretcher cases, being prepared to give his life for a wounded comrade. His Buffalo received a direct hit, and although it had wounded in it, he personally evacuated all of the casualties with complete disregard of the danger of fire and explosion from the ammunition and petrol, which had caught alight. His bravery and calmness under heavy fire were an inspiration to all there.'

This was the citation of Albert's Military Medal.

'Just what I told you, int it?' he said.

Forward Observation Officer Kenneth Ohlson of the 190th Field Regiment was once again in the vanguard, travelling across the Rhine by Buffalo with the commanding officer of the infantry battalion, and a special guest.

'A man called Wynford Vaughan-Thomas, a commentator, came with us, giving his commentary. It was quite a dramatic thing.'

Vaughan-Thomas was thirty-six years old at the time of the Rhine crossing, and one of the BBC's most celebrated war correspondents. He had gone into battle with British forces at Anzio, and flown in a Lancaster bomber raid over Berlin. In the recording of his passage with 15th (Scottish), one can hear the steady crackle of machine-gun fire, the sharp cracks and dull thumps of artillery, and the revving engines of the Buffalos, tracks clattering as they move down to the water's edge.

'We're coming now to the German shore. Side by side with us come the other Buffalos. We make a strange procession. A feeling of attack flooding across the Rhine. It'll take about three minutes, and believe me, every minute's going to seem a year.

'The first assault have gone in. It looks as though they've touched down.'

At this point the distinctive *zip* of an incoming bullet wings by. Machine guns continue to clatter in long, heavy bursts. Soldiers can be heard talking to one another, their calm voices marking them as veterans of many battles. The engines of the Buffalos then drown out all other noise as they rev hard and roar into the Rhine.

'We're in! The Buffalo dips its nose down, and now it's opening up full power! Three minutes to go, and we are racing across, and side by side with us go the other Buffalos, racing for that hell on the other side! The searchlights cast a white beam now right across the river, but ahead of us it's only red water.

'The tracer's making a path on either side of us, beating down the opposition. Now we're utterly alone, it seems. You get a complete feeling of detachment. Waiting all the time for the enemy to open up. Waiting all the time for them to spot us, as we lie helpless as it seems, out here in this wide stream.

'The Buffalo swings. Points its nose upstream. We're drifting, fighting the current to get over. You get a feeling of irresistible power, flooding now across the Rhine. In the light of the burning buildings, a broken pontoon bridge away to our right appears sagging in midstream. The sudden crack of a mortar burst as it falls on the bank just ahead of us. And all the time . . . the glare. The glare of the burning buildings. This is the welcome we've got to the German bank . . . that bank, which we've been thinking about so much during the last two weeks, is coming nearer and nearer.

'The signal flashes from the shore – the first Buffalos are up!'

Vaughan-Thomas stays quiet for a long moment, allowing the growling throats of the Buffalos to speak for him. All of a sudden the engines cut back, and in their place comes the sound of bagpipes.

'These are Scotsmen, who pipe their men into battle across the Rhine!'[1]

But the piping didn't last for long, as Kenneth Ohlson recalled.

'The water came over the top as the piper was playing, and this piper said, "Me peeps! Me peeps! The watar's got in me peeps!"'

The leading battalions found little opposition when they landed, but two shells dropped short and landed among the Royal Scots Fusiliers, causing more than twenty casualties. From early morning, as the leading brigades pushed inland, the reserve brigade began to be shuttled across on storm boats. DD tanks and bridge-building engineers also began to make the crossing.

Things were going well, but not entirely to plan. 10 HLI had been landed out of position and came into contact with a battalion of enemy paratroopers. A brutal fight developed, with A Company, 10 HLI losing all of its officers.

Three kilometres downstream were the 2nd Argylls. James Campbell, of the Anti-Tank platoon, recalled machine-gun fire coming from the German side as they crossed, and that Monty's Moonlight was lighting up the scene.

'All you could hear was people shouting, "Turn these so and so lights out," because we felt as though we were silhouetted on the river. If we could see a hundred, two, three hundred yards upriver and downriver, so the Germans could see us sitting out in the middle there like ducks. Lo and behold, when you got off the water it was absolutely pitch black.'

Sergeant Alf Wooltorton served in the same battalion. Across the river, it wasn't long before a shell scored a direct hit on the slit trench of one of his most dependable men, Reginald Sayer.[2] Alfred went to see what he could do, but the explosion had churned soldier and soil together.

'You couldn't have got him out, that was impossible. So we had to fill him in where he was.'

Thirty-year-old Reginald Sayer had been close friends with Alfred's former PIAT man, who had lost a foot to a mine on the Siegfried Line.

'Two really super guys, those two were. One from Suffolk, and one from Norfolk. If anyone was Mr and Mr Reliable, they were the two.'

But Alf and his men had little time to mourn.

'Like it was all the while, you moved on.'

'It was virtually close-quarter fighting,' said James Campbell. 'It was a case of just taking one farmhouse at a time.'

It wasn't until later that day that the Argylls realized that they were once again up against the German paratroopers with whom they had clashed in the Rhineland. Artillery fire from both sides crashed all around them, and James had a near miss from a shell that landed ten yards ahead of him, shredding a tree but leaving him unharmed.

Then, at 0930 hrs, all friendly fire missions stopped, and the guns fell silent. In place of their roar came the drone of thousands of aircraft. Tom Gore was waiting for his turn to cross the Rhine, and turned his head to the skies.

'Two divisions of Airborne troops flew overhead. A sight I should think it hard to see again.'

Somewhere up there were the 12th Devons, with whom Tom had served before being drafted to the Cameronians. He watched with bated breath as black puffs of anti-aircraft fire began to burst around the aircraft.

'A lot of 'em only had a one-way ticket,' he said. 'Sergeant Major Mashford was up there. He was to lose his life crossing the Rhine.[3]

'The gliders cast off just across the river, and the Yankee division went further down the river. Now the gliders went on out of sight, but the Dakotas, the tow planes, were very slow in turning, and a terrific lot of them got shot down. We watched them coming down, and (were) counting the crew that come out.'

Other men had planned on leaving their aircraft all along, and James Campbell watched the sky filling with the canopies of paratroopers. 'We could actually see them leaving the aircraft about five mile ahead of us.'

At 1345, the time came for Tom Gore and the 9th Cameronians to join the battle. They made their way to the water's edge and loaded into the storm boats.

'They were like small wooden boats with a put-put engine on the back. There was a Canadian (driver). He never said a word, he'd been across too many times, I suppose. I undone my equipment. Unlaced me boots. The idea being that if you got tipped out you had more chance to swim. This is what we got learned at Battle School.'

After suffering so many casualties in the Rhineland, many of the men in Tom's company were raw recruits, most of them eighteen years old.

'The new boys weren't comrades yet,' said Tom. 'That comes a little bit later.'

These 'new boys' struggled to comprehend what was happening around them.

'(The engineers had) started digging already to put the bridge across,' said Tom, 'and there was five dead engineers laid out there with blankets over them.'

It was the thought of lying dead with his boots sticking out this way that had caused Tom to go AWOL at Moyland.

'One of the new boys said to me, "Are they sleeping?" And I didn't want to disillusion him, because I knew that would come quick enough. I said yes.'

Tom's platoon moved away from the shore and came across three shallow graves on the corner of a minefield.

'They had their rifles stuck upside down. Two of them had steel helmets on, and one of them had a Scottish bonnet, with a Glasgow Highlander badge in. And you could imagine yourself there, really.'

Five days of fighting was about to begin for the men of the 9th Cameronians. Fifteen of them would be killed, sixty-one would be wounded, and seven would go missing.[4]

Tom's platoon were looking for a way to negotiate the minefield when a shell landed right in front of them.

'We all stopped, and you can guess who came to our rescue. Sergeant Rose, again.

'He walked on, and we all followed him. We got past the shelling, but the platoons that come after us weren't so lucky.'

Once the company was complete, they began to advance across the rural landscape. Their battalion's first objective was the village of Haffen.

'We got to a farmhouse, and all of a sudden a pig run out of there with a great lump out of his side. He'd obviously been caught in the shelling, and he was running around in circles. I aimed at him and put him out his misery.'

One of the 'new boys' did not recognize the act of mercy for what it was.

'E thee cruel bugger,' he said to Tom, to which he replied, 'You'll be the next if you don't shut your bloody mouth. And after the war, he often used to bring this up to me, and we used to have a good laugh about it.'

German families were found in some of the farm buildings, and Tom shared his boiled sweets with the children.

'We moved on, dug in against a wall of another farmhouse, and we were being fired on. The bullets was hitting the wall above us, so we kept our 'eads down. And around the corner, all of a sudden, came the (regimental sergeant major), stood up in a Bren gun carrier.

'I shouted at him: "*Incoming fire!*"'

The RSM ducked into the carrier and withdrew down the road.

'I sort of enjoyed this,' said Tom, as well he should have – it's not every day that a rifleman gets to shoo his RSM away.

Later, when darkness descended, Tom's platoon was ordered out of the farm and proceeded along a raised road.

'We were sitting targets, and all of a sudden they fired on us. Three of our platoon dropped down.'

Tom and the others took cover in the ditch beside the road, up to their knees in mud. They took stock of the situation, and their casualties, who were still lying on the exposed road. One of them was the Cockney, Rifleman Baker, who had told dirty jokes to the company at Nijmegen on the eve of the invasion of Germany. Baker lay moaning, unable to get himself into cover.

'So we pulled him to the driest part of the ditch, and stretcher-bearers come up. Squelched away with him.'

But Ronald Baker, twenty-three years old, did not survive his wounds.[5]

The platoon worked their way back to the farm where they remained 'for a day and a night' under shellfire. One mortar round came so close that it blew Tom's rifle across to the other side of the road. Tom crouched down into the bottom of his soggy trench, making himself as small as he could, 'and saying that inevitable prayer. A very short one. *Oh God!*

The man who shared the trench with Tom – Corporal Grant – had gone for a shave when the shell had hit. When Grant returned, and squeezed in beside Tom, he found a large piece of shrapnel beneath his feet, and where he would have been sitting – the battalion's grooming standard had saved his life.

Casualties mounted around the farm, but the shelling made it impossible to get them out. Instead, they were gathered in the cellar of the farmhouse, more joining them every day.

'Other companies that attacked through us, their casualties were all coming back and going in this cellar,' said Tom. 'God knows what it must have been like down there.'

It was 29 March before Brigadier R. M. Villiers visited the battalion and ordered maximum rest for all ranks, as the advance of the army had now completely passed 15th Division, who had won a hard-fought victory on the west side of the Rhine, creating a bridgehead that allowed bridges to be built and reinforcements to pour through.[6] 44th Brigade had 'smashed' the enemy's 84th Division so badly it was almost non-existent, and had captured 2,000 prisoners. They had then gone toe to toe with the veteran 7th Parachute Division, and linked up with Britain's own Airborne soldiers within five hours of their landing. The other brigades in the division faced fierce fighting of their own, 15th (Scottish) suffering some 1,000 casualties.

Luck played a part in who lived and who died. Not long after James Campbell was relieved from duty by one of his friends, the gun pit experienced a direct hit. 'Poor old Davie Morris was killed, so I lost another very, very close friend.'[7]

And loss was not confined to one's comrades. James recalled that a few days later 'I got a letter from my mother to say that my cousin, Frank Evans, who was in the Scots Guards, had got killed at Nijmegen in a bombing raid.'

Frank and James were of the same age – just nineteen years old.

'I lost six on my mother's side during the war. He was one of them.'

The 2nd Argyll and Sutherland Highlanders, the battalion of James Campbell and Alfred Wooltorton, had twenty-three men killed in five days of fighting. Tom Gore's battalion, the 9th Cameronian Rifles, lost sixteen.

Now out of the line came a time for reflection, remembrance and – God willing – smiles.

'We had a company concert,' said Tom. 'Major Nuthall from B Company, he sang "Trees". It went down very sentimentally with us.'

One can understand why. Sung in baritone, and with longing, it harkens to the beauty and divinity of our world – a world that must have seemed like a distant dream to the young men who were called upon to kill and die in a hostile land, far from home.

A further sentimental moment was to follow.

Tom was called in by his company commander, Major MacNeil, who a month earlier had given Tom twenty-eight days' field punishment for going Absent Without Leave. The final straw for Tom had been the battle at Moyland Wood, and the death of Corporal Jackman beside him. At the time of his arrest in Holland, Tom's regimental cap badge had been removed by the Military Police as a sign of his disgrace. Major MacNeil now handed him another.

'I hope you wear that with pride,' he told him. 'That was Corporal Jackman's.'

Tom took the words and the honour that he was given to heart, and would do so for the rest of his life.

'I've still got that badge. When I go on Armistice Parade, I wear that.'

CHAPTER 14

Red Devils

3rd and 5th Parachute Brigades during Operation Varsity
24–25 March 1945

'Speaking for myself, I was quite craven with fear. I felt survival was hardly likely. We knew this area so well now by briefing. We knew from the landscape that it was all wide open fields, barbed-wire fences dividing them, surrounded by woodlands. And so the thought of landing in the open, with machine guns in the woods, was a nightmare, and I don't know anyone who slept that night. One could hear the sharpening of knives on stones. It seemed one was going back hundreds and hundreds of years, to hear soldiers sharpening their knives on the night before going into battle. That terrible sound. The naked blade, and what it meant.'

John Petts, 224th (Parachute) Field Ambulance,
Royal Army Medical Corps

In the early morning of 24 March, weighed down with weapons and worry, D-Day veteran Walter Tanner climbed aboard his aircraft and squeezed down beside his comrades.

'You thought, *Christ – how's this all going to come together?*'

Across airfields in England and France, 16,000 British, Canadian and US Airborne soldiers contended with their own concerns. They were about to take part in Operation Varsity, and the largest ever airborne operation to take place on a single day.

'Then the engine started up, the orders come – "We're moving". It felt like a hell of a time before the aircraft took off.

'They reckon there was 1,700 aircraft, 1,300 gliders, and that wasn't counting the fighters that were zooming round us. The sight was magnificent, but all I thought of was my wife. We'd been married four months and two days.'

Twenty-nine-year-old Lieutenant-Colonel Napier Crookenden, from Chester, was a career soldier from a military family, and had taken command of the 9th Parachute Battalion in July 1944.

'On the green light from the tower the first three set off down the runway together and almost immediately behind them, the next three (and so on). A mass take-off by those American transport crews was a most exhilarating and impressive performance. It was a very fine piece of flying. We took off at about seven in the morning, due to land at ten.'

It was hoped that this daylight drop would lead to a greater troop concentration, and would occur when the enemy was already contending with the forces that had crossed the Rhine by water. The obvious downside was that the enemy's anti-aircraft gunners would have a clear view of their targets, and to this end known anti-aircraft positions would be heavily bombarded by British artillery prior to the drop, and receive close attention from the RAF.

The simultaneous landings of some 8,000 men from the 6th Airborne would take place over several drop zones (DZs) and landing zones (LZs). 5th Parachute Brigade would land at Drop Zone B and secure the Hamminkeln–Rees road. 3rd Parachute Brigade would land at Drop Zone A, east of the Wesel–Rees road, where they were to clear the nearby forests and seize a ridge of high ground known as the Schneppenberg. This latter brigade was made up of 1st Canadian Parachute Battalion and the 8th (Midlands) and 9th (Eastern and Home Counties) Parachute Battalions.

The air fleet of the 6th Airborne Division formed up over East Anglia, then crossed the Channel to link up with the US 17th Airborne Division that was taking off from France. It was a long flight made in less than luxurious conditions.

'We were all huddled up in our seats with this mass of equipment belted round us,' said Napier. 'Tea container passed up and down the line of men, and the urine tin. If you wanted to pass water, you had to burrow down through your equipment, jump jacket, Airborne smock, trousers, and then use this urine tin. Occasionally (a sick bag) went down for those who felt airsick. Then everybody started singing. As we got closer and closer to the scene of action, the singing died away. A lot of men went to sleep. They always did.

'I was sitting opposite the open door on the port side. Beyond the horizon, you could see the other aircraft and gliders of our 6th Airborne Division coming over the right and this vast armada, stretching back to the north-west. Out of the window on the other side, I could see the American 17th Airborne Division coming up out of the sky, right from the horizon, way down to the south-west. Above us and wheeling below us were the fighters of our RAF escort.'

The two formations came together over Belgium to form the greatest air armada of the war, numbering some 3,000 aircraft – transports, gliders, and fighters to protect them.

'We were flying in nine-ship-wide elements,' said Napier. 'Nine aircraft in a great arrow and then another nine (and so on), and the (US Airborne) were the same.

'Four minutes from the drop, as was agreed, the red light came on. We stood up, hooked up our parachute strops on the overhead cable, turned towards the door, and as was the drill, each man checked the strop hook of the man in front of him. Made certain the safety pin, which stopped the hook from undoing by mistake. And then from the back, No. 18, they shouted out, "Number eighteen! Number seventeen" and so on. I was jumping No. 1.'

Spread out below Napier were the battlegrounds of the Rhineland campaign.

'We passed over the terrible ruins of those German towns like Goch. The result of the Reichswald battle. I could see the great curving river of the Rhine below us. Almost immediately ahead of us was our dropping zone, exactly as our maps and models had depicted. On the ground, the parachutes of our other two battalions in the brigade, 8th Parachute Battalion, the Canadian Parachute Battalion, who had jumped three minutes before us. Men on the ground, running in towards their objectives.

'Then the green light came on and out we all went, into the sunlight and down into this beautiful March day. You could hear the occasional crack of a bullet going quite close, (but) not very many. Then I was down on the ground and I made my usual backwards landing. Picked myself up, looked around for my batman and my escort, and found the DZ full of my own men, making towards our rendezvous – the far-right corner (of the field).

'I could see, to my pleasure and delight, the blue smoke going up, which was our rendezvous signal put there by the regimental sergeant major. I made my way across there.'

By this time men were coming in from all over the drop zone.

'We all jumped out with no problems at all,' said Hubert 'Hugh' Pond, a platoon commander in the battalion.

'I landed on the DZ in what appeared to be a sort of smoky sunshine. All my troops were in a pretty compact group and we set off towards our rendezvous point, which was the edge of some woods near the drop zone.

'We watched planes coming over and dropping their parachutists. We also watched other planes coming in, either towing gliders, or fighter bombers strafing troops in front of us. One awful thing we saw was a glider that had been released coming into land. Something had happened, the glider had hit the top of some trees, turned turtle and out fell a light tank that it was carrying. It must have been a horrible death for those inside it.'

Paratrooper Paul Boxall, who had been wounded in Normandy, knew that getting down safely was a matter of luck, and odds.

'With the numbers that were coming down, they couldn't hit all of you.'

But it wasn't only the enemy that he had to worry about – Paul's parachute carried him into a wood where he became entangled in two trees, 30 feet off the ground. He managed to cut himself free and slid down one of the trees, and not a moment too soon.

'Part of the wood was occupied by the Germans. The first people that landed, landed into a firefight of some considerable ferocity. Once or twice I got fired at, but luckily they didn't hit me.'

Sidney Capon, a fellow D-Day veteran, also came down in woodland.

'I went to the right of the DZ and some very high trees. I hit the trees. I landed upside down, hanging by my right leg, and the Germans were firing through the woods. I shouted out, and one chap scaled the tree. He was a Canadian. A little Canadian with a moustache, a Canadian Para, and he cut the rigging lines and I hit the ground.'

The experience of hanging helpless as men tried to kill him had shaken Sidney.

'My mind had gone. Instead of going around the perimeter of the field to the RV (rendezvous point), I went straight across the field, with a plane coming down with a load of men hitting the woods on the other end.'

Bullets zipping overhead, Sidney made it to the blue smoke in the corner of the field.

'I got to the RV where Napier Crookenden was, waiting to advance.'

'We had to move off as soon as we were strong enough,' said Napier. 'Enough men were in to capture our first objective, which was a German gun battery on top of that hill. I urgently wanted to get my mortars into action, so as we moved off I had something to give us covering fire.'

The colonel needed to locate Alan Jefferson, a D-Day veteran and a ballet dancer in peacetime, who was the mortar platoon's commander.

'As I stood there watching the men coming (in) and being allotted by the RSM to their company areas for immediate defence of our rendezvous, I saw a soldier from the mortar platoon going past. So I grabbed him by the arm and said, "Where's Mr Jefferson?"

'"Oh," he said, "he's bought it, sir, terrible mess, right through the 'ead, head blown nearly off." Instead of saying, "Damn, I've lost Mr Jefferson, splendid chap," I remember feeling strongly – what a curse – *No mortar officer!* "Well, where is the mortar sergeant?" I ceased to worry about my friends, I wanted to get the mortars into action.'

A timely arrival was then made by the man who was supposedly missing his head.

'(Captain Jefferson) came prancing through the wood with his typical ballet dancer's walk, saying, "Good morning, Colonel! What a lovely day!" Some private soldiers do love bad news, and this lad's bad news about Alan Jefferson was totally false, much to my relief.'

More of 9th Battalion's paratroopers continued to arrive at the rendezvous.

'We had a very high proportion,' said Napier, '(half) of the battalion had arrived and were organized by their companies, including my own soldier-servant, Lance-Corporal Wilson, who arrived riding a horse he'd liberated from a nearby farm, with another one for me. So we mounted and we set off through the woods, against our first objective, this German gun battery. On the way, we passed one of our own gliders, which had crashed – turned upside down on landing. Inside it was an artillery piece and six gunners who were all dead, I'm sorry to say.'

The 9th Battalion reached the forested high ground of Schneppenberg and assaulted it from the rear, storming the artillery battery and overwhelming its soldiers.

'B Company, followed by Battalion Headquarters, rushed into the battery, shot anybody who bothered to resist, silenced the battery, and then we established our positions in that area,' said Napier, whose battalion took over 200 prisoners in the attack.

'The Germans went to surrender when we got up there,' said Sidney Capon, 'and one German, for some unknown reason, decided to run. He got shot. He laid not far from where I was on the perimeter of the woods.'

Taking the prisoners was the norm on the battlefield, but this could change if it was felt that a sense of 'fair play' had not been adhered to, as witnessed by John Petts, a conscientious objector and pacifist, who jumped into Drop Zone A with 224th (Parachute) Field Ambulance as an unarmed medic.

'Above my head was the colonel commanding the 1st Canadian

Parachute Battalion – hanging upside down, killed before he reached the ground. His parachute caught up in a tree.

'All the trees around – and they were quite big pine trees – were festooned with dead men, swinging gently in their harness – they had never reached the ground. Sitting targets up in the trees, with men underneath them with automatic weapons.'

Several of these Germans were killed in the fighting around John. The others then put up their hands and surrendered.

'That's the first time I have seen the dreadful murder of prisoners with their hands up,' said John.

'I have to say this because it's what I saw. After the Germans had either been killed or given up, it was discovered that there was a big bunker with men hiding in it, they were all ordered out of the bunker. As a row of men came out with their hands up, the Canadians just swept them with machine-gun fire. It was a terrible thing to see. Men expecting to be taken prisoner just murdered. Maybe it was just the heat of the whole issue at that time. The Canadians were so angry.'

Fellow medic Corporal Frederick Topham, from Toronto, jumped into Drop Zone A with the 1st Canadian Parachute Battalion. When the twenty-seven-year-old Topham saw two medics killed in succession as they tried to treat a casualty in an open field, he immediately ran forwards to take their place, continuing to work on the wounded man even after he was himself shot through the nose. Bleeding profusely and in intense pain, Topham carried his wounded comrade to safety. He refused treatment of his own wound, and for the next two hours he continued to come to the aid of stricken soldiers.

Later in that day, Topham saw a Bren carrier struck by a mortar shell. It was set ablaze, ammunition exploding in the heat. Topham ignored orders not to intervene and rushed to the vehicle to save the crew. One of the witnesses to this heroic act was Corporal Einarson.

'I saw a man jump on the carrier and literally lift the occupants out. I thought the person was absolutely out of his mind, being up on top of the carrier when the thing was literally exploding and burning and popping underneath him. As I moved down the road, I looked back and saw him jump off. Then the carrier exploded.'[1]

One of the three rescued men died soon after, but the others were saved. For his gallant actions that day, Corporal Frederick Topham was awarded the Victoria Cross.

German medics also risked their own lives to save those of others, both friend and foe.

'I called for a stretcher-bearer and a German POW, a medic, came over to take care of me,' recalled Corporal Flynn, who had been badly wounded in the thigh. 'We were going down the road when we were shelled by mortars. This German fellow threw his body right on top of me to protect me. I guess he saved my life.'[2]

Corporal Flynn was then handed over to 224th Field Ambulance, whose work seemed never-ending.

'I can only remember a whole chain of casualties, many of them very young men,' said John Petts. 'I rushed across to a man who was writhing on the ground – a lad of eighteen I would think. He must have had a grenade burst right close to him because I opened up his tunic and all his gut was completely smashed. As I opened up his tunic and belt and trousers, his whole gut just fell away. And he looked at this and said to me, "I've had it, haven't I?", and all you can say is, "No. No, don't worry, we'll see you're alright."'

What stuck with John was the sight of a coin lodged between the tendons of the soldier's leg, bearing the face of the king of the country that the young man was dying for.

'All I could do was hold him like a mother for a moment and give him a big shot of morphia. We carried morphia for such occasions. You knew how many grains would be an overdose, and send him on his way. The thing was to knock out his pain and his consciousness.

'I can't say that I have killed men by doing that, I have only made their inevitable death more bearable. If you say, who am I to make the decision of if the man was going to die or not, one only did this in extreme cases where the man was clearly not going to survive.'

While the Airborne's fallen had to be left where they fell, for now, the enemy dead were checked for intelligence, and loot.

'One of my soldiers was standing over a German artillery captain, lying dead on the ground,' said Napier Crookenden. 'As I passed he said, "Fine pair of glasses here, sir!" and I took a look at them. They were beautiful German artillery glasses. I said, "That's a good pair." I went to go on and he said, "You keep them, sir, no good to me." And I kept them. Twenty-five years later I lost them in Athens airport.'

There was nothing on the battlefield that was beyond 're-issuing'. After securing the high ground, Napier led an attack against the village of Lanchenoffer, to the western flank of DZ A. This required advancing over 500 yards of open ground, and all while under fire from infantry and a pair of self-propelled guns.

'A self-propelled gun came into our area and started blasting away with its gun,' said Hugh Pond, 'which wasn't very effective because it was an armour-piercing gun, so it wasn't doing us any damage. It was also spraying the area with machine-gun fire. A couple of our chaps crept up close on the sides and managed to plant some bombs in the tracks and blew the tracks.'

9th Battalion's war diary credited this action to Corporal Round, from B Company.

'Eventually the crew came up and surrendered,' said Hugh. 'One man I think was killed in the process.'

Hugh, an ex-Royal Tank Regiment man, was then ordered by Napier Crookenden to get the SP gun back into action. This he managed, but the vehicle was abandoned later in the campaign due to its high consumption of fuel.

By 1530 hrs, just five and a half hours after the landings had taken place, 3rd Para Brigade made contact with the 15th (Scottish) Infantry Division, who were pushing their way towards the Airborne.

'We were all established in our final positions by three o'clock in the afternoon,' said Napier, who would be awarded the DSO for his actions that day.

As his soldiers dug in for the night, Napier visited his companies who were in 'The usual layout – two companies forward, one in reserve, Battalion Headquarters in the middle. Our positions covered the main road from the Rhine, running eastwards. I was just going across the road, from B Company to A Company, to see all was well, when a jeep came up the road flying a Union Jack.

'A Union Jack means the Army Group commander, so I flagged it down, saluted and said, "Crookenden, 9th Parachute Battalion, sir," and of course it was Monty.

'He said, "GOOD GOOD GOOOD, thank you, thank you! Well done, Crookenden, I know your father," and we had a chat, very few words, and then he gave permission to his driver to drive on. So I said, "Stop, sir, just a minute. Fifty yards around that bend is the next German position. This is the frontline, we've only just arrived here." "Oh," he said, "thank you, thank you, thank you, thank you." He said everything three or four times. Turned around and drove back.'

It was not a moment that Napier would forget. Nor, it seemed, did Montgomery, and in later weeks Napier learned that the field marshal had written to his father on the very same day that he saw his son.

'What moved me very much was that there was Monty running a colossal operation, crossing the Rhine, but that night he took the trouble to write a postcard to my father – a retired colonel living in Berkshire, who he'd known for years, most of his life. It read like this:

"*My dear Arthur, I saw your boy and his battalion today. They were in good knick, Yours ever, Montgomery of Alamein.*"

Drop Zone B

James Absalom, 12th (Yorkshire) Parachute Battalion's Signals Platoon officer, stood up and hooked on in the back of his Dakota.

'When the green light went, we all started to shuffle out. All of a sudden, one chap stood at the door, couldn't go any further. I was friends with this bloke, and I shouted, "Boot him!" – I heard him say, "Oh no, oh no!" and I shouted, "Boot him!" and I booted him out.

'He went down and then we were all airborne. I remember lowering the kit bag and then realizing I was passing people in mid-air, and I thought, *I shouldn't be doing that, we should all be going down at the same sort of rate*, but I was hurtling past some people.

'I'd got a big hole in the front of my parachute, which meant I was travelling down much faster than everybody else. Looking up, I saw my batman above my head and he was pointing down to my parachute. I hit the ground with a bit of a thump but I was very fortunate.'

Less fortunate was a trooper tangled up in a tree.

'He said, "How do I get down from this?"'

James told the man to come down his kit bag line, not 'working out quick enough' that when the soldier released his harness to climb down, the kit bag would fall away to the ground, taking the line and the soldier with it.

'He fell about twenty feet. As we moved off, he come up to me and said, "That was a bloody silly idea of yours, wasn't it?"'

James also came across the man that he'd 'booted' out of the aircraft, who apologized for his hesitation.

'I thought that took more courage than actually jumping out the aircraft,' said James.

D-Day man Walter Tanner, 7th (Light Infantry) Parachute Battalion, had been apprehensive about the jump, and with good reason.

'Red came on, green came on, and out we went. The small-arms fire, I couldn't believe it. The amount of small-arms fire was unbelievable. I looked up and two of the rigging lines had been snapped.'

Walter had also been wounded in the hand by shrapnel.

'I thought, *Christ, they've got me*. There's nothing I can do about it and I came down, my chute landed across telephone wires on the unfinished autobahn.

'I released the kit bag, left that, jumped over the fence and then I teamed up with my platoon officer, and the other lads. Major Reed came on the scene and we made our way to the woods – that was our objective. When we got in there, you never saw a sight like it. These chaps were hanging in the trees. One of the lads went, "Hang on, lads, we'll let you down! *Jesus Christ, they're dead.*" They'd all been shot by the Germans.'

The sight of the helpless soldiers killed in the trees boiled the blood of the Red Devils.

'I have to say it, because the order came round – I don't know who started it, it wasn't our officer – the order came round: no prisoners. Anybody would realize why, when those lads are up there. Why should we give them buggers a chance?'

The US aircrews that delivered the paratroopers also suffered terribly – two of their aircraft were shot down on the approach, and a further ten as they banked to pull clear of the area. Seven more were badly hit and forced to make crash landings. All told, seventy aircraft – nearly all of those that delivered the 5th Para Brigade – were damaged to some extent by flak.

Gliders were also coming down in flames, and in pieces.

Major John Watson was the twenty-eight-year-old commander of A Company, 13th (Lancashire) Parachute Battalion.

'There were three gliders to each battalion, loaded with quartermaster stores and soldiers. Our three gliders were all shot out the sky as they were landing, with only one survivor – chap called Doug Baynes. Doug had been taken prisoner in Normandy. He'd escaped by digging through the floor of the railway truck he was being carted off to Germany in and dug his way through the floor with his fighting knife and got back to England eventually.

'Once taken prisoner, you didn't need to go into action again. There was no need for him to come with us but he did, being that sort of bloke, and he was in one of those gliders and he lost a leg. He was the only survivor.'

Casualties continued to mount once on the ground.

'They were firing anti-personnel airbursts,' recalled D-Day veteran Ronald Follett, 7 Para. 'A lot of chaps were wounded by airbursts.

'Our CO, Colonel Pine-Coffin, and the RSM were all in the same woods as me. Colonel Pine-Coffin was wounded, he had a huge slash of shrapnel went across his face and left him with a huge scar that he carried for ever.'

Nicknamed 'Wooden Box', Lieutenant-Colonel Richard Pine-Coffin had been involved in actions since 1942. He was awarded a Military Cross in North Africa, and the Distinguished Service Order twice – once for Normandy, and once for Operation Varsity. In photographs taken decades later, a deep scar is visible on his right cheek, running all the way from nose to ear, but the wound did not stop Colonel Pine-Coffin from remaining in command of the 7th (Light Infantry) Parachute Battalion and leading them to seize all of their objectives that day.

'That morning of the 24th was very alarming and very war-like,' continued Ronald. 'Lots of noise, lots going on, lots of casualties. A very war-like scene.'

Drop Zone B was thick with the sound of explosions, gunfire and the drone of the departing aircraft, but the Airborne's officers had a canny method of rallying their men in this din.

'I had my hunting horn with me,' said Major John Watson. 'We discarded our helmets and put on our red berets, so we must have looked a fearsome lot.'

'We got to the rendezvous,' said James Absalom, 'and it was my job to set up communications as fast as we could. We packed our radio sets very carefully, there was only one damaged out of the radio sets being used for all the battalion. We used to have a set at each Company Headquarters, backed up by a second set and then each platoon had its little 39 sets, which were outside my control, but the Company HQ sets were the important ones because they allowed Battalion Headquarters to get in touch with companies all the way we moved.

'My job was to tune in, make sure that the whistle I could hear in my earphones was at the right pitch, and then I knew that the transmitter and receiver of each set were properly aligned. It was during this time that one of my signallers was shot – chap named Harry Copeland.'[3]

Twenty-three-year-old Harry died on the battlefield.

'Several other people were injured,' said James, who was too busy to move to a safer location. 'My batman and I had already dug a slit trench and were cannibalizing sets in order to put together a set to replace the one that was damaged, and getting into contact with the companies as they moved across the dropping zone into their various positions.

'Just over the field, away from us, there was a detachment of German troops with a gun, and they kept firing at us. It was there where Phil Burkinshaw – who got his first Mention in Despatches – went across and knocked that gun out of action. Then we moved on to the first objective and we took a farmhouse.'

James would return to the farmhouse years later, in times of peace.

'I went across there and spoke with a large German farmer. His name was Wilhelm, and he said that he'd been there as a boy when we landed. I said to him, "What happened?" and he said, "We had two of our soldiers here, and one was on the roof and he kept shouting down to the other chap, who was drinking refreshments in our kitchen. He kept on shouting down, 'There's an aeroplane coming! It's British! There are thousands of aeroplanes coming! There are millions of them jumping out on parachutes!'"

'The next thing was the door burst open, and a very small parachutist looked at (him) and he said, "Hands up." (Wilhelm) said, "I stood up, and the parachutist said, 'You're very big. Sit down.'"

Harold Cammack's section in the 12th (Yorkshire) Parachute Battalion had lost two men on their drop.

'The majority of us, we rendezvous together then we linked up with the rest of the company and followed on to take our positions. I was just giving some directions to the section and next thing I know I just heard this *WHACK* and it sent me somersaulting. I turned round to this lance-corporal – they called him Steadman, always remember, came from Paisley. I said, "Okay, Bob, it's all yours." I just laid there and when the attack had gone through, some of the Germans who they'd captured, two of the Germans came up and put me on this door and took me to this big marquee. That's where the wounded were, there were German wounded, British wounded, we were all in there, maybe twenty-four hours or so, and they shipped me back to Bruges.'

By the middle of the afternoon of the 24th, 5th Parachute Brigade was firmly in control of the Rees–Hamminkeln road.

'The whole operation was successful,' said John Watson, OC of

A Company, 13 Para. 'The opposing forces were German parachutists, but within a matter of hours, we had secured all our objectives. By the end of the day, we were in a very solid position – all our objectives were taken.'

'At three o'clock in the afternoon, word came through that all our objectives had been taken,' said Walter Tanner. 'We got pushed out to a farmhouse where we had to dig in. I don't know who the clever bugger was, but he put us right beside a bloody dung-heap of all places; and with the midges and the mozzies out there, same as in France, they were buggers.'

Walter was then sent back to the Regimental Aid Post to see to a shrapnel wound on his hand.

'He put six stitches in but I didn't see anything because I passed out. I came to and saw the bandage round there and thought, *It's got to be a Blighty!*

In Walter's case, an evacuation back to Britain would mean a reunion with his beloved wife.

'I said to this corporal, "Does it mean I'm going back to Blighty?" "No, mate," he said. "You're alright. What hand do you write with?" I said the right hand. He said, "Well, you pull your trigger with your right finger, don't ya?"'

He was returned to his platoon and settled down for the night.

'When it got light, and we realized things had quietened down, orders came round and you smartened yourself up as best you could with the cold water that we had – cold shave, bit of a wash.'

The brigade was smartening itself up for good reason.

'We was waiting for the Second Army to come through, and somebody shouted out, "Bloody hell, tanks!" You could hear these tracks. When a tank (is moving) you can hear those tracks from a long way. So of course straight away, everyone is on the alert, everyone is ready to meet the onslaught, you see. But as luck would have it, it was a Bren gun carrier, followed by a few more, and who were they? The Middlesex Regiment.'

Walter, a Middlesex man himself, shook hands and shared greetings with the men of his local regiment.

'I was quite proud of that moment.'

The Airborne had achieved their objectives, but at great cost. More than 1,000 Allied Airborne soldiers were killed during Operation Varsity.

One of them was sapper William 'Bill' Hobson, whose body was collected and buried by his friend Bernard McDonough. Later that day, Tommy Hobson, who served in the same squadron, came in search of his twin brother.[4] Bernard had the horrible job of telling him that he'd been killed.

Major John Watson, who had jumped into Drop Zone B, recalled that 'an enormous amount of casualties' were suffered by the gliderborne element of the division.

'I think the thing that stuck in my memory was to see our gliders on the ground. The pilot and copilot were still sitting in their seats, roasted. I'll never forget that. I can still see that to this day, still holding their controls like a roasted rabbit.

'What a way to go.'

CHAPTER 15

Nothing Is Impossible

Glider Pilots during Operation Varsity
24–25 March 1945

'*The havoc those 88s caused amongst those gliders. You see a glider come in and then next minute it's cut in half. They never stood a chance, they had no chutes.*

Even when they landed they were still under heavy fire from machine-gun fire. If you come across any man that says he went to war in a glider, shake his hand, because you're shaking hands with a hero.'

Walter Tanner, 7th (Light Infantry)
Parachute Battalion

In 1942 the call went out across the army for volunteers to fill the ranks of the newly formed Glider Pilot Regiment. Arnold Baldwin, from Croydon, was serving in the Royal Engineers and eagerly applied.

'I wanted to get out of what was really a non-combatant unit into something a bit more active. As a communist I actually wanted to do a bit of fighting.'

Arthur had once tried to volunteer for the socialist republic during the Spanish Civil War. Instead, he would see his first action against fascism on D-Day, when he landed his glider at the Merville Battery. He also took part in Operation Market Garden, and escaped

Arnhem before the 1st Airborne Division – out of ammunition, full of casualties, and after nine days of continuous fighting – was forced to capitulate.

Having come so close to capture, wounds and death during these landings, Arnold knew that he was pushing his luck with a third.

'I wasn't very happy about the operation at all. I felt as though my invulnerability was open to question now. Feeling that you can't keep going on like this and not copping it sooner or later.

'Also, I felt that it was only too obvious. The Second Army was lined up on the riverbank, waiting to cross. So (the Germans) had the best idea where we were going to be landing. Added to that, my first-born son was only three weeks old at the time when the Rhine crossing took place. That worried me extremely too, as I'd very much looked forward to having a family, and I'd landed myself in a situation where I might leave the baby fatherless before I'd even seen him.'

These fears were well founded. So heavy were the losses of the Glider Pilot Regiment at Arnhem that pilots of the RAF were called upon to bring it up to strength.

'Initially, very few volunteered,' said Brian Latham, a twenty-year-old RAF pilot who had hoped to fly Spitfires. 'Then we were told if we didn't we'd either go in the infantry or down the mines – we'd never fly again. So we became voluntary conscripts and very bolshie.'[1]

Twenty-one-year-old Leonard MacDonald, RAF, was called onto parade with about 200 other trainee pilots.

'The flight lieutenant who took parade, after roll call, he drew himself up to his full height of about five foot seven, and he said "You lot have just volunteered to fly gliders." At a stroke, the RAF had got rid of two hundred surplus pilots, and we were sent off.

'The army glider pilots were soldiers first, and then they learned to fly gliders. We were pilots first of all, trained by the RAF, and they kept us in what was known in the RAF Element of the Glider Pilot Regiment.'

Lacking the rigorous battle training, and battle experience, of the army glider pilots, the RAF aircrews picked up tips from their new comrades that might one day save their lives.

'Where we learned how to conduct ourselves in a battle situation was in the Nissen huts at night,' said Leonard. 'They'd decided to mix RAF and the army pilots together, so you had a mixture in a Nissen hut, and round the stoves at night they would tell us about their experiences, including having to swim over the Rhine.'

This was the method by which some of the pilots had escaped the collapsing pocket at Arnhem.

'Another one was, if you get out of the aircraft, the first thing you do is get down behind one of the wheels of the aircraft.'

For Operation Varsity, Leonard was paired up with an experienced soldier of the Glider Pilot Regiment.

'I found out I was crewed with a Staff-Sergeant Penketh, but nobody knew where Penketh was. That's how clever the army were, you see. I eventually tracked him down, (and) he was in the sick bay. I went up to see him. There was Penketh, sat up in bed with a WAAF nurse on either side. I thought we'd never get this man to move.'

The Medical Officer gave Penketh the choice to be released from sick bay or a few more days to recuperate in bed. Penketh chose the bed – or, perhaps more accurately, the nurses.

'And I didn't blame him for that.'

Three days later Leonard prepared his aircraft for the operation.

'I loaded the glider up with a jeep, trailer, four motorbikes and about ten Royal Signallers, from the 53rd Light Regiment, Royal Artillery. We had the signals unit so they could contact the guns back west of the Rhine, to direct the fire where it was needed, so it was a fairly important load we had.'

Leonard then went back to the sick bay and reported to Penketh that the glider was ready.

'"Right-o," he said. "I'll see you at the flightline at 7.15 on Saturday morning."

'Take-off was about 7.40. He turned up, and as we're walking out to the glider he said, "By the way, I haven't flown for nearly nine months." How he managed to be there and not fly I don't know. He said, "Perhaps you better do the take-off."'

Penketh then stowed his pack and weapon in the glider. Rather than arming himself with a Sten gun or rifle, Penketh had brought along a Bren, and plenty of ammunition to go with it. This was a choice born of experience, as Vincent Penketh was no stranger to battle. A twenty-five-year-old former postman from Liverpool, Penketh had landed on D-Day, and later at Arnhem. In October 1944 he gave interviews to both the *Liverpool Daily Post* and *Liverpool Echo*, recalling how a bullet had narrowly missed his head during their approach at Arnhem, and how the 1st Airborne Division had stood toe to toe with the enemy for nine days:

'One day the Germans sent a loudspeaker van, and it said "You honourable British soldiers, you have done a good job. Surrender and you will be treated as honourable prisoners. The Reich is the real land of freedom." The van immediately became a target for all our arms and disappeared. Then Germans with Spandau machine-guns tried to mix themselves up with the hospital cases and fired on us, but we soon settled their hash.'[2]

To avoid capture, Penketh and others were eventually withdrawn across the Rhine beneath 'a pasting' from the German guns. His interview with the *Echo* had concluded: 'We gave a lot more than we got, and we held on. Our next objective is Berlin.'[3]

The operation to make that a reality was now underway.

'The RAF had devised a wonderful system,' said Leonard. 'The gliders were stacked down the runway, facing the way to take off. They were on one side of the runway and just behind them on the other side was number two, so they were staggered all the way down the runway. The tugs were facing the runway at an angle of about forty-five degrees and the tug would taxi out, take up the slack and they were off. They could get a whole batch of tugs and gliders off in about two or three minutes flat. It was absolutely marvellous. It must have been about thirty tugs and thirty gliders I think, known as combinations. Thirty combinations.

'I never went to any briefings whatsoever. I did get a map and was told my landing position was in Landing Zone P, which is west of Hamminkeln, and they pointed at a field and they said, "You should land there." I got that from the intelligence sergeant there, but having been late for getting up to (the airfield), we missed all the briefings.'

This was not as great a disaster as it would be for pilots in other situations.

'All the flying and change of direction was done by the tug pilot and his crew,' explained Leonard.

One of those 'tug' pilots was George Reid, from London. George had served in the RAF since 1935, first as an armourer, and then as a navigator in Bomber Command. In 1941 he trained as a pilot and began serving in the RAF's Transport Command. Varsity was his first time flying his Dakota as a tug in combat.

'We were much relieved to see that on the Rhine crossing we were putting the troops down almost within sight of the river. They were not far away from the bridgehead that was being developed coincidentally with their landing. On this particular operation, my (crew) was given the task of towing a Horsa glider.'

Inside the Horsa were thirty men belonging to the 2nd Battalion, Oxfordshire and Buckinghamshire Light Infantry.

'It wasn't a task we particularly enjoyed because a Dakota with a fully laden Horsa glider behind it was not a very manoeuvrable aircraft. It was extremely hard work, because they would drag you all over the sky.'

In the early morning of 24 March, not long after first light, the tugs began to throttle up their engines and roll forwards. Tow ropes pulling tight, the gliders came with them.

Leonard MacDonald was taking off for battle for the first time.

'We did the take-off and Staff-Sergeant Penketh must have been quite pleased with that, because he turned to me and said, "Do you mind if I have a kip?", and I said, "If you want a kip, you have a kip." I thought he was joking, but he wasn't. Gets into his Airborne rucksack, stashed beside him, pulls a blanket out over his head and promptly goes off to sleep. The RSM signaller who was in charge of the signals unit was like a cat on hot bricks, as you can imagine. He said, "Half the crew's asleep!" and I said, "Don't worry. If I need him, I'll wake him up."

And on they flew, to Germany.

Into Battle

'The air was absolutely full with aeroplanes,' recalled George Reid, RAF. 'I've never seen so many aeroplanes. The spectacle of all those aircraft, there seemed to be thousands of them. The Typhoons and Tempests were doing ground attacks and they would suddenly zoom up from the ground as we were dropping our gliders.'

Staff-Sergeant Penketh, Glider Pilot Regiment, had managed to sleep for the entire journey. Leonard MacDonald woke him as the Rhine appeared beneath a smoky haze.

'(Penketh said,) "Ah, coming up to the Channel, are we?" and I said, "No, that's the Rhine we're looking at." The only advice he gave me was, when we got the green light, "I wouldn't hang about if I were you." All he said. It was good advice because I put full flaps on. When you put full flaps on a Horsa, it tended to come down almost like a lift. It was a remarkable aeroplane.

'We came down pretty sharply, levelled off a bit. People came out of that smog heading for trees, high-tension cables, side of a farmhouse.'

Leonard was on the right line for his target, but didn't have the elevation to make it. He came down two fields short, but his first combat landing was a good one – he got down alive.

At the controls of his Dakota, George Reid released the Horsa he had towed from England.

'I looked down and the glider had gone about 300 feet below and went *boof!* Like that. Disappeared. Ox and Bucks Light Infantry, that was the end of their war.'

There were thirty infantrymen in the Horsa, and their crew of two pilots. George did not know how many survived, if any.

Harry Gibbons, Glider Pilot Regiment, had worked in movie studios before his call-up in 1942. Since then he'd escaped capture at Arnhem – a battle that would itself be immortalized on the silver screen – but his luck ran out on the Rhine.

'One of the wings hit a tree and we made a pretty rough landing. We had a jeep and about eight blokes in the back, they were all

OK, but immediately we came under small-arms fire. We'd obviously landed on top of a bunch of Germans. We got out of the glider as quick as we could but unfortunately by that time, two of the chaps in the back (had been shot and killed). Just alongside where we'd landed, there was a ditch and we'd managed to get in there. We fought them off for as long as we could but eventually they surrounded us, lobbed a few hand grenades over and that was it.

'I always remember "*Hände hoch*" – you know, surrender. The chap who had his rifle sticking up was a German paratrooper. He was shaking like a bloody leaf. He was more scared than I was I think. He was literally shaking.'

Harry was marched off and taken into captivity. Meanwhile, Arnold Baldwin wasted no time getting his Hamilcar glider down out of the flak-filled sky.

'As we crossed the river, I thought I'd pull off fairly quickly because we didn't have far to go into the country on the other side of the river, so I pulled off and I started a whole series of spiralling tight turns going down. Must have been a bit uncomfortable in the back. I'd got a jeep and a trailer full of six-pounder ammo and I'd got about four blokes from I believe it was the Bedfords, but I'm not sure about that. It must have been a bit scary for them.

'It was what would be known as a split-arse approach. When I finally pulled out of this dive, I realized that in spiralling round like that, I completely lost sight of my LZ. Nothing to do but land now. I could see Hamilcars burning on the ground. I thought I was bloody right about the Hamilcars – they're too easy to hit. Then I thought, *Well, perhaps I had saved our bacon by making this sort of approach.* I knew I wasn't on my LZ. In fact, it turned out to be I wasn't very far across the river. I was across the river, but not as far as I should have been.

'When I began to level out and look around I found that I was flying parallel to the edge of a wood, about roughly thirty yards or so from the edge of this wood. Then I suddenly realized that dead ahead of me was a solitary building, perhaps a farmhouse or something of that sort.

'I realized that I hadn't got enough speed left to pull up clear of this building. I could only try it, but I didn't think it was going to be very lucky. I couldn't turn aside one way or the other – too late to do that – so I just tried to stretch my glider, ease it a bit, and try and skate in just over the roof of the house.

'We didn't quite make it and the undercart caught the roof, and another of those little miracles that I get from time to time occurred, because on the other side, the far side of the house, which I hadn't seen on my approach, was a huge pile of brushwood. Just a few yards from the house, and it was quite as big as the house itself, great big pile of brushwood.'

The aircraft clipped the building before the nose dipped and buried itself in the brushwood. The glider came to a halt, intact, and with the pilots very much alive.

'I was rather pleased with myself,' said Arnold. 'I thought I'd bought it. I thought for sure we'd had it, but I didn't go in for any of that stuff where your whole life passes before your eyes or that sort of rubbish, or even start to say my prayers. I simply said to (my-copilot), "Well, that's fucked it, Jack."'

On the Ground

Arnold Baldwin called out to the men in the back of his crashed glider, 'Everybody alright?' He didn't know the men personally, but the young lieutenant and his three soldiers had all survived. As Arnold encouraged them to get clear and struggled to free himself from his harness, he saw a German officer and about six or eight men dash from the wood about thirty yards from the house. *That's not too good*, he thought to himself.

Annoyed over misjudging the landing, and feeling as if his luck was about to run out, Arnold couldn't help being a little impatient with the officer who may have been in his first action, saying, 'He didn't seem to know what to do.'

Arnold, his RAF copilot Jack Cod, and the four soldiers got clear of the glider and peered over the brushwood, searching for the Germans.

'They started to creep down the side of the house and their

officer, thinking we'd probably been killed in the crash anyway, rather boldly stepped forward.

'I said to (the British) officer, "Well, I think the best thing to do is knock him off." I couldn't get any response at all from the officer, I'm sorry to say. I think he was too badly shaken up. I thought, *Right, then I'll take him out.*'

Arnold raised his rifle, the sights of which had been damaged in the crash.

'There wasn't a lot of time for reconsidering what to do or anything, so I drew a bead on this bloke. I fired and down he went, and he spread himself on the path beside the house with a groan and I think he died then and there. The others, his men, they scooted back into the woods as fast as they could go. So I thought, *Well, I don't know how many troops there are in that wood. It may be full of them. We've got a glider in a huge pile of brushwood, with a jeep with a petrol tank full, and a trailer full of ammo, and we're sitting on a funeral pile here if we're not careful.*

'Looking across, opposite to that wood, we appeared to be on the edge of a field. Away off to our left was a copse. I thought we could take ourselves to there.'

Arnold told this to the officer.

'He seemed mentally paralysed. He didn't respond to me, he didn't make any effort to take control. Although we were always trained that we fought with the troops, you didn't assume command over an officer unless you were an officer (yourself), and I wasn't. So I was looking for a lead from him but I wasn't getting it. So I said, "The only thing we can do, we've gotta get out of this damn thing." I said, "We'll make a dash." There was some fairly long grass in this field between us and this copse. I said, "We'll make a dash and go a few yards and drop down, then the second party will leapfrog over us, they drop and we'll go over them" and so on. He said, "Alright."'

Arnold moved first to prove the route.

'I belted across a fairly short distance, barely fifty yards. Dropped down, and to my horror the grass was not anything like as long as I thought it was. I thought, *This is never gonna provide us with shelter if we try this leapfrogging, because they can rake it with machine-gun fire, and they'll kill the blinking lot of us like that.* I thought, *It's not gonna work.* So I thought the only thing to do is continue my mad dash for that copse. So I did.

'I upped and I ran like a maniac to that copse. I heard a few angry shouts from behind me. Obviously the blokes thought I was running away from them. But I couldn't stop and explain the position. I could hear the bullets were simply whistling past me, but I was quite unscathed when I reached my copse, and found to my surprise that it was a sunken area of rather marshy ground, with aspens I suppose they were, lots of very small trees. Choka-block with them. But it did mean it was like being in a trench, as it were. When I reached there I jumped, landed in the bottom of this, turned round and there was the bank, just about the right height of a trench parapet really.

'Now I've got to get the others to come over. Of course I was particularly worried about Jack Cod. I felt he'd been pitch-forked into this experience. I hadn't helped him with what I'd done and I felt as though I was responsible for him. I was terribly worried then.'

Arnold then heard the sound of fallen branches snapping in the copse.

'I thought, *Jesus, Jerry's in here as well.* I turned and two of them came towards me with their hands up. I thought, *That's just what I need, fucking prisoners.* I saw they'd thrown their weapons away, so I just signalled to them to stand to one side and wait there. Well, I then shouted across to Jack and I said, "Come on, Jack, make a dash for it!" Well, he was very reluctant to do it and I kept shouting and shouting. The distance was not much more than 150 to 200 yards, I suppose.

'Finally Jack decided to try it and I was horrified to see the bullets licking up. It was dry soil. As he was running towards me (I saw) all the spurts of dust. *Christ*, I thought. *Will he make it, will he make it?* As he was right over me I said, "Jump!" You never saw an expression on anyone's face as there was on Jack's when he saw these two Germans. I imagine he thought that they had taken me prisoner and I'd encouraged him to run in to be taken as a prisoner.

I said, "Don't worry about them, Jack. They're more shaken than we are."

'Then I called out to tell the others to make a dash for it, but there was no movement from there. They were laying in brushwood and so on and the glider was a wreck in the middle of the pile. I couldn't really see anyone.'

Suddenly a Canadian paratrooper appeared, having walked up a track at the edge of the copse.

'He was just standing out there and I thought he must be within range, but no one seemed to take a poke at him. He saw those two Germans and he said to me, "You're not taking those bastards prisoner, are you?", so I said, "What else am I going to do?" and he said, "Shoot the bastards," and I said, "I'm not shooting prisoners." He said, "They killed my mate."

'I said to him, "If you feel that you want to shoot them, I can't stop you shooting them, but no way am I going to shoot them. I don't believe in shooting prisoners."

'Well, he was really bluffing because he didn't shoot them. He said that a lot of his mates had been caught up in the trees, and they'd been dangling there, quite helpless, when the nearest Germans to them had just opened up on them and shot them. And he was so embittered about this that he wanted revenge, but he seemed to want me to exact that revenge and not do it himself.'

When it became clear that no one was prepared to shoot the prisoners, the Canadian directed Arnold to a nearby house, saying, '"There's quite a few of my mates there, there's quite a mixture, there's a few Poles I believe. There's a church nearby and they're using that as a first aid place." So I said, "Okay, well, come on, Jack, we'll take these two mugs with us and we'll go down there." We scrambled up out of this ditch and marched these two 'round.'

Arnold found the Canadians and handed over his prisoners, who were added to those being held within the high fence of a tennis court beside a house. Then there was a happy reunion.

'I found two mates of mine from B Squadron – Tommy Geary and Arthur Shakleton. They'd obviously landed some distance off the LZ as well as myself.

'I think they got their RAF seconded pilots with them, same as I had mine, so we were a group of six. The Canadians had commandeered this house in the first place and we were left to have the basement. There was no lighting in the basement. Certain amount of bedding had been pulled off beds upstairs and slung down on the basement floor. How many were finally in the basement, I don't know. For the rest of the day, we were up and about. One or two German civilians came by, middle-aged people or elderly.

'I was walking round this house, just surveying it. You knew where Canadians were because you just followed the trail of chicken feathers. They were very quick to grab chickens wherever they went and they were in the cook pot before you could say "Jack Robinson". I went round the back of the house and it was quite a fine, warm sunny day and the window was open. The ground-floor window was fairly high, and I saw an alarm clock on it. Well, my father-in-law, who was working in a shipyard in Poole, his alarm clock had conked out and you couldn't buy an alarm clock in England at that time for love nor money. He was always in trouble because he had to get to work and he had no means of rousing himself. I suddenly saw this one on the sill. I thought, *I'll have that.*'

Taking it came with a risk – looting Germans was one thing, but stealing from Canadians was another.

'I know what it was used for – the Canadians had put it on (the) sill and they were setting the alarm for their guard duties. (I) thought, *Well, my need is greater than theirs, or at least the father-in-law's is.* So I crept very cautiously past the window, lifted this clock off the sill and I was wearing what we used to call jumping jackets. They had large pockets, camouflage tunics, so I shoved this clock in one of the pockets, and fortunately for my life I wasn't seen by the Canadians because I'm sure they would just have soon killed me as not.'

Arnold then returned to the basement and carefully picked his way over the sleeping men.

'I tried to find a vacant place where I could bed down, or lie down rather, and all of a sudden this buzzing noise started and several shouted out, "It's booby-trapped, it's booby-trapped!" and there was a real panic in the dark.

'I realized that this buzz was coming from my pocket – it was this alarm clock that was going. So I said, "Settle down, settle down, it's alright, it's me, I've got something in my pocket that's making that noise."'

Arnold survived the battle, and seemingly the wrath of the Canadian soldiers.

Leonard MacDonald, RAF, had lived through his own descent and landing, but forgot a key piece of advice given to him by the experienced Glider Pilot Regiment crews: get down into cover when you get out.

'I was admiring the view and then – *BRRRR* – a Spandau shot past me. Penketh was immediately behind me and said, "GET DOWN BEHIND THE WHEEL," and I did.

'I had a .303 rifle. The RAF taught us how to fire, that was no problem. I also had a Smith and Wesson .38 revolver. Penketh had a Bren gun. He was a crack man with that.'

US Airborne troops had become intermingled with the British, and Leonard watched as they put in an attack on an enemy-held farm.

'They formed a ring and they charged this house. They were mown down like ninepence. There was a (British) officer there, I don't know what unit he was, but he wasn't taking charge.'

Leonard suggested that the infantry fire a PIAT round into the roof of the farmhouse to set it alight. The idea worked and the Germans came out with their hands up.

'We had more than a dozen prisoners that we didn't really want.'

The infantry then dug in around the position, and the pilots with them.

'Later that night there was a platoon of (enemy) troops trying to get back to German lines. I was out the back of this farmhouse in a slit trench. They fired at the front of the house. It whipped past my ear. I got up, crept round, more firing went on, and there was such a lot of talk going on, German and English.'

Leonard didn't know whether he should try to take the men

prisoner or surrender himself, but the experienced Staff-Sergeant Penketh acted without hesitation and 'got amongst' the enemy with his Bren gun.

'I think there was several killed and others wounded,' said Leonard. 'They surrendered. It was near the end of the war and I don't think they had the heart for it.'

Leonard, with no infantry training, then took part in the vicious fighting at Hamminkeln. After the 6th Airlanding Brigade were relieved on the evening of the 25th, many of the glider pilots marched back to the rear, but Leonard and Penketh caught a ride in a truck. Given Penketh's character and obvious charisma, it is easy to believe that he had something to do with this more luxurious form of exfiltration.

The glider pilots were later flown back to England, Arnold Baldwin returning home to his wife and their baby son he had never met, and with a prized alarm clock to boot.

'You could say that for me the war ended on a happy note.'

Arnold had come through D-Day, Arnhem and the Rhine crossing, beating the odds that thousands of others did not, and he would see no further action – Operation Varsity was the last major Airborne operation of the war and, as ever, it had come with a heavy cost. Twenty per cent of the glider pilots who took part in Varsity became casualties, and many of their passengers died with them. For the men of 2 Ox and Bucks, who had famously seized Pegasus Bridge on D-Day, their battle on the Rhine was nothing less than 'mass murder'.

CHAPTER 16

Mass Murder

2 Ox and Bucks during Operation Varsity
24–25 March 1945

'The ack-ack was terrific. All you could see was shells bursting through that, and then the gliders cast off, and all you could see was Dakotas coming down in flames, gliders coming down in flames. It was absolute chaos. Where we landed was all covered in smoke, the pilots couldn't see where they were landing. Gliders were piling on top of each other. They were going into the sides of houses. It was absolute murder. It was terrible.'

William 'Billy' Gray, D Company, 2nd Oxfordshire and Buckinghamshire Light Infantry

Lewisham-born Wally Parr was one of a handful of men who could claim to be first into Normandy on D-Day. Led into that battle by Major John Howard, D Company, 2 Ox and Bucks, had seized Pegasus Bridge in one of the British Army's most daring missions. Many more actions had followed, and many men were lost and wounded, but within D Company remained a core of veterans who could say with pride that, 'I was there, at Pegasus Bridge.' Tragically, a number of these 'originals' would be killed just six weeks before Germany's surrender, falling in the battalion's bloodiest day of the war: 24 March, 1945.

Now twenty-two years old, and a corporal in command of a section, Wally Parr had his reservations about the mission from the outset.

'We were introduced to our two glider pilots at the aerodrome and we just looked at them. The old man out of the two was nineteen years of age and his copilot was eighteen, in brand-new army uniforms, but (with) RAF insignia – they did not instil us with confidence.'

While the Parachute brigades dropped to their west, the 6th Airlanding Brigade, carried in 196 Horsa gliders, were to put down in the south-eastern corner of the division's assault. The 1st Royal Ulster Rifles would land on Landing Zone U to seize a bridge over the Issel and anchor the south-eastern corner of the brigade, while the 12th Devonshires would land on Landing Zone R to take and hold Hamminkeln. The 2nd Battalion, Oxfordshire and Buckinghamshire Light Infantry, would attack out of Landing Zone O. They were to seize the bridge over the Issel opposite Ringenberg, as well as holding the railway station and sidings to the east of Hamminkeln.

Wally Parr recalled that the Ox and Bucks also received a more 'informal' but persuasive order before they left England.

'The German (Airborne) helmet and the British Airborne helmet are very much the same shape, and sometimes you have to look twice before you know exactly what to shoot. So one of the Para battalions sent out a message: "To whom it may concern: when we land we're throwing our helmets away and we're putting on our red berets and we're going to shoot anyone wearing a helmet." We all got the message so we all had our red berets tucked in our smocks.'

Lieutenant Richard 'Sandy' Smith had been awarded a Military Cross for his actions at Pegasus Bridge, and later had to be evacuated from Normandy for wounds. He was, therefore, under no illusions about what it meant to go into battle by glider.

'I'll never forget that day, 24 March '45. I was in a headquarter glider, which carried a great deal of equipment and a few men. We consisted of myself as the officer in charge, two flight sergeants from the RAF, as glider pilots, a medical sergeant, a signals sergeant and about three or four signal men at the back of the glider. Between the front of the glider, where we officers and sergeants were, was a jeep and a trailer filled with 3-inch mortar ammunition, a motorcycle strapped to the bonnet of the jeep and a lot of signal equipment and medical stores. The three or four signallers at the back made up the whole total.

'Our purpose was to attack the gun emplacements about eleven miles the other side of the Rhine to prevent them from shelling the Rhine crossing. We had been promised by the RAF that we would not have much flak because they would neutralize it beforehand, but unfortunately that would prove to be a fallacy.'

At 0615 hrs, the battalion took to the air.

'It was a lovely morning,' recalled Sandy. 'We had a perfect run-up to the Rhine itself.'

'We took off in our usual fashion,' said Wally Parr, 'singing and laughing, but it was very comforting to see all these fighters about. We also understood that we were going to be joined over (Belgium) in the air by General Ridgeway's 17th Airborne Division. Ridgeway was in charge of the operation.

'All you could see, every time you looked out a hole, were gliders and Paras' planes. The Paras, as usual, had the doors open with their legs hanging out, and (were) waving.'

William 'Billy' Gray was a close friend of Wally's, and saw war for the first time as a London milkman during the Blitz. Billy had since turned in his bottles for a Bren gun and was the second man to rush Pegasus Bridge. By the time of Operation Varsity, he and the other veterans of D Company had learned a lot about war.

'There was a far different atmosphere from D-Day. After we'd sampled a bit of action, we weren't too keen to go in again like we were originally.'

D Company, now led by Major Tony Dyball, had received many reinforcements since Pegasus Bridge.

'Most of our platoon were new fellas,' said Billy. 'They'd never been in action.'

Henry 'Harry' Clark served in No. 25 Platoon along with Wally and Billy, and had fought beside them since Pegasus Bridge.

'The reinforcements appeared to be quite happy, but all the older hands were a bit apprehensive – they'd done it before and they didn't fancy it somehow. There was a sense of foreboding amongst us that something was in the wind. We guessed right, because shortly after that, we heard the glider pilot shout, "I can't see the landing field, it's obscured by smoke."'

As well as the British smoke screen on the west side of the Rhine, which was intended to give cover to the flanks of the amphibious landings, pilots had to contend with the effects of battle. The ruins of Wesel were smoking from its bombing the previous night. Shelling and fighter-bomber attacks also churned up dust and set off hundreds of smaller blazes, much of this Allied fire targeting the enemy's 800 anti-aircraft guns in the area. Those crews that survived now trained their sites on the Airborne armada.

'We met the most incredible flak from 20mm and 88mm guns,' remembered Sandy Smith. 'The actual effect of the RAF (attacks) on the gun emplacements seemed to me very, very mild. I saw several gliders being released prematurely because their tug aircraft had been hit by flak. What happened to them is difficult to say because of the heavy smoke which was on the ground as a result of Monty's smoke screen.

'When we eventually came near to the landing zone, the front of the aircraft was hit by a shell, and the first pilot was wounded in the shoulder, and then the rear of the aircraft was struck, and I heard one or two of the signallers screaming. Much more ominous was the fact that the jeep started to catch fire – it was smouldering. We had full petrol tanks on board, and the three-inch mortar ammunition in the trailer behind. I myself was nearly struck by flak because I felt a loud explosion and tug on my side, with wetness trickling down my side, and I thought that I'd been hit.'

In fact, it was not blood, but water – Sandy's bottle had been ripped off his hip by shrapnel.

'The second pilot turned round to me, I was standing behind him, and he said, "I think we should put this thing down very quickly, sir." The officer has to give the order to land because you don't want to land somewhere unpleasant and you really should know where you are. I told him to get down and we came down in a long field, and I think the pilot did a wonderful job, because compared to the Normandy landing, which was a very violent one, we had a smooth landing and bumped along the field. The only problem being that by this time the glider was well on fire and there was smoke inside the aircraft, inside the glider, and also that we were being shot at by small-arms fire as we came in. I distinctly remember hearing the bullets ping off the bonnet of the jeep.'

The glider set down 'in a field with four German gun emplacements, with 20mm flak guns, all of whom were firing at us and other gliders.'

Alfred 'Alf' Whitbread was a member of 27 Platoon, B Company who had been attached to Major Howard's force for the D-Day assault on Pegasus and Horsa Bridges. Shortly before take-off for the Rhine, and owing to a mix-up, Alf and two other men had been told to change aircraft. They said goodbye to their mates in the platoon, planning to reunite with them on enemy soil.

Now over Germany, Alf and his two comrades were the sole passengers in a glider sent spinning by a massive blast of flak.

'I can remember it touching the ground, terrific crash, then it broke in half. Back end broke off and it was thrown quite a way. It was only us three (in the back). We went one way. The other part of the glider just sailed on and crashed into a building and stopped. (The) crew were killed.

'I think I was unconscious for a while. I can't remember much except these German people, civilians, patting my face, touching me. I think the first I said was, "Am I alright?" I felt my legs.

'That day we had our crash helmets on, normally we didn't wear them, we wore the red beret. I think there was an instruction come that we've got to wear the crash helmets in flight. I was picked up and taken back by our medics.

'We were taken back to the landing zone where all the gliders had landed. They had a field station there. There was some terrible sights but we were lucky.'

When Alf later went in search of his platoon, with whom he was originally intended to fly, he was told that their glider had crashed, with no survivors.

These were Alf's best friends and comrades, many of them brothers in arms who he had known for years. They had relied upon each other. Fought with each other. Laughed with each other. And now they were gone, victims of a massacre in the air.

For those that survived the landings, the battle raged on.

On the ground

Wally Parr had harboured doubts about the young RAF pilots at the helm of this aircraft. 'Those two fellas, they flew that glider straight down, straight across a field, over another hedge, over another field and stopped it sixty yards short of a wood. It wasn't a very good landing but it was the best they could do.'

Harry Clark, who was in the same platoon as Wally, and quite possibly the same aircraft, named his pilots as Sergeants Stan Jarvis and Peter Geddes, and praised their efforts.

'I think we lost one and a half wings on the way down. (The pilot) went down into dense smoke. We just couldn't see the ground at all, we were looking out the little portholes. Suddenly we hit the ground with a terrific whack. We bounced, the wheels came off, (and) we skidded along on the skid.'

Shortly after the landing, one of the soldiers called to Stan Jarvis over the gunfire. 'I know that before you left the airfield we asked you to get as close as possible to the railway station, but if you had landed any closer we would have been in the ruddy booking office.'[1]

'We rapidly got out of the glider,' said Harry Clark, 'pulled the hand cart out with all the extra gear and ammunition in, and just as we got out, a German tank tore by, followed by a German motorcyclist. We don't know who was most scared, him or us. We immediately took up a position of defence around the glider and watched the appalling carnage that ensued. There were gliders crashing into trees, buildings, plunging into the earth. It's a sight I will not forget as long as I live. I took a vow there and then along with the others that never again would we travel by glider. It was mass murder.'

Harry also recalled seeing the bodies of American paratroopers, who had been dropped in the wrong position, mixed in with the British.

'The many dead, injured and seriously wounded in and around

the gliders were a horrific sight. At the front of one burning aircraft was its glider pilot, still wearing his headphones, arms outstretched and forming the shape of a crucifix in the flames. Fifty-three years later that still haunts me.'[2]

Wally Parr and his section ripped off their helmets and replaced them with their red berets.

'The railway sidings were on our left. I said, "GO!" There's a hedgerow over there, that's what you wanted. We went for it, we ran like hell across this field – there was machine-gun fire coming from all directions, you couldn't tell exactly where it was coming from.

'We got in the hedge and threw ourselves down, turned round and looked for Lieutenant Shaw and the rest of the platoon. He'd taken the least line of resistance, he went straight into the woods in front of him and that's the last I saw of him for the best part of that day.

'I was alone with the section. As we lay there taking stock and me weighing up the situation, we watched a glider come in behind us. It hit the ground and started to bounce across the ground. To our left was a very large building of three or four stories, and we could see the glider going like mad towards it.'

Wally's section watched in horror as the glider ploughed straight into the building, which collapsed on top of it. Muffled explosions came from within the rubble. No man came out.

'Some days later I spoke to Sergeant Rayner out of D Company,' said Wally. Rayner was one of those who uncovered the stricken glider. 'He said it's the worst experience he'd had. It was 22 Platoon – thirty bodies all mangled up. Not one of them survived.'

Lieutenant Richard 'Sandy' Smith's own glider was badly shot up and burning when they landed.

'The medical sergeant's duty was to do the opening of the door, but he obviously had had enough at this time and he was lying on the floor of the glider with his head in his arms. It was obviously no place to stay, so I got up and hauled the door up and to my relief found an (empty) German slit trench about five yards away. I dived into that, hotly followed by the signals sergeant. By the time I realized where we were, the two pilots had scrambled out on the other side of the glider and had run into a farmhouse, ten yards from them. Our nose of the glider was up against a road, which was a road and rail junction with a signal box. Behind us was the German gun emplacements, and some of the Germans were firing small-arms fire at us.

'The medical sergeant also escaped on the other side of the glider. Went into the farmhouse with the glider pilots. Unfortunately the signallers in the back were trapped and they were burned to death. We could hear them screaming but there was nothing we could do.

'The glider was blazing furiously and the ammunition inside was exploding, so it was extremely dangerous to put your head above ground. At this juncture, a German tank, preceded by two or three motorcyclists, came screaming down the road in an effort to get away from the landing zone. There was a German officer standing up in the cupola and he saw the glider blazing a matter of a few yards from him. He came to a halt, his motorcyclists dived into the ditch and then, to my astonishment, he gave an order, which I could hear quite distinctly, and the gun of the tank swung round and fired what looked to me like solid shot, straight into the nose of the glider, which was by this time almost disintegrated with the fire. He then saw me and the signals sergeant.

'I remember having a faint desire to surrender and I put my right hand up, which had a revolver, and waved it at him, and he shouted an order down and the tank's gun swung round, obviously going to shoot at us. So I shouted to the sergeant and we both got down to the bottom of the trench and the gun of the tank couldn't depress itself low enough to shoot at us, it was too near, and the shot went over the slit trench and landed on the ground behind us. The blast was tremendous. I then looked up to find that the German officer had shouted another order, looked at me, waved his hand and drove off with his motorcyclists in an endeavour to get away from the landing zone. By this time I'd had enough, so I shouted to the signals sergeant to get out of the trench and run round to the farmhouse, which we did.

'How many times we were fired at I just don't know, but we must have broken all records for the sprint. We charged into the courtyard of the farmhouse only to be confronted by a solitary German paratrooper – the 1st Parachute Division was defending that area – and we bumped into him. I remember feeling absolutely no fear at that time. The poor fellow was unarmed and we got him on the ground. The sergeant said, "Get off him, sir, get off him, sir!" and fired his Sten gun into the German.

'He must have been seeing his girlfriend, because he was unarmed. At that time, the girlfriend appeared from an underground shelter in the courtyard, saw her boyfriend dead on the floor and went absolutely berserk, charged at us, and we had considerable difficulty in bundling her down into the same underground shelter, where we locked her in. We then thought that it was time to find out whether there was anybody in the farmhouse, because although I'd seen glider pilots disappearing that way, I wasn't sure that they were in there, so we searched the farmhouse first for Germans and then for pilots, and found nothing, until we came to a trap door in the kitchen.

'I lifted the trap door up, and there was some stairs going into a darkened cellar. I proceeded down these stairs to find the two glider pilots lying behind some bags of potatoes, with their Sten guns over the top of the bags. One of them said that he would have shot had he not recognized my gaiters. We then found some champagne in the cellar and we drank some of that, which made us all feel much better.

'Then I went up into the courtyard again to try and find out really where we were. Fortunately, we were on a road and railway crossing. I knew that if we followed the railway south it would lead us to the railway station at Hamminkeln, which was our headquarters RV. I then went out onto the road and there met Huw Wheldon, of television fame, who was commanding a company of the Ulster Rifles, and a party of Devons. I managed to get them into the farm to hold him as it struck me as being one of the key points.

'With the signals sergeant I proceeded down the railway track to Hamminkeln railway station, and it wasn't too far away, a matter of about half a mile. I was there met by Mark Darrell-Brown, our commanding officer, who was moving with surprising agility, being chased by a 20mm gun, which was spattering the walls of the railway station just behind him. It was rather like a Wild West scene.'

Wally Parr and his section had moved off the landing zone and were digging in on the railyard among the carriages. They were under rifle and machine-gun fire from several positions, and Wally ordered Billy Gray to get into a carriage and suppress the enemy with his Bren.

'Billy jumped up into the truck above me, (and) his number two started manning the gun. Billy jumped down and crouched in front of me (and said), "You're never going to believe this. Look what we've got."

'"WHAT'S THE MATTER WITH YOU? GET OUT THERE!"

'And he said, "No, have a look." I had a look and (the truck) was full of aerial bombs, shells and crates of ammunition. The whole lot was an ammunition train.'

The section were digging in next to enough explosive to make them all vanish in a flash – a bad place to be in a gunfight. They scrambled out the other side of the carriage. 'I could see maybe 250 yards, maybe 300 yards,' said Wally, 'but I could see a road, hedgerows. I said, "Right, we go that way. Spread out."'

'Don't forget at this time we were wearing red berets. We must have been sticking out like bloody poppies. I think we made it about fifty yards when over on our right there was a shout of "Help! Help!"

'This fella come round and he had no uniform, no equipment, no helmet, and he's got both hands up. He said, "Help me, I'm an American citizen." So I said, "Cover him." We knelt down and he came galloping up and he said, "Oh my God, 6th Airborne Division" in a bloody Yankee voice and I said, "Yeah, that's right, you're way off, you're about three miles off course! Your outfit's over there, three or four miles away!" Billy Gray, he started to laugh.'

The American addressed Wally: "I'm a war correspondent. I'm in a Dakota up there, I'm reporting this battle. I came over with American paras, I'm recording the battle from the air."

'He's just doing his recording, there's a terrible bang and the pilot says bail out, and he bailed out with a notebook and pen and that was it. He landed right among us.'

The reporter then told Wally to take him to his commanding officer.

'I said, "Yeah, that's a good idea, mate, where is he?" He said, "Don't you know?" And I said, "No, I don't damn well know." "Take me to your company commander," (he said.) I said, "Look, mate, I don't even know where my bleeding platoon commander is! Can't you see what's going on here?" He said, "Oh my God!" Now if that bloke said "oh my God" once, he said it fifty times in the next three quarters of an hour.'

'(He) hadn't really expected it to be quite like it was,' Billy said of the reporter. 'He said to us, "Has anyone got a weapon you could lend us?" I had a German pistol from Normandy. I said, "Here, you can have that, but you'll let me have it back."'

Wally remembered the moment a little differently.

'I said, "Look, mate, stay with us, we'll do what we can for you, alright?" I said, "Billy, you've got a spare." We always carried a couple of spares. I wasn't going to give him mine – a spare revolver. Billy gave me a Luger that he picked up in Normandy, it was his favourite Luger. I turned to the Yank and said, "Here, cop a hold of this. Do you know how to use it?"

'He said, "I can't use this!" And I said, "No, you'll soon learn." And he said, "I'm a civilian. If they catch me with this, they're gonna shoot me." And I said, "Look, mate, they're gonna fucking shoot you anyway! So you might just as well have a go with it!"'

Wally then told his men to spread out and follow him – the reporter following hot on their heels.

'As we dashed the next 250 yards to this hedge, I've never seen a bloke look in so many different directions at the same time. His head was on a bleeding swivel.'

Wally had already picked his spot, where a large tree offered some cover. He spread the rest of the men along the ditch. Just before he left to take up a firing position, the telescopic sight already fitted on his rifle, the reporter came to life.

'I said, "What is it? What do you want now, for Christ's sake?" And he said, "My God, what a story I'm gonna be able to tell when I get back!" Billy Gray was getting his Bren gun up, and he turned around and he said, "Oi, mate, don't you mean *if* you get back?" And he said, "*Oh my God!*"

Now in the ditch, Wally's section continued to exchange fire with the enemy. This went on for 'about ten minutes solid' before Wally realized that something was missing.

'All of a sudden the Bren gunner got quiet. I suppose I was forty yards up the road so I shouted "BILLY! BIL-LY!"'

There was no answer.

'I thought, *Oh, Jesus Christ, no. Not Billy*. I got out of the ditch, doubled over with my rifle, trotted down.

The Bren gun was on top of the bank. Billy Gray was propped on one arm in the ditch with his number two, and there was this bleeding war correspondent, and Billy was saying, "And my mum and dad live at number so and so . . . and my girlfriend's name is so and so . . . and I'm going to get married . . ."

'I just looked: "I DON'T FUCKING BELIEVE THIS. WHAT THE HELL DO YOU THINK YOU'RE DOING?"

'He said, "Corps!" Now, Billy called me Wally on parade, but if he ever had a threatening attitude he called me 'Corps'. He said "I'm being interviewed!"

'I said, "I don't give a bugger what you're doing, get up (there)!"'

A few more minutes passed, then Wally began to hear more snippets of conversation. He ran over to find the reporter trying to interview another one of his men, and pre-empted the American with his own answers: '"Yeah, I'm married, I've got a wife and two kids, alright?"'

'I said, "Now, look, I don't want another bleeding word out of you, mate! I don't believe you!"'

If the reporter was upset, he didn't show it. Instead, he handed Wally a contact card and asked him to keep in touch after the war.

'Just then, coming up the road was about six blokes from the other platoon. By this time, (the Germans had) quieted down. I think they'd had enough.'

The six men, carrying a wounded comrade on a stretcher, asked Wally for directions to Regimental Headquarters and the aid post, which were located in Hamminkeln's train station.

'"You couldn't do me a favour, could you?"' Wally asked after telling them where to go. '"Take this bleeding Yank with you?"'

'I said, "Off you go, Yank. I'll see you about." That's the last I saw of the man.'

Wally then called Billy over to him. 'I said, "Right, let's try and find Company HQ." Billy said, "Where's the Yank?" and I said, "He's gone."

'"*Where's my Luger?*"

'I said, "He took it with him."

'"*The thieving bastard! I'll find him! That's my Luger!*"'

'He never did find him,' said Wally, who then led his section back to headquarters at the train station.

'There was burning gliders still going on. There was wounded everywhere. I won't go into the full details of that particular day, but it was the second longest day of my life.'

The Second Longest Day

Already depleted from their landings and initial battle, the Ox and Bucks now prepared to fight off counter-attacks.

'We had various objectives to hold,' explained Lieutenant Sandy Smith, 'such as a bridge opposite Ringenberg and at one or two strategic points along the railway line.'

The important bridge was a little over 400 yards north-east of Hamminkeln's train station, which housed the battalion's HQ.

'What was left of the regiment was placed in defensive positions.'

The battalion's war diary noted the companies' strengths at 2030 hrs that day – not one was above sixty men.

'We took stock of our casualties and we found that almost a third of the platoon had gone,' said Harry Clark. 'The platoon finally established itself in a house close to the position where the rail bridge which crossed the River Issel, which in itself was only a tiny fordable stream, but it was a deep anti-tank ditch. We took up a position of defence in the house, facing across to the town of Ringenberg.

'We were attacked on a number of occasions from the direction of Ringenberg and on every occasion we were able to call in rocket-firing Typhoon aircraft. In each case, they came over and broke up the attack almost immediately. These attacks continued throughout the day on the 24th.'

Billy Gray took up position in the attic of what he believed was a signals box.

'(We) knocked out a few tiles, and we put a table in the middle of the attic (to stand on), and had this terrific field of fire across this field and across an unfinished autobahn, which was right in front of us. Jerry came across at us from there, but we just couldn't miss. It was like being at a fair – you couldn't miss them. Hundreds of them. I got an idea that it was the German Home Guard because they were coming at us like in the First World War, with their weapons at the high port.

'They were doing fire and movement, but we had such a field of fire and stable platform for the Brens that anything you aimed at, you hit. There was a wall, it was about 300 yards from us, and there was a big gap in the wall, and Jerry sections were trying to get from one side to the other, and we were trying to anticipate when they were going to start running, so we would fire just before they started running and they would run right into it.

'Next thing, a Royal Artillery spotting officer came to us, and funny enough he had a sailor with him in battle dress and a sailor's hat with a radio set. This officer just said, "Having trouble, lads?" and we said, "Yeah, look at that lot out there.' He said, "Ah well, we'll see what we can do with them," and he just read a few numbers into the microphone and the next minute, the field just vanished, no sighting shots, nothing, just vanished in black smoke. I understand they were 55s firing from the other side of the Rhine. I never seen shooting like it – fantastic.

'It was like that all day. My mate Chalky White, who had saved my life in Normandy, he got killed there on the autobahn.'

Harry Clark recalled the moment that he learned of their comrade's death.

'Corporal Bill Bailey, a Normandy veteran, came over to tell me that an enemy sniper had just killed Denny White, one of my best mates. I was then told that another of my close friends, Don Fogarty, had been killed in one of the other Horsas that had crashed.'[3]

Twenty-one-year-old Dennis White and twenty-five-year-old Denis Fogarty both hailed from Dagenham.[4]

'Both were long-standing mates of mine,'[5] said Harry.

'By the evening, the Germans had recovered from the shock of the landing and they started to become aggressive,' said Lieutenant Richard 'Sandy' Smith. 'They must have realized that we were weak.

'(Colonel) Mark Darrell-Brown had sent me up to C Company, which was holding the bridge, and I had no idea when I arrived there that the Germans were literally across the very small canal. When I came up to Gilbert Rard, I said to him, "How's everything, Gilbert?" and he put his hands to his mouth and said, "Shhhh", and then I realized I could hear the German tank equipment, wireless equipment. They were just literally the other side. Hugh Clarke, one of the subalterns, was firing a PIAT at what we found out later to be Panther tanks. The PIAT didn't have much effect on the tanks but it stopped them coming over the bridge. He fired about six shots at this tank in the dark and that persuaded them not to charge us.'

Lieutenant Hugh Clarke was awarded a Military Cross for his actions that night, and was credited with scoring five hits on the tanks that were less than fifty yards from his position.[6]

'Nevertheless, during the night, further activity was heard and more tanks were heard to be marshalling up towards the bridge. Gilbert asked Mark permission to blow the bridge, which we did, much to the annoyance of the divisional commander.'

The bridge was blown at 2230 hrs on the 24th, which may explain what happened to Wally Parr.

'At half past ten that night I had a patrol out on the left, and the Germans started moving tanks. You only move tanks at night if you're desperate. I left the section there. I couldn't find anybody else. I went right. Looming out of the darkness was Bill Bailey.

'(I said), "I'm glad somebody else is here, where are you?"

'"I've got a section on the right."

'I said, "Well, who else is here?"

"'Nobody. They must have dropped back."

'Just then there was the most gorgeous explosion behind me and I flew forward into Bailey's arms. He caught me and he looked at me, and it was the fatal words – I've used them meself: "Are you alright, mate?"

'I said, "No, I ain't. Both legs."'

Wally was taken by Bill Bailey to a building that had been used as the Company Headquarters before they'd pulled back.

'He dragged me in there. There was a fella named Cook who was a medical orderly cum radio man, there were two wounded Germans, one bloke who had been blinded, and two other blokes laying on stretchers – whether they were alive or dead I don't know. But there was also smoke coming from everywhere. Bailey disappeared. I said (to Cook), "Open that door over there, it's coming through the ceiling."

'It was a barn full of hay, and it was burning. The whole bloody place was on fire. I got hold of Cook and said, "Get them on the radio!" He started the usual performance: "Able, Baker . . ."

'I said, "Sod the able baker! Give us it!"'

Wally snatched the radio handset and somewhat dispensed with the correct voice procedure.

"Get your arses back here and get us out of here! There's six wounded in here and we've got to get out – it's burning!"

'Five minutes later the door burst open and Billy Gray came in. A couple of them tried to take me back to the RAP. They picked me up in a stretcher, got so far across a ploughed field. I said, "Put me down." I staggered about 300, 400 yards. I used my rifle as a sort of crutch and I found the RAP. The MO was sat down and he had a Kerosene lamp on and was reading a book. There was a couple of bodies laying over there covered with blankets.

'He said, "Corporal Parr again? Where is it?"

'"Both legs."

'"You've just missed the ambulance."

'I said, "Sir, there's tanks coming."

'He said, "Yes, I've heard them."

'"Don't you think you ought to get out of here?"

'"No, I'll have some more customers later on. I suggest you take a walk down. On you go, there's a good chap." He never looked at my legs or anything, he just carried on reading the book, not a worry in the bloody world.'

Wally 'hobbled down the road' until he came to the building that was now being used as a battlefield surgery. It made for a grim sight, and smell.

'There were three tables with surgeons with butchers' aprons on working away. There was blokes lying and moaning and blokes propped up.'

Since the doctors were busy with more serious cases, Wally was told to make himself useful and brew some tea.

'That's how I spent the night – giving out cups of tea and fags.'

He and the other men were then collected by ambulance, but they were not out of trouble.

'Our ambulance lost its way and ran into a German patrol. They fired at us, red crosses and all, so we came back and went another way. I eventually wound up in the 21st General Hospital in Bruges.'

Denis Edwards, who was himself injured and for a while presumed dead, served in the same platoon as Wally, and remembered him as 'a real London character. He was frequently reduced in rank from corporal to private when not in action, since he was always getting into scrapes of one kind or another. He was never cut out to be a "spit and polish" conformist, but excelled as a fighting soldier.'[7]

When Wally was injured in Normandy, he had said to his comrades, 'Don't worry, lads, I'll be back.'[8] He was true to his word again, and rejoined his company following his wounding at Hamminkeln, remaining with them until the end of the campaign.

The fighting around Landing Zone O continued into the 25th, more than twenty-four hours after the battalion had landed.

'There were a series of attacks but they were weakening most of the time,' said Harry Clark, who recalled that a major push at dawn, supported by tanks, was broken up by artillery and rocket-firing aircraft.

'I saw the enemy force virtually annihilated as I watched. It was with some awe that I saw a lone enemy medic moving around his dead and wounded comrades. The courage and devotion to duty of this very brave man, under that hellish fire, held my attention for many minutes.'[9]

As the day wore on the enemy's attacks became weaker and eventually petered out. Just as it was getting dark, on the evening of the 25th, Billy Gray recalled hearing 'sort of strange voices behind'.

They belonged to the Jocks of the 52nd (Lowland) Division.

'They came up and it was just like on (Pegasus Bridge) with the 13th Para. They just patted us on the helmet – "Good lads." Professional attitude, they had. They gave the impression of confidence. Smashing load of blokes.'

One of those blokes was Cyril Butler, an eighteen-year-old replacement in the 6th Cameronians. The Rhine crossing was his first operation.

'It was raining (when) we got to this place called Hamminkeln. All the remains of war was there, all the Germans had gone, a lot of dead paratroopers laid about. It was a shock to the system. You don't mind seeing dead Germans, but to see dead English lads, it wasn't very good. You realized it was a war then. Before, it was a game. But like everything else you get used to it in time.'

D Company, 2 Ox and Bucks were pulled back into 'a big church hall' and rested there until the next morning. The soldiers had been in action for thirty-six hours and suffered appalling losses: over 50 per cent of the battalion had become casualties.

Harry Clark recalled that several men from No. 25 Platoon were killed, and others later died of wounds. Other injured soldiers survived, including the platoon's commander, Lieutenant Shaw, and its sergeant, 'Bob' Ollis, who had previously been injured in the landing of Glider Number 1 at Pegasus Bridge.

Sandy Smith reflected on the price of Operation Varsity, and its conduct.

'The regiment had lost 101 dead on the landing zone and 356 wounded, along with a lot of our ammunition, mortars and light anti-tank guns. Altogether we had a rather unpleasant twenty-four hours.

'I think that one of the lessons to be learned from an operation of this nature was that paratroopers should hold the ground to enable gliders to land without Germans being literally under their wings. Also, that the smokescreen to get across the Rhine was a tremendous handicap for any glider pilot trying to land in fields and woods with woods nearby. I think a lot of casualties were caused by bad planning of this type.'

The casualties that lived were evacuated. Those who had given their lives were now attended to.

Raymond Rayner, from Aylesbury, was a provost sergeant in the battalion. One of his duties was to supervise the burial of the dead, including three men from his hometown.

'I'll never tell people how I found them people. Their (parents), or wives. They was terrible. I would have rather been in the line than burying the dead, cause that was a horrible job. I used to have to take their identification disc off of them, and take their personnel effects off them, note it all down, and it give it to the padre to give to their next-of-kins.

'They sent me up with about eight blokes to dig the graves, but I sent them back. I relieved a labour camp, where there was Poles, all sorts in there. I asked them if they'd come and bury the dead for me if I fed them.

'They made a beautiful job of the graveyard. They put a cross up and everything. A wooden cross. Done it beautiful. All in line, the graves. I didn't do it. They done it. They made a marvellous job of it.'

A hundred and one men of 2 Ox and Bucks were buried in the German soil. Their average age was twenty-three.

Relief

As the assault divisions fought to establish and enlarge the bridgeheads across the Rhine, engineers toiled night and day to create the crossings that would enable the movement of an army, and the supply chain that followed it. As shells exploded around them, the sappers set to work soon after the first wave had crossed on the night of the 23rd, risking their lives to build a lifeline to those already on the other side. A Class 9 folding boat bridge, suitable for lighter vehicles but not armour, was opened around midnight on 25 March. Three Class 40 Bailey bridges, capable of bearing tanks, were constructed in the vicinity of Rees, at the northern end of the bridgehead. The first, 'London Bridge', began taking traffic at midnight on the 26th, followed by two more Class 40s – 'Blackfriars' opened on the 27th, then 'Westminster' on the 28th. Further bridge construction followed in the vicinity of Xanten. To the south, the American engineers were 'throwing up' their own bridges. As each construction was completed, troops flowed across the spans, coming also by small boat, raft, Buffalo, DUKW, and landing craft of the Royal Navy. Montgomery was building up his forces for a breakout, and this, of course, made the crossing points a high priority for the enemy's guns and aircraft.

Frank Brodie, 1st East Lancashires, was moving towards a bridge as it came under attack.

'I had this young recruit with me, driving. We were going down this field. It were downhill, and pontoon bridge were in front of us. There was tapes down each side of us (to mark the track), and every so far there was a pile of mines. Teller mines. Big ones.

'I'm watching these (German fighter aircraft) bombing and strafing over (the) bridge like, and I'm watching what's going on, and this lad, he's going down this track, and next thing I see this tape is being dragged up, and he's heading straight for this pile of mines! I grabbed the steering wheel and pulled him away.' Frank laughed.

'It were all this action what were going on like, you know? He (was) scared. You're heading for this damned pontoon bridge and these bloody things are diving at you.'

As the soldiers of the reserve divisions crossed the Rhine and pushed north and east, they came across the detritus of the battles fought to seize the bridgehead.

Alec Fieber, 1st Manchesters, remembered it as 'quite an unpleasant kind of experience'.

'I remember seeing a glider with the people who had been in it, the soldiers, lying in a circle. The glider had totally burned out, and it was quite horrific, because the flames had reached the crew and the Airborne soldiers and burned them halfway down their bodies. I remember the brass straps on their gaiters were still glittering, and their boots were polished, and yet the top half of them was no longer a man, if you get my meaning. Such little scenes as these, I find, stick so much in the memory.'

Nelson Taylor was a private serving in 1 HLI and saw what could happen if the dead were not treated with dignity.

'Some of the Airborne lads came along with about twelve prisoners.'

One of these prisoners, 'a big six-foot German', pointed to the red berets resting on the freshly dug graves of Airborne soldiers and snidely called them 'women's hats'.

'This one Airborne chap took the red beret off the cross and made this German carry it with his hands up. They took them to a building, disappeared in there. The Airborne chap came back with this German and made him put the beret back on the cross. He marched him some six foot away, and he shot him.'

In the few days of fighting, 16,000 Germans had been taken prisoner, and thousands more were killed and wounded. The Allied forces had suffered their own heavy casualties – some 4,000 British and Canadian, and almost 3,000 American. As many as 2,700 of these were sustained by the Airborne.

Mary Haddie Swan, Queen Alexandra's Imperial Military Nursing Service, was attached to No. 3 Casualty Clearing Station, 81st General Hospital.

'The Rhine crossing, I remember, was awful. We had masses of casualties in there. Masses of casualties. It was so busy, and I remember quite a lot of bigwigs came in to see what was happening. And I remember saying to them, "I haven't got time to talk to you."'

Mary was very fond of the men whose lives and limbs she sought to save.

'They were terribly good, and very, very grateful. They were extremely brave, and very funny. They were very funny about it usually.

'They were very keen to bring out their photographs and show you pictures of their wives, and their sweethearts, and tell you all about them. One of the first things they did was dive into their pocket and get out their photographs.'

The casualty clearing station often came under shellfire. This did not worry Mary. The suffering of her patients, on the other hand, was 'terribly upsetting'.

'I used to go down the whole line of stretchers with my watch, making a note of what time they'd died, and getting to the end of the ward and uncontrollably—' Mary cut herself off there, but one can imagine what she meant. To witness death and suffering was a possibility for every soldier. For medical staff like Mary, it was a guarantee.

Mary, who was awarded a Mention in Despatches for her work on the Rhine, was asked if she was ever scared during this time.

'We were never frightened,' she said firmly, 'because you can conquer fear. Fear is very easy to conquer. Probably at first I was frightened, but you can conquer fear, and you can face things. Don't you think?'

The proof of her statement was clear to see – frightened soldiers had conquered fear to cross the black water of the Rhine, and capture its towns street by street; frightened paratroopers had leapt into the sky, then fought their way out of their bloody drop zones; frightened sappers withstood storms of shells and diving fighters to construct their bridges. Tens of thousands of individuals had faced their fear, and conquered it, and by their actions the Battle of the Rhine was won. British forces now flowed inexorably across the mighty river, and just a few days after the opening shots of Plunder had been fired Montgomery had four of his corps across – more than 200,000 men, the majority of them motorized and armoured.

Now the breakout could begin, and the race to end the war.

PART 3

The Race to Victory

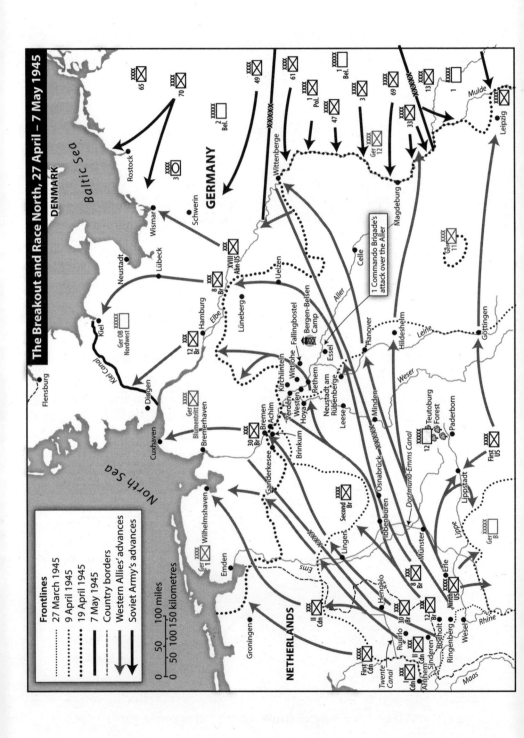

CHAPTER 17

The Mosaic of Victory

Clearing the Dutch/German border
27 March – 11 April 1945

A hundred yards from Yorkshire Bridge lie soldiers and civilians who died in the battle for Weeze.

These are not the proud white headstones of Commonwealth War Cemeteries, of which there are many in Germany. Rather they are the size of a book cover, and set into the ground. Wipe away the decaying leaves and you might be able to read a name on the weather-worn stone, and wonder at their story. Just as likely you will see the words, "*Unbekannter Soldat*".

Unknown Soldier.

There is no doubt that this cemetery was designed with great care. Three mighty stone crosses watch over the rows of war dead. An information board bears a black and white photograph of its consecration, and the crowd is large, and sorrowful. What's unsettled me is that while the grass has been cut, the names that should face the heavens have instead been left covered in leaves. As someone so used to Commonwealth War Graves, and the attentive care they receive, the oversight seems almost unconscionable. Right or wrong, I feel that those that lie here have been forgotten.

This sense grows as I travel from battleground to battleground across the country. Only at Hamminkeln do I find the kind of memorial that is so commonplace in Western Europe. And this stone and plaque, laid by comrades of the Ox and Bucks, seems grossly dwarfed by a bright white FedEx sign a few yards to its side. At Rethem, the only clue to the end of lives are the patched-up pockmarks on its disused train station. At Ibbenbüren, a few bunkers hidden by forest on a high ridge. And then, at Lüneburg Heath, where a surrender brought an end to the slaughter, the memorial stone is 400 yards from where the moment took place, and lying behind a few information boards are bags of fly-tipped waste.

It worries me. And not because I want this victory to be celebrated, but because I don't want another to ever be needed again. If those that forget history are doomed to repeat it, then we that forget war's cost are doomed to bear it.

Of course, there are many ways to remember. It is simply my opinion, right or wrong, that the dead of both sides are deserving of memorials in the places where they fell. To be taught something in a classroom is one thing. To know that people bled on your streets so that you could walk them without fear is another. And in Britain, we are also guilty of this same neglect when it comes to this period of the war, and it is not born of any ill intention. There are understandable reasons why the battles of April 1945 have never received the same attention as those in previous months and years, chief among them the fact that the war was won in May. Who wants to look back on painful days when bright futures lay ahead?

But only some of us get to make that choice. Others would always look back, because their sons, their husbands, their fathers, their brothers died within weeks of the war's end.

I met one of these people on Remembrance Day. He knew little about his older brother's death, other than the date. The soldier's end barely warranted a mention in the unit's war diary, because his death was not abnormal. I visited his grave, in Becklingen, where he is laid to rest with thousands of others. If April was 'the race across Germany', as it's often described, then the fuel of that race was blood.

Those that died in April could feel the promise of peace, but fell as they reached out to touch it.

Bocholt

Through February and March, the 21st Army Group had suffered 5,180 men killed, 21,170 wounded and 2,850 missing. All told, these losses are the equivalent of more than thirty-five infantry battalions.[1] A heavy toll had been paid to reach the Rhine, and cross it.

The 53rd (Welsh) Division came over the bridges on the 26th, spending a night among the smashed gliders of the 6th Airlanding Brigade before pushing through Ringenberg to capture Dingden. As part of XII Corps, their eventual destination was Hamburg.

After a night of 'heavy stonking', and supported by tanks of 7th Armoured Division, the weight of the entire 53rd Division was then launched against Bocholt. Two and a half miles from the Dutch border, the small town was an important communications centre protected by minefields and roadblocks, and had already been heavily shelled and bombed.

On 28 March, 2 Mons and 6 RWF made a direct assault on Bocholt while 158th Brigade – which included 1 East Lancs – made a left-flanking manoeuvre onto the town. At 1700 hrs, D Company of the East Lancs had established themselves on their objective, but A Company were held up by stiff opposition and SP guns firing from their left flank. Worse was to follow.

Bob Atkinson remembered the moment. 'There was another company coming through, and Company HQ was right behind us, and this shell come over, dropped right in the middle of them.'

It was a devastating moment for A Company. Sergeant Major Montgomery, who had won the Military Medal in the Ardennes, was killed outright.

'Montgomery had gone all the way from the landings (in Normandy),' said Bob. 'He was A Company Sergeant Major when I joined them. He was a regular. He was alright, was Monty. He was a good sergeant major.'

Major Joe Cêtre MC, the respected leader of A Company, was badly wounded in the leg. Bob and others carried him into a barn to escape the fire that continued to pour onto A Company. It was the end of Major Cêtre's war, but not his time in the army, and he would go on to serve in Malaya, Burma, Palestine, Egypt and elsewhere around the globe. He retired in 1967 with the rank of lieutenant-colonel, became a professor of English, and struggled with the wound he received at Bocholt for the rest of his life.[2]

Thomas 'Tommy' Neary served in D Company, and had missed the battalion's heavy action in the Reichswald having been wounded in the Ardennes. He rejoined the East Lancs at Goch, learning that many of his friends and comrades had been lost during his absence. More fell at Bocholt.

'We found out that A Company had been flattened,' said Tommy. 'Major Cêtre, CSM Montgomery, Dickie Lee, (Thomas) Oddie, and they were all killed bar Cêtre.'[3]

Tommy had been close friends with twenty-eight-year-old Richard 'Dickie' Lee. 'Grand lad, he were.'

D Company were up against it themselves, advancing at 2130 hrs to the village of Bielefeld, on the outskirts of Bocholt.

'One of the lads up front shouted, "Tanks!" We turned around, and we said to the Sherman behind us, "Tanks! Tanks!" They opened up, the Jerries. Three of (our) tanks went up in flames. The six-pounder anti-tank (gun was hit). Company jeep went up in flame. We were on the side of the road then, in t' ditch.'

Pinned down with wounded men beside them in the ditch, Tommy, carrying a radio, followed his lieutenant into a nearby farmhouse.

'We were up in t' loft so we could see the tanks, but the battery I had had run down. I went back across the fields, onto the main road to get a battery out of the jeep, but it were on fire, you know.'

Tommy was able to recover a battery and map from the flames and returned to the loft. The lieutenant gave him the map reference for the tanks, which Tommy passed on to the artillery. 'We got the guns to fire, and we shooted them.'

At this time, Sergeant Charles Hatton – who was acting as Company Sergeant Major – was in command of C Company while his Major was away with the leading platoon. On seeing the two tanks, he seized a PIAT and worked round the flank of the tanks, stalking them alone until his was able to sight the weapon. The citation of his Military Medal recorded that:

'At almost point-blank range, he destroyed a MkIV tank with his first shot. The tank was completely burnt out; four of the crew were killed inside and the fifth man who jumped out and tried to escape was shot dead by Sergeant Hatton whilst he was running away.'[4]

Sergeant Hatton then stalked the second tank, which withdrew before he could destroy it.

Regimental stretcher-bearer Private William Pickard, already known for his coolness and bravery, was also awarded the MM for running out over a hundred yards of open ground to recover a comrade, with bullets and shells striking the ground all around him.[5]

The East Lancs suffered forty-three casualties that day, eight of them killed.[6] The army may have been across the Rhine, and the writing on the wall, but the enemy fought doggedly on.

'Progress was made slowly,' said Sidney England, 3rd/4th County of London Yeomanry, whose tanks were supporting the 53rd Division as they pushed up from Bochalt, their objective to cross an unfinished autobahn and push north to seize the Dutch town of Winterswijk.

'On Friday 30 March, which was Good Friday, I was leading tank. Somewhere along one of the sideroads, or sidetracks, the wireless radio in the tank went all peculiar. I could receive, but we couldn't send out. I halted, and called the tank that was behind me to take the lead. Shortly afterwards, going along a track in the woods, the tank in front of me was hit, and I could see that the problem came from the right amongst some farm buildings.

'What turned out to be an SP gun in the farm building fired down the line behind me, which was mainly composed of troops of the Ox and Bucks Light Infantry riding in the Kangaroos. This SP just fired and it shot up nine Kangaroos behind me.'

The enemy armour had ambushed the British column just as it was reaching the autobahn.

'We lost quite a lot of people that day,' said Kenneth New, 1 Ox and Bucks. 'It was quite a bad day, that one was.'

Desmond Milligan, of the same battalion, would later write of the ambush and the burning Kangaroos, 'Men were tumbling out, screaming and burning, others trying to beat out the flames of their burning comrades. It was a terrible sight.'[7]

Thirty casualties were suffered, many of them 'wrapped up in bandages and looking like Egyptian mummies'.[8]

Ten soldiers from 1 Ox and Bucks were killed that day, three of them eighteen years old. Given that others were so badly burned, it is likely that more did not survive their injuries.

Andrew Wilson MC would become a journalist and writer after the war, but in 1945 he was commanding a troop of flame-throwing Crocodile tanks in 141st Regiment, RAC. His memoir *Flame Thrower* was written in the third person, allowing him a sense of detachment from memories that were both raw and unpleasant. Some of these experiences came during the advance from Bocholt to Winterswijk.

'Kangaroos were being hit one after the other. A Sherman was alight. From out in the darkness came a clash of Brens and Brownings and Spandaus. When the noise at last died down, and situation reports came through, it appeared that the infantry had got one side of the autobahn with the Germans still clinging on the other. Phase Two was to wait until morning.'[9]

This would involve Wilson's troop supporting the infantry in an attack on a village that lay on the other side of the unfinished autobahn. It was launched the next morning at dawn.

'The landscape was littered with dead and burnt-out vehicles. A few feet in front of a knocked-out Kangaroo lay a dead German, still gripping the discharger rod of a Panzerfaust.'[10]

Wilson recalled that German dead lay everywhere, some of them crushed beneath the tracks of his tank.

'One after another, buildings swept into the path of the flame as the Crocodile ran down into the face of the village. There was no time to stop and no time to choose targets.'[11]

As buildings went up in flames, Wilson was seized by what he described as an 'unfeeling madness'. He made four runs on the village, leaving it ablaze and in ruin. It was an attack that the enemy could not withstand, and those that still lived now surrendered.

'Eventually the trouble was cleared,' said Sidney England. 'I went into a farmhouse, and down in a cellar. I found quite a number of Dutch people hiding, and I was kissed by two of the young ladies in their early twenties, being the first Englishman they saw, and became known as their liberator. I am still, even at this stage now, fifty-one years later, still kissing those two young ladies. In fact, I did so only last week. So something came out of it. I have made very good friends in that area, and frequently go back there to see my friends.'

The price of that liberation was horror and death. Andrew Wilson recalled the moments that followed the enemy's surrender in the village.

'The Germans began to bring out their wounded, blinded and burned, roughly bandaged beneath their charred uniforms. Some of them looked at the Crocodile. What were they thinking?

'He went back to refuel. At the rendezvous point he remembered his letters. One was from his mother. It said: "We are proud of you."'[12]

Stadtlohn

On 30 March, seventeen miles east of Bocholt, 5th Royal Inniskilling Dragoon Guards and 9th Durham Light Infantry attacked Stadtlohn, with the aim of seizing its bridge.

'It was a town built on a very steep hill,' said Corporal John Dobbs, 9 DLI. 'But to get to this town we had to cross over a series of railway junctions, and they had been heavily bombed.'

The craters and debris caused considerable difficulty to the Dragoons, who had knocked out twelve enemy SP guns in the previous two days of action as they approached the town. The infantry clambered over the obstacles and pushed ahead.

'Eventually we got into the town and we had to do house clearing. Half the platoon went down one side of the street, and the other half on the other side. In order to do house clearing we used to go in in pairs.'

John and 'one other lad' went into one house while the rest of the section stood guard outside. 'We went in, we raced up the stairs, and on the landing there was two doors. I nodded to my mate, and we both rushed and kicked the doors open and we fired a burst as we went in. It's a wonder we didn't kill each other, because both the doors went into the same room. That was a bit of a shock, I can tell you.'

The platoon continued to go house by house until they reached the end of the street, where they came under fire.

'Another one of our Welsh pals got badly wounded. He was called Ivor Buttle. He died of his wounds on the spot.'[13] John and Ivor had been friends for five years, serving in the South Wales Borderers before being drafted into the DLI.

'Then we come out in the open country, and there was a few Germans in a hedgerow there, and they had bazookas. They were ready to fire at our tanks, but we didn't have any tanks with us at that particular time, so we opened fire on them, and we got rid of them, and that was Stadtlohn.'

Sergeant Tom Myers was commanding a platoon in 9 DLI.

'When we set off it was our platoon what had to lead the company attack to probe in first, and with us we had the troop of tanks. The section on the right was fired on from this house, so we just signalled to the tanks to fire at this 'ouse, and they blasted it with everything they had. HE (high-explosive) and armour-piercing (ammunition).

'We fetched the reserve section up and I went in with them into this 'ouse. Went in, and the door on the left, just an ordinary house, we lobbed grenades in there. Nobody in there. Door on the right, we lobbed grenades in there. And looking straight ahead, there was a door.'

Tom deduced that this led down to the cellar from which they'd been taking fire.

'Well, when we opened this door we heard such a noise of shouting and bawling. They came up with their hands in the air. There were two or three German army, and the others looked to me as though they were Home Guard. We lined them up, and oh dear me, some of them dirtied themselves. They were paralysed with fear (about) what we were going to do.'

An English-speaking prisoner told Tom that two SS men remained in the cellar.

'We lobbed some grenades down, and I sent a lad along to the tanks and got a jerry can of petrol. We poured that down, got a lighter, lit a bit of paper, flung it down and shut the door. We more or less burned them to death in this cellar.'

The platoon then continued on through the town beside the tanks, who were especially vulnerable in the rubble-strewn streets.

'A Panzerfaust on the left fired,' said Tom, who watched on as the tank's turret was struck. The lethal Panzerfausts had accounted for 6 per cent of tank losses in Normandy, but that figure rose to 34 per cent in the Battle for Germany.

'I've seen nothing like it in all my life. (One of the crew) just shot out like a champagne cork flying out of a bottle. He was dead when he landed.'[14]

Tom's infantry killed the Germans who had fired the Panzerfaust, while a second tank pushed the first out of the road. Tom's platoon then came under small-arms fire from a cellar.

'We directed the tank onto it first. The left-hand section went forward then to clear it out. Well, they couldn't get in. The tanks had made such a mess (of the building). But they heard this moaning and groaning. The bloke that had been firing through that cellar window, they dragged him out. It was a German warrant officer. He spoke in English. He said, "We're never finished till the war's won, and we're gonna win it." He must have been a real fanatic.'

It was not an uncommon opinion encountered in the latter stages of the war, particularly among the most fanatical element of the Wehrmacht – the Waffen-SS – even as the Reich collapsed around them. The more realistic, 'defeatist' attitude of elderly Volkssturm, on the other hand, often meant that they were kept separated from the nation's youth who had been pressed into service. This was so that they were unable to convince the boys to surrender, and survive a doomed cause.

Tom's company encountered both kinds of men as they continued to battle through Stadtlohn, Tom talking to the Dragoons' crew through a telephone on the back of the tank.

'I just says, "Hit every bloody house there is until we stop ye. While we've got the power let's use it and smash them." It was continual fighting, all the time.'

It wasn't until 1745 hrs – some fourteen hours after the attack was launched – that Stadtlohn's bridge was seized.

'Fortunately for us there wasn't no German artillery or anything come onto us. It was all small-arms fire all the time.'

Tom recalled a large number of enemy dead 'laying about. I think some of 'em was just shootin' them when they were wounded as well. They'd had enough of the Germans by then. They were just sick and tired of them.'

Tom shared this view.

'We took no chances whatsoever. We says, "No, let them shoot the buggers."'

Prisoners were taken, mostly older members of the Volkssturm. Others were killed by their own side before they could surrender.

'SS somewhere fired on them,' said Tom. 'Shot them. You knew it was the SS, they were trying to make them fight.'

Such acts had been witnessed by British soldiers in Normandy and other battles.

A total of 104 enemy dead were counted in the town, and more than a hundred taken prisoner.[15] The 9th Durham Light Infantry lost five men killed and nineteen wounded. Casualties would have been heavier if not for Lieutenant-Colonel John Mogg DSO, who had taken command of the battalion during a bloody action in Normandy, when the previous commanding officer was killed. Mogg was often to be found in the thick of the action himself, and used whatever tactics he could to both achieve the battalion's objectives, and preserve his men's lives. Mogg's plan at Stadtlohn was an unorthodox one, as explained by David Rissik, a historian of the DLI:

'Instead of the usual drill of holding the enemy frontally and working round the flanks, (Mogg) ordered one company to drive a wedge into the centre of the town – which it did – and then two to move off to branch off to the flanks in a sort of 'Y-shaped' movement. This surprised the Germans and met with immediate success.'[16]

Tom Myers was in the 'wedge' company, and was full of praise for the tanks who had supported them in the street fighting. 'Oh, it might have taken us days (without them). Your tank was your big weapon. It was the hitting power behind ya.'

And while this was true, the enemy were more than capable of hitting back.

Life on the Line

By the morning of 26 March, seventeen tanks of C Squadron, 4th/7th Dragoon Guards had crossed the Rhine by raft. It was a hairy trip for Austin Baker, a crew member of a Sherman that he'd christened *Shaggy Dog*. One of Austin's comrades in the squadron, artist Edward 'Ted' Payne, had painted a suitable mascot on the side of the tank. In later years Ted would be known around the world for his stained-glass art. One wonders if he ever crossed paths in the army with John Petts, 224th (Parachute) Field Ambulance, who would also gain international acclaim for his work in this field.

Austin recalled that naming a tank was considered unlucky by some, and as *Shaggy Dog* was rafted across the river, it looked like they might be right.

'We were going across and a German plane came over terribly low. We were right out in the middle of the Rhine, which seemed like a sea when we were all on it.'

Austin couldn't decide whether to climb inside of his tank for cover or keep out in case the raft was sunk.

'I crouched (in the turret) half in, half out.'

Across the river, 4th/7th Dragoons and other units of the 8th Armoured Brigade joined the fighting around Rees before pushing north with their old friends, the 43rd (Wessex). Both formations were part of XXX Corps, under General Brian Horrocks, with an eventual destination of Bremen.

'We found out that we were detailed to lead the advance on the other side of the Rhine,' said Austin. 'What the advance consisted of was the squadron of tanks interspersed with Kangaroo personnel carriers. The (advance) was one road wide.'

By 30 March, this advance had reached the vicinity of Sinderen, Holland, and was approaching the village of Vasseveld.

'Two ('Honey' reconnaissance tanks) were in front of us, and we were the first tank of the actual squadron.

'We got a report of a tank in the neighbourhood from air reconnaissance, and they gave a map reference, and they said there's a Tiger. When I looked on the map I saw it was only in the next field. We plugged on and we came to a village called Sinderen, in Holland. We discovered there was smoke drifting across the road. When we went round the corner, the second Honey was in a ditch and the commander was lying dead on the turret, Lieutenant Sheehan, and the first one had disappeared altogether. So we went gingerly on.'[17]

Ronald Sheehan was twenty years old when he was killed, his three remaining crew taken prisoner. After passing their knocked-out tank, Austin's crew fired a few shells into a nearby windmill in case it was being used as an OP.

'We moved on a few more yards and there was a tremendous crash. We'd been hit by an armour-piercing shot. The gunner and myself, a chap called McCarthy, we came out of the hatch together more or less.'

Tracer fire zipped and bounced all around as the men sought cover in the lee of a house. *Shaggy Dog* continued to be struck by shells but did not brew up. Austin believed this was down to it having a diesel tank, rather than petrol. Under fire, he and McCarthy took shelter with a platoon of the Wiltshires.

'There was a German infantry attack on this house, which was beaten off by the chaps, the infantry, with Bren guns in the back room. Two Germans lying dead in the garden.

'After a bit, our driver, who's certainly the coolest man I've ever come across ever, Bert Morsley, he said what we all need is a cup of tea. We knew that in the back of this battered tank there was cups and tea-making equipment. And so he actually got out, and went on all fours across the road to get the stuff to make a cup of tea, and as he rose to get the tea out, a German rose out of a ditch with a bazooka, and put a bazooka round through the front of the tank. It didn't hurt Bert and he ran back in, but we didn't have the tea after all.'

Austin remained with the infantry on foot as they patrolled forwards with more tanks.

'Suddenly a mine went off under the track and the tank rolled over into a ditch. There were anti-personnel mines about, and an infantryman got his leg off.'

William 'Bill' Bone, 12th Battalion, King's Royal Rifle Corps, had been fighting in Normandy when his second child was born. Tragically, the baby died soon after, and Bill could not be spared to go home to his family in Hackney. It was several more months until he saw them.

'I was picked out of the hat, I was lucky, for seventy-two hours in Blighty. Mostly married men who got it, and I come home to see the wife. It was nice to see the boy, but it wasn't very nice to go back again, though. Your life is on the line in the infantry. If I was a bloody cook or something like that, it wouldn't have been too bad, or a bloke in the stores, it was alright, but in the infantry, I mean your life was on the line every day.'

On 31 March, Bill was again in action in the Dutch town of Ruurlo.

'We had a right battle there, street battle, with the 43rd (Wessex) Division in support.

'We heard these guttural voices – German voices – in this house, and one of the chaps said, "Well, we're not going in there, Corporal, we're going to throw a couple of grenades in there, mate. See what happens." So I said, "Fair enough, do that." So they slung a couple of hand grenades in there, and we never heard no more afterwards, so we continued clearing the rest of the houses. It was either them or us, you know what I mean?

'When we used to take prisoners, a lot of them towards the latter part of the war was the SS, and no doubt about it, I'm gonna fucking swear, they were bastards, they was. And they used to say to us ("I'm not a Nazi"), and I said, "You're a fucking Nazi alright." I mean, my mates used to say, "Give him one, Corporal. Go on, give him one." They never used to like us. We was winning the war and they didn't like it.

'We settled in (Ruurlo) for a few days, then we went on again, and we come to the canal called the Twente Canal.'

This battle, involving both British and Canadian soldiers, took place on 2 April. Bill's company, led by Major Bill Deedes, was tasked with taking a bridge that was believed undefended.

'When I come up with my section there was Spandau bullets all over the place,' said Bill Bone, 'and there was like a little block-house on the bridge. We had a Bren gun up there, cause Hitler Youth was in a woods up top, and they was putting up a right fight, the Hitler Youth.'

With one platoon pinned down on the bridge, and the rest of the company held up behind them, Lieutenant Andrew Burnaby-Atkins sprinted across the open bridge, firing from the hip, before taking up a firing position to cover the withdrawal of the lead platoon. It was an action that would earn the young officer a Military Cross for the second time in the war.

'He was brave, I well agree,' said Bill. 'He ran across the steel bridge on the girders and got to the other side. I remember seeing him going into the smoke.

'So anyway, I got my section lined up, and all of a sudden the air bursts are coming over. We all scrambled to cover. All of a sudden I felt a searing pain in me shoulder. My mate said, "Bill, you've been hurt! You've been hurt!"'

The reserve platoon, waiting behind the canal's bank, suffered ninety per cent casualties from shelling.[18] Bill had shrapnel wounds to his head, arm and shoulder.

'"Bill, you've been hurt, mate!" "Fucking hell," I said, "*Oorrrrrhh*." Next thing I know I'm on a Red Cross van being taken out of the field.'

Bill was 'patched up' in Brussels and rejoined his battalion a few weeks later, though many of the faces he had come to know over the years were gone. Despite Major Deedes' brave efforts at the bridge, which earned him a Military Cross, almost half of B Company had become casualties, twenty-two of them killed. Some, like twenty-two-year-old Lieutenant Barry Newton,[19] had been with Deedes since Normandy.

'When he was killed I think everyone in the Company who knew him felt a few years older, and the funny things in life seemed much less fun,' wrote Deedes.[20]

The battle to seize crossings over the Twente raged for several more days.

Ernie Leppard's regiment, the Sherwood Rangers, had been part of the advance on the Dutch town of Hengelo, which sat astride the canal, and was liberated on 3 April.

'(On) 4 April we reformed as a new troop. I had a new tank commander, Sergeant Freddy Jones, and a new troop leader, Second Lieutenant Ken Hunt, he was straight out of England.'

On 11 April, Ernie's troop was told to take the lead of 8th Armoured Brigade's column. With the troop leader being new to war, it was decided to put a more experienced crew at the front.

'So my tank was asked – wasn't asked, bloody ordered – to lead. You're leading and the whole bloody army is behind you. There's Germans either side of you in the forest, you've the KRRC (King's Royal Rifle Corps), who are your own personal infantry, trying to keep pace with you and to keep the Germans from coming up to the edge and firing their Panzerfaust. The tank commander is looking over the top, he's got a Sten gun, the gunner's looking in front and firing at everything that moves in front, I'm looking over the left and I've got grenades and I'm chucking (them) into the forest because occasionally you're getting fired at by this parachute infantry. We're crawling along.'

Then the tank crew were contacted by HQ via radio:

'"Will the troop's leader please take over and speed up the things, we must push on to get ahead. Regardless of our position, push on."'

The lieutenant acknowledged the message and took over the lead himself. Ernie recalled that the officer's tank had not gone more than twenty yards when it was struck by the enemy.

'Because he's new to the game, he gets Panzerfausted – the tank's hit. He's killed. Two in the turret are killed. The driver, who was a friend of mine – Charlie Stamp – he had bailed out. We had one of these funnies with us, the ARV.'

The Armoured Recovery Vehicle was a Churchill tank equipped

with lifting jibs and a winch, and was operated by soldiers of the Royal Electrical and Mechanical Engineers.

'(The ARV) comes up to my tank and he says to the sergeant, "One of your crew come up with me to get the chap out the tank up the front." So my sergeant turned to me and went, "You go."

As the Shermans raked the woods either side of the road with machine-gun fire, Ernie removed his headset and climbed out of the tank.

'I wasn't going to get up on the (ARV), it was a bit exposed, so I jumped down (into) a ditch on the left-hand side. I think our tank had backed up because the tank was about a hundred yards in front. I got about fifty yards and then there's a German kid – he was younger than I was, (and) I was only nineteen. A German kid with a stick grenade. He pulls it out and chucks it at me but I think he was more nervous than I was because he forgot to unscrew it and arm it and just chucked it.'

The enemy soldier then ran away, and Ernie was able to clamber up onto the stricken tank of his troop leader and peered into the turret. Lieutenant Hunt was dead, as was the gunner, Trooper Alfred Tyler.

'The wireless operator had lost both legs but was still alive, so we got him out.'

Ernie then went in search of his friend, Charlie Stamp, who had bailed out of the tank. Instead, he found a nearby slit trench still occupied by the enemy and aimed his revolver at them. The heavily armed Germans chose to surrender, which was lucky for Ernie.

'I'd unloaded me revolver when we was in Hengelo,' he said, seeing the funny side of it many years later. 'I had an unloaded revolver! That didn't do my nerves a lot of good.'

Ernie took some Dutch money from the prisoners, and a wristwatch. As he was bringing them in they were spotted by a heavy-weight boxer in the squadron.

'He was gonna pan these (prisoners), because the crew had been friends of his. He was gonna hit these two Germans that had panzerfaust our tank. One of our troop leaders had to pull a revolver on him to stop him.'

As ever, the dead of the regiment were collected and buried by their padre, Reverend Leslie Skinner.

'Our padre was burying the dead in the corner of this field,' remembered Ernie. 'He said, "I'm burying the dead and I'm buggered if about twenty Germans didn't come out and surrender to me."'

Ernie was reunited with his friend Charlie Stamp later that evening. 'He was always the troop leader's driver, and this was the fifth troop leader he'd had killed on 'im.'

The soldier had come to the end of his tether.

'"I've had enough. The fifth is enough," he said "I can't go on any more." He'd grazed his leg badly bailing out of this tank. He said, "I'll have to see if I can give meself a Blighty." So he got some cow muck and rubbed it in this graze. He said, "That'll go bloody septic soon and I'll get sent back."'

But the wound healed quickly, and Charlie soldiered on to the end of the war. 'He said, "I've never known a cure like it,"' Ernie chuckled.

The long months of campaign, and the enemy's reluctance to accept defeat, was taking its toll on many men, and the ambush that day was a final straw for Ernie.

'I think at that point I'd lost my nerve. I'd been alright up till then but, for the rest of the war, I'd lost my confidence.'

The Dortmund–Ems Canal

Cyril Butler, 6th Cameronians, had been shocked by his first sight of a frontline, at Hamminkeln, but over the next few days things started to look up.

'I would think we travelled forty miles and never fired a shot, until we came to the town of Rheine.'

Captain Coutts, 4 KOSB, explained the 'superb rumour' that went around the 52nd (Lowland) following the capture of the town.

'Due to a little fancy map-reading the (Divisional Mobile Laundry and Bath Unit) did, by devious side roads, enter Rheine without opposition and, finding a railway bridge intact, set up shop ready to serve showers, according to regulations. When one of the leading platoons arrived, holding close to the wall in single file, imagine their astonishment when they were offered a shower and a change of underwear!'[21]

Cyril Butler and his comrades were glad to see them. 'When we got there they said, "Right, lads, go to the baths." We all had a shower. Clean socks, clean trousers, new uniform, couple of shirts. Beautiful.'

The author of the 52nd's Divisional History, who was himself greatly enamoured of this story, conceded that 'The strict historian would ignore this pleasing moment as an accidental irrelevance. In fact, troops of other formations had ventured into Rheine before the Lowlanders relieved them and completely secured the town.'[22]

Only the western side of Rheine was held, and even here there were German infiltrations. On the night of 2 April, 5 KOSB fought their way up to the banks of the River Ems, across which the town's bridges had been destroyed. That same night, the 7th Cameronians crossed by soft-skinned boats to seize the other side.

Eighteen-year-old Ivan Markwell had seen comrades killed for the first time during the relief of the 6th Airborne a few days earlier. Crossing the River Ems would be his first attack, his company providing fire as another crossed by boat. Seven of the battalion were killed in the action, and another twenty-three wounded. Once a bridgehead had been seized, the other companies passed through, including Ivan's.

'A friend and I happened to stop outside this house and there was a woman putting her head out the window and she said, "Are you English soldiers?" speaking in perfect English. She was an English woman who had married a German. She was chatting to us about England while we stood there for a few minutes.' A German neighbour came over and asked the Englishwoman to speak to the soldiers for her. 'She turned to us and said, "This woman has got two Germans in her house. They want to give themselves up. Would you go and get them?" So we said, "Yes, alright."

'So we followed this woman over to the other side of the road and she came out with these two young Germans, two young lads. We had a rifle on 'em, and my friend searched their pockets to see what they got on them and that sort of thing. You could see they were frightened.'

These were two of sixty-five prisoners taken that day. More German soldiers were lying in defence of a second obstacle that lay two miles north-east of Rheine, on the high banks of the Dortmund–Ems canal. The country on the Rheine side of this canal was flat and open, while on the other side there was farmland dotted with copses and farmhouses, the fields intersected by ditches, wire fences, streams and hedges. The 52nd's Divisional History concluded that this sodden terrain was ideally suited for the defender.

'And since the enemy had the obvious line of the canal as a simple base for his calculations, he had every small feature ranged to a foot for his cunningly concealed mortars and SP guns.'[23]

With the few boats they had available, the 7th Cameronians began to make their crossing of the canal in the early morning of 4 April. They came under withering fire from snipers and machine guns, which had been placed in enfilade so that they could rake along the length of the water.

'We were the platoon to take the lead and I was given the job of being a boatman,' said Ivan Markwell. 'They were these canvas boats and there was about half a dozen of them, and we had to quietly lower them into the water because the Germans were on the bank the other side. Then we had to quietly get the lads to fill in, and quietly paddle them across. As soon as they got to the other side, everything was breaking loose – grenades, machine guns, everything was flying across that bank.

'We were taking the chaps backwards and forwards as boatmen. That was a terrible and frightening experience.'

By 0800 hrs, a bridgehead 150 yards deep had been created by two of the Cameronians' companies, but now in the daylight they were held up by air-bursting shells, machine guns and snipers. Ivan and his platoon took shelter in the only cover they could find – an old dyke half-full of the water.

'It was so bitter cold that you had to keep moving and stretching your legs because we were stuck in there for about four or five hours. You just couldn't move. There was snipers about, we could see Jerries moving around. We were stuck until someone else could come and take the front.

'There was one lad, he kept getting up and stretching himself and a bullet struck the bank behind him. A corporal was near and he said, "You wanna keep down, there's a sniper got an eye on you. Keep down whatever you do, don't keep moving about."'

But the soldier was so cold that he moved again, and the sniper fired.

'This bullet went right through his shovel (on his pack) and the corporal said (again), "Keep down whatever you do."

'Anyway, he couldn't take it. He moved again and the next one was right between his eyes, and that was the end of him. The rest of us were stuck in this ditch until eventually another company went in front of us and cleared the way, made an attack so we could then pull out.'

5 HLI crossed the canal in the late morning, and succeeded in expanding the bridgehead's depth to 700 yards in places.

'There was dead and dying laying all over the place,' said Ivan. 'We managed to get out the ditch and dig a slit trench on top of the bank. I was in the slit trench with the corporal and we had a Bren gun between us. That would only fire single rounds, useless thing, and so he said, "No good hanging on to this thing, might as well just have your rifle." He said, "We'll go and see if we can get another one."

'The front area had been cleared now so it weren't so bad, you could walk about a bit, you could stand up without thinking you might be shot at, so we went over and saw the sergeant major. We told him we got this gun that was no good and he said, "There's a chap with one over in the ditch, he got a new one, take it off him."

'We went over to this ditch and there was a lad sat in there. His tin hat was off his head, and his head was all caved in like an egg with all the yolk. He sat there with this Bren gun and his brains were all over the gun.

'We got this Bren and cleaned it up with some grass as best we could and went back to the section again. It was then that we could pull out because this other company had gone through us.'

Ivan and his company returned to the canal.

'Out of about half a dozen of these canvas boats, there was only about two left afloat. The rest were full of holes and had sunk.'

After crossing back, and as they were pulling back to the barn where their operation had begun, the company came under attack from an enemy gun.

'An 88, you don't hear. There's no shriek. Suddenly there's a big explosion and that's it. We all dived as quickly as we could into the bank or laid flat. I remember throwing myself into a ditch, and I could remember feeling shrapnel striking the hedge all around me and a chap two or three down yelled out. A big lump of shrapnel hit him in the back and he didn't last long.'

Later on, when Ivan was checking his ammunition, he discovered that his bandoliers may have saved his life.

'A piece of shrapnel had cut this bullet nearly in half, and if it wasn't for that, I think that would have gone somewhere into my back, and I might have been killed.'

Cyril Butler, 6th Cameronians, passed into the bridgehead later the next day by way of a Bailey bridge, which had been constructed by sappers working tirelessly under enemy fire. Their objective was the village of Drierwalde, which was held by Hungarian Waffen-SS.

'We got over this Bailey bridge, couldn't believe all the dead lads on the other side – it seemed like a hundred laid on the roads. We got over and there wasn't a shot fired at us. We must have been a lucky battalion I reckon.'

Thanks to the Bailey bridge, the troops across the canal were now able to receive the support of tanks, a troop of Scots Greys joining the Cameronians for their attack on Drierwalde.

'We made our way up the road and up come three Shermans. The first one got hit by an 88 and blew up. The last one turned round and cleared off. We were laid in a ditch next to the second tank and we were shouting, "Bugger off! Clear off!" We didn't want another 88 hit him with us (nearby).'

But instead of retreating, the tank crew charged.

'He took off and he cleared the 88 out, and everything else!

This one lone tank! We captured our objective and never fired a shot. Unbelievable. That was my first (attack) – I never fired a shot.'

The 52nd (Lowland) Division's history records that this tank was commanded by 'an unknown and resourceful corporal of the Greys'.[24] One hopes that he was recognized for his courage, though such acts were often overlooked by the awards system.

General Horrocks, the commander of XXX Corps, took great issue with how the army awarded medals for gallantry, particularly for other ranks.

'I remember on one occasion, when visiting a forward battalion, I asked a young Lance-Corporal commanding a section, with no medal ribbon on his breast at all, how many attacks he had taken part in. He replied, "Seven or eight." Yet there was I, living in comparative safety at Corps H.Q., with a chest shining like morning glory. For this reason I often felt quite ashamed when visiting forward units.'[25]

But Horrocks did what he could to ensure that his men received their just recognition, and the actions of one of his officers, on 3 April, deserved nothing less than the Victoria Cross.

It was two months later that the *London Gazette* reported:

'Captain Liddell was commanding a company of the Coldstream Guards ordered to capture intact a bridge over the River Ems, near Lingen. The bridge was heavily defended and prepared for demolition. Captain Liddell ran forward alone to neutralize the 500 lb. charges. Unprotected, and all the time under intense fire, he crossed and re-crossed the whole length of the bridge, disconnecting the charges at both ends and underneath it. The bridge was captured intact, and the way cleared for the advance over the river. Captain Liddell's outstanding gallantry and superb example of courage will never be forgotten by those who saw it.'

Forty of the enemy were killed at the bridge, and Horrocks believed that its capture saved two days in the corps' advance. He visited the site himself, and was talked through the action by Captain Ian Liddell, who Horrocks duly recommended for the VC. Horrocks had tried to secure the award several times for his soldiers, but Captain Liddell's award was his sole success. Tragically, the young

Guards officer would not live to receive it. Eighteen days after his heroic actions at the bridge, Captain Liddell was killed by a single bullet. Horrocks recorded it as 'a stray bullet'. Other sources attribute his death to a sniper, while another, who served in the same battalion, believed he had been killed by a young German boy. Regardless of the cause, a brave man was lost, and before he was ever aware that he had been awarded the medal.

Horrocks recalled that this was often the case for Britain's gallantry award winners, and criticized 'some mysterious committee in the UK who had little, if any, experience of the conditions prevailing on the modern battlefield.' They were so slow that by the time the award arrived the recipient was usually no longer around to receive it, being either in hospital, dead or posted elsewhere. 'Consequently, it was quite rare to see anyone in the frontline wearing the ribbon of a medal awarded for gallantry.'[26]

But what was missing from the chest of a man's battledress was remembered in the hearts of comrades like Alan Pemberton, a fellow officer and friend of Ian Liddell's.

'I knew him very well. A very amusing man. Enjoyed life. Great raconteur. Played the piano brilliantly. Great fun. Not an obvious person who you'd expect to win a VC.'

Ian Oswald Liddell was twenty-five years old when he died on 21 April 1945. The inscription on his grave speaks not only to his own selflessness, but to his family's, who knew full well the cost of war:

INTO THE MOSAIC OF VICTORY WE PLACE THIS PRECIOUS JEWEL OF HUSBAND AND SON.

Both XXX and XII Corps had made steady progress from the Rhine, and the enemy were pulling back to take up new defensive lines behind the rivers of the German plain. Away to their south-east, VIII Corps' own breakout battle had led them to a place where the fate of German peoples had once been decided, almost 2,000 years ago:

The Teutoburg Forest.

CHAPTER 18

For Valour

The Teutoburg Forest and Ibbenbüren
1–7 April 1945

'People get frightened, but when they've smelled blood, and tasted blood, and killed, they wanted to kill all the time. It was in me. Once I'd killed I wanted to kill. Wanted to kill.'

Sergeant Tom Myers, 9th Battalion,
Durham Light Infantry

Forest of Ghosts – 11th Armoured Division

Three days before Captain Ian Liddell VC's heroic actions on the Ems, 11th Armoured Division encroached on the town of Ibbenbüren, where a vital road crossed through the low hills and forests of the Teutoburger Wald. It was in this forest that the future of Europe had once been changed in dramatic and decisive fashion. Three Roman legions and their auxiliary forces entered the Teutoburg Forest in September of AD 9, but only a few scattered survivors emerged. It was perhaps the greatest defeat that Rome ever suffered, ending its eastern expansion in North West Europe and shaking an empire that had up to that point seemed all but unstoppable. The ancient battleground, steeped in German lore, was held by the Wehrmacht's Nr. 471 Division, made up of two battle groups – one of infantry and artillery replacements, and the other of infantry NCO trainees, who were particularly well motivated and well trained.

The first attempt to dislodge them would be made by the Black Bull – a nickname of the 11th Armoured Division whose insignia was a fierce bull on a yellow background.

Patrick Delaforce served in the division as a Forward Observation Officer with the Royal Horse Artillery, and was twice mentioned in dispatches. He had been 'fairly badly wounded' in a mine strike that killed his driver, and would be wounded again in late April. Four of his school friends had been killed in the war, and more wounded.

'So in a quiet, determined sort of way I wanted retribution for Hitler's evil regime. Perhaps exacting a form of revenge is almost happiness?'[1]

Patrick dedicated much of his life to writing histories about the war, including one about the Black Bull, where he described the events that unfolded at the Teutoburger Wald on 2 April 1945.

'The battle that followed had two very different characteristics. 3 Mons with 1st Hereford had the unenviable task of clearing the thick woods in the north-west area of the Ibbenbüren Ridge. Although 2nd Fife and Forfarshire blasted the outskirts of the woods with HE, and divisional artillery rained down stonks, it was to little avail.'[2]

Roy Vallance, from Suffolk, was a tank commander with the 2nd Fife and Forfar and in action that day.

'A Squadron were the leading squadron, and I think I was the leading tank. The road went through a high ridge. About halfway along, it was densely wooded. We went to approach and we were fired upon. I swung off left, I remember, immediately, in a big circle left, and put out smoke, crossed the road again into a farmyard where we were under cover. The other tanks in the troop all swung off right where the ground was boggy and they all got bogged.

'I was ordered by somebody to go on foot and see what was up the road. My driver came with me. We crept up by the hedgerows and so on. Couldn't see a thing, so after a while we went back and said we couldn't see anything. It wasn't our role – we felt really naked going up on foot.'

This 'naked' role, devoid of armour, belonged to the infantry. The 3rd Battalion, Monmouthshire Regiment set off to capture the wooded ridge, but it was not to be. In conditions that were almost jungle-like, where visibility could be no more than a few feet, companies lost touch with platoons, and platoons with sections. Every stretch of open ground was covered by snipers, who picked off officers, NCOs, radio men and machine-gunners first.

Corporal Edward 'Ted' Chapman, a twenty-five-year-old section commander, had worked in a colliery in the Rhymney Valley before the war. He was advancing with his section when a machine gun opened up at close range, and several of Chapman's men went down.

Roy Nash was a Bren gunner in Chapman's section, and recalled how the ambush was just the beginning of a brutal struggle.

'It was the worst I had experienced in ten months of action. Many were killed and wounded and the terrible screams of the wounded will haunt me to my dying day. I kept firing until I ran out of ammo. I lay down behind the wall, picked up thirteen empty bullet cases and pushed them into the ground in the shape of a cross.

'Suddenly I felt pain, terrible pain, wicked pain and I cried, broken-hearted for my mum.'[3]

The back of Roy's hand had been shot away.

'Corporal Chapman told me to lay down and that the stretcher-bearers were coming. He then picked up my Bren gun, put on a magazine, and said, "I'll kill the bloody lot of them."'[4]

Firing the Bren gun at the hip, Corporal Chapman charged the enemy. He killed several at point-blank range, and put the remainder to flight.

Chapman had saved his section for the moment, but they were alone, cut off from the company, and in danger of being overrun. The re-gathered enemy, with bayonets fixed, made determined attacks on Chapman's position, their movement covered by a heavy weight of machine-gun fire. Undaunted, he stood to meet every assault with his Bren gun until he was almost out of ammunition.

Chapman's section reacted bravely and brought up more ammo under the cover of his fire. Grenades now came flying in, spraying shrapnel, splinters and dirt. With a fresh magazine on his Bren, Chapman attacked once again, charging the enemy and driving them from the position.

He then turned his attention to his company commander, who had been severely wounded earlier in the action. Chapman covered fifty yards of exposed ground to reach his officer, every step through a storm of bullets. Reaching the company commander's side, Chapman was wounded in the hip by a bullet that also struck the wounded officer. Ignoring his own wound and pain, Chapman carried the officer back to his own lines, where it was discovered that he had not survived. Corporal Chapman, who had already done all that could be asked of a soldier and more, refused to be evacuated and continued to fight for the next two hours.

The battalion's war diary makes clear the frequency of the casualties that day, particularly among its officers:

'1430hrs: Commence second phase. D Coy leading. Advanced through wood (South East) towards road, and hold high knoll halfway towards objective, suffering casualties by sniping. Captain V Mountford killed. B Coy follow and gain high ground overlooking road. Suffer casualties again by snipers, including 2nd Lt Driver, killed. B Coy have counter-attack against them, Major Lyons, Captain Dixon, Captain EA Campbell, Lt Elliot, 2nd Lt Evans, 2nd Lt Joiner wounded . . .'[5]

The exhausted soldiers then spent a miserable night dug in as pouring rain turned their slit trenches to mud. At 0930 hrs on the morning of 3 April, A Company was attacked in force and was compelled to withdraw from the slope that they had shed so much blood to take. The 3rd Monmouthshires now received support, with a battalion of the Devonshire Regiment going in on their right flank, and tanks and infantry on the left. This, combined with heavy artillery barrages put onto the top of the ridge, finally forced the enemy to withdraw. Eighty-five prisoners were taken, all cadets of the German Army School, Hanover. Patrick Delaforce wrote that 'the Dorsets of 131 Infantry Brigade trapped two companies of the German NCOs and killed them all.'[6]

The 1st Herefords experienced their own difficult and bloody battle at the Teutoburger Wald. After taking the high ground in the woods, they suffered several attacks and were surrounded. A fighting withdrawal was carried out at high cost – forty-three of the battalion were killed or wounded, and a further thirteen taken prisoner.

There was no danger of Britain's army being destroyed in the forest, as had befallen the three legions of Rome, but the fierce and brave German defence had stalled the advance of VIII Corps, and particularly the 11th Armoured Division. It was now decided to disengage so that the corps could continue the race east.

But 3 Mons would not be going with them. Two days after the battle at Ibbenbüren Ridge, their commanding officer was called to Brigade HQ. On his return he addressed first his officers, and later all ranks, informing them that, owing to their heavy casualties, the battalion was no longer able to be classed as a First Line Fighting Unit, and was to be detached from 11th Armoured Brigade. 3 Mons would spend the rest of the war out of the line, conducting duties in the rear areas, such as searching houses for weapons and guarding the bridges on the Rhine. The brigade's commander visited the battalion soon after, addressing those who had fought since D-Day and expressing his sorrow at losing them for the rest of the campaign.

J. D. Hutchison, a decorated officer of 2 Fife and Forfar, held 3 Mons in high regard. 'They were very tough, and brave.'

It was a sentiment echoed throughout the 11th Armoured Division, and no wonder. 3 Mons lost forty-one men killed and eighty wounded in the Teutoburg Forest, and they had suffered more than 1,000 casualties since landing in Normandy (a casualty rate of over 100 per cent), including 267 dead. Three times they had lost their commanding officer killed, and six consecutive officers commanding C Company lost their lives. Although their final attack of the war did not end in success, the contribution of 3 Mons to the final victory in Europe has never been in doubt.

Corporal Ted Chapman survived the battle, and the war, and was awarded the Victoria Cross for his actions in the battalion's final battle. Tom Griffiths, from Blaina, had served with him in 2 Mons before Chapman's wounding in Normandy, whereupon he had been reassigned to the 3rd Battalion. 'Oh, he was a lovely, delightful little gentleman,' Tom said. 'He wouldn't say boo to a ghost, you know, but he had something about him.'

Dai Edwards, 2 Mons, was another pal of Ted Chapman's both during and after the war.

'He was a quiet-spoken fella. He liked fishing, and he liked horses. He kept ponies as a young chap. I know, on one occasion, a reporter said to him, in my presence, "You're a sort of Rambo, Mr Chapman." And he said, "No, no, no, no. I am not. I am absolutely not." And he wasn't.'

Dai remembered some post-war get-togethers for veterans of the Mons who were preparing a trip to Europe. They'd pick Ted up at his house, 'and his wife would say to him, "Ted!" "Yes, Rhoda?" "Come here, Ted." And he'd go over to her now, and she'd get a comb, and she'd comb his hair down. He'd be looking at us, and he'd be looking up at the ceiling as she parted his hair. So that's not the image you get (of a VC winner).'

Ted Chapman VC passed away at the age of eighty-two, his local newspaper reporting that 'the soil of Wales took back one of its most valiant sons . . . The service was simple and dignified as befits a quiet and gentle man of whom, as a comrade said, much was asked and a very great deal rendered in return.'[7]

The Battle Continues

With the departure of 11th Armoured Division, the battle for Ibbenbüren was handed over to XII Corps, and in particular, the 7th Armoured and 53rd (Welsh) Divisions. It would take them a further three days of fierce fighting before the north-west corner of the Teutoburg Forest was cleared.

Sergeant Tom Myers, commanding a platoon in 9 DLI, realized that they were up against a different kind of enemy at Ibbenbüren when his company was charged by a single soldier.

'He had a Spandau at the hip, firing. And we're all there, like, a full company.'

Tom got behind his half-track's .50 calibre. 'I started firing. I must have knocked him to bloody bits, him. I said, "What kind of blokes are these? One man attacking about a hundred of us!"

'One of my lads said, "Look over there!" There's one walking up the hedge. So I says, "Fire that Bren." Down he went, and then he crawled along a bit, and then he stopped. He had all the camouflage kit on.'

Tom took a captured German rifle with a telescopic sight and shot the crawling soldier. 'I pumped another two into him. That stopped that. I told the corporals, I don't know who these blokes are that we're up against, but these is the hardest we've bumped yet.'

Tom, a hard man himself, found that there was no quarter given in Ibbenbüren, and witnessed stretcher-bearers – usually respected by both sides on the battlefield – being shot down by the enemy. He was then ordered to put in an attack on the houses where the firing had come from, one of his men going down just before they reached the buildings.

'They fired and hit the corporal in the leg, and he fell on the garden path. And when he was trying to crawl away, this lad, they just riddled him.'

The six German defenders then withdrew into the cellar, but grenades encouraged them to surrender.

'They come up with their hands up, and the first one, Big Jock, he pointed at this (dead Corporal), much to say, *look what you've done*, and he grabbed him right in the face.'

The six prisoners were then lined up on the road between the houses.

'I said (to the platoon), "Train your Bren guns on them, train your rifles on them."

'They tried to run, and they just riddled them. And I went around with me Sten and blew the heads off them.'

Tom said that this killing brought out a change in his men.

'People get frightened, but when they've smelled blood, and tasted blood, and killed, they wanted to kill all the time. You could have taken them to Berlin after that.

Tom himself said that once he'd killed he wanted to kill again, and was asked if he regretted this.

'No, I didn't at all! What they'd done to that lad, what they'd done to them stretcher-bearers in the field. They'd shot them in cold blood. Well, how can you treat a man then? You can't treat them.'

Two more houses remained to be cleared. Tom told the supporting tanks to 'blast them, until they're on the bloody ground. Whether there's anybody in them – we didn't care if there was civvies or not – blast them. Knock them down. Knock hell out of them.'

The next day Tom came across a German lying in the road with his arms outstretched. From long experience, Tom smelt a ruse – the man's neck was pink, meaning that his blood was pumping, and he was only feigning death.

'I put me Sten gun onto single shot and fired one in his heart, and his body jumped. (I fired another) to the back of his head, took his face off.'

He then got his Bren gunners to riddle the body so that it rolled over: 'And he had some grenades. What he was gonna do I don't know.'

It wasn't the only enemy ruse that Tom came across at Ibbenbüren.

'I looked down the road, and there's these two (British) staff officers coming up in their service dress. Brown shoes. The red braid. I says, "There's sommat funny 'ere. Look at 'em." They both had officer's canes, but they were swinging them in their left hand. British officers always swung it with their right arm and put it under their left if they had to salute.

'I says, "Get your Bren guns ready." I stepped out. I said, "Where you goin'?"'

Tom then had an exchange with the officers, who failed to answer his questions or his curiosity. 'I says, "You buggers are Germans." They tried to make a bolt for it. I just shouted to Corporal Down, "Fire!" We didn't half blast them an' all.'

Tom went over to the bodies. 'They were still gaspin' an' one thing and another. I just pulled their jackets open and they had the German uniform on underneath.'

The battalion's padre then came upon the scene.

'Well, they were a waste of time, you know, padres. A waste of grub. I wasn't a heathen, but my faith had gone in all forms of religion.'

The padre then asked about the bodies piled at the side of the house.

'He said, "You're a butcher!" to me. "You're a butcher! I'll have you court-martialled!" Well, I was a bit foul-languaged to him and told him where he could go, and take his bible with him.'

Lieutenant-Colonel Mogg arrived on the scene and saw the padre's reaction. 'The colonel shouted across to us, "I think he's war-weary. He's gone a bit bomb-happy." He got him sent the hell out of it.'

In the same battalion as Tom was Corporal John Dobbs.

'When we went down this lane and came out in the open we found two British soldiers lying dead in the road. We didn't know who they were because they didn't belong to us. We couldn't stop to identify them. We had to keep bashing on.

'We got down towards this farmhouse and we came under heavy fire, and we dived into this ditch, and that was half under water.'

Due to a lack of officers, John's platoon was commanded by Sergeant Redpath.

'He was wounded. Blood was spurting out of the centre of his back.'

After a while the enemy's fire 'cooled off' and a white flag appeared from the farmhouse, whereupon 'about forty' of the enemy surrendered. John got his men to lift a gate off its hinges and used it as a stretcher for the sergeant. Both Sergeant Redpath and the prisoners were then handed over to the troops behind them.

'I never knew what happened to him after that.' After seeing Redpath on his way, John returned to the platoon and discovered that Lance-Corporal Hopkinson, a husband and father, had been killed.[8] 'There was another Welsh lad there called George Baker. He was a private soldier, but because we were so short of NCOs, (he was acting) as section leader. Unfortunately, he got wounded.

'I realized that I was the senior NCO left. I didn't want to lose any more of the platoon, so I said to the wireless operator, "Get through to HQ on the blower and tell them that we need support straight away."'

But the wireless op complained that he could not get the correct frequency.

'I played hell with him. I said, "If I wanted bloody dance music, you'd get that quick enough."'

John then heard the sounds of tanks approaching – they'd come to retrieve the platoon. John saw his men and wounded onto the first tank, which went on its way, then climbed onto the second with the two remaining men.

'We were sat with our backs to the turret. Private Cox was on one side of me and Private Dickson was on the other side. They moved away and after a while I heard what sounded like the crack of a whip. I knew what that was because I heard it so often.'

Someone was shooting at them.

'I heard gasps, and both Dickson and Cox had been shot through the head.'

There was nothing John could do for the men. 'Dickson was already dead and Cox was in convulsions. He didn't last very long.'[9]

The enemy's defence of Ibbenbüren was so fierce that it wasn't until the 53rd Division also joined the battle that the balance was tipped. As was so often the case in Germany, the use of flamethrowers was required to overcome the strongest points of resistance.

'Really, that was quite a thing to see those in action,' said Bob Summers, Royal Engineers. 'I remember seeing these Crocodiles flaming the houses, and you think, *God, there's some chaps inside there*, you know. It's pretty horrible, really. But still, part of the act.'

Douglas Waller, 1 Rifle Brigade, was in action around Ibbenbüren with his Wasp flamethrower. Though deadly to the enemy, the Wasps also posed a danger to their crew.

'You've only got to get a hit on the (fuel) tank and the damned thing would explode or go up in flames.'

Douglas agreed that the flamethrower was a 'pretty horrific weapon'. '(It was) not nice. Not nice. You were glad you weren't on the other end of it, but at that time, I'd say, it was obvious to everybody that you were approaching the end of the war. Nobody was sort of worried, as long as you stopped alive, that was all your concern was.

'You got very edgy. You were very careful. If you got into a village, you no longer picked things up. There was a complete disregard for the building, or anything like that. In Germany, nobody cared. It was their fault – they started the war.'

And with its end in sight, and salvation near at hand, the behaviour of the British soldiers was changing.

'It was no good them saying, "We want volunteers" for a patrol, because nobody would have done it. Everybody was thinking, *I just want to keep me head down, and keep alive.*'

On the German side were many soldiers who welcomed the chance to surrender, and survive, but others fighting for the Third Reich held a very different attitude towards war and death – they were not only prepared to die, but welcomed it, as recorded by Lieutenant-Colonel Burden when he spoke of Ibbenbüren:

'The Nazi cadets seemed to prefer death to capture, exposing themselves to the full blast of (machine guns) or flamejets from the crocodiles, as they chanted Nazi slogans to the last, obstinately determined to die for Adolf Hitler.'[10]

Against such a foe there was no escaping the cost of war, and the journeys, and lives, of many an old soldier would come to an end breaking the enemy's next defence line, out on the bloodied flood plain of the River Weser.

CHAPTER 19

More Bloody Bridgeheads

VIII Corps on the River Weser
27 March – 9 April 1945

'As we entered one particular place, there were some huts at the side of the road, obviously army huts, and we were fired at from these. We got down from our tanks quickly and a platoon went in to clear the huts. The commander of the platoon was someone who had been seconded to us. He obviously didn't know what he was doing – he walked past a window, straight up instead of ducking below the window, and he was shot through the head and killed. The danger was, towards the end of the war, some chaps got a bit complacent and that was a dangerous thing to do, because you were always likely to meet up with a group of Germans who were hard fighting professionals.'

James Absalom, 12th (Yorkshire) Parachute Battalion

The 6th Airborne Division's part in the Battle of Germany did not end after Operation Varsity. With several of its battalions now heavily depleted, the division was assigned to VIII Corps to bolster its infantry contingent, as was the 17th US Airborne Division, which had also suffered great loss on the Rhine crossing. They were now to push on to the River Elbe, by way of Osnabrück. Corporal Walter Tanner, 7th (Light Infantry) Parachute Battalion, recalled the manner of the Airborne's advance.

'We used everything we could get to carry everything – prams, wheelbarrows. Anything that was on wheels that could carry anything, we used it. We don't know where the officers got the horses, but half a dozen of the officers found horses. And away we went and we had to pass the Guards. Of all people, we had to pass the Guards. Now everybody knows what the Guards are like, they are smart, and always will be. Even then they looked as though they were ready to go on parade. What their regimental sergeant major thought of us I don't really know. He must have had heart attack after heart attack.'

'We had great admiration for the Guards,' said James Absalom, the signals officer of 12th (Yorkshire) Parachute Battalion. 'We got on very well.' James had first come into contact with the brigade of Guards on attendance of a drill course in England, where he had been left in awe – and fear – of a certain Drill Sergeant Evans.

'I was stood at the side of this road when the Guards Armoured came to give us a lift. I didn't wear any marks of rank if I could avoid it – it was a dangerous thing to do, because the German snipers picked on you.

'I heard a voice scream out, "Take your hands out your pockets, that man!" and my hands came out my pockets very quickly. I turned around and it was Drill Sergeant Evans.'

The Paras were in action almost immediately at Erle, twelve miles east of Hamminkeln. Walter Tanner was ordered to assemble men for a night attack on an enemy gun position.

'Tommy Sanderson came from York. Wonderful chap. I went to his sergeant, Sergeant Cherry, and I said, "Tommy's got to bring his Bren gun, we're going out to take the place." He called Tommy over and said, "Get your gun, son, you've got to go on this patrol." I can see Tommy right now doing it – he took the sling of his Bren gun (and) he said to Reg Cherry, "Here you are, give that to the next bloke. I won't be needing it."'

Sergeant Cherry tried to stamp out the soldier's fatalism: '"Don't bloody talk like that, man."'

'(But) Tommy never spoke a truer word,' said Walter. 'We went down, we attacked these guns. There was eleven in all plus Schmeissers, Mausers. Six Jerries were killed and I think it was thirty or forty-odd prisoners taken and Tommy was killed – shot by a machine gun right through the head.

'Whether that man had a premonition or not it's hard to say. We buried old Tommy the next day. There were no flags, no television camera, no ordinary camera, no crowds, no music, no bugles, we just buried Tommy. He was only a Para but he was a smashing bloke, he was one of our mates. When a Para dies, the others feel. We do have tears. We can cry, you know. He was the only one that was killed there.

Lance-Corporal Thomas Sanderson was killed on 27 March 1945.[1]

'Lofty (Lieutenant Hinman) was Mentioned in Despatches, he was also put up for an award but he never got one. Private Meckin got the MM and Corporal Noble got the MM out of that.'

James Absalom was also involved in the capture of Erle.

'We were going across ploughed fields and at one point, we'd not had much sleep, we'd obviously slowed down. We had to get there for dawn to carry in the dawn attack and we did one of our famous night marches to get there, but it was all across soggy fields. We all carried a little Benzedrine tablet, we were told to take one Benzedrine to keep us going. That put me off drugs for life because it gave me a terrible headache the next day. Anyway, we took it and as we approached, a large ammunition lorry, German ammunition lorry came along the road and everybody in the battalion started shooting at this. Eventually it went off with a big bang and the officers, myself included, were screaming at the men to cease fire. I think the blokes were enjoying the fireworks, but we managed to get control and we went into Erle.

'I was supposed to be signals officer, but when you go into a position like that, when you're attacking a village, in a way it's every man for himself. You get in and get on with the job and then reorganize as quickly as you can afterwards.

'There were some blokes lying down the side of a garden and I stepped out past them and there's a big barn to my left. As I stepped out, obviously silhouetted against this barn in the early morning light, I was fired at by it seemed like twenty or thirty enemy soldiers, who were down the back gardens, further away from me. I stepped back again (and the bullets) went all around the wall. How I wasn't hit, I don't know. I stepped back, and I said to these soldiers, parachutists on the ground, "Get up and follow me!" and they said, "We've been told to stay here, sir."

'You always expect parachutists to argue with you at the wrong time. A voice from down behind me said, "What's up, sir?" and it was Corporal Walker from the platoon I used to command when I was a platoon commander, and I said, "I've just been shot at and they're all down there. We've got to sort them out." He says, "Alright, we're with you," and most of my platoon came down. We went down to a wall and I said, "Hang on a minute, I'm going to chuck a grenade over this wall. You get out with that Bren gun to that plot there, fire and we'll all go down shooting and clear them out of the slit trenches."

'I chucked the grenade over (and) I said to the Bren gunner, "Get out with your gun," and he and his mate went out and they set up covering fire and we went out from behind the wall, shooting as we went, but the Germans were already out their slit trenches with their hands up. There were a couple of blokes in the black uniform of the SS.'

One of the SS men lay dead, killed by James's grenade. The force of German soldiers was a motley crew, and also included regular German army soldiers, and elderly Volkssturm.

'They decided that it was best to give up, and I would have done the same in their position. Round the other corner came Frank Boucher, the second in command, and he shouted across, "Alright, Jim, you enjoying yourself?" and I said, "Yes, sir," and I saluted. Then he joined us. The sergeant major, Sergeant Major Partridge, came with me and we cleared the houses right down through the back of Erle. I heard noises in a barn and I said, "Alright, keep going," and I shot at a vase, a big pot of plants which was on a ledge over the huge doors of this barn. Knocked that down and the biggest horse I'd seen in my life came charging through the doors and scattered us as it ran away from all the noise.

'We went down then to a farmhouse and this German couple

came out and they'd got a young chap with them and asked if we could help. His leg was shot away at the top and to me it looked gangrenous. Whether he was a German soldier or not I don't know, but he was in civilian (clothes). We sent him up to our medical officer, Doc Wilson, who looked after him.

'Erle was clear and we knew then that the Germans would stonk us, start to shell us at intervals, usually ten or twenty minutes. So we quickly got ourselves underground, either slit trenches or cellars. There was one incident where all the prisoners we took were in a barn. The regimental police were there and one regimental policeman suddenly collapsed – a shell had fallen nearby and four pieces of shrapnel had hit him at the base of the skull and killed him.'

The advance from Erle continued.

'We experienced a lot of skirmishing,' said James. 'Most of the skirmishing was done by German soldiers who had seen a lot of action. Some of it was carried out by Volkssturmers. The difference was the chaps who'd seen a lot of action carried on shooting and fighting right to the last and you had to knock them out to make an advance. With the Volkssturm, when things got too hot, they very rapidly surrendered.'

During VIII Corps' advance the infantry were often carried on the back of 6th Guards Armoured Brigade's tanks. On 30 March, Robert Keenan, a gunner in the 4th (Armoured) Coldstreams, spotted an armoured vehicle in the distance, partly obscured by a hedge. Unable to make out whether it was friend or foe, he said to an American paratrooper sergeant, '"Wouldn't it be a good idea to send a couple of men up there to see it?"

'I didn't like the look of it, but they just sat there. So, I went up to this tank destroyer in front of us – it was British, they had a better telescope than us. But they just said, "No, it's alright, it's one of ours." I wasn't happy about it at all, (but) I couldn't do much about it.

'Anyhow, we sat there, and I was still watching this thing. I couldn't make it out. It wasn't a Tiger, it wasn't a Panther, I couldn't make out if it was an SP or a tank. There were chaps there – I couldn't even make out their uniforms. Then all of a sudden there was such a bang. It was a German tank the whole time.

'An American had been sitting on the tank behind us, and the shot had gone through his legs and penetrated the armour. It didn't hit anybody, but it set the ammunition up in flames. Sergeant Nesbit, he had shot out of the turret like a jack-in-the-box. He had shot out, the crew had got out, (and) by this time the tank was a mass of flames.'

Robert's tank and others quickly rushed down the road.

'I was in a heck of a state. I was filled with "I could've had him, I could've had him."'

Robert recalled that 'Sergeant Nesbit was alright, he said he couldn't remember touching the side of the tank,' but that the American paratrooper died of his wounds. More loss was to follow as they continued on in the direction of Münster.

Robert's troop came under a second ambush as they closed on the city.

'Suddenly (my) tank commander said, "Gunner right, quick! Anti-tank gun on the right!"

'So we turned the turret round, and in this field there was a big gun pointed right at us. Why they didn't fire upon us first I don't know, they were sighted right on us. (I) fired the first round, and it went over the top and exploded behind him. Another round in, fired again, and that hit the gun shield and they ran away. Then we machine-gunned the whole area.'

Robert and his crew succeeded in knocking out the gun and continued the advance.

'Some firing came from the right. I was firing the machine gun, and as I fired the tank went forward. We went on past (a) house. There was firing coming from behind that house somewhere. You're sitting in your turret and you sort of have a panoramic view. And the next thing I knew, something was coming down on the top of me, and I thought, *My God! I've been hit, something's happened and my head's split open!* I had blood pouring down me, horrible. I'll never forget that.'

Robert suddenly begins to cry. The interview, conducted fifty-five years after the event, is paused. He then continues to recount the death of his tank commander, twenty-two-year-old Lieutenant Robert Brand, who had returned to the troop after he had been wounded in the Rhineland.[2]

'I turned round, and his head had gone. He slumped forwards, and I pushed him back, and sort of looked around. The wireless operator was trying to get out, but his hatch was jammed, or half open. He managed to get out. I was gonna follow him, and when I got halfway out the turret I could see there was a German outside with a submachine gun. You don't know what to do. I thought, *Well, if I go out there, I'm going to get shot. But if I stop in here, is whatever hit us going to fire again?*

'I got down in the turret and I prayed to God, I did.'

Robert tried to send a message by radio, but the tank's communications had been knocked out.

'I got into the front compartment and thought, *Well, if there's any Germans coming in here, they're going to have to fight me.* I got the Bren gun out. When the driver got out the front hatch, he left the hatch open, so I could look out, but I couldn't see anything. I saw someone run across the field, it was a German, and I could hear the Americans firing at them. I knew that Germans were round here – *Are they around the tank?*

'I lay in the front compartment, (and) I could hear someone climbing up the back. I thought, *Well, is that a Jerry? Is he going to drop a grenade in? Is he going to come and shoot me if he sees me in here?* Then I could hear somebody looking in the turret. Then I could hear this person – I didn't know who it was – climbing back down again, then I didn't hear any more. After a while, I looked out the escape hatch and I saw these American troops coming (towards me through) the field, and I knew it was alright then.'

Robert climbed out onto the tank's front deck.

'The battalion commander, Lieutenant-Colonel Smith, came up to the front of the tank and he was going to the turret. I said, "Sorry, sir, there's nothing you can do for him."

'I found out that the person who had clambered up on the turret was one of our other crew, Jim Nixon, and of course he saw

Lieutenant Brand was dead, and he saw me lying down there and thought the same of me.'

The tank was moved off the road, and the crew taken into a farmhouse, Robert covered in the blood of his officer and friend.

'Next day they had got the German prisoners of war to clean the mess out of the tank, but when you went inside there was still a horrible smell, and spots of blood. My khaki belt had bloodstains that I never seemed to get rid of. Whatever hit him, he didn't know anything about it.

'After that I would say my nerve was shattered. I remember that after that, the nerves were not the same. Something goes. Before you get hit, you think, *Well, that's not going to happen to us.* But something did happen to us.'

When the tank's driver, Bill Chiddy, was sent on leave, his co-driver Glen Grace took over with a replacement co-driver joining them. As they were moving down a road with mortar shells going off on the flanks, the new co-driver panicked, wanting to get out. Reacting with uncharacteristic anger, Robert shouted at Glen Grace, telling him to '"Bloody well shut him up! Hit him with a spanner and bloody knock him out!"

'He was panicking, and I knew that if he didn't stop I would've joined him.'

On the Weser

Most actions ended with tragedy. A treasured few, with laughter.

On 3 April the two Para brigades were joined by their elite comrades of No. 1 Commando Brigade. Their mission was to capture Osnabrück.

'We was landed with the job of attacking the big barracks, and it *was* a big barracks,' said Walter Tanner, 7 Para. 'Buckingham Palace was small compared to it. Well, if you put yourself in my place, you're going across the barrack square, you've got to take this palace and you're thinking, *Christ, why aren't they firing?* It's in your mind all the time – *For Christ's sake fire, let us know where you are!* We was three-quarters of the way over before the penny dropped

– nobody was there. They'd scarpered. God was on our side, it's as simple as that.

'Anyway, we still had to check the place out because the German soldier was a past master of booby traps, he really was – you could pick up the simplest of things thinking it was nothing – he'd booby-trap it. Pens, pencils, who would think a pencil could be booby-trapped? He knew how to do it – take the rubber piece off the top, he'd have something inside, just to cause a hand injury. Down the corridor going with my section, one of the boys shouted out, "There's some Jerries down here."

'You could hear German voices talking, but I can't speak German so I don't know what they were saying. So I left these lads behind, (while) myself and two others crept forwards with hand grenades.'

Walter and his comrades threw the hand grenades into the room, but instead of hearing the screams of wounded, or the silence of the dead, the German voices continued uninterrupted.

'So we charged in ready to shoot, and what was it? *A radio room* – they'd left the radio on. It took us nearly three weeks to live that one down.'

At the beginning of April, VIII Corps' subdivisions had been given a number of objectives, with the primary aim of securing bridgeheads over the River Weser. The 6th Airborne and the 6th Guards Armoured Brigade were to take and hold bridges at Minden and Petershagen, while 11th Armoured were to secure a bridgehead in the area of Stolzenau. Meanwhile, No. 1 Commando Brigade was to complete its clearance of Osnabrück and, if needed, send one of its Commandos forward to support the 6th Airborne. The 15th (Scottish) was to be ready to move to a concentration area on the Weser as yet undecided.

On 4 April, the 3rd Para Brigade advanced on Minden – a town that holds an important place in British army lore. The Battle of Minden, fought in 1759 against the French, resulted in an Anglo-German victory. Its anniversary on 1 August – known as Minden Day – is celebrated by several regiments, whose soldiers adorn their headdress with a rose to mark the occasion.

Approaching the town some 200 years later were soldiers of the 8th (Midlands) Parachute Battalion carried on the back of the

Grenadier Guards' Churchills. An enemy Panther and several SP guns were spotted pulling back into Minden – an inauspicious start. The enemy armour reappeared soon after, and with deadly effect.

An SP gun fired and hit the leading Churchill, the armour-piercing round penetrating the turret ring and killing three of the crew. The 8 Para soldiers made a right flanking attack on the position but came under heavy fire and could advance no further without artillery support.

The battle was then decided in an unusual manner – at least, as far as the experience of the British soldier in the Second World War was concerned. Throughout history, it was something of a norm.

One British and two US officers approached the historic town beneath a banner of truce. The Germans respected the white flag and received the delegation, who delivered a simple message: 'Surrender the town or it will be shelled out of existence.'

It was a compelling argument, though one not often heeded in total war. In this case, however, the enemy's force pulled back. The 6th Airborne cleared Minden at 0230 hrs on 5 April, finding that the bridges had been demolished. Still, it was something of a day for some of VIII Corps' soldiers.

James Campbell, 2nd Argylls, recalled that, 'The King's Own Scottish Borderers, who had been at the Battle of Minden a way back years and years ago, actually stuck roses in their steel helmets as they marched through the town.'

Walter Tanner had a less romantic memory of Minden, and remembered a dead German still sitting behind a machine gun at a crossroads. 'Believe it or not, somebody had written a notice and (hung) it round his neck – "Got any fags chum? I've been here a long time." It's callous to say it, but this was the wit of the British Tommy – there's always someone in your section, your company, who's got the wit. You'll find one.'

Further south, 6th Airlanding Brigade secured a bridgehead across the Weser at Todtenhausen and Wietersheim on 5 April. A difficult battle ensued throughout the night and into the next day, the reinforcements coming across the river exposed to the enemy's shelling. In the coming days the men of the Airlanding Brigade would also face counter-attacks from both Panther and Tiger tanks, and without any of their own armour in support. Arthur Taylor, a young soldier in the Devons who were holding the village of Bierde, recalled the lack of effect that their PIATs had against the German heavy armour.

'If we had been with pea-shooters, we would have created just as much effect on those tanks. The PIAT rounds just bounced off the armour plate. Even direct hits had no effect. In other words, we were sitting ducks. Opening up with their machine-guns, they began firing at us as we flattened our bodies, forcing them down and digging with broken fingernails into the earth.'[3]

Somehow coming through the attack alive, Arthur was left with the question that haunts many survivors of the battlefield:

'Why is it that comrades either side of me were killed, some terribly wounded, yet I was left untouched? I saw the ugly bullets raking the ground just inches in front of my eyes. One of my mates, the lower part of his face missing and pouring blood, looked up at me for comfort and help, and then his head fell forward.'[4]

It was a one-sided battle, the tanks firing point-blank at trenches that their guns could depress enough to destroy, and crushing the others with their tracks. Fifty-one soldiers of D Company, 12th Devons, surrendered in the face of these insurmountable odds and were taken prisoner.

Two miles south, Billy Gray and 2 Ox and Bucks were seizing the village of Frille.

'We crossed the Weser on canvas boats and we got to the other side and up this big hill, a field, then there was a hill, then there was a village or small town on top of the hill. We lost two or three blokes getting in there. We laid low until it got morning and we heard a tinkling of a cycle bell.

'We looked out and saw this German, he was an army man but he looked like a postman and he was old and fat and riding along on his bike. The officer we had, he was a reinforcement officer – we had about four new officers out there – he just put his pistol into (the German's) side and shot him. There was no need, obviously a postman, but he was in a German uniform so he shot him. I don't think there was any need for it. The war was nearly over in any case.'

Billy referred to this incident as an 'atrocity', and believed that there was a commonality in their occurrence.

'I think the trouble was that we had very few officers. If you got a new officer, he was bleeding killed or wounded in a couple of days. We never had a platoon sergeant.'

Both Billy's platoon sergeant and commander had been wounded during Operation Varsity.

'My number two on the Bren gun, he was about the most senior bloke we had – lance-corporal.

'It's not like the First War where it's the whole company together, you're in individual sections and you never see an officer. Think we'd have gotten along better with discipline with more officers about, perhaps even better-class officers we'd have done even better than we did.'

Some twelve miles north of Frille, the 11th Armoured Division was attempting to seize a bridgehead between Stolzenau and Leese, villages on the west and east of the Weser respectively. Panzerfausts had already claimed several tanks and the lives of their crewman, and across the river more German soldiers lay in wait in prepared positions. An experienced and decorated *SS- Oberscharführer* of the Training (Ersatz) Battalion, 12th SS Panzer, gave detail of his defence on the Weser's banks.

'I lined my platoon along the railway embankment. This stands about twenty feet above the ground between the River Weser and the village of Leese. The first British probes were easily repulsed – our field of fire was excellent. We could see every movement that the Tommies made. I had my mortars behind the railway embankment with the reserve sections and three tripod-mounted MG42s on fixed lines. The battalion had ammunition enough. We had been ordered to hold to the last.'[5]

First across the river on 5 April were G and H Companies of the 8th Battalion, Rifle Brigade. Major Noel Bell MC was the officer commanding G Company.

'Reading the English newspapers at the time, one would have

thought that fighting had virtually ceased and that all we were doing was to motor along and take thousands of prisoners. This annoyed us to no small degree. Valuable lives were still being lost daily, and we wished that some of these war correspondents who were sending back these totally inaccurate reports could be up with us to see what was really going on.'6

At around 1540 hrs, ten minutes after the companies had crossed the Weser, a lone Luftwaffe aircraft appeared over the bridgehead, reconnoitring the British positions. It was the first of many enemy aircraft that G Company would see that day, several of its men becoming casualties from Luftwaffe attacks.

'There was no sign of the RAF nor had we any Ack-Ack protection. Our Brens and Brownings chattered constantly against the marauders, but they were quite futile, the tracers visibly bouncing off the armoured bellies of the Boche planes as they swooped low over the rooftops.'7

A relatively quiet night followed. Then, just before dawn on 6 April, a section of H Company were overrun by about forty SS-Hitler Youth attacking out of their outpost on the embankment. For the remainder of the day the two sides sniped at each other, H Company losing six killed, including a platoon commander and a platoon sergeant. All told, the two companies suffered fifty casualties, including eleven deaths, during their first thirty-six hours in the tiny bridgehead.

Luftwaffe attacks continued throughout the 6th, and enemy flak guns were fired in the direct role at the bridgehead. British gunners of the 58th Light Anti-Aircraft Regiment put their own flak up over the bridgehead, through which Tempest pilots of the RAF chased the Luftwaffe at great risk to themselves. Two Tempests were hit by their own side, but fortunately neither pilot was killed, and those remaining hunted down and destroyed the enemy aircraft – gun camera footage of which is held by the Imperial War Museums.

No. 45 (Royal Marine) Commando arrived on the Stolzenau side of the river that morning, and Lieutenant David Ward, a section leader in E Troop, went to receive his orders – the Commando was to cross the Weser that afternoon, and support the Rifle Brigade in pushing on Leese. After going down to the river to recce the crossing point, David returned to his troop, and quickly lost his temper.

The majority of the men were drunk.

It transpired that the sleep-deprived commandos, who had been rushed to the area and without a meal, had found a stash of German Army issue beer, and had it for breakfast.

David, and the other officers and Seniors NCOs who had been away for the briefing, cajoled the drunken men down to the river, carrying and rowing the boats themselves, and all while under fire. One would have imagined that this action might have sharpened up the men, but several were drunk to the point that they were incapable of digging a slit trench. Despite the noise of battle several fell asleep, which at least allowed David the chance to search 'the sleeping beauties' and remove any more bottles.

The rest of No. 45 Commando crossed shortly after midday and pushed south along the river, David's 'bedraggled lot' following behind. The Commando was only able to advance some 200 yards to the embankment and the enemy's outpost before being pinned down, several of the men shot through the head as soon as they exposed themselves.

'It was obvious that to look over the bank would be fatal,' said David, 'so we engaged in a grenade-throwing match. The next troop forward was able to snipe into the German position.

'The fighting in the bridgehead had become nothing more than desperate. A furious hand-to-hand struggle resulted. It was during this short, sharp engagement that Captain Dudley Coventry was credited with striking a German soldier dead with one blow of his fist.'[8]

Francis Burton, from Liverpool, had been wounded in Holland but rejoined his 'family' in the Commandos as soon as he was able.

'I can remember seeing a line of Germans running across the top of the bank, and two of our (machine guns) had set up. This chap started at the back of this group of Germans and just mowed the lot of them down. Went right through the line.

'(Our engineers) were trying to make headway on the bridge, but we could see them under fire. They were getting killed. It was tragic. It was terrible to see it, really. To see them being killed trying to do their job.'

Despite the bridge and its surrounding area being subjected to near-constant shelling and air attacks, including sorties made by Messerschmitt Me 262 jet fighters, the Royal Engineers had been working night and day to span the Weser. Several of the sappers had been killed and wounded, and on the evening of the 6th a Stuka dive bomber scored a direct hit on the half-completed bridge, taking thirteen more lives and convincing the British commanders to halt further construction.

'That bridge had symbolized all of our hopes,' said Major Noel Bell, whose G Company now seemed trapped across the river. 'As one sank, so did the other.'[9]

A Black Day for 7 Para

The right flank of VIII Corps had fared much better than the left. Despite the armoured counter-attacks that had cost the 12th Devons so dearly, 6th Airborne was across the river and firmly established in Petershagen.

On 7 April, 7th and 13th Parachute Battalions, mounted in lorries, pushed out of the town en route to Neustadt am Rübenberge. They reached Wunstorf airfield at 1430hrs and, as the airfield had been reported clear, proceeded to motor across it, with B Company in the four leading trucks.

'All hell broke loose,' said Sergeant Walter Tanner. 'I've never seen lorries cleared so quick in all my life.'

Now out on the ground, the Paras found little cover from the incoming fire.

'You've got to imagine what an airfield is like – it's not bumpy, it's dead flat. You try hiding behind blades of grass while someone's firing at you.'

Walter could hear truck tyres popping and deflating as they were struck by the swarms of bullets.

'The Bren gunner got hit. I took the Bren gun and it was just a question of firing anywhere in front of you – at the woods, at this house that was on the other side of the road, because they were firing from there. Then I heard somebody from the back shout, "Christ, they're firing from their aircraft!" There was these aircraft parked and they were firing from these aircraft. I don't know where they were firing from, actually, I never took the trouble to find out.

'Anyway, I fired away and I heard this moan.'

Walter's friend had moved to a firing position beside him and was instantly struck through the neck and shoulder. Walter, believing that the enemy had been aiming at him, later named his eldest son after the man who had unknowingly saved his life.

'Eventually, Tiger Reed, our company commander, gave the order – everybody with bayonets, fix. Now that means you're going to do a charge, and it's not a nice thing. No British soldier, whatever rank he is, likes to do a battalion, company or platoon charge. It means one thing – standing upright, holding that rifle in front of you, your bayonet, and charging and hoping you'll get away with it.'

The entire battalion was about to rush the enemy, and a smoke screen was laid to at least give them some cover from view.

'Then came the order to charge,' said Walter. 'I covered the fastest 200 yards that anybody will ever cover in this world today. I mean that, because I've never run so fast in my life. As I'm running I'm saying, "It's gotta be the next (bullet), it's gotta be the next, it's gotta be the next."

But Walter, unlike many others, was able to make it across the open ground.

'And who's in front of us in the ditch? Colonel Pine-Coffin and the second in command, Major Taylor.

'My platoon sergeant, Sergeant Kealy, he said to me, "Sergeant Tanner, take the men to that house and clear it." Now as we got to get up he said, "I'll come with you," so he led us in. We got to the side of the house and when everyone was tucked in safely, he said, "Right round this side." And as he went round, the Germans come out the door, but he got the shot in first – that (German) died where he stood.

'The next job we got was room clearing. It's not a very nice thing to do really because the only way you can clear a room is open that door, throw in a grenade, or couple of grenades, whatever you can – shut the door, wait for the explosions, open the doors, if anybody's alive, just shoot. Again it comes back to one thing – survival, you or them.

'After we'd done that we checked all the rooms, (and) the dead that was in the rooms. I can't say if we caused their deaths or whether they might have been killed with all the stuff that was being fired at the house and the woods you see. But none of them got out of it alive.'

But someone had taken prisoners, and Walter recalled that they were far from second-rate soldiers.

'What I did see was too many black uniforms with their SS badges, arrogant bastards. I've got to say this, because that's what they were. The mood of the chaps was – kill them. They knew what we were going to do when they saw all the blokes cock their rifles and the Stens and point to them – they knew what was going to happen, make no mistake about that.'

7 Para had lost six men killed and twenty-one wounded in the ambush and wanted blood, but one of their highly respected medics now stepped in.

'His argument was this was the price of war – they were doing a job the same as we were doing a job. They were fighting for what they believed in, and we were doing the same. He stepped forward and he said no, he wouldn't have it, just would not accept it at all, that's not the thing to do.'

These words, coming from 'a wonderful chap', were heeded. The Paras lowered their weapons, and the prisoners lived.

As well as men, a large amount of enemy equipment had been captured at the airfield, including nineteen Messerschmitt 109s, four Fockawulf 190s, two Junkers 88s and two Junkers 52s.

Wishing to waste no more time, the battalion quickly pushed on to Neustadt am Rübenberge to seize its bridge. At some point, as the Paras were quietly patrolling into the town in the darkness, two German soldiers became mixed up with the company.

'We can't say whether they were infiltrating or whether they (thought we were) German troops on the retreat,' said Walter. 'Unfortunately they were both killed, quietly dispatched with knives.'

The town's bridge was found intact, and two of B Company's platoons raced across shortly after midnight.

'My platoon, 6 Platoon, we were kept in reserve and 4 and 5 Platoon were moved up.'

As these men were crossing the bridge, one of the Paras noticed what looked like bombs, and urged the others to move faster, but it was too late.

'I was on (the near) side of the bridge with a couple of my chaps. We got blown off our feet, but it still didn't register the fact that the bridge had gone up. (We assumed) it was a shell that he fired, an 88 or something like that.

'Then we heard these cries. When we got to the bridge there's debris falling and everything. You couldn't believe it – two whole spans had gone. We tried everything we could to try and get across these spans, but we couldn't do it.'

Two of the Paras, one of them named Phil Crofts, volunteered to swim across the river to take medical supplies across, a courageous act given that the Speyerbach was almost in full spate at the time.

'Over the other side of the bridge to the right, there's a house,' said Walter. 'The woman that lived in there, Erika, there was just her and her daughter in there and she turned the whole house over as a first-aid post. Bob Allen, a mate of mine, he was one of the first to cross, he got away with it. He was a Bren gunner but his Bren gun barrel was bent by the force of the explosion.

'He said that this woman was a marvellous woman. She might have been a German, but she looked after the boys, she tended them. One of them died in her arms calling out for his mum and he heard her say, "I am your mother," and he died in her arms.

'Every sheet that was in the house, anything they could tear up for bandages and so forth, she gave it up.'

Walter recalled that Major Reed provided this courageous and kindly woman with a letter, requesting that the army replace everything that she had given up to help the Paras.

B Company, who had already suffered the majority of the six

killed and twenty-one wounded at the airfield, lost a further nineteen killed and nineteen wounded in the bridge explosion.[10] Six other men were missing, and never found.[11] It was a black day for the 7th Parachute Battalion, who had fought so valiantly from D-Day and beyond.

'One thing I've got to say, when we buried our boys the next day with a full military funeral, who's coming through? The Highland Light Infantry, and I've got to say this to those men – those that could stand in their lorries all stood up and saluted, and to us that was a marvellous gesture I'll never forget.'

No Quarter Given

The same day that 7 Para had their battle on the airfield, 11th Armoured Division moved down from Stolzenau and crossed the Weser at Petershagen. Brigadier Mills-Roberts, No. 1 Commando Brigade, noted that the armoured division could not launch its attacks to the north-west until Leese had been taken. The situation around the village had not improved, with the men of 8 Rifle Brigade and No. 45 Commando still pinned down by the river, where they suffered constant sniping and shelling.

After a delay caused by a shortage of boats, the remainder of No. 1 Commando Brigade crossed the Weser that night. They then marched down the river 'like rats wading through the main sewer',[12] and looped around Leese so that they could attack from behind the enemy at dawn. Mills-Roberts, who was sick of 'the ordinary way' of doing things in war, had come up with another plan that surprised the enemy, and in less than twenty minutes they had been driven off their defence line. Sixty-nine of their number, teenagers all, would never leave Leese, and are buried in the village's war cemetery.

No. 3 Commando, now with the support of a squadron of the 23rd Royal Hussars, then pushed a half-mile north to seize a factory that was shrouded by woodland. A fierce fight ensued and Captain John Alderson MC was killed.[13] No. 3 Commando's CO, Lieutenant Colonel Peter Bartholomew, climbed up onto a tank to direct its fire, his runner mortally wounded as he sat beside him.

As Brigadier Mills-Roberts moved into the wooded area he noticed wagons in a railway siding, and was surprised to discover that each was loaded with a V-2 rocket, one bearing a hand-scrawled message: 'To England. Victory at any price.'

A more startling discovery was made in a nearby forest, as Mills-Roberts recalled.

'This forest – that looked so innocent from the air – was composed of large buildings with slab-like roofs of concrete and tracks running close underneath. On top of the concrete was five or six feet of earth and in this earth fir trees and other vegetation sprouted – it was the most convincing piece of camouflage.'[14]

The Imperial War Museums hold film footage of the V2 installation in the woodland, including of the graffitied rocket.[15]

'The entire establishment of the V-2 factory was in our hands, including technicians and research staff. It was a valuable find.'[16]

With a firm bridgehead now established across the Weser, and Leese seized, the other enemy pockets in the area were cleared in a series of violent actions.

On 8 April, the 4th Battalion, King's Shropshire Light Infantry, supported by the 3rd Royal Tank Regiment, advanced into the village of Husum. It was to be the first British contact against members of the 2. Marine-Infanterie-Division, who were bolstered by SS youths. At first the advance of 4 KSLI and 3 RTR encountered little opposition, but soon a battle was joined that would cost seventeen German and thirteen British lives, with more than thirty British soldiers wounded.

Captain Corbett, who served with 4 KSLI, recalled that the tanks had no mercy on the civilian buildings.[17] These dwellings caught alight from tracer, and much of the village of Husum was burned to the ground. The 11th Armoured were again in action against the 'Steel-Eyed Boys', as they called the SS youth, in the village of Steimbke, where the Germans were surrounded on three sides by tanks as the 8th Rifle Brigade cleared the houses one after the other – the teenagers of the SS suffering 150 casualties.

'The SS fought fanatically and every house had to be cleared individually,' wrote Major Noel Bell. 'Our stretcher-bearers were fired on, which spurred us on even more. No quarter was given or asked and very few SS prisoners lived to tell the tale of the battle for Steimbke.'[18]

Some foreign field

With D Company, 2 Ox and Bucks, Harry Clark had taken part in one of the most well known actions of the Second World War, but like thousands of other 'D-Day men', his war did not end at a celebrated bridge, or on a famous beach, but in one of the thousands of streets and fields across the breadth of North West Europe.

Shortly before crossing the Weser, Harry had a 'strange premonition' that he would be killed that night, and wrote a letter to his mother. He told her that everything was OK, and not to worry. A few hours later he was in action on the eastern side of the river.

'Having got through the village, we were advancing down the road. Suddenly a burst of machine-gun fire rang out and before I knew what had happened, I got two bullets in me right hand and two in me left leg. It knocked me to the ground and I received a nasty electric shock from some cables that were on the ground.'

Harry was able to pick himself up and get back into the village of Frille.

'I had a close look at myself and the whole of the centre of my right hand was shot away. One of the lads took me into a house and he said, "Do you have a smoke?" and I said, "I don't smoke," and he said, "Have a smoke, it'll do you a world of good. Make you feel better."

'So I sat and smoked and smoked and smoked and I finished sick as a dog.

'I got down into a cellar because there was a bit of shelling going on and I lay in the cellar all night. I was in considerable pain, there was no morphine available. The following morning, probably it would be some two or three hours after daybreak, a jeep came up to the house. They managed to get a jeep across on a raft. I was put on the jeep, handed a Sten gun and told I would guard six prisoners in front while the driver was driving.

'I don't think I had the strength to pull the trigger so it was a wasted exercise. Having got down to the river, the MO had just come across and he looked at me (and) said "What, you again?" I said, "I think it's my last time, though." He gave me a dose of morphine, got me on a stretcher and he instructed a couple of his men to carry me down to a raft. I remember this old German woman came out of the house and snatched the pillow that was under my head and ran back into the house with it. Captain Smith chased her into the house and got the pillow back. This sticks out in my mind.

'Then I was put aboard the raft, and on it was either the brigadier or the divisional commander, and a newspaper correspondent. I was covered with a German greatcoat as a blanket. I can recall one saying to the other, "Who's that?" and the other saying, "It's a German prisoner." I distinctly recall saying, "I'm not a bloody German, and I'm not a prisoner."'

After crossing the river, Harry was loaded onto a stretcher and placed on a jeep.

'By which time I was feeling really bad. I was driven for some hours to an advanced dressing station, and I was there for some time. A doctor looked at me eventually and I received no treatment. I was loaded onto the jeep again and we were driven for some long distance. I felt like death and I thought my premonition was right.'

Harry eventually arrived at a surgical unit in an old farmhouse and was put on the table.

'Looked like a kitchen table covered with blankets and a kind of mattress. Two RAMC doctors came in and one of them picked up my hand, sniffed it and he whispered to his colleague, "Gangrene." Although he whispered it, my hearing was so acute it was as though he shouted it.

'Then he said, "We'll start straight away, we'll get some drips and that in, and if he's still here at eight o'clock, we'll operate." I assumed with that loss of blood, I'd been bleeding all night, and the gangrene, that I was in a desperate way. This was further confirmed a few minutes later when the padre came in and said, "Not to worry, son, we'll make sure all your personal gear will be sent home to your parents." I thought, *This is it, I must be close to death.*'

In fact, Harry's life was saved, but not without cost.

'They amputated my hand, they dressed me leg and they found a further bullet hole through my foot. So I'd been losing blood through three sources, so I must have been fairly weak. They'd obviously given me transfusions, got rid of the gangrene in the hand by amputating the hand and I felt a thousand per cent better.

'I woke up the next morning at five a.m. I was in a large room, surrounded by casualties on stretchers, and I immediately demanded of the first orderly that he see that I get a strong cup of tea and something to eat. I felt as fit as a fiddle then.

'They moved me further back, near to the town of Cleves, which was just a ruin, everything was bombed. I stayed in a tented hospital there for a further three days. We were in the care then of the army nursing sisters and I can recall them picking me up and carrying me to the toilet. Terrific strength. Much to my horror, we were driven to an airfield outside Cleves and they said we're flying you back to England. After my previous flight on the Rhine crossing, the last thing I wanted to do was to fly. I was filled with dread (at) the thought of flying. They put us in a Dakota and we flew back to England.'

Harry – known as Nobby to his mates – eventually made his way to a hospital in Salford, where he was a patient for three months. It was here that Harry met his future wife, who was a night nurse on the ward. There was also a happy reunion.

'I was suddenly awoken by a voice saying, "Nobby, Nobby!" and I awoke and I saw Charlie Godbald, his nickname was Claude.'

This was a comrade of Harry's whom he had presumed dead.

'I thought perhaps I'd died and I'd joined him in heaven, but when I fully woke up I realized he was there in the flesh, so we had a grand reunion. Although I was bedridden, we managed to scrounge a wheelchair and cross the road into the local pub.

'Much against the doctor's orders, I imbibed a few pints.'

At the time that Harry was wounded, the 53rd (Welsh) Division were approaching a town 130 miles distant from where they had crossed the Rhine two weeks earlier. When one recalls that it had taken the division ten days to push through the seven-mile-wide Reichswald Forest, it is easy to understand why some of the men now believed that serious enemy resistance had crumbled, and that all that remained was a 'swan' across Germany, and then peace.

That belief, and many lives, would end at Rethem.

CHAPTER 20

For Freedom

Actions on the River Aller
9–15 April 1945

'They attacked us all night from every side. The buildings had been set on fire, and you'd got a backdrop of all this glowing and this crackling and sparks and things. It was like some sort of weird movie.

They finally got into the courtyard, the Germans. This is without exaggeration – in one case, there was a three-tonner (truck) with some of the cook staff, lying in the three-tonner, firing at Germans, and Germans under the three-tonner firing at the British.

All the time the heavy armoured cars of ours were firing out over the perimeter, and eventually it died down, and it all stopped. Miraculously, I think there were only three or four casualties throughout the night on our side. There was quite a number of German casualties, I can assure you.'

Joe Abbot, 53rd Reconnaissance Regiment

After leaving the Teutoburger Forest and Ibbenbüren, the 53rd (Welsh) Division were ordered to seize Rethem, a small town of strategic importance, with a bridge that spanned the River Aller, and a major road passing through to Hamburg. They were then to push north and seize the important crossroads and bridge at the village of Verden.

The division's first obstacle to achieving this was the River Weser, which would need to be crossed and bridged to allow the division to 'shake out' and deploy for the assault on Rethem and the villages that surrounded it. Patrols were sent out across the river, both to reconnoitre the enemy's strength and positions, and find possible crossing points. One of these patrols, belonging to 4 Welch, came to disaster on the night of the 8th, when their boat was shot up while crossing the river. Of the seventeen men who left on the patrol, only four returned.

On 9 April, the 6th Battalion, Royal Welch Fusiliers were tasked with seizing the eastern side of Hoya, the western side of the village already in British hands. Hoya was bisected by the Weser, and the enemy had entrenched themselves on the other side after blowing both the road and rail bridges. On the north-eastern corner of the village was an airfield, now disused, which attested to the level nature of the countryside.

Bruce Coombs was turning twenty years old that day, but instead of enjoying his birthday with his family, and sharing a few pints with his pals back home in Kidwelly, Bruce was spending his youth at war, just like his father had done. In the morning, heart in his mouth, Bruce and his comrades carried a few soft-skinned boats down to the river's steep bank. Two companies were going across the river, while the rest of the battalion gave fire support from the western bank.

'As luck would have it, the river was so fast flowing we went down further from the village than what we should have done, and we crossed onto the middle of the airfield. Well, it was a good thing really, because if we'd have crossed further up, we'd have had more casualties.'

The Germans were firing on the two companies across the river, but were so far away that they were struggling to hit their targets. They were also having to contend with the artillery barrage laid down on top of them.

'One lad from Manchester had a bullet in his foot,' recalled Bruce, who was hitting back at the enemy with his Bren gun.

The enemy's fire became a lot heavier and more accurate as the Fusiliers entered the village. Bruce and his assistant gunner – known as his number two – laid down suppressing fire as their comrades fought house to house. The enemy put up a fierce defence in a manor house that perched on the river, but Hoya was cleared that morning, and construction of a Bailey bridge was soon underway.

'My number two, he went to run across the road and he got killed. He fell with his head on the pavement like a cushion, and they put bullets into him when he was on the road as well.'

Bruce's battalion suffered twenty-one casualties on his twentieth birthday, four of them killed. Their ages were twenty-two, twenty-one, twenty-two, and nineteen. 6 RWF was a pre-war Territorial Battalion, but the men who died at Hoya included one soldier from Middlesex, and another from London, giving insight into the decimation of its original ranks, and how the face of Britain's 'county' regiments had changed so drastically after the ten-month campaign in North West Europe.

With Hoya secured, the sappers of the Royal Engineers began to span the Weser with a Bailey bridge, which would allow the rest of the division to cross for the attack on Rethem and its surrounding villages. Unbeknown to the British, a full-strength German marine regiment had arrived in the town on 7 April. Converted to the infantry role from their previous occupations in the German navy, these marines were mostly aged seventeen to twenty-three, and well motivated. The regiment didn't waste any time setting up defences in the nearby villages, and in and around Rethem itself. As was often the case as new defence lines were formed, some unlucky farmers had their houses and outbuildings turned into strongpoints, as one resident recalled: 'We were christened Strongpoint Elfriede when the first defenders occupied our house. The establishment of the defences telegraphed no good, and we were to experience everything that a strongpoint could experience in war.'[1]

The civilians of Rethem were soon to witness all the horror of battle. We should also remember that many of the soldiers on each side of the coming battle were civilians themselves until drafted by their respective nations. Many had not volunteered for the war, but would have to fight it, regardless, if only for their own survival, and that of their friends.

Rethem

In the early hours of 10 April, the metal spans of a Bailey bridge rang with the tramp of hob-nailed boots as soldiers crossed the Weser in their thousands.

The 53rd Division's plan to seize Rethem called for a series of staged attacks by its battalions, who would follow each other over the single Bailey bridge at Hoya. 7 RWF would clear the village of Hassel, followed by 4 Welch, who would take Eystrup and secure the division's right flank. 1/5 Welch would push through to seize Rethem and its bridge over the Aller, while 1 East Lancs would secure Hohenholz, and clear the nearby woods. Compared to the division's experience in the Reichswald it was a straightforward plan, and a swift success was expected.

It all started well enough, with 7 RWF securing Hassel by 0300 hrs. 4 Welch pushed through, and the village of Eystrup was secured an hour later.

The men of 1/5 Welch had a ten-mile march to Rethem, some of it along the sandy tracks of pine forests. At 0830hrs the soldiers heard the rumble of guns as the 25-pounders of the 133rd Field Artillery began their bombardment of Rethem's Old Town, which caused an outbreak of fires. Recognizing the bombardment for what it was, the flak guns of Rethem's defenders began firing into likely forming-up points and start lines that could be used to launch the attack.

The leading soldiers of 1/5 Welch began to come across communication wires running through the woods, and heard the sound of vehicles bringing food to the marines in the forward positions outside of the town. At 0900 hrs they came under light fire from the enemy in the woodland, but pressed on.

C Company then hit the first of the farmhouses-cum-enemy-strongpoints, and were subjected to withering fire from machine guns, as well as the flak guns on the outskirts of the town. C

Company were ordered to deal with the strongpoint itself, while B Company wrapped around their left flank to enter the town from the north.

At first the going was good, B Company hidden by a mist rolling across the flat and featureless fields. But then the mist began to burn away and, to the men's horror, they were still a quarter of a mile from the edge of the town and, worse, trapped in the fire of two strongpoints. The German gunners likely couldn't believe the target that presented itself in front of them, and opened up. Caught in a crossfire of machine guns and flak, B Company were pinned down, and started digging into the ground with their fingernails.

Major Bowker, who had taken command of 1/5 Welch after Lieutenant-Colonel Morrison-Jones had been killed by a mine a week earlier, now made the bold decision to send three Bren carriers and two Wasp flamethrowers headlong into Rethem along the main road.[2] This task force was commanded by Sergeant Douglas Moses, and through a combination of speed and surprise, coupled with the marines' inexperience at handling Panzerfausts, the force was not only able to enter the town, but succeeded in eliminating the crews of three anti-tank guns on its outskirts. They raced on into Rethem itself, hosing down buildings with their flamethrowers and machine guns, until they were stopped 450 yards short of their objective: the bridge over the Aller.

Both sides traded heavy fire. One of the Wasps was then hit by a Panzerfaust with the loss of all crew. A German officer was covered in flammable liquid, which failed to take light. The gallant attack had stalled and the task force had to withdraw, with three men killed and three missing.

'Sergeant Moses commanded the force and brought havoc and death to the stern opposition,' said the author of the recommendation for his Military Medal. 'All the while, the force were under heavy small-arms fire from all sides.'[3]

Meanwhile, a possible bridgehead on the Aller was secured when 4 Welch, supported by the 5th Royal Tank Regiment, took the village of Westen in the face of light opposition. Westen could be developed as a bridgehead if necessary, but for now Rethem remained the division's main focus.

After a reconnaissance flight was made over the town and confirmed that its bridge was still intact, 1/5 Welch were ordered to resume their attack in the late afternoon – this time, with three regiments of artillery in support.

The enemy's strongpoints continued to dog the attackers, and the capture of the Strassengabel farmhouse was all-important. It was finally taken by C Company after bloody fighting, only to be lost in a counter-attack by the German marines. The gallant officer who led the attack, Leutnant zur See Wittman, was fatally wounded in the stomach and asked his men to end his agony. They refused, and the remaining ten German defenders were overwhelmed by C Company at 1505 hrs.[4] They would have a short respite before joining A Company in the resumed attack on Rethem at 1735 hrs.

Artillery pummelled the town, but proved ineffective. Barely had the companies risen at their start lines than they came under such a weight of fire that they were forced to ground – the attack was over before it could begin. The battalion withdrew under cover of darkness, having suffered one officer and forty-seven other ranks killed or wounded. When B Company extracted from the open field where they had been pinned down since early morning, a roll call was taken:

Only twenty-four men answered their names.

Death in the Woods

In the evening of 10 April, 6 RWF and two troops of the 5th Royal Tank Regiment were ordered to push from Hoya to Anderten at best speed, dispensing with their usually cautious protocols. Sources are split as to why this decision was made. Some say it was complacency; others that it was an acceptable risk as it would deny the enemy, who were retreating from several places, any time to reorganize. Given that the division had been experiencing heavy fighting all day at Rethem, and remembering that 6 RWF had lost twenty-one casualties just the day before, the suggestion that the

Planes and parachutes fill the skies east of the Rhine at the onset of Operation Varsity, when the British 6th and US 17th Airborne divisions dropped en masse, 24 March 1945.

Airborne soldiers take cover in the wreckage of their glider during Operation Varsity, 24–25 March 1945. Harry Clark, 2 Ox and Bucks, described the landings as mass murder.

The wreckage of gliders lies all around the rail yard at Hamminkeln, where Pegasus Bridge veterans Wally Parr and Billy Gray found the stranded American journalist. Over half of their battalion, 2 Ox and Bucks, became casualties during the Rhine crossing, including Wally.

Left: 97 per cent of Wesel was destroyed by bombing during the war, but it was still an important hub of the Rhine defences and took around forty-eight hours of fighting to secure between 23 and 25 March 1945. *Right:* Some of the 850 prisoners that No. 1 Commando Brigade took during the battle are gathered in a bomb crater prior to being taken back across the Rhine, which can be seen in the background.

Soldiers of the 6th Battalion, King's Own Scottish Borderers cautiously advance past the bodies of German soldiers, east of the Rhine, 25 March 1945.

A Bailey bridge over the Rhine nears completion, 24–25 March 1945. The sappers braved shell fire and air attack to build the lifelines that would support the army as it broke out beyond the river.

Members of No. 45 (Royal Marine) Commando show off trophies captured at Wesel, 28 March 1945.

Soldiers of the 2nd Battalion, Monmouthshire Regiment at Bocholt, on the Dutch-German border. The graffiti on the wall reads: 'Now more than ever: Heil Hitler!' 29 March 1945.

Tanks pass through Stadtholn following its capture by 9th Durham Light Infantry and the 5th Royal Inniskilling Dragoon Guards, 31 March 1945.

88mm anti-aircraft guns at Rethem, knocked out by 5th Royal Tank Regiment and the artillery called in by Major Richard Hughes MC, 13 April 1945.

Churchill tanks of 6th Guards Tank Brigade with infantry, carriers and half-tracks of 15th (Scottish) Division wait to advance towards the River Elbe, 13 April 1945.

A Bren gunner takes cover behind a First World War memorial as Uelzen burns, 18 April 1945.

Armour and infantry advance into Bremen, 26 April 1945. For many of XXX Corps' soldiers, the battle to seize the city and its satellite towns would be the last time that they fired their weapons in anger.

Left: Scots Greys tanks on Wismar's town square. Murray Walker, a troop commander in the regiment, was one of the winners of the race to the Baltic and helped prevent Denmark from falling under Soviet occupation, 2 May 1945.

Right: Sapper Griffiths, from Bootle, shares a drink with a Russian tanker at Wismar, 3 May 1945.

Below: Field Marshall Montgomery meets the German delegation at Lüneburg Heath to discuss their surrender, 3 May 1945.

Top left: Bob Parker Atkinson, 1945. *Top right:* Bill Lingard and Arthur Jones (facing camera) of the 5th Battalion, Duke of Cornwall's Light Infantry, working on the tracks of a universal carrier before the Rhine crossing.

Ted Rutland, who served in the Royal Armoured Corps, pictured in late 2024.

decision was born of complacency seems wide of the mark. Rather, it was most likely one of the many difficult decisions made in war, where risk is weighed against reward. Make the right choice, and the decision is remembered as tactical brilliance. Fail, and men die.

Of course, the old soldiers of 5 RTR had every right to be cautious – some of them had been fighting since the desert, and were reticent to push their luck. The regiment's war diarist recorded that a troop leader objected to the infantry company commander about moving through a thick wood without some sort of foot recce, 'but it was considered that there would be no opposition and speed was essential.'[5]

Sergeant George Stimpson, a desert veteran of 5 RTR, recalled that during their briefing they had been told that infantry had already patrolled into the wood that morning, and that it could therefore be considered clear of the enemy.

'With this in mind, the first few miles would be carried out at the double, with the infantry riding on the back of the tanks.'[6]

When Allied fighter bombers were spotted in the sky, George's troop stopped to display their recognition panels, while 11 Troop – unaware of this change of circumstances – continued into the wood. Shortly after, George heard the sounds of gunfire and explosions. 11 Troop had driven into an ambush that would prove tragic for both 5 RTR and 6 RWF. Two of the troops' tanks were able to pull back out of what had quickly become 'a terrific and bloody battle', but of the other two there was no sign.

One of these tanks belonged to George's great friend, Jake Wardrop, and George was granted permission to go in search of him and the other missing men. Volunteers to accompany him were not in short supply, and George was soon heading into the woods.

'It was rather quiet and frightening, but there was no signs of the enemy. The two tanks were still and quiet and there were bodies of British soldiers everywhere. I found Jake's body at the side of his tank. They were gunned down as they tried to escape.'

Interviews with survivors, recorded close to the time, give an immediate insight into the events. Nineteen-year-old Fusilier William Haley, 6 RWF, was riding on the tank at the head of the troop.[7]

'When approaching a T-junction I observed movement on the right-hand side of the junction but it was not possible to communicate with the tank commander due to all the noise.

'We turned left at the junction and up ahead we could see a tree blocking the road. We approached slowly, still aboard the tanks. We dismounted – I was on the right-hand side of the tank – and moved up to the obstruction, following in line. Suddenly a lance-corporal doubled back towards me saying, "There are Jerries up there," and kept going. Then the action started. Panzerfausts knocked out the second tank, blocking the first against the obstruction; this tank must also have been hit, as I immediately dropped flat in the shallow, roadside gully and was joined by the first tank's crew. My first reaction was alarm that I appeared to be the only one armed in this little group. I took up a firing position and the face of a young German popped up just a couple of yards in front of me. I fired and didn't see him again.'

William's rifle jammed, and he wasn't able to clear it without exposing himself to the heavy fire that seemed to be coming from everywhere.

An unnamed Fusilier from B Company, 6 RWF, recalled that: 'The enemy fired all he had at us, and we did the same, keeping their heads down while we obtained good fire positions. The only support we received was from our tank, which fired one burst as it turned round and retired the way we had come, instead of putting up a fight with us as we had hoped. We were left by ourselves. Underneath the knocked-out tank was one of the dead crew and another badly wounded.

'We thought at first we might be able to hold Jerry off until support came. No support did come, however, and more of our boys were killed and our platoon commander, Lieutenant Castles, was wounded in the face, shot through the shoulder and again through the wrist. He was bleeding badly, as was the fellow by the tank, but we could do nothing for them.'[8]

'The noise of action was all around,' said William Haley. 'Sniper fire from the treetops was "pinging" about. After a while – it seemed an eternity – I heard our officer shouting, "*Kamerad, Kamerad!*"

With the enemy creeping up on them from all sides, and with casualties mounting, Lieutenant Castles made the decision to surrender before his men were wiped out.

'The Germans took over,' said William. 'They seemed a mix bag; young and old. We were taken through the forests and one wounded tank crew member was left in a forest cottage to be looked after by civilians.'

The group of prisoners eventually arrived in Rethem, 'where we received the usual hostile welcome for POWs. After a few kicks, etcetera, we were told to empty our pockets into our helmets and wait for interrogation. I went in before two officers, one of whom spoke very good English.'

This man asked William what he was fighting for.

'And I replied, "For freedom," but I must admit I felt a little foolish. He got angry and said, "Bloody Englishman, get out!" We were then marched to Stalag XI-B.'

Historian John Russell makes the convincing argument that this ambush was likely carried out by marines who were making their way to Rethem following their eviction from Hoya – the very men that the mixed force and tanks were trying to find, and cut off. One can pore over the reasons why events unfolded as they did, and who was to blame (if anyone), but in the end it is nothing but a moot point. What matters most is that the soldiers of both 5 RTR and 6 RWF suffered the loss of dear friends and comrades, and that these men would never return to their families.

One of those killed in the ambush, Sergeant Jake Wardrop, had kept a diary during the desert campaign. It was recovered from his stricken tank by George Stimpson and later published, providing one of the most immediate and intimate accounts of the war.[9] A letter written by Jake to his mother, explaining his decision to remain at the cutting edge of battle, was also passed down to us. It speaks to the man who would not leave his comrades, and the price that might be paid for that unwavering loyalty.

'I am a tank commander, and I shall continue to be one until the end. Should it be the wrong one, don't worry, I played the game as it seemed to me the right way to play it. I have respected the women, and given my rations to the little children because they were hungry, and have shot the Germans down and laughed because of lost friends. And in any case, they started it.'[10]

"Kill! Kill! Kill!"

War is an exhausting business. During the first day of the 53rd Division's Rethem operation the infantry had either been marching to battle, fighting one, digging slit trenches, or standing watch against counter-attack. Sleep, if it happened at all, was measured in minutes.

'A number of our new reinforcements were very young and all became quickly exhausted,' wrote Captain Cuthbertson, 7 RWF. 'It was the only time that I observed soldiers asleep standing up, leaning on their rifles.'[11]

1/5 Welch, who had seen the heaviest fighting, were again ordered to make an attack on Rethem on 11 April. H-Hour was 0445 hrs, and the battle no less savage than the previous day. A civilian in the cellar of the von der Kammer farm, now a strongpoint, remembered that 'It came to hand-to-hand fighting – we could tell by the noise. Ownership of the house changed on several occasions. During a quiet period I crawled out and saw a mountain of bodies.'[12]

At times the different floors of the farmhouse would be held by different sides, with British below and Germans above them. The civilians took this opportunity to leave, which the 'English soldiers' let them do.

'At the next strongpoint the German soldiers prevented us from going further and told us we had to turn back as they were concerned we would betray their position. We had to return and hid under a dung-heap near the house.

'Heavy fire forced us to leave our hide in the dung-heap and we crawled through the plough furrows. The children gave us the most trouble. Even though we must have been recognized as civilians we were fired on by German soldiers. One of the women had a pram with her which was pierced by a bullet but luckily the baby was not hit. I dragged a child on top of a pillow behind me.'[13]

The attacks were no less bloody and no more successful than those made the previous day, and after two hours the companies of 1/5 Welch fell back, withdrawing under cover of their own artillery. Casualties were so heavy that A Company had to be broken up, its survivors distributed between the other companies to bolster their dwindling numbers.

Leslie George was an old hand in the battalion's anti-tank platoon and had been awarded the DCM for an action in Normandy, where he had single-handedly engaged an enemy tank, amongst other heroic acts. Leslie was regarded as 'a bad bastard' in the battalion, akin to the term 'badass' in today's language, but even he was shocked by the fierce resistance at Rethem.

'I remember it was a total shock, especially for the younger intake who had not until then encountered heavy action.'[14]

In little more than twenty-four hours the 1/5 Welch had lost seven officers and 186 other ranks – nearly a quarter of a battalion's full strength. They were the victims of circumstance – the presence of fresh and determined troops had been unknown – and perhaps, more tellingly, the wearing down of the Second Army from months of near continual combat.

By April the 53rd Division was – in some respects – as green as it had been when it landed in Normandy a little over nine months earlier. Veterans remained in the ranks, but what was absent was the years of training that it takes to gel old soldiers with new, replacements coming into the division by the thousands. The rate of loss for experienced NCOs and officers, in particular, was incredibly high – there were only so many times that they could put themselves in the most dangerous positions to lead, and get away with it. It was a problem felt across all of Britain's infantry divisions.

'Some of our reinforcements were not even infantry,' recalled Freddie Graham, a battalion level officer in the 15th (Scottish) Division. 'The number of people still serving who had landed in Normandy with us were quite small. So a combination of lack of trained leaders and trained manpower meant that simple tactics had to be employed. From this time on, attacks were like the infantry assaults of World War One – anything more ambitious would have been beyond us. The trained leaders were no longer there. That was the instrument with which we had to complete the campaign.'[15]

This may explain what happened next at Rethem, when the 2nd Battalion, Monmouthshire Regiment, were detailed to take over from 1/5 Welch and attack the town in a frontal assault. They would be supported by B Squadron, 5 RTR.

Edward Wilson, a troop commander, recalled that the ground over which the assault force advanced was better suited to a medieval battlefield than a modern one. In front of the railway embankment, where the enemy had placed their deadly flak guns, was a flat, open area some 600 yards wide and 1,200 deep – it was over this killing ground that the tanks and infantry were expected to advance – and this in daylight. H-Hour for the attack was 1600, and would be preceded by twenty-four rocket-firing Typhoons, followed by a twenty-minute artillery barrage.

Major Richard Hughes MC was the commander of 497 Battery, 132nd Field Regiment.

'We had a fairly large amount of artillery available to us. Regardless of how the Hun reacted, we were going to need it because our advance to the town meant crossing about one and a half miles of flat, open country, all in full view of the enemy.

'Across our approach to the town ran a railway line. It seemed reasonable to assume that there would be a line of resistance at or around that area. I therefore arranged for six Medium regiments to "treat" the railway for fifteen minutes. As part of the fire plan I ordered 2,000 rounds of smoke shells.'[16]

Richard, who had first seen action in 1940, wondered if the war's slaughter would ever end, but until that long-awaited moment he would have to continue to play his part. Otto Pfister, a German marine, was on the end of the artillery fires that Richard ordered. 'It was terrifying. The moans and the screams of the injured still ring in my ears.'[17]

One of the 2 Mons soldiers assaulting the embankment was Dai Edwards. 'They shelled it and shelled it to such an extent that we found out later that the crews of the 88s had cleared off, but the

20mm ones hadn't. They were still there, and they caused some real problems.'

Just 450 yards short of the town, the assault force came under a massive weight of fire from both flak guns and infantry. They gave as good as they got, particularly because a rumour – later disproven – had gone around that the German defenders were killing British prisoners. 5 RTR's tanks engaged the enemy's guns on the embankment with machine-gun fire and high-explosive shells. The dead piled around the guns, but as soon as one crew was killed another seemed to spring up in their place.

And yet, despite the opening barrage and the support of 5 RTR, a third of B Company, 2 Mons had soon become casualties.

'We were digging in with our fingers,' said Dai Edwards, 'scratching the ground away to get into some sort of cover. There was a German lying about fifteen yards from me, and he was raising his one hand, and then down it would go. And then he'd raise it, as if he was waving to somebody. The stretcher-bearers eventually got to him.'

5 RTR's crews continued to engage guns, infantry and even a train that was attempting to build up steam. One troop made it onto the embankment before a hail of Panzerfaust projectiles forced them to withdraw. Their ammunition expended after two hours of battle, B Squadron was relieved by C, who continued the engagement. One would imagine that after losing nine of their comrades in the woods the previous day, the men of C Squadron went into the battle with a mix of trepidation, and the desire for revenge.

The attack was, however, doomed to failure. After stalling at the embankment, momentum was never regained, and the infantry were withdrawn under the cover of the tanks and artillery. Richard Hughes, who longed for an end to the war, coordinated the guns. 'While our troops were coming back I again leathered the town with medium, heavy and field artillery, with one thought in mind – Kill! Kill! Kill!'[18]

Casualties were collected and piled into B Company's Bren carrier, which was commanded by Corporal Dawson and driven by Private Wild. After darkness had fallen the battlefield continued to be illuminated by the blazing buildings of the town, but, undaunted, Dawson and Wild returned to within fifty yards of the enemy to check every fallen body, bringing back those who showed signs of life. For this heroic action both men were awarded the Military Medal. Lieutenant Mackenzie, who had continued to encourage his men despite suffering six wounds, was awarded the DSO.

Withdrawn behind the road from where they'd started the attacks, the tankies of 5 RTR and their colleagues of the 'Poor Bloody Infantry' shared brews and grumbled about the absurdity of that day's plan. It was at last decided that further attacks on Rethem would be held off until bombers and Crocodile flame-throwing tanks were made available, and this delay now provided the infantry with an opportunity.

Those that could closed their eyes, and slept.

No Headlines

On the morning of 12 April, George Stimpson, 5 RTR, returned to the battlefield to recover one of his troop's tanks that had been abandoned the previous night. Stopping his four tanks 200 yards shy of a level crossing, George and his Sergeant Ted Lines decided it would be safe enough to recce ahead on foot. They dismounted, and with their two hull gunners, proceeded to patrol into the town. He described the events that followed in a letter to historian John Russell.[19]

'We soon reached the level crossing with no trouble and were able to have a closer look at the dead soldiers lying in the field. There must have been a whole company of them and I don't think I have ever been so saddened as I was that morning.'

Seeing no sign of an ambush, George called the four tanks forwards. They were just around the next corner when a party of civilians appeared carrying a white flag. With them was Rethem's mayor, who let it be known that most of the German defenders had withdrawn, and the town wanted to surrender.

'I said OK provided all arms were laid down and the remaining troops formed up on the road. Failing this we would shoot the lot!'

Word was sent back to 5 RTR's commanding officer, Lieutenant-Colonel Leakey, who quickly came forward. As he was awaiting the CO's arrival, George Stimpson was taken to the basement of a large building that was being used as a hospital staffed by German nursing sisters. He estimated that there must have been a hundred wounded on the floor, and half of them British. Seventy-year-old Doktor Hoffmeyer saved the lives of many of these men. 'His heroism was talked about long after the war's end,' said John Russell.[20]

Once he had reported to the incoming Squadron Leader, George and Ted Lines went forward to inspect the bridge, which was found to be blown – apparently it had been struck by a rocket fired from a Typhoon, which caused the demolition charges to blow, and had hampered the retreat of the marines leaving the town. They instead escaped by small boats, through woods, and used a ferry, which they then scuttled.

A handful of the enemy had remained in Rethem, either by accident or to hamper the British advance. When a German marine took a shot at Lieutenant John Gwilliam, who was dismounted from his tank, the big Welshman disappeared around the corner and reappeared moments later, carrying the young German by the scruff of his neck. He had spared the marine's life because he was 'much too small' to shoot. [21]

John Gwilliam went on to win twenty-three caps for Wales, thirteen as captain, and enjoyed victories over Australia and the All Blacks, as well as winning a Triple Crown. It will not surprise fans of the sport that his position was No. 8.

As morning wore on, 2 Mons followed the tanks into the town and found a scene of devastation.

'I remember seeing an old (man) and his wife, I assume,' said Dai Edwards. 'They'd been crossing the road when they'd been killed. They were lying there, holding hands. There was lots of that sort of thing.'

George Stimpson had served in several campaigns, but was still capable of being shocked by the brutality of battle, and its aftermath.

'When I walked into Rethem with Sergeant Ted Lines I saw by far the largest number of dead and wounded British soldiers that I had ever seen. Although it can never be compared with the larger battles of the war, a fair-sized battle involving heavy fighting took place (at Rethem) but it never made the headlines; in fact, it has hardly warranted a mention (since).'[22]

1/5 Welch and 2 Mons suffered a combined 251 men killed, wounded and missing at Rethem. The German marines defending the town lost seventy-three men, an unknown number wounded, and 339 taken prisoner. Fifteen of Rethem's inhabitants were killed, including Inge, Hilde and Horst Bassman – their ages nine, seven and five years old.

Many of those killed with weapons in their hands were little older than children themselves. Captain Eric Wilde, 5 RTR, recalled that they looked to be sixteen to eighteen years old. In a letter to John Russell he wrote, 'Even then, when one was pretty hardened to death and suffering, we all, I think, felt pity for such young lives being sacrificed.'[23]

Across the Aller

On 11 April, with Rethem still unoccupied by the 53rd Division, 4 Welch went into action at the riverside village of Barnstedt. C Company's first attack on the village had been fought off, and when a second was launched the leading platoon became pinned down in Barnstedt's outskirts.

Seeing that the platoon was cut off and in danger of being surrounded, acting Company Sergeant Major Roy Finch ran forwards alone and was immediately engaged by a machine-gun crew firing through the cover of a nearby bank. Without hesitation Sergeant Major Finch charged the position and, despite being wounded in the arm, killed the gun team. He then immediately charged and silenced a second machine-gun post. Seconds after taking the position, a grenade exploded only yards away, breaking his leg and blowing the fingers off one hand.

By this time Finch was within ten yards of one of the leading platoon's sections. When two men came to carry him into the cover of a barn, Finch ordered them to lie him next to the slit in the wall, from where he continued to encourage his men and engage the enemy, firing one-handed and having his weapon reloaded by one of the section. By taking out the machine-gun nests Sergeant Major Finch had turned the course of the battle. He was recommended for the Victoria Cross, but was awarded the DCM.

That night the East Lancs moved to Westen, a village north of Rethem, which had been taken by 7 RWF. Westen lay on the Aller, and in the early hours the East Lancs began to cross by boat. First to cross was A Company, led by Major Whiteside, who had replaced the wounded Joe Cêtre.

'We crossed in the early hours of the morning,' recalled Bob Atkinson, who was now the second in command of a section. 'It was a swift-running river, and D Company had a boat turned over when they were crossing. There were twelve drowned.'

'It were light then, and you could see they were underwater,' said D Company's Tommy Neary. 'Swept away like that, they were. Only two got out.'

Despite this immediate tragedy, the East Lancs pushed on across the fields towards the villages of Otersen and Wittlohe. They were supported by a barrage fired by 25-pounders.

As Bob Atkinson advanced he saw a large group of men emerging from behind a hedgerow. 'They were in brown uniform, and they had Spandaus and all sorts, and they're putting their hands up. I think the artillery had frightened them. They were shouting "*Hungar! Hungar!*"

Not recognizing the men's accents and appearance, Bob replied, "'I don't give a damn if you're Home Guard!'"

In fact, the men in brown uniforms were Hungarian soldiers serving with the German forces, and some of the sixty-five captured by the East Lancs that day. Some surrendered readily, but others put up a fight.

'I remember seeing a chap I knew well, Sergeant Major (Edward Potts) DCM, and he got sniped. Killed by a sniper,' said Tommy Neary, who came close to being shot himself.

'I could feel my pants (flapping), and I could hear this shout behind me.'

Bullets had passed through the material of Tommy's trousers and struck the leg of the man behind him.

Sniper Owen Butcher remembered stiff opposition, and 'quite a few casualties. I think there was about six killed and twenty wounded.'

All told, the East Lancs suffered twenty-one men dead that day, many of them drowned when their boat had overturned on the Aller. After the East Lancs had crossed over, 555 Field Company had begun building a Class 9 folding boat bridge at the scene of that tragedy.

'When we got there we were under machine-gun fire from the opposite side,' said Bob Summers. 'We built this bridge mostly under machine-gun fire. I don't think they were Germans, I think they were Hungarians, actually.

'By the grace of God we'd had no casualties, I can't understand why.'

Several Hungarian prisoners taken on the Aller claimed that they had been deliberately firing high. This may be true in some cases, but it's also in a prisoner's best interest to convince his captor that he wasn't trying to kill him just a few moments before. Whatever the reason, the boat bridge at Westen was built, and 7 RWF pushed across to expand the bridgehead.

No sooner had one bridge been completed than Bob Summers and his men were called down to Rethem, where 244 Company were building a Bailey bridge capable of bearing tanks.

'We got down there at about midday, I suppose, and the place was being shelled like anything. My job was to build what they called the landing bay on the far side. To do that we had to keep on crossing the river. Shells were all over the place.

'In the end we had to stop (because of the shelling), and we went back at night.' At that time the troop was visited by the most senior engineer in the division, a lieutenant-colonel, who began making suggestions. The troop sergeant must have been a believer that too many chefs spoil the broth, and told his superior officer in no uncertain terms that "I'm in charge of this bridge. Bugger off."'

'And the lieutenant-colonel did as he was told,' Bob chuckled.

'The thing that annoyed us (was that) it was obvious the war was going to finish only one way, and yet the silly fools were blowing up bridges, and doing all sorts of things, causing themselves no end of destruction, which was completely unnecessary. German soldiers, fighting right to the end.

'At Rethem, the German soldiers just committed suicide, really. It was terrible. But on the other hand, they were the enemy, and they had to be shot.'

Richard Hughes, whose artillery had played a large part in the killing at Rethem, was ordered across the Aller the day after the town was taken.

'Understandably we were all getting very weary: Drive on – Attack! – Drive on!!! Will it never end????'[24]

At times like these it must have seemed that the only way out of the war was through death or terrible wounds.

'We were going out and bumping into enemy all the way,' said Joe Abbot, 53rd Reconnaissance Regiment, 'and they were dug in all the way once you'd gone a mile or two (from the river), so it was obvious we weren't going to get very far.'

On the night of the 13th, a series of determined counter-attacks were made against the 53rd Division's units that were across the Aller. C Squadron, 53 Recce, were located at a farm some 500 yards east of Wittlohe.

'We took up positions around HQ,' said Joe Abbot, who was known as 'Bud' to his mates. 'About eleven o'clock at night, well, I was making my way from one trench to another trench to see that everything was OK, and then the bazookas came over. The blast caught me and lifted me up and put me over the bonnet of a (vehicle). I heard somebody say, "Bud's had it!", and that was it. Nothing for a minute, and then I sort of gradually came around, and fortunately all I'd got was a cut across my knee.

'The next thing I remember was Goldsmid[25] coming over to me saying, "Corporal Abbot, get your men together. Go and help 6 Troop." We got there just as the Germans were attacking, and a bloke in the German side was shouting, "You might as well give up, the war's over for you." Well, I won't tell you what reply he got. It wasn't printable, I'm afraid.'

There was no surrender, and the battle raged on all sides of the farmhouse and its outbuildings.

'They attacked us all night from every side,' said Joe. 'The buildings had been set on fire, and you'd got a backdrop of all this glowing and this crackling and sparks and things. It was like some sort of weird movie.'

Close-quarter battle ensued, but C Squadron were able to kill or drive back the enemy, including those who had made it inside the courtyard.

'We learned later that these were some German marines, and German paratroops, and others. We had a chap called Rockfield, he was a White Russian, and he was dashing about shouting orders in German, to confuse the Germans, but unfortunately he was one that got shot, so I don't know quite who shot him.'[26]

The fighting was heavy across all of the division's positions. 7 RWF, in particular, were in danger of being overrun, and fought a close-quarter battle through the night to hold their ground. Had the attacks succeeded, the new bridges on the Aller, paid for in lives, would have been in danger of destruction. Instead, they could now be used to carry men, supplies and armour for a push on Verden.

Bob's Number Comes Up

Bob Atkinson, 1 East Lancs, recalled the terrain between Rethem and Verden as being 'typical English country. Farming country, I'd call it.'

On 16 April, he was up at the front of the battalion as they approached the village of Kirchlinteln. This was part of a push by two of the 53rd Division's infantry brigades, as well as 4th Armoured Brigade.

'There was myself, my Bren gunner, and his number two, and this corporal was behind us. There was eight of us, going up the road.'

The enemy opened fire, and five of the eight fell down dead, or wounded. The call went out for a stretcher-bearer, and one lone man came up.

'He had nobody, he was on his own, so he had to get one o' t' lads to help. A young lad had "volunteered". I said, "Come on, we've gotta have somebody to take it." He got volunteered. Picked it up. Took about half a dozen steps. He got hit by a sniper right in t' head. He went down. Anyway, another lad. I said, "Come on, somebody has to get hold of him. Lad can't go on his own wit' stretcher. Somebody'll have to help.' A lad called Geordie Cave got it. He got hold of the stretcher. Sniper fired again. It ripped (Cave's helmet) open, like a tin opener.'

The soldier immediately turned around in the direction that the sniper had fired from.

'I'm not telling a word of a lie. He said, "You silly bastard, get your sight straightened!"

'Anyway, he took him back, did Geordie.'

A Company then continued its advance.

'We were crossing open ground, and it was woods in front,' said Bob Atkinson. 'This machine gun (and) rifles opened up at us. We'd no cover. We'd no cover whatsoever.

'I said to (my officer), "If you don't get the Crocs in and burn them out, they're going to finish your platoon off, cause we got a lot of casualties there." I used a few words beside, I think, but still.'

The Crocodiles soon appeared, and lashed long tongues of flame into the woods.

'You could hear them screaming when this fire hit 'em. No doubt about it, it was fierce, but it was your life or theirs. You either lost all your men, or you got someone to stop 'em.'

A few lucky enemy escaped the flames and were captured. Bob recalled the manner of one.

'He was impudent. "You haven't won the war yet," he said. "We'll still beat you."'

The prisoner's war was over, but Bob and his comrades had to push on and begin clearing the village. A Company lost their company commander in the fighting, the battalion's war diarist mistakenly typing the name 'Major Cetre', which is perhaps an indication that Joe Cêtre's presence was still felt in the East Lancs. In fact, it was Major Whiteside who had been injured, along with

Lieutenant Burton and Lieutenant Stewart, who Joe had singled out for praise in the Reichswald. Ten other ranks were wounded from A Company and three killed, their names unrecorded in the war diary.

'The officer, Mr Burton, he got some machine-gun bullets across his shoulders, his back. We were knocked from a full company – well, they say full. Sixty, seventy men – down to twenty-odd.'

For every soldier injured, several others were required to carry them back for aid.

'I was the senior NCO in the company, as a corporal. There was (another) corporal, but he was one that we'd had come from the ack-ack,' said Bob, meaning that he was one of the replacements who had come from the Royal Artillery. 'He didn't know nothin' about infantry work, so we didn't count him. There was him, and a lance-corporal, and meself.'

That same day, Lieutenant-Colonel Crozier, Manchester Regiment, recorded: '158 and 160 Brigades are played out. Some (battalions) are less than 200 strong (in the four rifle companies). And they are very tired.'[27]

On 17 April, Verden fell to 1 Ox and Bucks. The 53rd Division's long battle, that had begun eight days earlier at Hoya, was over. It had been a hard fight for Bob Atkinson, but one that ended on a happy note when he was given an unexpected week's leave to Britain. 'I never thought I'd get a leave until after the war,' he said, referring to how the order of selection was based on a draw made earlier in the campaign, when each man picked a number, the lowest of which would have priority for leave.

'Mine was five hundred and odd, but we had that many casualties.'

Fix Bayonets

On 10 April, twelve miles south-east of Rethem, VIII Corps were attempting to force their own crossing of the Aller. The fight to seize the eastern side of the bridgehead began when the 159th Infantry Brigade and tanks of the 2nd Fife and Forfar began clearing the villages south of Essel. This was the same force that had launched the first assault on the Ibbenbüren Ridge a week earlier, and they found the enemy on the Aller no less determined. Essel's road and rail bridges were held by SS Hitler Youth and marines, and backed by panzers, the eastern side of the river thickly wooded and to a defender's advantage.

Around noon, Brigadier Derek Mills-Roberts, commander of No. 1 Commando Brigade, was visited by 11th Armoured Division's commander, General Roberts, whose troops had been held up by the enemy at Essel.

'If he pressed on in the ordinary way and succeeded in driving the Germans out of Essel they would retire across the river and destroy the bridge in passing. The Germans would then defend the river bank and an organized crossing in the face of this would necessitate an inevitable delay. Time was valuable and this was the last water obstacle before Luneberg – a most important objective. If a snap crossing of the river could be made it would save invaluable time.'[28]

Mills-Roberts suggested that No. 1 Commando Brigade attempt to cross over the rail bridge, some one mile north of the road bridge, and then come down through the forest to take the road bridge from the rear. Both Mills-Roberts and Roberts agreed that the plan had little chance of success, but if the commandos could get across the rail bridge, they would have, at the very least, a foothold across the Aller.

That evening No. 1 Commando Brigade was brought forwards in trucks, disembarking close to the destroyed villages, and digging in along the road. Smoke, thick with the stench of burning flesh, hung heavy across the battlefield from the previous fighting. Under cover of darkness the commando brigade made its silent approach along the railway embankment, with No. 3 Commando and Mills-Roberts in the lead.

'Suddenly there was a terrific explosion in front of us. The first span of the large steel railway bridge lifted high into the air and fell a crumpled mass of girders and metal.'[29]

The vigilant enemy had blown the rail bridge as No. 3 Commando approached. They may have believed that this would put an end to the attack.

It did not.

James Griffith, from Brigade HQ, volunteered to swim the river. On the far bank he searched for, and cut, any wires that he could find to prevent further demolition. A recce was conducted onto the bridge itself, finding a shattered stone pier, but enough of the spans intact that the bridge could be crossed. Machine-gun fire was coming overhead, but to the mind of Colin Rae, adjutant of No. 3 Commando, it seemed high. With Arthur Wardle (OC 3 Troop) and the leading section of 3 Troop, they charged across what remained of the bridge and opened fire in the direction of the enemy's muzzle flashes.

Two machine-gun posts were assaulted and taken, and No. 3 Commando's remaining men began to pour over the bridge. Colin Rae was awarded a Military Cross for his part in this early action, and received a gash in his leg from the enemy's fire.

Stan Scott, No. 3 Commando, recalled one instance of meeting the enemy on the other side.

'A party of Germans was coming down the road,' he said, clapping his hands. 'Well, you don't believe that sort of thing. It don't happen. They didn't know we were there.'

Hidden in cover, one of the commandos called for the Germans to surrender. They raised their weapons instead.

'Now they were in a column, and they're marching down a road. And the leading people have opened fire,' he chuckled. 'Now what the bleeding hell? What sort of tactics is that, you know? Sorry. We just opened up. We just let fly. That were that.'

True to form, Brigadier Mills-Roberts was in the thick of the action, encouraging his men and providing immediate solutions to problems. Even at this critical point of the battle he found moments to spare for the welfare of his commandos.

'There was one poor chap, a corporal of 3 Commando, on the enemy side of the bridge waiting to be picked up by (a) stretcher party; he had been shot in the stomach and was asking for a drink of water. All I could do for him was to wash his mouth out with water as a drink would be fatal.'[30]

Mills-Roberts then had a hurried conversation with James

Griffith. This twenty-six-year-old, whose real name was Kurt Glaser, was a Jewish German national who had fought for the loyalists in the Spanish Civil War.

'(Griffith) had been leading the patrol which had to swim the river and snaffle the sentries on the enemy side of the river. I asked him how he got on. He said that the enemy sentries had been alert and he was in the process of stalking one of them when the bridge blew.'[31]

Griffith had been wearing gym shoes for the purpose of quietly stalking the sentries, who would have been killed by the commando's daggers if all had gone to plan. Now that a battle was raging he removed these shoes and replaced them with a pair of boots taken from a German corpse. Griffith would himself be killed shortly after dawn, shot by a German sniper firing from up in a tree.[32]

From one of the enemy prisoners taken close by the bridge, Mills-Roberts began to understand the full extent of their opposition, which included a strong force of infantry and tanks in a nearby village. The enemy defenders held the belief that they would be tortured and killed if taken prisoner, and fought hard, and bravely.

'The opposition was so heavy,' said John Carney, No. 3 Commando, 'it caught us by surprise, really.'

By 0630hrs the commando brigade had failed to capture the road bridge, and now faced vicious counter-attacks by infantry and panzers. It would take almost three hours to drive these attacks off, and resume bringing reinforcements into the area. Mills-Roberts knew that his brigade was in danger of losing the initiative completely. He sent a message to Tony Lewis, the commander of No. 6 Commando, and told him to clear the ground between No. 3 Commando and the road bridge.

Lewis's plan to accomplish this was simple, yet tried and tested.

'They decided that the Commando would line up and we'd have a bit of a bayonet charge,' said Andy Brown, who served under Lewis. 'We all got in the line and positioned to charge the enemy, and when they give the order to fix bayonets, mine had a little bit of a problem with going on,' he laughed, referring to his nerves. 'Or seems like it did, you know. Bit of a shake on.'

'I don't think we were any (less) frightened than the Germans who were in the wood,' Geoff Scottson agreed with a smile. 'It was about equal.'

Lieutenant-Colonel Lewis and two other officers blew hunting horns and the commandos charged, screaming their war cries.

'(The distance) must have been two hundred yards,' said Geoff. 'It cleared as we got towards the bottom, and they were behind trees trying to surround the area of the bridge on their side. They stood up firing at you until the last minute, then they threw their hands in the air.'

'I'd never heard such blood-curdling yells in my life,' said Peter Fussell, who was with Brigade HQ. '6 Commando went in with the bayonet and they cleared these woods in a matter of about five minutes. There were a number of casualties on both sides, obviously, but there were a lot more German casualties than there were in 6 Commando.'

'When we charged them they broke and ran,' said Andy Brown. 'We went through 'em like a dose of salts. There was a lot of them got bayoneted. All the way down this hill to the road there was German dead. There was about forty prisoners taken.'

'We first started getting prisoners in, and we suddenly realized how young they were,' said John Carney, No. 3 Commando. 'They were the real cream of the German youth, you know. They were dedicated youngsters.'

'I think at that stage, the Germans had just gave up defending the area,' said Peter Fussell. 'They lobbed one or two smoke bombs in the trees where we were. Derek Mills-Roberts, who was in the trench next to mine, he was firing an American Garand rifle, semi-automatic. I know for a fact that he knocked out about six people in that wood.'

The commandos began to consolidate their position, but their hold on the road bridge was tenuous. Geoff Scottson and 3 Troop were ordered to clear the woods on the other side of the bridge. 'And that's when I was wounded.'

Geoff was shot through the left arm – a through and through that fortunately did not hit bone.

The commandos' ammunition was dwindling after a night and morning of battle. It was a welcome sight when their quartermaster – who had served in the First World War – arrived with a jeep and trailer full of ammunition and food.

'We had the entire brigade with us,' said Peter Fussell, 'so we were fairly strong and we were all tightly packed into one area.'

Nevertheless, attacks and counter-attacks would continue into 12 April. That same day, events began to unfold that would shock both the British soldiers, and the world.

Under a flag of truce, at first light, two German medical officers crossed the lines and reported to the headquarters of 1 Cheshires at Engehausen. Their purpose was to inform the British army of a nearby camp that was suffering from an outbreak of typhus.

Then, at 0900hrs, two German staff cars flying white flags crossed the bridge at Winsen, which was still held by German forces. The two emissaries were taken to HQ of 159th Brigade, where they explained that they had been sent by orders of the Reichsführer-SS, Heinrich Himmler, to discuss the establishment of a neutral zone around the camp, the name of which will never be forgotten: Belsen.

CHAPTER 21

Liberation

*The liberations of Belsen and Fallingbostel
12–16 April 1945*

'The first thing I saw was a whole collection of German guards, stripped to the waist, barefooted, with no belts, carrying naked corpses from the pits where they had been flung into a newly formed burial ground on the other side of the road, and the Germans were being beaten by the British guards with their rifle butts.

I went into the headquarters established by the (Military Police), who had taken charge of the camp. The major who was there said, "I have no control over my troops."

This was the beginning, and you really couldn't blame the soldiers. It was a most horrific sight. You were taken to a shed, absolutely full with bodies. Your reaction is "what a lot of bodies". What else can you say? It numbs the mind.'

Lieutenant Richard 'Sandy' Smith MC, 2nd Battalion,
Oxfordshire and Buckinghamshire Light Infantry

The Third Reich will for ever be synonymous with the act of genocide, but for the British soldiers battling their way through Germany, the discovery of concentration camps came as perhaps the greatest shock of their young lives.

Major William 'Dick' Williams was a staff officer in the Supplies and Transport branch of VIII Corps.

'For many years Belsen has been at the back of my mind, and it wasn't until I saw a complete misrepresentation of the conditions under which we were introduced to Belsen, the reasons for it, and what we found and what we did, that I felt that the record should be put straight.'

Dick Williams recalled the purpose of the two German emissaries to VIII Corps as being 'to negotiate on the basis that there was a concentration camp in 11th Armoured Division's line of march, and that on humanitarian grounds, and the fact that typhus was rife, there should be an area set aside around the camp, so that no fighting went through the camp, no artillery would fire into it and there would be no artillery firing out of it.'

The initial German terms were unacceptable to the British, who sent Brigadier Taylor-Balfour, of VIII Corps' staff, to present the British terms. These were also rejected, as it would allow the British to outflank the German forces still fighting on the Aller. Instead, a gentleman's agreement was reached with several officers, including Oberst Harries, deputy commander of the Bergen training area.[1]

Dick Williams recalled that, while the negotiations were ongoing, VIII Corps' commander asked Brigadier Glyn Hughes, the chief medical officer of the Second Army, to form a reconnaissance party and to go forward into the camp and assess the situation.

'My colonel called for me,' said Dick, 'and said, "I want you to go with Glyn Hughes and check out the numbers (of people in the camp), what food there is, what cooking equipment is there and anything else for supplies." We hoisted white flags on the vehicles and off we set. The map reference we were given was just a small side road off to the left in a forest area. We got there and there were no signs of anything at all. But fifty yards down (a track), there was a German sentry box, and a Hungarian soldier.

'He just lifted the pole and waved us through. Immediately on the right, there was a small brick building and outside were grouped a lot of German army and SS people, outside the main area which at first sight was a huge barbed-wire fence, which you couldn't really see through, with a double gate, with wooden reinforcements on it. It turned out that the senior person waiting for us there was Josef Kramer and he had Irma Grese with him, who was the senior lady of the SS.

'Brigadier Glyn Hughes instructed Kramer to provide escorts for us and two were allocated to me – two SS, who were still armed at that time. I went to look at the food and cooking equipment side.'

The British party were led to a camp in a hollowed-out area in the middle of a forest.

'We went through the gate, into the camp proper, and it was a sight that I will never forget. There were bundles all over the main concourse which was just dry earth, no grass anywhere. There were just bundles, looked like rags, but turned out to be dead inmates.

'As we went in further the stench of the whole place came at me, coupled with the fact there was an acrid haze over the camp formed from the inmates setting fire to their straw palliasses and wooden floorboards, anything they could make to burn. There were inmates or DPs (Displaced Persons) hanging on the wires, fallen beside it, grotesque positions, and you just had to pick your way through them. Two were walking and came towards us and the SS escort just shot them. I couldn't understand at the time what that meant, because we were there under a white flag. I'd got a .30 calibre revolver at my side but there was nothing I could have done at that time.

'We went further on into the camp and see these corpses lying everywhere, you didn't know if they were living or dead. Most of them were dead, some were trying to walk, some stumbling on hands and knees. They were lying in the doorways, trying to get down the stairs and falling. Just died on the spot. It was just everywhere. Going (deeper) into the camp, the stench got worse and the numbers of dead, it was just impossible to know how many there were.

'There had been no attempt to collect the bodies. All the bodies were above ground. The only place where there had been anything attempted was outside the hospital area.

'There the bodies had been stacked naked, nose to tail, about eight or nine corpses high and about fifty feet in length. Must have been about five or six such piles. The rest were just everywhere where they'd fallen and died. It seems that they'd had no water for about eight days and they'd have been on short rations of very poor food. About ten days they'd have been without food. It was just impossible to believe that no action had been taken either to provide water or to do something on the sanitary side to collect the bodies. They'd just been left where they died.

'When I reported back to Brigadier Glyn Hughes, I told him that there were thousands to feed and thousands to bury. My estimate at the size of the camp was about the size of three football pitches.'

Belsen was originally a prisoner of war camp, but became a concentration camp in 1943. By 1945 it was extremely over-crowded with the addition of inmates who had survived death marches from camps on the ever-encroaching frontline in the East, including Auschwitz. John Fink, a German Jew from Berlin, had been an inmate of several concentration camps since 1943, and corroborated Dick William's version of events.

'Glyn Hughes, who was a medical officer, was sent there and there was a colonel and other British and they saw what was going on. They weren't prepared for it, but they tried to get relief supplies. It was an experience for them too. They'd never liberated a concentration camp. Kramer himself, he took the English colonel, Taylor I believe, took him around and explained, "Those people are sick people, there is typhus," and "Don't send your men in, they will die."

'Confusion started in earnest because the SS disappeared slowly; only certain troops stayed there. Kapos, the privileged prisoners, left – that was on the 13th, 14th. By that time, I was almost a skeleton too. I was about 80 pounds by that time.

'On 15 April, it was in the afternoon, it was a sunny day and I understand it was a Sunday. Somehow we saw different military vehicles with the white star on there and then a loudspeaker car came in, one of your field ambulances, and it had loudspeakers on.'

Kenneth Trafford, who served in the 63rd (Oxfordshire Yeomanry) Anti-Tank Regiment, Royal Artillery, was one of those who arrived at Belsen that day, having driven through the frontline under the protection of white flags. After the convoy passed through, 'All hell broke out behind us. They started fighting again.

'We drove up to Belsen. On the outer cordon guard were Hungarian guards. They didn't present any opposition at all, they just (put) down their arms as soon as we appeared. The next line of defence around the camp was old German retired soldiers – they didn't give any opposition at all. Inside, a different matter was the SS. We've been criticized for letting the SS retain their arms, (but) at that stage we had no idea what a concentration camp was. The Germans had told us that there was typhus loose in the camp and there was a danger of the inmates breaking out and spreading typhus across North West Europe.'

It had been stipulated in the truce that the Hungarian troops would remain in the area indefinitely under British command. Points relating to the SS guards dictated that they should continue custody of the camp until 1200 hrs on the 13th. Any SS guards remaining after this time were to be treated as prisoners of war.[2]

'As soon as we saw the piles of dead bodies, circumstances changed,' said Kenneth. 'We disarmed the SS. The commander was a bloke called Kramer – horrible, most objectionable character. Our commanding officer, Major Ben Barnett, locked him in a refrigerator compartment in the basement. There were also a lot of female SS guards. The most notable was Irma Grese. Very hard woman. Next morning, Ben Barnett woke up and realized he'd forgotten to release Kramer from this refrigerator unit. He came out looking pretty ill. After that the MPs (Military Police) came up and took that lot away. They left us with the rank-and-file SS men and women to assist us in the burial of dead bodies.

'The dead bodies all had to be picked up in piles all over the camp, picked up in lorries and buried in pits which the engineers had dug to bury these bodies. There were literally thousands of bodies, all in piles all over the place. Horrible sight.'

Kenneth recalled that one of the inmates called out to a British officer walking around the camp.

'Anne Maria was her name, something like that. She had been

working in his family's household before the war. Although we were not allowed to let any of the inmates out of the camp, he spirited her away. I think he got her back to the UK within a few days of that happening.'

Inmate John Fink recalled that he was sitting inside a barrack block when the British soldiers arrived.

'The barrack was full of dead and half dead and people were out of their minds after such a long time.

'I'll never forget, the English troops came in. The simple English soldier – those people would give away all their rations to us. There was no British Red Cross here, there was only the soldiers the first one or two days. They gave us their milk, their chocolate, the emergency ration. You would take this and it would come right out because you couldn't hold any food. People were sinking on their knees when a soldier came and kissing their hands. Of course those who talked English, they would tell the people what was going on.'

Gertrude Meaney, a Jew from Brno, had been imprisoned in Theresienstadt concentration camp in October 1941, then moved to Auschwitz and, finally, Belsen.

'I can't describe it,' she said of the horrors. 'We didn't get anything to drink, and we didn't get anything to eat. We are waiting to die.'

Derrick Sington, an officer of the Intelligence Corps, entered the camp with the 63rd Anti-Tank Regiment in a vehicle equipped with loudspeakers, and asked for English-speaking inmates to come forward.

'We were four girls,' said Gertrude. 'Lottie, Bettie, Ruiza and I. I had the courage to lift up my hand, so I did. All four of us were then working for the British.'

Agnes Sassoon was taken from Czechoslovakia as a schoolchild. When the British arrived at Belsen, the twelve-year-old was pulled from a pile of people both dead and dying. 'When they came in I was opening my eyes,' she said. 'They took me off because they see I was alive. I was collapsed somewhere and they just put people on the heap. Many of the people were alive.'

William Essex served in the 23rd Air Construction Group, Royal Engineers, and found a living inmate among a pile of the dead.

'We did find a woman, she was hidden about four feet in a big mound of bodies. How we come to find her, it's only the fact we shut the tractors down for something and we just hear murmuring. We couldn't make out where it was coming from but we listened and we got her out, she was in about three to four feet in a mound of bodies. We got in there and we pulled this one woman out. She was about dead but we managed to save her. That's the only one we ever found like that.'

William's unit was tasked with moving the bodies of more than 10,000 dead into mass graves.

'We made some Germans help us. They were guards in the camp. They couldn't pick them up (because of the disintegration of the bodies). We couldn't handle the bodies at all. We wanted to lay them to have a decent burial. There were dead everywhere.'

William recalled that more decomposed bodies had to be pushed into graves by a tractor.

'When you disturbed them, the smell was horrific. We changed our clothes every night. (It went on for) three weeks. It had to be done so somebody had to do it.'

'We stayed in Belsen for about a week to ten days, burying bodies,' said Kenneth Trafford, Oxfordshire Yeomanry. 'The (male SS) picked up the bodies and put them in the lorries. The women SS unloaded the bodies and put them into the pits, then a bulldozer came along and bulldozed over the top.'

The living were at first attended to by British army medical staff, and later aided by Red Cross personnel and nearly a hundred student doctors who had volunteered to come out from Britain.

Frederick Simpson served in No. 32 Casualty Clearing Station. 'There were swarms of people trying to get on every stretcher. The medical officers went inside and just sorted out the ones who needed hospitalization immediately. The others had to stay behind. Of course they all tried to get on the ambulances. (It was) a fight to get them off. The ambulances used to come in with clean blankets, go down to the main camp, load up the victims, bring them back up to this reception area, then they were taken from there, washed and loused by German nurses we had conscripted. One time we washed and de-loused 960 people in one day. They were laid out on stone slabs and we got buckets of hot water and soap and the German nurses washed them down and we powdered them with DTT powder and all body hair was shaved off.'

Frederick recalled that the German nurses were offered the same inoculations that the British had been given. One of the three who refused died of typhoid.

'We had a laundry unit that would boil the water day and night. We worked from dawn in the morning till dusk at night, till it got dark anyway. My job was to see that the clean blankets that were washed in the laundry unit were used in the sectors that went down to the camp and the dirty blankets were taken back and washed so there was no lice on them. People came up and were covered in lice and excrement. Horrible sight. (The inmates were) cringing and crawling.'

Frederick believed that this behaviour was a response to having lived so long in fear of beatings, and worse.

'Just like animals, brutalized by the Germans.'

Frederick Riches, Royal Army Service Corps, was on his way into Belsen in a convoy of lorries and ambulances when the column came under attack by the Luftwaffe.

'We were in our vehicles, waiting for the order to move out, and these two (German) aeroplanes come over. Sergeant-Major says, "Don't worry, we're on neutral ground." They come round the camp, come in through the left-hand side of us and just strafed us, machine guns bursting all over the place. One of the ambulances was hit, one of our chaps was caught on the ankle. Meself, we had our rifles, I just pulled it back and I was aiming up and the sergeant major said, "If you do that, you'll be on a charge."'

Cecil Warren, 11th Field Ambulance, also recalled the attack.

'Three Jerries came over, they machine-gunned all along the tents, the cookhouse, up and down two or three times.'

One of Cecil's friends, twenty-one-year-old Frank Phillips, was caught by the aircraft's fire.[3] 'Frank died during the day, he had all his side shot away. He was one of the few, us ten, who went on D-Day.'

As VIII Corps resumed its push to Hamburg, Major Dick Williams and a few other members of Corps HQ, including Brigadier Glyn Hughes, remained at Belsen to continue to coordinate the relief of the camp.

'What those medics did was fantastic. Gradually all the fitter people were moved out.

'The whole camp was quiet. This was one of the things which struck me when I first went in, that the whole camp was quiet, and yet there were so many people there. You couldn't hear anything. There was some movement from those who could walk or move but it was just so quiet.

'There was one hut, quite a big one, barn shaped, which didn't seem to have any particular purpose where it was. I went into it. Very dull inside, bunks on either side five or six high. I don't know what prompted me, but I shouted out, "Any British here?" and six people answered.

'I had tried to find out who they were but I think that still may be a military secret. I think they were people who had been captured earlier on in France and been gradually moved back. It wasn't part of the concentration camp itself but it was just on the fringe, so they were obviously prisoners there, but not under the same harsh treatment as the concentration camp. I would say (their condition was) reasonable. Could have done with a square meal and a good wash and brush up, but on the whole I think they would have survived much longer.

'Belsen itself was not an extermination camp. It was built as a transit camp. There were no gas ovens, there was nothing to suggest this was the end of the road for people going there. It ended up as a death camp but it wasn't built as an extermination camp.'

Josef Kramer and Irma Grese were both tried, and hanged in December 1945. Other members of the SS were killed in Belsen.

'I did witness two SS trying to make a break for it through the wire,' said Dick. 'They were shot down and their colleagues were sent after them, brought back, and their bodies thrown onto the pile on the trailer.'

Dick did not believe that any of the SS guards who had remained in the camp came out alive. He also recalled how prominent members of the nearby town of Bergen were made to come to the camp to witness its horror.

'Overall, I believe that it was right that they should bring in Burgomeisters to see the camp. The looks on their faces means that whether they knew or not knew was immaterial – seeing it there, they had to believe it. This is one of the things you must never forget – that the Holocaust did happen.'

Dick was recalled to VIII Corps HQ after a fortnight at the camp. 'I must admit it was a relief to be away from Belsen. It certainly had an effect on me. Remember, I was twenty-four at the time. It was one of those things which you look back on – *Did I really go there, did I really do that, did I really see this?* You begin to question as to whether it had happened. When colleagues asked about it, you would tell them and they would say, "You're exaggerating, surely." And I would say, "No, I'm sorry this is the truth." Even at a military headquarters such as VIII Corps, it was something they had to contend with. They had no idea of what was in that camp and what we actually were doing. All they knew was there was a constant call for more support, in terms of medics and ambulances and those sorts of things, in order to cope with it all.

'I think the whole episode really bypassed the army. It was something we did on the side, rather than part of the main war. It had no real effect on our advance. Our divisions pushed on, bypassing Belsen. There was still stubborn resistance from the German army and we had to fight our way up to Hamburg.'

Around 37,000 people died in Belsen between May 1943 and April 1945, including a Dutch schoolchild named Anne Frank, who perished a month before the arrival of the British soldiers. Sixty thousand people were liberated on 15 April 1945, but more than 13,000 of them were too ill to survive.

Leslie Hardman was a Jewish chaplain in the British Army, and was asked if what he saw in the camps made him question his faith.

'It made me question,' he said, 'but I got no answers.'

Several soldiers interviewed by the IWM agreed that their attitude towards German civilians hardened after receiving news of

Belsen and other concentration camps. Some even witnessed the horror themselves.

Sandy Smith, 2 Ox and Bucks, was taken by jeep to see Belsen two days after its liberation. After seeing the piles of bodies, the numbers of which 'numbed the mind', Sandy was taken to see the former camp commandant, Kramer.

'He was known as the Beast of Belsen. He had been very badly beaten up and again he was without shoes, and without belts, just sitting in his cell, very badly bruised, he was eventually hung. The woman (Irma Grese), she hadn't been beaten up to the same extent, but she obviously had been given a beating. It was the most extraordinary few hours and I've never forgotten it.'

Sandy was asked if the experience had changed his opinion of Germans.

'It has to. I remember a day or two later, in Celle, in the market square, the British authorities had taken photographs of Belsen and had put them up on the notice boards to show the population what had been going on under their very noses.

'An old woman had been looking at these photographs, she had come out to get some potatoes or whatever, and she didn't know I was behind her. When she was looking at these photographs, she says, "Ach, propaganda," and I just seized her by the back of the neck and pushed her face into the photographs and said it wasn't propaganda. I remember losing my temper. You are bound to be affected by things like that, you can't possibly escape not being affected.

'The thing that everybody asked was how on earth could a massive camp of that type be fed and watered without the population nearby knowing, it's almost unbelievable. But when you asked any German they said they didn't know what was going on. It was a stock answer.'

Peter Fussell, No. 1 Commando Brigade, also recalled a change in the behaviour of himself and his comrades after learning of the Holocaust.

'We captured about twenty-one German SS people and I would suggest that if it was not for the artillery regiment that was in support of us, I reckon that we would have cheerfully lined these people (up) and shot them. (The artillery troops) said, "No, we'll send them back down the line." We were fully prepared to knock them out.'

The anger was shared by their commander. Peter described an incident that occurred at the end of the war, not long after the commandos had found evidence of further atrocities at Neustadt on the Baltic.

'(Field Marshal Milch) came to surrender to Brigadier Derek Mills-Roberts, and it's the first time I've seen a field marshal's baton being smashed on a German field marshal's shoulder. Derek Mills-Roberts was absolutely livid with this man. Not against him personally, but for the atrocities that he'd seen in Belsen.'

Mills-Roberts himself makes no mention of the incident in his book.

Milch was later interviewed by United States Army psychiatrist Leon Goldensohn during the Nuremberg Trials, and claimed that Allied atrocities were just as bad as German ones. 'When captured, he himself was beaten up by an English general. It was inconceivable, he said, that a field marshal could be beaten. Why was he beaten up? I asked. Because the English had just captured a concentration camp.'[4]

Now working with the British, former inmate John Fink remained in Belsen until 21 May. After the final inmates had been either evacuated or buried, what was left of the concentration camp was burned to the ground.

'I was standing right behind the British officers and British soldiers who saw that. Only after the last barrack was burned, the British flag was raised. It was symbolic. The British flag should never be raised over such a place.

'It was very emotional.'

Prisoners of War

Dick Williams was back on the staff at VIII Corps HQ when a report came through that some RAF personnel had been seen in a small wood, about thirty miles from HQ. 'Colonel Blackie said,

"Go off and find out what's there and do what you can." So off I went and all I could see in that area was a small copse of trees in the middle of a field and the only thing out of place seemed to be some bales of straw.

'As I went up towards this I shouted out, "Have we got any British people in this area?" An airman appeared and it seemed there were about thirty of them. They had been moved backwards and backwards as the pressure had come from the West, and they had been abandoned in this area. I told them to hold fast, went off and an hour or so later was back with a truck, chocolates and cigarettes and things and waved them on their way. So there are happy incidents, and those incidents help to break the horror of what had gone on the previous month.'

Around 170,000 British troops had been taken prisoner by German and Italian forces during the many years of war. More and more of them were liberated as the Allied armies advanced across Germany, while those still in captivity were often shuttled from one place to the next in an attempt to thwart their liberation.

Arthur Topliss, from Skegness, had served in France and North Africa with the 4th Royal Tank Regiment, where he witnessed the actions of Victoria Cross winner Captain Philip 'Pip' Gardner. The regiment was captured at Tobruk on 21 June 1942, and Arthur would spend almost three years in captivity in various POW camps in Italy and Germany. He was moved to Fallingbostel camp, near Soltau, in September 1944.

'(In mid-April) the Germans opened the gates and took us all out on the march. We were on the march for three days. All we had to eat was a little handful of grain, oats or barley. No water or anything. At the end of the third day we saw a flight of Mustangs go over. We heard a lot of machine-gun fire. The Germans downed their arms, left us where we were. They said, *You can please yourselves what you do, the bridges are blown, you can't go on. You can please yourselves to stop here or go back.* We were on the plain outside of Fallingbostel. We'd marched three days and only covered about thirty kilometres in those three days.

'We marched back in about three hours (over what) had taken

us three days to cover. We pitched our bivouacs on the sports field outside and was there for about two days, and we heard a tank battle during the night. The next morning we woke up and we found an armoured car of the 8th Hussars just inside the camp, British flag on it, and they said they'd come to set us free.'

John Lindsey (a name he adopted to protect his identity) was born in Dusseldorf in 1922, and fled Germany as a fifteen-year-old to escape the Nazis' anti-Semitism. After a period as a internee in Australia, he had joined the Pioneer Corps and eventually the King's Royal Irish Hussars. Now he was one of the first to liberate Fallingbostel on 16 April 1945. 'It was a tremendous day, of course, especially as we had our own people in there. Our regimental sergeant major was there. I think they'd had reasonable treatment, as most prisoners of war did.'

'Some of the prisoners had been captured on the desert, including a friend of mine,' said Tom Hope, one of the liberators of Fallingbostel, and commander of a Cromwell tank named *Ambassador*. 'I had a very good crew. My wireless operator, Michael Jones – not his real name – was an Austrian of Jewish blood. We had a number of Austrian and German people in the regiment. They were first in the Pioneer Corps, and later joined the Armoured Corps. These Austrian and German people were very useful to us, as they all spoke German. Although they had lost their homes and were aware of what the Nazi regime really meant, and had good reason to hate the Germans, they nevertheless treated them very fairly. I remember someone took a watch off a German prisoner. Michael reported it to our captain, who made him give it back.'

Glider pilot Harry Gibbons, who had been captured during Operation Varsity, was at Fallingbostel for a few days before he was marched east.

'Myself and a lot of others (were) taken out on the road and marched for several days, until we came to the banks of the River Elbe, somewhere south of Hamburg.'

The next morning, Harry was told that they were now changing direction to avoid the approaching Red Army.

'We did a smart about-turn, marched back the way we come

more or less, and after a couple of days we ended up just outside a town called Zarrentin. In the morning there was a hell of a commotion outside, lots of shouting and hollering going on there.'

The source of the commotion were Red Devils of the British Airborne, whom Harry had fought beside at Arnhem and the Rhine crossing.

'And we were released, just like that. Marvellous.

'What do you do (now)? There's no organization or anything. We were just told to make our way in that direction, that they'd come in. Two other chaps (and I), we collared one of these German motorbikes with the sidecar. We drove in the right direction until we were told to stop and we were gathered up. We were taken to a camp where we were deloused, we could have a wash and that sort of thing, and eventually flown back to England.'

April was a month of liberation for hundreds of thousands of people held captive in Germany, but what was a new beginning for some meant the end of everything for others.

At the same time as VIII Corps was liberating Belsen and Fallingbostel, XXX and XII Corps were about to fight the last great British battles in Europe.

CHAPTER 22

Die-Hards

XXX Corps' capture of Bremen
13–27 April 1945

'There was some heavily defended places. There were a lot of old men, and young lads fighting, and they're die-hards, you know? Young fanatics.

Everyone knew war were over, and you were keeping your bloody head down, weren't ya, you know what I mean? Fellas were getting knocked off. Our company commander, he got hit. Major Pemberton. Back end a' war, like.'

Albert Holdsworth, 2nd Battalion,
East Yorkshire Regiment

Closing in

George Rayson had landed into the carnage of Sword Beach with the Suffolk Regiment, and was now a few weeks away from surviving the war.

'It wasn't like it was in France, it was nothing near as intense, if you know what I mean. We got shelled day after day in France, we didn't get shelled so much in Germany. Little bursts didn't do us any good, mind you.'

But even a rapid advance came with its difficulties.

'After we crossed the Rhine, we was going about eighteen hours a day,' said Frederick Ridout, 4th Wiltshires. 'We were supposed to dig in when we got in at night but we just sat down on the ground and fell asleep.'

'The main thing about it was lack of sleep in those particular weeks up to the end of the war,' agreed Arthur Rouse, who had won a Military Cross with the South Lancashires. 'Chaps began to fall asleep at the wheels of vehicles.'

Each of these men were part of the drive on Bremen and its nearby port of Bremerhaven, both of which had long been a target of the Allies. An important industrial centre and communications hub, Bremen received its first 'thousand-bomber raid' in June 1942. Almost three years later more than 4,000 residents had been killed by bombing raids, and two thirds of the city's accommodation had been lost.

Approaching the shattered city that mid-April were the 3rd, 43rd, 51st and 52nd infantry divisions, as well as the 8th Armoured Brigade and elements of the 4th. Standing in their way were a mixed force of German paratroopers, second-grade troops such as the Volkssturm, an SS training regiment, some 2,000 naval personnel, and a powerful force of anti-aircraft artillery that was equally as useful at destroying tanks and infantry. The remnants of the 15th Panzergrenadier Division were positioned to defend the area between Bremen and Hamburg, including the important highway.

On 13 April, the 3rd Division became involved in a bloody action at Brinkum, an important town and road junction just south of Bremen. Four SS companies in the area, each of 200 men, were determined to fight to the last and halt the British advance on the city. D-Day man Kenneth Powter, acting as a Company Sergeant Major in 1 Suffolks, described the tenacity of the enemy in Hallen-Seckenhausen, some 1,500 yards south-west of Brinkum itself.

'We had tried to capture the crossroads, which was being held by fanatical Hitler Youth, Hitlerjugend. Major Claxton – he'd already won the MC, he'd been wounded several times – took a patrol up towards this (crossroads) prior to our attack on it and he'd been killed there.'[1]

The SS then launched several counter-attacks, and the fighting at Hallen-Seckenhausen degenerated into a bloody stalemate that lasted for two days, the two sides so close that the Suffolks could hear the enemy singing in their positions.

'Several companies had tried to attack and capture this crossroads,' continued Kenneth. 'It seemed that each company that attacked it were very vulnerable and exposed and consequently we had casualties. But eventually orders came that C Company, my company, were going to attack it. There was a ray of hope because we were going to secure, if we could, Crocodiles. If they didn't (arrive) at the appointed time, we were going to attack anyway.'

The Suffolks breathed a sigh of relief when the flame-throwing tanks came rumbling along to the start line. These Crocodiles of 7 RTR were joined by tanks of the Staffordshire Yeomanry and 4th/7th Dragoons, and supported by five regiments of artillery. It was a weight of fire that not even the most fanatical fighters could withstand.

'We attacked this crossroads with these flamethrowers and eventually captured it,' said Kenneth. 'I was at that time acting sergeant major, and I'd got the signallers and the stretcher-bearers in a farmhouse, which was only about 100 yards back from the crossroads, or 200 yards. My company commander, Major Vines and another lieutenant, we were at the Company HQ and we were observing our forward platoons going in. We stood at the gable end of a cow shed. Fortunately for me, I'd walked to see the signallers again, just got my foot on the step of this house, and a shell hit the end of this gable building and killed Major Vines and wounded this officer.'[2]

1 Suffolks lost seventeen men killed in the three days of fighting at Brinkum, including several who had marched across Europe from Sword Beach.

On the same day, twenty-five miles west of Brinkum, the enemy launched a counter-attack against the 43rd (Wessex) Division's bridgehead outside of Ahlhorn. Two hundred German infantry and tanks succeeded in overrunning some of the division's forward positions. Shelling was heavy, and the ferocious battle lasted for two hours before what was left of the attacking force was driven off.

Ronald Clack, a Normandy veteran in the 112th (Wessex) Field Regiment, Royal Artillery, recalled a number of casualties that day.

'Lieutenant Skinner, he went down this lane to go to a farmhouse to see if he could have a gun position there and they were machine-gunned from behind. The friend of mine who was the radio operator, he got wounded quite badly in the arm and various parts of his body – he lived but he was very shook up.

'German 88s were up this road and they fired shells on (our battery). The casualties were not many but they were quite severe.'

Among the dead was Sergeant Major Albert Ramsden, forty-three years old, from Woking.

'He could have been out the army – he was twenty-odd years in the army – he could have been home with his wife, but he was killed by the shellfire of an 88.'[3]

Seventy per cent of Ronald's signaller section were either killed or wounded. 'It was pretty awful.'

Hubert Essame, who was a brigade commander in the 43rd Division at the time, wrote that a complete enemy battle group had been destroyed.

'Later in the day, when the advance was resumed, old men and women emerged from the woods and neighbouring villages to carry away their dead, who lay in long rows in front of the Worcestershire's position. Many were young boys; others were old men who had been hurriedly pressed into uniform. It was a sombre scene, pathetic in its utter futility even to the battle-hardened troops of the division.'[4]

Ahlhorn was seized that night, and the 43rd continued onwards towards Bremen. The 51st Highland Division were themselves closing on the city from the south-west. Ian Hammerton, 22nd Dragoons, was in support.

'That was the first time that I'd seen undamaged houses that had been gone through by the Highland Division, and it was an eye-opener. They certainly went through them. And everything that was in drawers was out of drawers on the floor, cupboards emptied and so on.

'I was just climbing into the turret, and I got one boot in, and a salvo of mortar came over, and one of them landed on the turret. Fortunately on the forward slope, and it exploded downwards, mainly. Filled my face with small bits of shrapnel. I found myself lying on the ground. I hurriedly climbed in again, but I wasn't really badly hurt at all. Bit shaken. The driver found bits of shrapnel in his beret.'

Ian's squadron then went into a 'small attack' where his corporal knocked out an SP gun. 'There was a lot of bullets whizzing around, and I remember a little German girl had been hit in the forehead by a bullet. She and her mother came across the road, and she was streaming blood, so I bunged her on a scout car and we took her up to the first aid post. I think she was a child of about twelve, or thirteen. But she was alright. They looked after her.'

Back in the area of Brinkum, on that same day, 2nd East Yorkshires captured Heiligenrode and Gross Mackenstedt. Eighteen-year-old Ray Robinson was left out of the battle but watched it unfold from a distance.

'To see an actual assault going in was marvellous, really. This tank with a bowser at the back, and it was shooting flame out about 150 yards, and all the lads following up at back. They won the day.'

The East Yorks went through the villages in house-to-house fighting, often calling upon the Crocodiles to burn the enemy out of buildings. After a series of attacks made by other battalions of the 3rd Infantry Division, Brinkum and its surrounding villages were finally secured by 20 April.

It was a bittersweet moment for the men of 2 East Yorks. Major 'Banger' King, who had resupplied the surrounded soldiers at Yorkshire Bridge, was badly injured in a mine strike on the night of the 16th. Lieutenant-Colonel Bill Renison, the battalion's commanding officer, recalled what happened next.

'Early the following morning, the news I had been dreading came though – "Banger" had died during the night.

'All of us had come to regard "Banger" as invulnerable . . . that he as a Regimental Officer should become a legend almost throughout the Army was no more than his due.'[5]

'All the battalion would have followed him through hell,' said young Ray Robinson.

A pre-war regular, King had stirred his men during their run into Sword Beach, reciting to them the Saint Crispin's Day speech from Shakespeare's *Henry V*. One of his soldiers, Wilf Todd, said that 'Banger was a father, mother, big brother, you name it, all rolled into one.'[6]

Major Charles King DSO was forty years old when he was killed little more than two weeks before the end of hostilities. He was missed both by those who knew him, and those who wished that they had.

'A Bit Much'

After the hard fighting around Verden, the Black Rats of 4th Armoured Brigade came back under control of XXX Corps, and pushed north-east to Bremen. It was not an easy path. On 18 April, enemy 88s hidden by woods and a nearby farm opened fire on the armour. Sergeant Fred Cooper's platoon of the 2nd Battalion, King's Royal Rifle Corps were given the order to take them out.

'Unfortunately, (our platoon commander) set out a tactical plan which to me was something out of the First World War. He had my section on his right, with himself in the centre, Corporal Butler's section on the left. And he had a further section behind, with the platoon sergeant behind him with the two-inch mortar, which is always there. If you get in difficulty, it smokes you out.'

Fred may have been dubious about the officer's plan, but he had no doubts about his courage – Lieutenant Hugh Elgar had already won a Military Cross for his actions in the Rhineland. 'He earned it,' said Fred.

The platoon moved off, the farmhouse and the 88s to their front. Fred was told by his lieutenant to move across the track because a fence was hindering Butler's section, 'cramping him up'.

Just as the order was given, the enemy opened fire.

'And I knew it was close because there are times when you hear the whistle of a machine gun, the whistle of the bullets going by, but there are other times they're so close you can hear the twirl of 'em. And I could 'ear the twirl of 'em.'

The soldiers 'hit the deck'.

'Normally, under those circumstances, whoever is in charge asks,

"Is everyone alright?" But there was nothing coming from him. So, we waited for a while. Nothing.'

Fred asked, 'Is everybody alright?' One of the men called to say there was a casualty. Fred crawled over, finding Lieutenant Elgar badly wounded.

'When I got to him, I said, "Are you alright, sir?" He said, "No." He said, "I'm finished." He said, "You know what you've got to do, now get on and do it. Don't worry about me, I'm finished. I'm finished." And with that he just slumped.'

Twenty-one-year-old Lieutenant Hugh Elgar died on the battlefield.[7] The platoon was without their leader, and still under fire 200 yards from the objective.

'So I thought to meself, *This is no good.*'

What Fred did next would later be described as showing 'an initiative greater than can be expected of his rank'.[8] But while Fred did not have an officer's pips on his shoulders, he did have several campaigns and countless actions under his belt.

'I had learned, from previous experience, that infiltration is the thing. Get behind 'em and they'll come out.'

Under fire from at least one machine gun, Fred moved his section into the ditch that ran along the track to the farm. 'I said to the Bren gunner, "When we move, give us covering fire. Doesn't matter what you're firing at as long as you're firing, but keep it well clear of us."

'I got up and run like bloody hell to this farmhouse down this ditch. Eventually got behind (the farmhouse). And they come out all over the place. Think we must have captured about sixty.'

With the rest of the platoon following, Fred began to consolidate on the farmhouse.

'The company commander came up with the platoon sergeant. We started a run of bad luck after that.'

As Major Roland Gibbs arrived, the farm's roof was struck by mortars. A row of roof tiles came sliding down and struck Fred on his helmet. Moments later, both Major Gibbs and the platoon sergeant were deafened by an 88mm shell that exploded above their heads. There was clear discharge coming from the sergeant's ears, so Major Gibbs sent him back to the aid post, leaving Fred now in charge of his platoon. With no time to waste, Gibbs sent Fred to clear the woods with the aid of a tank.

'Our tanks came up a road and unfortunately, what had happened, the tank commander of the leading tank had come 'round the bend too much. (They were) within view of this 88mm gun. The tank commander was out of the turret, consulting his map.'

The enemy gun fired, the shell decapitating the tank's commander. Fred heard the lad behind him give a loud cry and looked to see 'his eye's in the back of his head and it's pooling with blood. Another lad got a bit of shrapnel in his arm, and there's another one laying on the floor. All from this one shell ricocheting off the turret of the tank.'

Fred went to the man on the floor, who had 'a big hole' in his back.

'I know he survived, but he must have lost a kidney. They were pulling bits of his pullover out dripping with blood.'

The platoon – already depleted from previous actions – had now suffered several casualties. 'You've got three wounded, so you need three people to look after them, which means you're gonna lose six. So anyway, I nominated people, you've got people in mind to do this. People who are gonna be the least valuable if it come to a fight.'

The other platoons had made good progress by this time, and Fred was ordered by Major Gibbs to bring the survivors of his own back to Company HQ. Fred, who was 'quite upset' due to the casualties the platoon had sustained, was then approached by one of his company officers, Captain Thomas Trenchard MC. Thomas was one of the sons of Hugh Trenchard, widely recognized as the 'Father of the Royal Air Force'.

'He come out of company office, and I saluted him, and he said to me, "Very well done, Sergeant Cooper, very well done." It was the first time it dawned on me – you know, you're so absorbed in what you're doing – I'd done something creditable in the battle. And later I was awarded the Military Medal.'

Previous actions were also listed in the award's citation, which praised Fred's 'outstanding, consistent courage'.[9]

'I've since thought about it,' said Fred. 'It didn't seem such a risk at the time, but with the machine-gun (fire), charging over two hundred yards of ground was a bit much, you know?'

Ganderkesee

On 20 April, the 51st (Highland) Division were approaching the village of Ganderkesee, an important junction some ten miles west of Bremen. Alfred Leigh, 2nd Seaforths, recalled coming under mortar fire and running like hell for the shelter of some nearby houses.

'Across the fields was this German flak gun. We're in the houses, and he just couldn't depress himself enough to get at us. AP (armour-piercing) shells were coming through (the top) of the room. HE (heavy explosive) was busting against the wall. We're laying flat, like, you know. Doggo. But he did manage to knock out one of the Middlesex Bren carriers. Anyway, a shell come up and knocked hell out of him. He's knocked out.'

The following day, 'we came up (with) these Churchill Crocodiles. A squadron of them. My section were with the second (Crocodile) flamethrower, and we went in (to) Ganderkesee, and proceeded to burn the village down.'

The flamethrowers aimed at the thatched roofs of the houses, and burning blobs of thatch and flammable jelly began to bounce back towards the advancing soldiers. One landed on the helmet of Alfred's friend, Paddy, who now reminded Alfred of a candle.

'I start singing "Happy Birthday",' he chuckled.

Other memories of that day were not so pleasant.

'We come across this trench, two German wounded screaming their heads off.'

Alfred's platoon were told to leave them and press on. They then found civilians who talked with them and offered the soldiers sausage, but Alfred declined so as not to deprive them of their food. Enemy soldiers were still in the village, and others began to infiltrate in.

'I looked out of the window and down the passage, and I seen this German paratrooper telling the old boy to get down the shelter.'

Alfred did not hesitate, and brought his weapon up to his shoulder.

'I shot him. It must have been about thirty yards away. He went down.'

He then saw a second paratrooper who was in cover, but slowly edging out of it.

'Eventually he came out two steps, and I shot him and all.'

Alfred went to recover the submachine gun of the first man – a prized souvenir. As he was lifting it off the body he spotted a third paratrooper who was unaware of his presence.

'So I said, "Well, I'll knock this bugger off and all."'

Rather than using his own single-shot rifle, Alfred decided to use the captured submachine gun.

'So I run up to him, and I fired, and I only got one round off. The damn thing jammed.'

One of Alfred's corporals ran up and shot the German, who was hit in the leg.

'Shattered, it was. Completely open. Broken bones and everything, and he's screaming like hell, he was.'

A few moments earlier Alfred had been ready to kill the man.

'I changed me mind. I said, "Give us a hand, Andy." We dragged him along the cobble passage, and he's screaming blue murder. I told him to "Shut up, you bastard."'

Once inside the platoon's positions, the wounded German began asking after his comrades. Alfred gave him the bad news.

'I said, "*Kaput*."'

The soldier understood, and let out a moan of anguish. Alfred then dressed the man's wounds and made a splint for his leg. 'And he said to me, "Have you a cigarette?" I had one cigarette left, and I gave this German my last cigarette, but I also took his wristwatch in exchange.'

After a near brush with two M-10 tank destroyers that the Germans had captured from Americans, but which were shooed away by a civilian with a white flag, Alfred and two of his comrades went 'on the scrounge'. He had a few eggs in his pocket by the time he met a group of Russians who had been put to work in the area as slave labour. They offered the British soldiers some of their home-made vodka.

'And we're drinking it like water. We left their camp, but somehow, well, boozed up, we fell asleep in this ditch.'

Alfred woke in the early hours with a pocket full of smashed eggs. Worse was to follow.

His company had been called back to the battalion and were nowhere to be found. Alfred and his fellows made the best of the bad situation, with two of them sleeping in beds, while the third – who Alfred described as 'a bit bomb-happy' – slept in the cellar.

'The following morning this corporal come. He'd just joined the company, bit of a glory-seeking boy. Busted open the door and said, You're under close arrest." Obviously I busted out laughing. Reached for me cigarettes, and he said, "No smoking, you're under close arrest."'

The three men were told to smarten themselves up, then marched back to Regimental Headquarters. The charge against them was severe:

'Desertion in the line.' Alfred laughed. 'Not intentionally. We just got drunk.'

Alfred was given a slap on the wrist – fourteen days confined to barracks, which was not enforced. The company still had a war to win, and needed every man it had.

Peter White, a platoon commander in 4 KOSB, had found a third of his platoon rendered 'totally incapable' by alcohol during the advance.

'The whole battalion was incessantly faced with the problem of drink. What punishment could awe a chap with whom death and mutilation were constant companions in prospect or in fact week in, week out?'[10]

Twenty miles east of where Alfred was nursing his hangover, Peter's own division was putting in an attack on the town of Achim.

Achim

Eighteen-year-old Cyril Butler, 6th Cameronians, 52nd (Lowland) Division, was so new to his platoon that the sergeant didn't know him by name. This came in handy when the sergeant was looking for 'volunteers' to go on patrol, as Cyril didn't get picked so long as he stayed out of sight. Survival was the name of the game, but escaping the attention of his sergeant could only get him so far.

'You never knew the next minute when you were going to be fired on. The first big battle (on the way to Bremen) we were to capture this wood. About ten tanks came up on our right and they fired the machine guns into this wood while we moved. It was that sort of ground where there was a barbed-wire fence about every fifty yards. We were being fired at from the flanks, you could hear the bullets popping as they passed over your head. I was carrying the Bren.

'We got to maybe a hundred yards of the wood and it was every man for himself. I opened up with the Bren and then out of these trenches came these Germans with their hands up. We still kept on firing, even though their hands were up. They'd been potting at us for a hundred and fifty, two hundred yards, and as soon as they seen the colour of our eyes, they run out. Those that didn't get hit just run away back.

'We wandered around this wood for quite a while and spotted these two young Germans in a trench and they had never fired a shot. Young kids, maybe about fifteen, sixteen. We took the guns off them, gave them a kick up the backside and sent them off back.

'We lost a few lads there but we never knew whether they were just wounded or dead because you just went on, you see.'

Ivan Markwell, 7th Cameronians, recalled that they rounded 'up some men and young chaps' and held them in a hotel, but some of these prisoners refused to listen to their captors and take their orders.

'And there was one Jock lad there, he was rather bad-tempered, didn't take a lot to upset him, so he told them to shut up or else. They just laughed it off – they didn't think nothing of it. After a few minutes, he didn't mess about. He came out with his pistol and he shot one through the leg, and that quieted them down. They behaved themselves after that and we had no more trouble from them.'

The 52nd's Divisional History recalled that at Achim:

'It was discovered that the railway telephone to Bremen was still intact. Using this, with the local stationmaster as intermediary, divisional H.Q. did its best to persuade the garrison commander in the city to surrender. The stationmaster also did his best to urge the cause of reason, but Bremen was firm on holding out; and the negotiations broke down when 800 heavy bombers came in and cut the line.'[11]

Ray Robinson, 2 East Yorks, could hear the growing rumble of the bombers coming over the horizon, and watched the cascade of high explosive falling onto the already ruined city.

The attack on Bremen was underway.

Into Bremen

Godfrey Welch had won the Military Medal at Hill 112, Normandy after his tank was knocked out, and he had continued to fight on despite his wounds. After a period of convalescence Godfrey had rejoined his unit, the Scots Greys, and was with them on the march to Bremen, often in the dark about how events were unfolding in Germany.

'We don't know what's going on in other areas. You just know what you get told. *We're pushing on to so and so.* Sometimes you make it, sometimes you don't. And sometimes you meet resistance. Heavy resistance. You lose people and equipment. Other days you can go two or three days and not encounter anybody aggressive.

'Everything stopped on the outskirts of Bremen. We had a few days' lovely rest.'

But rest from action did not mean that they were idle.

'Your first love was your tank. That always had to be up to par before you do anything yourself. That had to be kept operational at all times.'

On 25 April an artillery barrage was laid down on Bremen, and the Scots Greys moved off in support of the 52nd (Lowland) Division from Achim. It was a slow process to clear the rubble-strewn streets on the city's outskirts, and the infantry were shelled and sniped at.

'You drive up with your infantry,' said Godfrey. 'The infantry go through the houses. You go up the road. And any opposition firing at you, you give them the heavy weaponry.

'There was a lot going on, street fighting-wise. Different areas had different amounts of violence. I don't think we were too bad, although we didn't see the end of Bremen, because we got knocked out, you see. We got a bazooka, or Panzerfaust, in the engine, from behind us.

'When the old Panzerfaust hit, you got this terrible bang, and the (tank) fills up with smoke. You've got to bail out, haven't you. Now that's the moment of truth in street fighting. Opening up the hatches and bailing out. Because if they've been near enough to fire a Panzerfaust, they're near, aren't they.'

Godfrey had seen tracer fire passing through the body of his commander as he'd attempted to bail out on Hill 112. Thankfully, their exit at Bremen came without casualties – the crew ran into a building with an open doorway, and fell in a pile on top of each other. They were unhurt, but without a single weapon between them.

'So we had to stay in this big house until the infantry came up,' Godfrey laughed. Seventy-two hours later they had a new tank, and rejoined the squadron as the battle for Bremen was drawing to a close.

Ian Hammerton, 22nd Dragoons, had also enjoyed a short rest before the attack.

'We were there for a short while, parked in the ground of a very large house. There was a beautiful grand piano inside, and some rather disgusting photographs that the owner had taken of his wife.'

Ian was then tasked with escorting members of T-Force to the nearby Focke-Wulf factory. T-Force was a joint US–British operation to seize German industrial, technological and scientific assets, and Ian recalled his experience with them in Bremen as being 'rather hairy'.

'There were parties of Germans skulking around in all directions. Sniping going on. We got into this area, and we had to stay put overnight. The next day we were firing at some enemy nearby and we saw a white flag waving. A scout car appeared right in front of us.'

Sitting in the vehicle was the unit's new CO, who was less than popular with his troops.

'I had to physically restrain my gunner from training the Browning on him. That was the reputation he'd already built for himself in that short time.'

As they pushed into Bremen, the Dragoons came up against the defences that the enemy had prepared – some of them were unmanned, but no less deadly.

'The Germans had built huge concrete walls with a gap between, and then had rolled a large concrete block into the gap. So I fired at it, and it just knocked chips of concrete off, so I called the AVREs up to ask them to Petard it, which they did, and the AVRE commander said, "Right, we've done our job. After you, Claude."'

This was a reference to a BBC radio comedy, *It's That Man Again*.

'I said, "No, after you, Cecil." He went through, and he got a few yards on the other side and there was an almighty explosion, and the Churchill went straight up in the air. And the jeep, which had been following right close behind him, just vanished altogether.'

D-Day veteran Fred Hartle, 1 KOSB, observed an SS officer walking by their positions. At first Fred thought the man may have wanted to surrender, and while Fred didn't say why he changed his mind on this, it's quite possible that he came to the conclusion that the German was using the confusion as a chance to recce the British positions and numbers.

'I says, "Shoot him." So we shot him. Then I went and fetched him in. I looked in his inside pocket, and his credentials. He was a colonel in a Todt organization,[12] and he were eighty-two years old. We put him on a stretcher. I think he died.'

Leslie Gibson, who had fought across Europe from Normandy, served in the same section as Fred. Their objective on 25 April was a barracks in Bremen.

'There was some buildings before the barracks, and we were told to go up there, and when we got near the barracks we had a lot of fire incoming from some of the windows up on the top part of the building. I think one of the anti-tank guns had a go at it, and they blasted a hole in, and I think the Germans got a bit fed up of this and sort of left the barracks.

'We went in through one of the side entrances. We was very careful to go in there, cause you didn't know what was what, and we took cover in this building. We started crawling around the one side to where the fire had been coming from, and we found out that there was no Germans there at all. I think it must have just been a handful who had been left behind to cause problems. Probably these young Nazis.

'Another part of the building, there was a high window. We did spot one or two Germans there. Everything seemed a bit on the quiet side, as though nothing was going to happen anymore, as though the war had finished, you know?

'We was just taking it easy, waiting on this other regiment to come. We were sitting there and all of a sudden all hell was let loose. They'd come on the sides, they'd come on the flanks, and they must have had two sections on each side. Anyway, they come in, they was blasting away at us, Spandaus going, mortar bombs.'

'One of the lads gets hit in the head, and he gets killed,' said Fred Hartle. 'Another gets wounded. Another gets wounded. I'm shouting to (the) PIAT man, "Put a bomb in that building up there," and as soon as I shouted I was hit myself.

'I was hit in the right arm and I was losing a lot of blood. I can remember looking down and seeing this gaping-wide hole in me arm, and I started losing consciousness.'

'Fred got two or three rounds (in his arm),' said Leslie. 'Another chap got one through the side of the head. Two was killed.'

Only Leslie and one other soldier were unharmed, 'but we were both quite shaken, you know. We'd never been under this concentrated fire and having so many casualties at the side of us. We managed to get them out of the way, safely at the side of this building. The stretcher-bearers came up and took 'em away, then the other regiments arrived, and this is when the Germans started really pulling back.

'There was hardly any opposition in Bremen after that. You'd think the war had ended then. But it did a short while after, which we was quite pleased about.'

The two soldiers killed with Leslie and Fred that day were William Houston, twenty-seven, and Martin McDowall, eighteen.[13] Fred was collected by stretcher-bearers, but didn't remember anything until he got to the airstrip and was being loaded onto an aircraft.

'I heard a voice say, "Oh, I know him! That's Fred Hartle! His wife lives across road from me mother!" They called him Billy Hill. He were in RAF and he were a navigator on this here aircraft.'

The aircraft was only going as far as Brussels, but Billy was about to go on leave and promised to let Fred's wife, Mary, know what had happened to him.

'When I went in the hospital I were feeling sorry for myself, cause I thought, *It's tail end of war and I've got done!* he chuckled. 'Anyway, when I went on the ward and seen all these lads with arms and legs off, I thought, *Well, I really have been lucky.*'

Fred was returned to the UK and demobbed in 1946.

Back at Bremen, the British soldiers continued to secure the city and its satellite towns. Lieutenant-Colonel John Corbyn, commanding officer of the 4th Wiltshires, led his battalion into an attack on the 26th.

'I can't remember exactly what the 4 Wilts history said, but the fact was we were doing a two-battalion attack astride a road towards a military barracks in Bremen and my battalion, 4 Wilts, got on rather better than 5 Wilts. I was standing on the road with my command vehicle, which divided the two battalions, when they put down a salvo of shells which landed right beside the road. With the first salvo I got a slice taken out of my trousers but I wasn't hit myself, so I tried to get my carrier to the other side of the road, but another salvo landed and I was hit in the back and that was the end of my time in the war.'

Vic Sayer, a platoon commander in the 2nd Battalion, King's Shropshire Light Infantry, was in action that same day on Bremen's southern tip, at Dreye.

'It was actually nice spring weather by then. We knew it would probably be the last battle a division fought. At that stage, at the end, it was obvious.'

Vic recalled that two long-serving officers were badly wounded by the same shell, and that there was 'mayhem' at Dreye as an attack went in on a factory.

'I do remember having an altercation with a tank officer about who should move across a space. He obviously didn't want to get hit by a Panzerfaust, because in a built-up area that was a tank man's worst fear, and I didn't want any of my platoon shot at. He and I were not on the best of terms.'

In the end the battle for Bremen was not decided by fighting in the city's streets. Rather it had been won in the towns and villages that lay on the approach to the city, and its outskirts, these actions degrading both the enemy's strength and will to fight. *The Times* reported that, on the evening of the 26th, the surrender of the city was offered by its chief of police, who was acting on behalf of the mayor.

Parts of the garrison, however, continued to fight on. On 27 April, the 7th Cameronians were ordered down to Bremen's docks to clear out the die-hards.

'We loaded onto lorries and away we went for a long ride,' said Ivan Markwell. 'Going along the country roads, every now and then there was a stop. Presently the lorry stopped. I flew up in the air and without realizing it I'd been shot through the leg. I got up and everybody got up because we'd been warned that there was snipers about and that sort of thing and if anything happened we were to get out of the truck and take positions on the side of the road.

'We all got up and started to get out of the truck when someone shouted out, "It's alright, it's alright, sit still, we're moving off." I couldn't move off because blood was running down my leg. Up come the ambulance, I was man-handled out to the back of the truck. The MO come up, gave me a shot in the arm and put me out. I was shovelled in the back of the ambulance. It was done so quick because they didn't want to stay so long.'

'The next thing I knew I was coming round in a house and they were asking me my name, rank and number and all the rest. I was shipped back into what seemed to be a big hall with lots of wounded laying about on the floor.'

That same day, the 4th Wiltshires captured General Siber, Bremen's garrison commander, as well as 'the Nazi bishop of Bremen' who had been taking part in the fighting. The organized defence of the shattered city was now over.

Major Raymond Birt, 22nd Dragoons, would become the archdeacon of Berkshire in later life. 'In disbelief we saw ourselves surrounded by acre after acre of ruin that either fire or high explosive had created. It seemed to be a signal not only of the defeat of Germany but also the death of civilization.'[14]

Other soldiers felt differently about the destruction.

'We didn't think too much about any of that kind of thing, really,' said Arthur Hicketts, 4th Wiltshires. 'I mean, they bashed us about a bit, didn't they? And we had no pity for them. I had no pity for them at all. I don't think any of us did, really. We were just thankful that we got through and were still alive, and it was (a) "you or them" attitude, you know?'

George Rayson, 1 Suffolks, came across one of Bremen's bunkers while on patrol.

'(We saw) an air-raid shelter that was almost as big as a football pitch. I think the concrete was about five foot thick, and a big runway leading up to it. I go up there with these blokes and four or five women ran to us, they put their arms round us and kissed us. They said, "*Nichts mehr bomben*." We knew what that meant: the bombing was finished.'

Arthur Rouse, 1 South Lancs, discovered that at least some of the city's civilians had a greater fear than Allied bombers.

'One of the things they did say is, "Why do you stop here?" They were obsessed with the idea that communism was the great enemy. And everyone, all the Germans we spoke to, although we didn't speak to very many, all said, "Why are you stopping now? Why do you not go on to Moscow?" They were obsessed with the idea that America and Britain should continue to Moscow.'

XXX Corps remained in Bremen and, with the city in British hands, soldiers were billeted in such houses as were still standing. 'They turfed the people out and put the troops in,' said Arthur Blizzard, the pioneer sergeant of 1 Suffolks.

The garden of the house where Arthur was staying showed signs of being freshly dug over, raising his suspicions.

'So we dug it up and found all these here pictures of Hitler, so we was in a proper Nazi house. Then the company commander rang me.

'He said, "Sergeant Blizzard, looks like we've come to the end of our tether, boy. Do you know where the brewery is?"

'I said, "Yeah, I passed one up the road."

'"You did? You've been having some?"

'I said, "I had a tipple to see what it was, that's all."

'So he said, "Could you get enough to give the battalion a drink?"

'And I said, "I don't know about that."'

When Arthur got to the brewery, the staff told him 'No, *kaput*' in response to his first attempt to liberate some booze. Not believing them, he uncovered a store of potent cherry brandy.

'So we made them wash all the barrels out, fill them up. I think I got about six barrels, enough to send round to the companies. I kept one back myself, (and) I gave one to the officers' mess. That was it, it was lovely.'

John Duddle, Royal Engineers, had less happy memories of Bremen.

'Talk about wiped out. London was bombed, and bombed, and bombed, and bombed, but you could still go through areas of London and not see where they'd been. But Bremen, there was hardly a building that you passed that wasn't blown away or really damaged, and you could smell the dead. There must have been thousands of Germans dead underneath all the rubble. You could smell the rotten bodies.'

They were not the first German civilians to be killed in the war, nor the last.

A hundred and twenty miles to the east of Bremen, British soldiers were 'wreaking vengeance'.

CHAPTER 23

Final Days

*XII Corps' capture of Hamburg, and VIII Corps'
race to Wismar
15 April – 3 May 1945*

'The troops were so bitter. They were bitter about the casualties we took. There were rumours that we had been shopped by some of the civilians. They bust into this town with flame-throwing tanks and set fire to the place. It was pretty horrible. There was a feeling of wanting to wreak vengeance. There's no doubt that some of the houses were unnecessarily burned down. One woman had gone quite mad and was nursing her dead baby.'

Philip Stein, 2nd Battalion, Glasgow Highlanders

The town of Uelzen, forty-five miles south-east of Hamburg, was one of the many casualties of April.

The battle to take the town had gone badly from the beginning. At the nearby village of Stadensen, the Glasgow Highlanders, with a mixture of supporting arms, were counter-attacked by Panzer Division Clausewitz. In a brutal battle that lasted several hours, the Glasgow Highlanders suffered fifty-four casualties, including twenty-tour taken prisoner. Sixty-three British vehicles were destroyed, most of the village was set alight, and many civilians were killed. The attacking German force also suffered heavily, losing twelve SP guns and ten half-tracks, some of them destroyed by

Major Stephenson, 530 Battery, who won the Military Cross for knocking out enemy vehicles both with a PIAT, and a 25-pounder used in the anti-tank role.

At noon on the 15th, 10 HLI entered Veersen, the southern suburb of Uelzen, with the 2nd Gordon Highlanders on their right. Both battalions became pinned down by heavy fire, including from flak guns, and were unable to advance further. The next day, the 9th Cameronians pushed through. Tom Gore was with them.

'We got to a road, and something I had learned at Battle School was never to hang around when you're crossing a gap, so we dashed across. The next section opened up with their Bren gun. The enemy were pulling out up the road.'

An SP gun fired back and caused 'three or four casualties' in the second section. Tom moved on, his own section mostly made up of replacements who'd been with him since the Rhine crossing, coming under intermittent fire. They then used their picks to knock holes through the walls of terraced houses, and advanced within the cover of the buildings.

'We got through pretty quick taking turns on the pick. Dropped grenades down the stairways. Dashed down, and there was a light coming from the cellar. I was short on hand grenades so I fired a burst of Sten gun and dashed down to the cellar on me own. And there staring at me was fifteen to twenty children, and two nuns, and my mouth went really dry. Thank goodness I'd run out of bombs.'

Tom's bullets had struck within a foot of the children, but caused no casualties. After taking off his helmet and trying to say a few reassuring words, the nineteen-year-old soldier left to catch up with the rest of the section. 'I couldn't stay there and look after them, because I'd have been Absent Without Leave again. You had to make these split (second) decisions when you're in battle. If it's right, or if it's wrong, you just had to do it. So I left them.'

Tom caught up with his section and continued to clear more buildings. In the confusion of the fighting, one of the neighbouring platoons threw a phosphorous bomb into one of the rooms where two of Tom's comrades were taking shelter. Fortunately, both men escaped with light injuries.

The platoon then joined up with tanks to push on to Uelzen's main square.

'There was a dead body of a civilian laying in the road, and the tanks were swerving to miss it. So we got hold of his legs and dragged him across the road and put him in the gutter. And there was a blue reddish mark, a skidmark of blood, right across the road.

'We moved on through Uelzen, went around a corner, and there was two ruddy great Panther tanks there. One of the engines was running, and their guns was pointing right at us, so we made a hasty retreat.'

A white flag appeared. It belonged to an escaped British POW, who told them that the German crews had only just abandoned the tanks and run up the road.

'Luck was with us again,' said Tom. 'The biggest tanks I ever seen.'

The escapee then led them to a school that was full of POWs.

'Now, when you see prisoners of war freed, they're always cheering and shouting and joyful. But there was no joy with these here prisoners. They seemed sort of dumbfounded, or something. I suppose it was the shock.'

And no wonder. The men were survivors of the 51st (Highland)'s stand at Saint-Valery, and had been in captivity for almost five years.

With resistance crushed in Uelzen by 18 April, and much of the town in flame, Tom's division pushed on to Lauenburg.

Desert Rat

John Donnelly, from Kirkaldy, saw his first action of the war in June 1942 at the Battle of Knightsbridge, in the western desert. Two years later, in Normandy with 1 Royal Tank Regiment, John not only survived an engagement with a Tiger tank but knocked it out. Promoted to sergeant for that action, John was a highly respected soldier in the regiment, and had been rewarded with some time in the UK before the Rhine crossing.

'I wished to hell I hadnae (gone back). I felt really worse then. I said, "Well, to hell coming back to this, and it's getting near the end."'

On 18 April, John and A Squadron, 1 RTR, went into action in the area of Tostedt, some twenty miles from Hamburg.

'Our infantry were being held up in this wood, and tanks very seldom went into woods, but they were being held up by a machine-gun post.'

Confined by the trees to a single track, John's troop went in to support the infantry with his tank in the lead. They'd just reached a crossroads when they were contacted by the enemy.

'I was hit by a bazooka which glanced off the top and blew off my mapboard. Another one hit the turret, it hit the gun, and the 75mm gun was oot of action. You just seen a big flash. You didn't know what was hitting. I told the driver to reverse back.'

The tank moved back and out of the enemy's fire while the battle at the crossroads continued to rage. When the track proved too narrow to allow the tanks behind John to move by his own, and despite his tank's weaponry being knocked out, John ordered his driver to go forward again to the crossroads, where the enemy waited in trenches.

'All that we had was hand grenades in a wee box, so I got the hand grenades out and I lobbed them into the trench, and they started to run. I had the Thompson machine gun, so I started shooting at them. I coulda been shot just as easy, but ya didnae think about that at tha' time. Yer just firin' away.'

A report written by one of John's officers recorded that:

'He stayed there, personally killing five enemy until the infantry could extricate themselves and their casualties and then returned to the attack in company with flame throwing carriers and finally cleared the wood.

'On this, the eighth occasion in this campaign on which Sergeant Donnelly has been hit by a bazooka, his personal courage and offensive spirit accounted for the destruction of the enemy post holding the wood, and also undoubtedly saved the infantry from considerable casualties.'[1]

'I withdrew and we came back at night and I thought nothing more about it,' said John.

But his actions were recognized by his commanders, and John was awarded a Military Medal.

'I was amazed.'

At the end of the war, Field Marshall Montgomery himself would pin the medal on John's chest.

'He said to me, "Congratulations. I take it you'll be staying on in the army?" I said, "No, sir, I'm a Territorial Army man, I've served my time."'

And at the end of April, that time was fast coming to an end. Only a few obstacles remained between the soldiers and peace, and the capture of Hamburg was one.

Hamburg

Situated on the River Elbe, the Hanseatic city of Hamburg was an essential communications hub, and seaport. The city had been extensively bombed by both the British and American air forces since 1943, with estimates of civilian deaths at around 37,000, and half of its homes destroyed.

Capturing the city would be no easy task. The remnants of the 1st Parachute Army, which had fought the British tooth and nail since the Siegfried Line, were waiting. The 12th SS (Hitler Youth)'s reinforcement battalion, naval personnel and militarized police were also available for Hamburg's defence, as well as a large number of anti-aircraft artillery that could be used in a ground defence role.

A British force of 7th Armoured, 15th (Scottish) and 53rd (Welsh) Divisions crept ever closer to the city. On 20 April, the 7th Armoured captured Daerstorf, eight miles west of Hamburg, and Vahrendorf. Here they dug in for five days – British commanders were not about to throw away lives needlessly.

The same could not be said of the enemy's command, and on 26 April, an attack led by the 12th SS Division's reinforcement regiment clashed with the Devons, leaving sixty German dead on the field. Two days later, the 5th Royal Tank Regiment, 1st Royal Berkshires and the 9th Durham Light Infantry seized Jesteburg and Hittfeld and reached the autobahn outside of Hamburg.

Twenty-one-year-old Tony Colgan, a Londoner in the DLI, had

been fighting the Wehrmacht since Sicily in '43. Outside Hamburg he awoke to find a German POW sleeping at his feet.

'He was a young lad of fourteen. He spoke English. He'd been told to lie in wait for a tank, with a Panzerfaust. He was obviously going to be written off, you know. But anyway they caught him before he had a chance to fire.'

The young soldier was told to speak into a microphone, and encourage more of his comrades to surrender. 'We had huge speakers, you could hear them quite a distance.'

These loudspeakers were part of psychological warfare operations that aimed to end battles before they began. Leaflets were also dropped and fired onto the enemy's positions, detailing the impossible situation of Germany and promising safety to those that surrendered.

Later that morning, Tony's war almost came to an end by the hand of his own side.

'A Cromwell tank came along with infantry on it. It saw us and swung its turret and fired on us. Knocked out the platoon truck. Wounded one of our sergeants. Suddenly realized what he was doing. Centred his turret, and just poodled off again without an apology. It was quite an interesting morning, you know.'

Sergeant Tom Myers, of the same battalion, recalled one day around Hamburg when they were coming under shellfire, and they spotted what was a likely enemy OP. Their commanding officer, John Mogg, led the patrol to take it out himself. 'There's a whole battalion to pick from,' Tom said, still impressed that Mogg would choose to put himself in the line of fire. 'He was a marvellous man, the colonel.'

Mogg and the patrol crawled to the OP in the trees and fired a few bursts into the branches to encourage their surrender.

'They came down,' said Tom. 'They're both in civvies. One was equivalent of a major, and one was equivalent of a lieutenant. A woman. And the colonel says, "You've been spotting for the artillery."'

The two soldiers – who were breaking the laws of war by wearing civilian clothing – did not disagree. The sentence for such activity was death.

'So (Mogg) says to us, "Put your rifles on ready. I'm now going to convey a field court martial."'

'It was just like that, touch and go, whether he said fire,' said Tom. 'We'd have shot them. If he hadn't been there, I'd have shot them. I mean, if anybody's gonna disguise themselves as civvies and have you fired on, you're going to do something.'

Instead, Tom recalled that Mogg ordered the pair to be taken back and handed over to Division.

On 28 April, the 3rd Regiment Royal Horse Artillery began to shell Hamburg, adding to the destruction caused by the bombers. They hit a rubber factory which had been turned into a military hospital by a Dr Hermann Burchard. The factory owner, Albert Schäfer, and Burchard went to the military commander of Hamburg, General Wolz, for permission to approach the British and ask them to spare the building. Seeing a chance to secretly open communication with the enemy, Wolz agreed, and gave them an interpreter, Leutnant Otto von Laun. On 29 April the men drove to the British lines, a white flag on their car, and were taken prisoner. They were ultimately driven blindfolded to a guesthouse on Lüneburg Heath, where intelligence officer Captain Lindsay met them. He agreed to stop the artillery attacks on the hospital, a sweetener for the deal he really wanted to negotiate: the surrender of the city.[2]

That same day, the 2nd Argylls lost almost a company's worth of men in an instant.

'A shell landed in a quarry where we were assembling,' said James Campbell. 'It really was awful.'

Eight soldiers from the battalion were killed in the shelling and between fifty and sixty were wounded.[3]

'These things happened,' said James, who turned twenty that year.

The following day, 30 April, Adolf Hitler killed himself in his bunker as Russian forces overran Berlin. The Führer was dead, but the war did not die with him.

Before his death, Hitler had denounced both Göring and Himmler as traitors, and after Goebbels' own suicide, the next in line for the leadership of the Reich was Admiral Karl Dönitz.

Knowing that the Reich was doomed, Dönitz's aim was to continue fighting in the east for as long as possible, thus allowing troops and civilians to flee west and surrender to the Western Allies.

On the same day that the world was well rid of Hitler, Schäfer was sent back to Hamburg with a letter from Major-General Lyne to General Wolz hidden in his shoe. The letter demanded that Wolz surrender, and threatened a bombing raid if he did not. On 1 May Wolz sent two letters in reply, carried by a Major Andrae and translator Captain Link. One letter thanked the British for not targeting the hospital, the other offered to meet with them to negotiate terms. Lyne wanted Wolz to be at the British lines at Meckelfeld the next evening, but then agreed to give him an extra twenty-four hours. The message was duly taken back by the German delegation. On 2 May, Wolz was busy ensuring that the military forces in the city would fall into line. He also had the backing of the city's Nazi gauleiter, who had been attempting negotiations of his own. Catching wind of what was happening and unable to prevent it, Dönitz pretended it was his idea, and that evening he ordered that Hamburg should be declared an open city.[4]

Wolz left Hamburg for the British lines at 2100 hrs, along with Major Andrae, Captain Link and a retired mayor. Meanwhile Tom Myers, 9 DLI, was ordered to lead a patrol to the edge of Hamburg, to confirm that the autobahn was passable.

'(Colonel Mogg) said, "I don't think you've anything to worry about." I was nearly shiteing meself! There's gonna be all sorts in there!'

Tom led the patrol up to the edge of the city, where a lone policeman appeared and offered the surrender of the city's police force.

'Word came up that there was a German general and others coming down, to go to our Division HQ to offer the terms of surrender. They were in the big open staff cars. Well, we stopped them. I says, "Out, everybody out."'

Tom took a sword-dagger from the general. 'And I took his medals off him, and I took his watch. I said to the lads, "Take what you want. Take their medals, take their revolvers and everything." And I said, "When you get them off, hide the buggers, because there'll be hell about this."

'As far as we were concerned they were finished. Oh yes (they objected). I said, "You're not entitled to wear medals, you're not entitled to wear that revolver, or that dagger." I said, "You're beaten soldiers. You're finished." I says, "We've come right back from the beaches of Normandy up here," and I says, "You're finished."'

Skirmishing and shelling continued as the negotiations were held. While clearing a wood on the Elbe, Tom Gore's battalion, 9th Cameronians, lost two men killed and sixteen wounded, and took 175 of the enemy prisoner.

'They were really scared. We had to pull them out of their trenches. A boy of about fourteen was setting up his Spandau machine gun. An officer saved our lives. He shouted and run and kicked the machine gun and dragged the youth out.'

That evening the battalion received word that a ceasefire in the area would come into effect at 0800 hrs the following day – Hamburg's garrison had surrendered. On 3 May, the 7th Armoured Division entered the city unopposed.

'My colonel and I went into Hamburg the day it surrendered,' said Edward Palmer, Bedfordshire Yeomanry. 'It was desolation. The place then had of course had these great firestorms, and so on. To be honest – we approved. We thought, *Good*. It was good to see how much they'd suffered after all the time we'd suffered. One had no sympathy for them. No sympathy at all, at that time.'

John Donnelly, 1 RTR, recalled the scene that he witnessed in one of Hamburg's hospitals.

'It was pitiful. There was men minus an arm. Minus a leg. Minus an arm and a leg. And this was all done from the Eastern Front, from Russia. They were that severely injured that they were just amputating.'

The 53rd Division also joined the 7th Armoured in the surrendered city. Dunkirk man Frank Brodie, 1 East Lancs, took some adjusting to the new state of affairs.

'I walked into this room and there's these Germans, supposedly police. One on right-hand side of room jumps up and (gave the Nazi salute). Everybody jumped to attention. I turned around and kicked him in t' bloody shin.'

Bruce Coombs, 6 RWF, was billeted in a civilian home.

'We were in this house, and there was a German with one arm missing. He'd had his arm off in the Russian front. He was a school teacher, and he could speak perfect English.'

The German told Bruce stories about the bombing of the city, which might have claimed as many as 40,000 lives.

'(He said) there was such a fire in Hamburg that people come down to the river. There was a vacuum of oxygen in the air because the fire was so great, and they all died on the bank there.'

It was a plight that would move Bruce in his later years, but not as a twenty-year-old infantryman who had fought his way to Hamburg from Normandy, losing hundreds of comrades to death and wounds along the way.

'I think you felt like they'd done it to London, so, you know what I mean? And you weren't worried about anything else. All you were worried about was survival yourself.'

The Race to the Sea

Britain and the United States were Allies of the Soviet Union, but it was a marriage of necessity rather than one born of shared ideology. As the end of the war drew near, all armies raced to secure as much of Europe as they could. Though agreements had been made at Yalta as to who would control what on the post-war continent, there was a great fear that the Soviet Union would occupy Denmark, which was then under German occupation. This was unconscionable to the Western Allies.

On the evening of 1 May, 3rd Parachute Brigade, in the area of Lauenberg, received orders that they were to race to the Baltic port town of Wismar, fifty-five miles to the north-east, and secure it against enemies and allies alike. The brigade was to set off at first light the following morning. To rapidly cover the distance, tanks of the Scots Greys would provide battlefield taxis for the Airborne.

Murray Walker was a troop commander in the regiment.

'The Greys and the 6th Airborne Division were instructed to head for Wismar on the Baltic coast, and we went for it. It was an incredible experience. At the rate of some 5,000 troops an hour, the German army was heading west as fast as possible to avoid being captured by the Russians, while on the same single carriageway road we were hammering east absolutely flat out. With the British and the Germans going their different ways just feet away from each other, there was no fighting, no acknowledgment even. At one point our headlong gallop was brought to a halt by the sheer weight of traffic and, sitting on the top of the turret eating a tin of Spam, I found myself looking down onto a vast open Mercedes-Benz staff car containing four obviously high-ranking German officers. It was hardly the time, place or occasion for a cheery chat; we studied each other dispassionately and not a word was spoken. Then the column moved on, so did they and that was the last we saw of each other.'[5]

The 11th Armoured Division, who until 29 April had been under the impression that they would go on from the Elbe to Berlin, were instead ordered to strike for the Baltic and the town of Lübeck, where the eastern side of the Danish peninsula joined the 'mainland' thirty miles west of Wismar.

John Buchanan, 2nd Fife and Forfar Yeomanry, noted the mood of the unit's replacements around this time.

'They were all dead keen to get into action, make a name for themselves before the war finished. That included officers who wanted to get their MC before the war finished. We, being old soldiers by that time, our main effort was to keep our nose clean. We wanted to end the war as we were.'

John, the old soldier, was twenty-one.

'We had this young officer. He was a nice chap and quite level-headed but he wanted to get on. He kept moving whether there was something in front or not. We were lead tank again. I could see all these Germans in the ditches beside us and I say to him, "Shall I brass them up?" If it were (my last commander), I wouldn't have bothered, I would have just shot them. He says, "No, it's OK, carry on." I was getting apprehensive. I had the gun turned round, pointing at the ditches. He said, "No, hold your fire."

'As soon as the first two tanks had passed, the Germans stood up with their white flags. They let the first two tanks past and they stood up. We took thousands of prisoners – told them to walk back and the infantry behind us took them on.

'We're coming into Lübeck and there's an aerodrome on the right-hand side and I saw a Junkers, one of these passenger planes, taking off and I fired at it. I hit it, but what happened to it I really don't know, it was foggy. By this time we were coming into the suburbs of Lübeck.'

The inhabitants of Lübeck were going about their business, and nobody seemed bothered by the British tanks that trundled into the city on 2 May.

'We kept on to this big bridge and we were told to hold the bridge.

'There was nothing to do, the advance had stopped. The officer had disappeared. We were sitting there. Down at the bottom of the bridge there was a pub. Anders says, "Ach, I'm going for a pint." I says, "I'll come." Norman, he stayed in the tank. He was like me, he didn't like leaving the tank, but I thought it was safe, the war was but finished.

'We went into this pub and it's like the Wild West. We banged the doors open and we were like the three cowboys walking into a saloon – everything stopped, all the voices stopped. We wandered in and went up to the bar and said, "Schnapps."

'I think the consensus was, "there's a war on, you cannae get schnapps". So he says he had beer, so we had a beer. It was lousy stuff, rusty water. When he realized we weren't going to do anything else, just sit there and drink, he opened the flap of the cellar and out stepped two German buxom blondes, the real German (look) with pigtails round their back and that German dress they have. Really plump, big bosom. About eighteen or nineteen. When they realized they weren't going to get raped or something like that they came out.

'The pub was full of German naval officers, young, they all had their leather coats on down to their ankles, carrying briefcases. When they realized they weren't going to get shot, they came en masse to our table to surrender. Some of them pulled out small revolvers. So we told them to go to some park we'd been told to tell (surrendering Germans to go to). We left them to it. The beer was lousy anyway.'

Thirty miles east, pacifist and conscientious objector John Petts, 224th (Parachute) Field Ambulance, was closing on Wismar with the 6th Airborne Division.

'We realized that there must be a hospital nearby, because many patients had clearly got out of their beds and put a blanket round them, and were staggering along the roads to get away from the Russians. Side by side with civilians pushing wheelbarrows, containing a few belongings. Anyone who could walk was staggering along, including German soldiers who apparently were disobeying orders and were in retreat. All this mixed up into an incredible hodge podge. The German soldiers, without exception, were panicking and in a great hurry to give themselves up. It was a tremendous moment really in my whole service as a pacifist in the British army to be handed loaded weapons with relief from the soldier, eager to hand them over.

'There were one or two of us who stood in the middle of the road while a queue of soldiers came, handing us their weapons, mainly rifles. We held them – after checking that there wasn't a bullet up the spout of course, we held them by the barrel and smashed the butts on the road and chucked them on a heap. We ended up with a great heap of smashed weapons, which was good to see. That's the only bit of destruction that I joined in during the whole of the European Holocaust.'

The British Army reached the heavily bombed town of Wismar on 2 May 1945, and not a moment too soon. The Red Army was only a few miles away.

That same day a Russian officer and his driver found themselves stopped by a roadblock manned by the 1st Canadian Parachute Battalion. It was the first of many encounters that could turn sour very quickly.

6th Airborne's commander, Major-General Bols, instructed the CO of 9 Para, Lieutenant-Colonel Napier Crookenden, to officially rendezvous with Soviet forces. In Napier's words, Bols told him to, '"Take your truck, go out to the east and find me a Russian general."'

Napier took with him a Canadian Doukhobors* sergeant, who was fluent in Russian, and his driver, Private Sayers, and set off east towards the Russian lines.

'After ten miles of empty countryside, we saw round the next bend, or on the next bend, a great long barrel of a Russian tank looking at us, so I furiously waved the white sheet out of the window. Sayers slowed down our truck and there was this little group of Russians, tank crews on the side of the road. We had a tremendous meeting, everybody kissed each other and so on.

'I said through my interpreter, "Where's your general?", and as I said that, a group of tanks came down the road, I thought at a very high speed, covered in infantry, and the leading tank flying a great big red flag. In the afternoon light, it looked really impressive, a picture of tanks at speed, rushing through an enemy countryside.

'We eventually found the senior officer, I put him in my car and pursued this group of tanks. They were going about thirty (mph) or something. Private Sayers was a very good driver and I said, "We must pass them," so at rather high speed and very often in or out of a ditch each side, he passed these tanks. This Russian senior officer, some sort of general I think, kept on gripping me by the arm, he was so nervous of Private Sayers' driving.

'We came into Wismar, (and) it was getting dark then. The Canadians had lined up, blocked all the road, had anti-tank guns pointing at the Russians. The tanks stopped, I got this Russian out, went into the Divisional Headquarters, a house they'd established temporarily. General Bowles and the Russian and his staff had a long talk and although I didn't know at the time what they were saying, what the Russian was saying, we were told almost at once (that) the Russian was cursing Eric Bowles quite rudely and saying, "I have a whole armoured regiment, my objective is Copenhagen. You are in my way, out of the way." Eric lost his temper, they'd been talking for about an hour, and said to his interpreter, "Tell this useless oaf, if he is not back one mile from my outpost, inside

---

* A sect of Russian dissenters, some of whom fled the country and settled in Canada.

of one hour, I shall open fire. I have with me a complete division, I have an Army Group of Royal Artillery of 250 guns, so if there's a question of who's the strongest, I am. So get back now."

'Straight away the Russian gave a smile, he'd had several whiskeys, and said, "At once, General." He read the form and of course that's the way they understand. They went back and we had no more trouble."'

Wismar remained in British hands, but its citizens were not entirely saved.

'We had a whole load of healthy civilians who were running, sighing with relief that they were now in British hands,' said John Watts, the commander of 195th (Airlanding) Field Ambulance. 'There were three German nurses pulling casualties with wounded that couldn't walk. Fortunately we were able to help them because there was a civilian hospital and we had plenty of ambulances. They were so delighted to be in British hands. They didn't know that three days later we (would) move out and let the Russians in.'

The war in Europe, which had claimed the lives of more than 30 million, was only days from its end.

CHAPTER 24

Victory in Europe

The final days the of war in Europe, and the first of peace
May 1945

'Somebody in my vehicle was killed on virtually the last day of the war, which was very sad. I mean, we'd had chaps killed on the gun position, but not in my personal vehicle, my forward team. We were just recce-ing a forward position right up on the banks of the Elbe, in open fields, when I saw a couple of aircraft flying very low towards us. Up to that time they'd all been British. We'd had air superiority. And suddenly I heard firing.

My driver and I leapt out just in time. My signaller, who was in the back of the vehicle, couldn't get out, was killed. That was two days before the end of the war. Which was a blow. Having to write to his parents. A chap I knew very well.'

Edward Palmer, Bedfordshire Yeomanry

Final Days

In the first days of May, Ian Hammerton, 22nd Dragoons, was supporting 51st (Highland) Division's assault on the town of Bremervörde. Survival for Ian, who had fought across Europe from the first wave on Juno Beach, was almost at hand.

'After the battle of Bremen we were told to go carefully, and when we got to Bremervörde we were told to go *very* carefully. Not to stick our necks out.'

Ian's troop of Shermans were moving along a road sided by deep ditches and interspersed with farmhouses – 'a horrible place for tanks to move' – when his leading tank spotted a self-propelled gun and quickly knocked it out.

'Almost immediately afterwards there was another shot from further down the road, and (the leading tank) was hit.'

Ian's own driver swiftly went into reverse.

'There was a Bren carrier right behind us who didn't know what was happening, and we banged straight into him and pushed him backwards.'

Ian's driver then swung the tank to get off the road. 'And as we did so, another shot came up the road and clipped the telephone pole right above me, and I had all the wires crash down on the cupola over my head.'

The three remaining tanks got off the road and found cover around the farmhouses.

'The (wireless) operator and the driver of Sergeant Stirling's tank came running up to me. They'd managed to get out. They reported that the gunner and commander had both been killed. The commander by a HE that had burst right on his cupola, and the gunner by an (armour-piercing round) that had gone clean through the turret and out of the back.'

Ian sent the two survivors back on foot, while he and his tanks remained to search for the enemy who had killed their friends.

'The infantry had already filtered forwards. Just as we got into the farm a German Volkswagen came hurtling up the road, towards the direction that we'd come from, and there was a burst of Bren fire, and a few minutes later a very dejected German lieutenant and his driver came walking into the farmyard with their hands on their heads.

'It was, I think, the Seaforth Highlanders who were the chaps we were with,' said Ian. These infantrymen 'dealt with' Germans who were hiding in the farm building while Ian and his tanks continued their search for the SP gun.

'We spotted it reversing down the road, and we both fired at it.'

One of the tanks fired a HE shell which struck a branch on a nearby tree, causing it to explode in front of them. 'And of course I got the benefit of the bang, and I was deaf for several weeks after,' said Ian, who worried that he'd never regain his hearing. 'But they turned out alright. Must have tough ears.

'Whether we hit the SP or not we never knew, but the infantry continued across. We shot them into the next objective. I remember the company commander – who'd been a (platoon commander) four weeks before – walking forward with his walking stick, and leading his men across the field.

'We shot them into the next farm, which caught fire, and then we were told not to go any further.'

The reason for this halt was developments taking place eighty miles to the west, at Lüneburg.

On the morning of 3 May, a German delegation headed by General Admiral von Friedeburg crossed British lines near Hamburg and travelled with a British escort to Villa Möllering in Häcklingen, the headquarters of General Miles Dempsey, Commander of the British Second Army. It was made clear that Friedeburg represented General Keitel, chief of *Oberkommando der Wehrmacht* (Armed Forces High Command) and Großadmiral Karl Dönitz, who had succeeded Hitler as head of the German state, both of whom wished to organize a surrender. Also in the delegation was General Kinzel, representing Field Marshal Busch, head of Army Group H, and Rear-Admiral Wagner, who was one of von Friedeburg's senior staff officers.

Four officers from the German delegation were brought to Field Marshal Montgomery at his tactical headquarters at Lüneburg Heath, an area of high ground inside a rural Wehrmacht training area. They were made to wait outside beneath a large Union Flag and once Montgomery came to meet them, he asked through his interpreter, almost petulantly, who they were and what they wanted, then proceeded to exclaim he'd never heard of them.

The German delegation proposed the surrender of Army Group Vistula, containing 500,000 soldiers deployed north of Berlin, an area that was earmarked for the Soviet occupation zone. Montgomery refused this proposal, either not wanting to expend resources on an army that was not in his area of operations, or not wanting to too overtly interfere with the Soviet sector. Instead, Montgomery proposed the unconditional surrender of all German forces to his army's north and west, including those in the Netherlands and the Jutland peninsula.

After the German delegation was treated to a lunch made of British ration packs, they were given a briefing by Montgomery on the overall military situation in order to reinforce the notion that further defiance was futile. However, the delegation felt they didn't have enough authority to give unconditional surrender and so Admiral von Friedeburg and Major Friedel, one of Kinzel's staff officers, returned to Dönitz to ask for it, the other officers remaining at Monty's HQ.

Friedeburg and Friedel returned the next day, on 4 May, and agreed to Montgomery's terms. After Montgomery hosted a press conference at 1700 hrs, the delegation was paraded in front of a Union Flag for photographs. A number of Allied fighter bombers flew low and fast above them, as though to underscore the point of Allied supremacy. The delegation was then escorted into a carpeted tent and the surrender was signed at 1830 hrs, coming into effect at 0800 hrs British Double Summer Time on Saturday 5 May 1945.

Richard Leatherbarrow, Army Film and Photographic Unit, had rushed to Lüneburg Heath after getting word of events.

'I felt at the time, I was conscious, that something was taking place that was of some historical significance, even if it was only a preliminary run-through. I knew that getting it down on film was of considerable importance.

'It was a glorious day out for a still cameraman. The Union Jack flying outside Monty's caravan, and six figures just standing still.

'It was just the four surrendering Germans, Monty and his colonel aide, and two or three cameras going at it.'

Word of the surrender was sent out to soldiers on both sides. It was a long process, the information needing to be disseminated down through many levels of command before it reached the squaddies on the frontline.

Acting Company Sergeant Major Harry Simpson, 7th Battalion, Black Watch, was in the area of Meckelstedt, between Bremerhaven and the Elbe, when he suffered one final brush with death.

'I laid the company low in a field at the top of this rise, by a farmhouse behind a wall. I said, "Well, I'll go forwards and just see if the road's alright."

'I got about fifty yards from the underpass when this bugger opened up from the left, shooting at me, so I turned about and ran like bloody hell back again, and jumped over the wall.

'A chap said, "Are you alright, Sergeant Major?" I said, "Aye, why?" He said, "You got a bloody hole through your pack." I said, "Have I what?" He said, "You've a hole through your pack." A bullet hole. It had gone right through.'

Two of the company's signallers then came over.

'They said, "Sergeant Major, we've a message here and they want an instant reply."

'I said, "What is it?"

'"It's from Battalion Headquarters. That with effect from the receipt of this message, you've to stay where you are and cease fire. There's a ceasefire in operation."

'"Well," I said, "the company commander wants that. Where's the company commander?"

'"We don't know."

'"Well," I said, "when did you see him last?"

'"Oh, it's a while ago down the road there."'

Harry told the signallers to forget that they'd given him the message about any ceasefire, 'because if we stay where we are, we're in a bloody open field, and we'll be sleeping in the open tonight.' He then moved the company off towards the village.

'The two Germans who had fired on us, they must have got the message as well, because they ran across the fields. We entered the village and that was it.'

The company occupied a number of houses and made themselves comfortable. The war was over, and against all odds, Harry Simpson had survived.

'That evening we got the message through that hostilities were to cease,' said Ian Hammerton. 'Anything that could fire fired straight into the air. I've never seen such a barrage go up in all my life. People who'd never had a chance to fire a weapon in anger fired them then.

'That was the first time I saw jet aircraft. Two Me 262s came whooshing straight over us.'

The enemy aircraft did not fire onto the packed road, along which refugees and surrendering soldiers came streaming.

'That evening the Seaforths brought up their band in full dress uniform, and they beat the retreat in the field alongside the road. Pipers, and the drummers, marching and counter marching with a battery of field guns at one end of the field, and as the German refugees and the soldiers got near that field, the entire column went across to the opposite side of the road. They were petrified.'

Ian had lost two men killed in action three days earlier, both of them 'old soldiers' who had come so far from the beaches: Trooper Edwin Taylor, twenty-six years old; and Lance Sergeant George Stirling, thirty-six, a married man.[1] A young officer who had been under Ian's wing for some time was also killed by shelling at Bremervörde.

'Lieutenant Hickey, he was very badly wounded. He died on the aircraft on his way home.'

Lieutenant Brian Hickey was nineteen years old when he succumbed to his wounds on 14 May. His older brother Bill was killed two years later during the occupation of Germany.[2]

'I was very upset,' Ian said of his friend's death. 'I felt a certain responsibility for him.'

More than 6,000 British soldiers of the Second World War are buried in German soil.[3] Their deaths, in the words of the late Captain Ian Liddell VC's family, were pieces 'in the mosaic of victory'.

On 7 May, an unconditional German surrender was signed by Admiral Dönitz to General Dwight D. Eisenhower, Supreme Commander, Allied Expeditionary Force in Europe. The next day, the heads of the Allied states took to balconies and the airwaves to address their nations. Of the many speeches given on Victory in Europe Day, perhaps the few lines that best encapsulate the British achievement are these, given by King George VI in a radio broadcast that night:

'In the darkest hours we knew that the enslaved and isolated peoples of Europe looked to us; their hopes were our hopes; their confidence confirmed our faith. We knew that, if we failed, the last remaining barrier against a world-wide tyranny would have fallen in ruins. But we did not fail.'[4]

The war in Europe was over.

VE Day

Bruce Coombs, 6 RWF, had once harboured doubts about Britain's ability to achieve victory.

'In Normandy I did, yes. Thinking of the 1914 war my father was in, they were there in France for all them years, hardly moving, back and forth, and all them lives were lost. I thought we'd be the same in Normandy, until we had the breakout. Then as you went further on, you knew then that the (end) was coming.'

Bruce recalled the day that the war ended, receiving the news from a passing tank.

'Their officer came out of the turret and he said, "The war's over!" It was the happiest day of my life.'

As soldiers are wont to do when they're happy – or sad, or anything in between – many of them now broke open the bottles that they'd been saving for the occasion, or went in search of fresh supplies.

'I got no personal celebration whatsoever,' said Bob Summer, who had taken over a platoon of Royal Engineers in late February. 'I was trying to keep the peace. My blokes went out into the town and got themselves into no end of trouble, and I spent all of VE night trying to find them and bring them back. In the end I got so fed up that anyone who'd got false teeth, I took them. I thought, *They won't go out again now.*'

James Absalom, on the other hand, had to be rescued by his men in 12 Para's Signals Platoon.

'My signallers were excellent blokes. We managed to pick up Winston Churchill's speech announcing the end of the war. We did this by using some of the bigger sets we'd got. It was broadcast and then the CO had an interpreter speak to all the Germans in this village and tell them what the form was.

'The colonel decided we'd have a victory party, so we had a big bonfire built on a piece of spare ground and the colonel found a white horse, a charger, and another lieutenant and myself did a stirrup charge through the village. He went at the full gallop and we're hanging on with our feet off the ground en route to the site of the bonfire. Sergeant Bailey, who'd been a bookie in civvy street, arrived with cigars sticking out his pockets. He was donating cigars to everybody and taking bets on some imaginary race.

'I remember being carried back to my billet by some blokes and I don't remember much after that. At this stage, I'd now got to the position where the experiences were having a bad effect on me. I felt cynical about a lot of things and found that soldiering wasn't really the thing I was cut out for, and war seemed to me to be a bit of a nonsense.

'My own soldiers felt the brunt of my temper at times, this was all because of what we'd been through. How they felt, it was difficult to understand. I was not the bloke I was when I started off as a young soldier.'

The loss of innocence, and of comrades, was felt heavily across the army.

John Donnelly, 1 RTR, had first seen action in the desert three years earlier. He finished the war at Hamburg with one of his few remaining close friends, Tommy Harland. 'A nice wee lad, and a very good soldier.'

Tommy Harland was awarded the DCM in April 1943 and received further recognition by being commissioned from the ranks. In August, 1945, now Lieutenant Harland DCM was made Chevalier of the Order of Leopold II, with Palm and Croix de Guerre, effectively making him a Belgian knight for his services in liberating that country. His citation notes that he had led his troop in every action since 7 June 1944, twice continuing actions in which his tank had been destroyed, and had been recommended for a further two gallantry awards in North West Europe.

When peace was declared, Tommy had looked around at the faces of his squadron and said to John that 'I couldn't see anyone that I'd known for any length of time other than one sergeant, who'd been together (with me) from El Alamein.'

That sergeant was John, who knew that the odds of survival had always been against them. 'There wasnae very many troop sergeants and troop officers who went through the war like we did and got away with it,' he said.

Two days after victory in Europe was declared, the commanding officer of the 2nd Argylls, Lieutenant-Colonel Hank Morgan, addressed his battalion, thanking them for their efforts, wishing those that would be demobilized the best of luck, and expressing his hopes that he would see those who remained in the army again. He then asked those who had been with the battalion since the battalion landed in Normandy to remain on parade, while all others were dismissed.

When Colonel Morgan saw how few remained, 'he burst into tears and dashed off the parade ground,' said James Campbell. 'Most of (the survivors) were all cooks and clerks. My platoon, there was only seventeen of us left out of the fifty-three at the start of the war, plus all the reinforcements that had been killed and wounded.'

'We'd suffered quite a lot,' James said simply. 'It was rather sad.'

But this did not dissuade James from remaining in the army after the war, and transferring to the Parachute Regiment. He served in Palestine, Korea, Cyprus, and the Suez Crisis, by which time he had risen to the rank of regimental sergeant major. One can only imagine the awe in which he was held by his young soldiers.

'I finally retired from the army on 13 January 1965. I wish I could do it again.'

Tom Gore, 9th Cameronians, ended the war on the outskirts of Hamburg. 'The company commander came around, Major McNeill, and he said it's just come over the radio that all hostilities will finish.'

The major poured a drop of wine in the men's bent tin mugs, and toasted to victory. It would be understandable if Tom, who had gone AWOL for a time from the frontline, regretted his experiences in the war, but this was not the case.

'We've discussed this a lot, me and my friends. And I don't think we would have missed it, really. But it took a great chunk out of your life. Four and three-quarter years out of your life, which was the prime part of your life, actually.'

Tens of thousands of British soldiers had died in that prime, their loss weighing on the comrades who had survived them.

'It was a time for reflection, really,' said Vic Sayer, whose brigade had suffered heavily at Kervenheim. 'I always think, when I see these pictures of celebrations in Piccadilly Circus, it wasn't quite like that in a battalion.'

The soldiers were also well aware that while Germany had been defeated, the war against Japan raged on. Vic recalled that this led to a rechristening of the British Liberation Army that summer.

'Burma Looms Ahead.'

Burma Looms Ahead

Many of the soldiers who ended the war in Germany had years left on their mobilization contracts, and were still liable for service in other theatres of war. In the summer of 1945, their likely destination was the Far East.

Having dealt with the initial refugee and prisoner problem brought about by the end of the war, 6th Airborne Division remained in the Wismar area until 17 May, when they were relieved, in stages, by the 5th Infantry Division, and began to make their way back home, retracing familiar ground until they came to Lüneburg Airfield. Here, the elements of the division that could be flown home to England waited until aircraft were available to carry them, while the motor transport elements made their way to Calais, and then across the Channel to Dover. A further few members of the division left Europe in a rather unconventional way, as recalled by Hugh Pond, 9th Para.

'We had discovered in this Baltic town, Wismar, a very fine yacht club. All those people keen on yachting had started taking these boats out and sailing them around the harbour. Somebody in the division made a deal with the navy, it must have been someone on board the cruiser *Birmingham*, that if we supplied them with a convoy of champagne, would they take some of these boats back to England? Because we wanted to start an Airborne Forces yacht club. This was pure piracy.

'This was agreed, so a load of trucks set off to Denmark, where the *Birmingham* was in Copenhagen harbour, then volunteers were requested to sail some of these yachts to Copenhagen, who had had experience of sailing. I had dinghy experience in the River Thames, so I said, "Yes, I can sail." They couldn't find anybody else better so they took me.

'Off we went and I thought we were going vaguely in the right direction – going north on my handheld compass. Eventually the mainsail split from top to bottom, bearing in mind these sails had been stored in a loft or something all the war. There we were left with a very small jib, making hardly any headway at all. Eventually we saw some land. My corporal said, "I'll jump overboard, swim to shore and see if I can get any help." He swam ashore and as he landed on a very rocky shore, a whole lot of Danes came up and started hitting him, thinking he was a German. It took quite a while, a couple of minutes I suppose, to convince them he wasn't a German. Then a boat came out and towed us in.'

Hugh then bartered for a tow to Copenhagen in return for diesel.

'We set off, being towed, but I remember the little daughter, she must have been six, seven or eight years old, and it was May and she tied a bunch of daffodils to the mast of the boat. Which was very sweet. Off we set. We were buzzed a couple of times by Allied aircraft and eventually we steamed into Copenhagen harbour. We saw the *Birmingham*, big cruiser. We also saw two German pocket battleships – the *Gneisenau* and some other, which were still fully armed, and they had refused to formally surrender because they hadn't had their orders from Admiral Dönitz, so it was a very tricky situation in Denmark at that time.

'Anyway, we were hauled aboard the Birmingham and immediately taken into the chart room and very closely questioned where we'd come from, how we'd come, what was our route. The Dane who'd towed us showed the route and they said, "You are extremely lucky because you've come through about three acoustic minefields. Why you didn't set those mines off, we will never ever know. You're extremely lucky."'

Peter Fussell ended the war at Neustadt on the Baltic. His brigade, No. 1 Commando, were soon withdrawn to England for onward travel to the Far East.

'Needless to say, we had loot in the form of German weapons. P38s, Schmeissers, Mausers, knives, bayonets, fighting knives, swords, dress knives. When we came back by this (ship), we were awaiting to approach Tilbury docks, somebody said, "Customs are coming aboard and anybody caught with a German weapon is going to get court-martialled." So you can imagine the whole of the English Channel was festooned with loot – cameras, watches, the lot – lock, stock and barrel. I've never seen so much loot go over the side of a ship in my life.'

The long-awaited, and dreaded, invasion of the main islands of Japan was avoided when Japan gave its unconditional surrender on 15 August 1945. The Second World War, which might have claimed as many as 85 million lives across the globe, was at an end.

384,000 British service personnel and 70,000 British civilians had been killed.

The end of the Second World War did not mean that all of Britain's soldiers would come home – even those who had been conscripted. In 1946, tens of thousands of men who had seen action across Europe were sent to Palestine as part of a 'police action'. The two-year conflict claimed the lives of almost 800 British service personnel, many of them called up for the Second World War and killed during the 'peace' that followed. There are also examples of regular soldiers who had survived Dunkirk, and all that followed, being called up from the reserve list and sent to the Korean War of 1950–53.

The British army would continue occupation duties in Germany until 1949. It was an enjoyable time for many soldiers, some of whom went beyond casual liaisons and married local girls. Others bemoaned their time spent in this 'police force'. At the end of the war there were millions of Displaced Persons in Germany, some of them bent on revenge against the citizens of the nation that had treated them so appallingly. When this resulted in rape, and murder, the accused stood trial and, if found guilty, were executed by firing squad.

Ronnie Henderson, who had returned to his unit after being wounded in the latter stages of the Rhineland campaign, took part in the execution of two men. He then served in Palestine, where he lost yet more comrades to terrorist attacks carried out by Jewish militants, and was finally demobilized in 1947. Ronnie's lasting impression, from his final day in uniform, was of the beauty of our natural world.

'The daffodils were in full bloom at the time. I'll always remember the daffodils at York station.'

PART 4

After War

CHAPTER 25

The Price of Victory

'I believe, once you're in the army, the army's got you for life, whether you're a civilian or not. You're still in it. You're there. You're there until they put you under the ground.'

Alfred Leigh, 2nd Battalion, Seaforth Highlanders

Through the use of personal accounts, I have tried to tell the story of the Battle of Germany as chronologically as possible, but this has presented me with a problem that I have struggled to find the answer to – what to do with the stories that didn't include a date, or place, other than 'Germany, 1945'?

As many of the soldiers alluded to, they were often in the dark about the big picture beyond even their section. They were also dog-tired, and more concerned with staying alive than with knowing the name of the town or village that they were fighting to take. And yet these stories, unanchored by time or place, are often the ones that shaped these men the most and should be remembered as part of their story.

And this first problem begets a second – when exactly does a soldier's experience of war end? When a surrender is signed? When a soldier demobilizes? Or when he goes to his grave?

That is for the individual soldier to decide, and because many of them spoke of having their lives changed for ever by war, and the Battle of Germany, I have included their stories here. It should also be noted that several soldiers spoke of having no ill effects from a war they were glad to have fought in. In fact, there were few who regretted anything, even if they continued to pay a price for their service. There is a lot to be taken from that – by and large, these soldiers felt that it was a just cause and a necessary war, but that does not mean that they revelled in it.

Throughout these chapters there has been ample description of horror – we know that it is hell, even if observed from a distance of eighty years – but when we conclude with the moment of victory, perhaps that horror begins to be replaced by a sort of elation. We wouldn't be human if we didn't feel this way, to some degree or other. Britain came back from the brink. A great evil was defeated. The lives that we lead today are shaped by that victory. And so, let us remind ourselves of what that victory cost – death, and the willingness of our soldiers to deal it.

'The aggression that you'd got took quite a lot of time to come out. To get rid of,' said Roy Hubbard, who had served as an infantryman. 'For instance – it's not very nice to say, but it's true – I were only courting, and we'd been to the pictures up here and we were arguing over something, I can't think what it was, I just picked her up and threw her over this privet hedge. Now, that was pure and simple cause she'd wound me up, but that's a reaction what you get in the army.'

Post-conflict societies tend to have higher rates of domestic violence. Explanations range from men returning home having been brutalized by their experiences and actions – many of which had been necessary for survival – to frustration at the difficulty of re-integrating into peaceful society, particularly with people who cannot fathom their experiences.[1]

John Petts, pacifist and Airborne medic, long pondered the question of the morality of the war. An end to the violence did not mean that all was now made well.

'One looked ahead with a deep sigh, and a determination. To take up one's life again was not easy. There's no question of taking up quite where you left it off.

'There was the burden of facing life again. There was also the problem of putting behind you all that you had suffered and all that you had thrust down, hopefully beyond pain. Hopefully, self-defensively, beyond self-realization of damage. But the damage was there. I'll never forget coming home on leave, although it wasn't the end of one's war service, having bottled up so many horrors, to be met and greeted by my dear love, Kusha. We went into a field and we sat under a hedge and I just broke and collapsed with my head in her lap. This was really the caring and, one would hope, curing, ameliorative meeting and homecoming of the man damaged by war. Not physically damaged, but by his experience of horror.

'I would have to say with a sigh that it appears that in a case like Hitler's mess of Europe, that there had to be violence. I suppose if they had let me volunteer, I might well have allowed myself to go and try and kill Hitler, just to kill that one madman, I might have worn that on my conscience. I also think, philosophically, that you can't really force the passage of history, as I quoted Alan Lewis saying "This great boil, this sickness, has to be lanced, and the boil is pain and danger and aggressiveness, and the lancing is aggressive and painful, but it is to allow the poison to get out, to burst out and be cancelled, and to leave the body with a chance to mend again". In relation to Hitler one means by the body, the body of Europe and the body of the world in relation to the Japanese aggression.

'One thing I did learn about watching violence occur, one terrible aspect to me about the human nature, was to discover to my mind that essentially war and violence is only possible to the angry and the acquiescent and the sick. We know about the angry, those who are full of righteous anger and have to go and do something about it when faced by wrong. That is understandable. We know about the acquiescent – the people who went conscripted, doggedly trailing their feet, go along with it, because there's nothing else you can do and they haven't got the force of personality to resist orders, so to speak, and to be out of step with their community and their time, which requires a certain moral courage.

'The third has never been mentioned, to my mind. By the sick, I mean those people who have violence in them, don't ask me who they are – just pick up any newspaper any day and follow the criminal cases in the courts. There are those who have the sickness in them to destroy, to smash, to harm, to hurt, and it is there. Of course the terrible realization is that never do all those people have such an opportunity to let this out, to act, as in the case of war. I have seen men doing things to men and women, by members of all sides. I have seen British soldiers doing things I wouldn't wish to describe on record, because they were sick.

'Under all the chaos of war, a man is able to do things and get away with it when, in peacetime, he would be arrested and imprisoned. I could list examples, but they would only sicken you. I could list thousands of examples.

'I'll give you one, if you like, to show the strength of my observations and memory and the truth. I'm talking about real sickness, you see? A man can kill another man in anger or because he's commanded to, which is part of war – he's a German so you shoot him. But if you're sick, you go up to his body after you have killed him, and picking up a spade or a rifle, you smash and smash and smash his face into a pulp until someone pulls you away. That's what I mean by sickness, that's what I mean by sadism at the level of madness. Yes (I saw that happen myself), and similar things.'

John was then asked about his own personal compromise in joining the 'military machine'.

'By my compromise, you mean my willingness to go into it. It seemed a strange thing to do in a way, but I had no awkward conscience about it. I was a part of the military machine, but I was not. It enabled me to do some things that I would never have been able to do. To meet some wonderful people that I would never have met, and to learn to grow up and to discover good things and bad things about the human condition.'

Billy Gray, the second man to rush Pegasus Bridge, also learned much of this condition, and was asked if killing the enemy had 'bothered' him.

'No, it didn't, funny enough. I just don't know how we did it, you know? I mean, looking back, I can think, *Well, blimey, I was nineteen year(s) old, how did I do it?* Whether they'd put something in our coffee, I don't know. Why were we so sort of free and easy? Just like going to a football match, something like that. I just don't understand how we found it so easy.

'When it came to the Rhine crossing it became much easier. I mean, we'd lost mates, and I didn't give a toss (about killing), really. If they were there, well, they were going to be shot, and that was it.'

Billy had been a milkman before the war, and was in London during the Blitz.

'I didn't feel bitter about the Germans so much. We all expected, *Well, some of us are not going to make it, some of us are.* It was just one of those things. I thought the Germans, whatever I read of now, weren't the terrors they were supposed to be. I noticed in Normandy that if we had any of our medical orderlies (go) out after wounded, and they had a red cross, that they weren't fired on. I won't say the same about German Red Cross (being respected). I think when they talk about German atrocities, they've got to go a long way to beat British atrocities. I think, and I've always said it, that some of our blokes were like bloody animals. I think they were cruel, they were greedy. They'd search a body to take the cash and whatever they could, or jewellery. I've seen wounded shot by our own blokes.

'People wouldn't believe it now if I said I'd seen wounded (Germans) begging for mercy and being shot. But it happened. I've seen 'em, a bloke chopping another bloke's finger off just to get a ring. And all I hear of is about the bad Germans.'

Billy then recalled several incidents in detail, including one of a German soldier who had surrendered to him.

'He was shaking and crying, so I gave him a cigarette. Just as I was lighting it for him, another one of our blokes came up, snatched it from his mouth, and pushed him over. I just turned round and give him a right hander.

'I mean, I've got some German friends now, and they're just like us. There's nothing bad about them. They had to do the same job as we did. I mean, they didn't ask for the war, I'm sure. We didn't ask for it.'

Ronnie Henderson, 13th/18th Royal Hussars, had mixed feelings about the Germans.

'German prisoners that were captured in action, they were welcome to a cigarette or whatever. They were soldiers as we were. They weren't beaten or anything like that. We tret them as part of us. As we would hope that we'd be tretted if we'd have been taken.'

Ronnie also befriended several local women when he was stationed in Berlin. They gave him tours of the ruined city, including to the Reich Chancellery – 'We saw Hitler's toilet, and used it' – and one can almost hear the smile as Ronnie recalled those days, adding, 'There were lots of (other) things, things I can't really say on here, because you don't know who's going to listen to it, but we had some marvellous times.'

There was a darker side to the memories, too. And many of them came from Belsen.

'We were told not to give (the inmates) any food. We wanted to give them food, we're only young. We wanted to help. We wanted to give them sweets. We wanted to give them everything.

'It was their eyes, you know, they looked up at ya . . . ' at this point in the interview, after hours of unfaltering recollections, Ronnie suddenly stops talking for a long moment and can be heard to swallow several times. 'They knew that . . . that we were there to help.'

He was then asked if what he saw at the concentration camp made him feel horror, and anger towards the Germans.

'I still have it today,' he said emphatically. 'I still have it today. I'll never forgive the Germans. And these people that are on about Germany today, and getting together, they want to go around all the cemeteries, both First World War, and Second World War, and see all those graves. And it'll have been for nothing if Germany takes over and makes a federal state of Europe. It'll all have been for nothing. It's only my opinion, but it's a shame.'

Stanley Whitehouse, 1 Black Watch, had thought that the war to defeat Nazi Germany would be a great adventure and noble crusade. After eight months of action, his feelings had changed.

'I spotted a fine-looking automatic rifle on the ground. Picking it up to admire it, I noticed it was in immaculate condition, with the bolt area still greased. Then, inexplicably, a wave of nausea swept over me. Why was I admiring this weapon, whose sole purpose was to kill people? I was sick of killing people. Barely able to stop myself from vomiting, I smashed the gun against a wall several times and threw it into the nearby undergrowth.'[2]

Stanley lost thirty close friends during the war, and many comrades. He recalled one incident in the wake of shelling on his company's position, when he heard a faint moan of 'help, somebody help' coming from a nearby dugout.

'Nothing prepared me for the dreadful scene I now beheld. The nearest bodies were so compacted that it was impossible to pull them apart, and the heads and necks were the same width. Right at the back, in the covered part of the dugout, was a blood-covered apparition, calling out faintly and trying to struggle over the bodies of his mates.'[3]

One death in particular stood out in the interview of Alf Wooltorton.

'John Little took a patrol out, and he took a guy who I'd become quite attached to. He was a corporal who'd been wounded way back. His name was Miller. (He) had a girlfriend in the Land Army, and they were going to get married after the war.'

The plan, like so many others made by loved ones during the war, came to a violent end in an unknown field. That night, Alf went with a stretcher party to recover the body of his friend, Corporal Robert Walker Miller, who was twenty-five years old when he was killed three weeks before the end of the war.[4]

'He'd laid there for some time, and by that time his rigor had set in.'

John Little, a former Glasgow policeman, had some experience with the dead and broke Miller's arm so that his body would stay on the stretcher.

'And I suppose I showed some sort of emotion,' said Alf, his voice beginning to break, 'and when we got back, John said, "I took you because I thought you of anyone would be alright. I had to break his arm,"' he said.

'I said, "I know you did. It wasn't what you did, it was *him*. It was because it was him."

'We buried the poor old boy next day,' Alf said softly, fifty-five years on from that day, 'it wasn't that often that you could do that.'

Alf begins to cry. The recording clicks off, then restarts, his voice now firm.

'And having done that, we moved on again. As you always did.'

It wasn't only the deaths of one's comrades that could haunt a soldier's memories.

'I often think of this,' said Fred Cooper. 'In one occasion we're led down by a ditch and we were pinned down, and our people had set the 'ouses alight. You know, they were blazin'. We knew that in these circumstances, all the families got together in one house, 'cause the cellars in these houses are (large).

'This house was alight, and we knew that this particular house had been used by the people of that area, and they were all down there. Women, children, and we could hear squealing.

'It was too much for me and a couple of the lads.'

Fred and a few of the soldiers tried to rescue the German civilians but they were driven back by machine-gun fire.

'We tried about three times, but in the end we had to give it up, but because we were pinned down we had to stay there, and you could hear the dying shrieks of these women and children, which haunted me for about five or six years after the war. You know, when you think of people burning up, dying, and shrieking, women and children, I used to wake up at night, shoot up in bed with the shrieks in me ears.

'It's past, thankfully. I haven't had it in donkey's years, but it did used to bother me.'

The deaths of enemy soldiers could also be hard to bear.

'I don't think I really hated the enemy,' said Ray Ashton, who remembered killing a German soldier at close quarters, and the moments that followed.

'I realized that he'd actually got his hands up. So, I mean, this quite shook me, and I had to live with this for quite a long while. People will say, oh well, that's war, it's an accident. But I remember walking across and having a look at him, and he was only a young lad. But thinking about it, he was probably about the same age I was. I looked upon him as a young lad, thinking I was now a man, you know? But I was probably only the same age he was.

'I just think, he was somebody's son. They're going to be upset.'

Alan Tate had fought his way across Europe as a nineteen-year-old officer in No. 45 (Royal Marine) Commando. After the war he became an architect.

'I was very fortunate in one or two respects. First of all, I knew what I wanted to do in civvy life and I say this because some people I knew found it quite impossible to settle down in civvy street. They didn't know what to do.

'I think (it's) because (war) is such an all-embracing activity in which you're completely immersed. Nothing in one's life ever seems as important as being involved in the war, doing your best for your own chaps, killing as many as you can of the other side. It becomes a sort of instinctive way of life. You never think of any life outside of the little group.

'I think to have been in any branch of the service in peacetime would have struck me as rather pointless.'

Alan did not become involved with ex-service associations, but visited Normandy for the 50th Anniversary of D-Day so that he could pay his respects.

'(I got) all involved with talking about D-Day, and what happened, and so on. During the night I had a violent nightmare in which I had to approach a door. And I had a feeling there was something terrible on the other side of that door. And when I opened it there was a great black cloud, which came out and rolled me over and over and over, and pinned me against a fence, and at that (moment) I fell out of bed.

'I had that dream in various different forms I should think a dozen or fifteen times.'

At the beginning of the war Alan was certain that all Germans were 'bad', and he had killed many of the enemy himself in the line of duty. He them recalled one night towards the end of the war, when he stayed in a German farmhouse. At the time he was nineteen.

'What I then thought was an old woman came in. She was probably about forty-five. She looked at me, didn't say anything, held her hand out, took my jacket and started sewing my button on. I didn't say anything either. Behind her there was a big sideboard, and on the sideboard there was a picture with a wreath around it. It was a picture of a young man in uniform. German uniform.

'I stood up, and she helped me put my jacket on. And then I pointed at the picture. It was her son.

'Do you know what? She put her arm around me. Just like that.

'That's it. That's the end of the story.'

Body and soul

'War is certainly a strange phenomenon,' said Jim Stockman, who served in the Seaforth Highlanders, SOE and the SAS. 'It fills you and dominates you when it rages, and there seems to be nothing else in life. Yet when it ceases, as it did so suddenly, the man who was for several years a furious combatant and legalized killer becomes abruptly disorientated and lost. You wonder if it was all worth it, and then why you did what you did. Above all else you wonder how you managed to get through alive.'[5]

An entire generation of Britons came of age during the Second World War. Many carried its scars for the rest of their lives.

As a teenage boy Ray Robinson lived through the Blitz, his hometown of Hull wrecked by German bombs. Then, on his first day in action as an eighteen-year-old replacement, Ray saw his battalion take more than 150 casualties in a single day.

'I went back to work in the January of 1948. I took all my leave. I always said, and a lot of the lads used to say it, I'm gonna take all my leave. I'm gonna live a bit of life, cause we didn't have no youth, you see.

'It might have been later on in '48, I started getting very nervous. For instance, Bonfire Night. I wouldn't go to Bonfire Night. You had the impression, every time a bang went off, you was going to hit the floor. And this was true with me. Oh, I was then very nervous. I got that bad I was feeling pains all over me, especially me chest, me throat. Dry throat.'

Ray's symptoms gradually improved over time. 'But I've always been, even now, I'm always that bit nervous.'

The war also took a toll on Ray's parents.

'I always said that the war shortened my mother's life. I think with the bombing, and of course, when I got called up. She had three sons in the war, you see.'

Bruce Coombs rarely wrote letters home while he was at war.

'I didn't realize how mothers worry like, you know? You don't, do you? As you get older you realize, if it was your child, my boy being there, I'd have been feeling hell not hearing from him.'

Bruce found life after the war 'good', but 'hard-going'.

'You were stressed out. I had an obsession about work. Couldn't stop working. Worked my holidays and all, seven days a week. It takes a long time to adjust, you know. A long time. I don't think I ever got out of it properly.

'Mental is the worst. I found the mental worse than anything. It's funny, it takes a while to get back into a system, doesn't it.

'I can't say I get nightmares. You get *thoughts* all the time. It's there with you all the time. Even today you get it, you know.'

Bruce had battled with the elements as much as the enemy, but said that he had no physical ailments from his service. Robert Keenan, on the other hand, who had served in the confines of a tank, was left 'with a weakness. You always get back aches and everything. But I managed until about 1970, around about that time I had back problems again and I had to go in and have another operation in the local hospital. There you are, you put up with it.'

The injuries of others were far more obvious.

'I met one of our ex-troop in London. Walking through the tube station, he got off the train and walked towards me. And I said to him, "I heard you were dead," and he said, "No, I wasn't dead, I lost my leg." And he walked off that train, perfectly.'

Ron Hann, a veteran of El Alamein, lost a leg himself while attempting to bring help to his platoon in the Reichswald.

'I don't think I would change anything. I wouldn't like to go through it again. I wouldn't wish it on my worst enemy, to go through any of that. No one in their right mind wants anything to do with that again.

'It doesn't really affect me. After the first sickening feeling, after (my leg) was off, it makes you sick a bit, but after that, I said well, that's it. Can't cry over spilt milk.'

Commando Stan Scott met his wife while he was stationed in Brussels. He remained in the country as a civilian, repairing bridges that had been damaged during the war. Stan had suffered a fair amount of damage himself – both by shrapnel and gunshot.

'I've got scars to prove it. Don't matter. I reckon it was well worthwhile.'

'It was a war worth fighting, wasn't it,' said tank crewman Austin Baker. 'And I'd be very sorry now not to have played a part in it.'

One of the things the veterans missed most was the great comradeship that they experienced during the war, and where they came of age together.

'I met some wonderful people,' said Kenneth Ohlson, who won an MC in the Rhineland. 'Other ranks, and officers. It was a wonderful growing up experience. I didn't go to university, but I can't help feeling that five years in the army is as good a university as you can get.'

'I was an uncouth seventeen-year-old when I went in,' said Arthur Jones, 5 DCLI, whose nerves were worn down after months of continuous combat. 'When I come home I was somebody that used to drop under a table when anybody dropped anything for the first twelve months. I didn't used to take a lot of chances (after the war), I can tell ya.

'You used to think twice before you done anything stupid, because you'd been so used to looking after yourself. Put it this way. At the frontline, you had an ear cocked all the time. All the time for shellfire. They reckon your ears grew another six inches,' he chuckled. 'Oh yes, it certainly altered me. I've never been the same since, I don't think.'

Tom Myers DCM, went back to work in Durham's coal pits after the war, but found that the experience of the army, and its culture, remained with him for life.

'You get institutionalized in the forces as to a way of thinking. You seem to be in a circle, and when you tread out of that circle you were lost.

'(War) didn't improve me any. It didn't worsen me any. It was just a bit of time in your life, something that had to be done, and you did it.

'Now, if I was the same age, and the same thing happened, I would like to do it again.'

Alfred Leigh returned to the site of the Reichswald battle to visit the graves of fallen comrades, and noted how every one was adorned with flowers laid by Dutch civilians.

'The Dutch children, they know what the war's about. They've been taught that the liberation of their country is a great thing.'

He did not believe that British children have that same level of understanding.

'I don't think they're up to scratch of knowing about the war, and why the war was fought for them. So you've gotta go through the process of learnin' them.'

Joe Abbot, who'd served in the 53rd Reconnaissance Regiment, hoped that later generations would learn the dangers of unchecked power, and hate.

'I think in many ways I'd become a bit more tolerant in some ways to some, but perhaps a bit more intolerant to others. I can forgive genuine mistakes, but I'm not very happy about overlooking mistakes that are done intentionally, with the idea of somebody else being at the brunt of it.'

Joe was asked if he'd recovered from his experiences of war.

'Recovered? I don't know, it's a funny word, that. I mean, it sounds as if I was a bit mental to start with,' he laughed. 'Have I recovered? Let me put it this way. For people to turn around and say, oh, they want to forget all that, that annoys me, because anybody that has experienced it can never honestly say they forget it. I would say that anybody who served in the front, or in anything connected with the aftermath of the frontline – that includes medical services and that – will never forget it.'

The interviewer then thanked Joe – their time was over.

'Is it? Oh. That's the end of the lot, is it now? Well, it's been nice having you, and it's nice of you to listen. It's not often that I get anybody to listen. And I can't make you a cup of tea or anything now, can I?'

The recording ends.

EPILOGUE

Eighty Years Later

In November 2024 I was invited into the home of one of our nation's heroes.

Ted Rutland was twenty years old when he went to war as a trooper in the Royal Armoured Corps. Now 101, and a tall man, I ask Ted how he ever managed to fit inside a tank.

'I couldn't stand up,' he laughed. 'Gunner's seat were best for me.'

But what's best for soldiers and best for the army are not the same thing. It was decided that Ted should serve as co-driver, and in this role he was sent to France with 148th Regiment, RAC.

'The Germans used to put dead bodies on the road, and they'd put a mine in the soft ground. And the co-driver, his job was to get out and move this body, because we wouldn't run over a dead body.

'You just didn't take much notice of it. You used to do the job and that were it.'

But there were pleasant memories, too. Even while under fire.

'We was in a field, about a mile north of Pegasus Bridge, and they shelled us. They dropped a shell on a cow in a field, and everybody ran across and cut pieces off. Farmer were playin' hell,' Ted chuckled.

When they got the chance to rest, the crew slept beside each other under canvas beside their tank. Spending every moment of every day in each other's company, and under the most stressful conditions, brought the young men closer together. 'We got on very well.'

Tragically, many of Ted's comrades did not survive the Battle of Normandy. Not only did they suffer losses at the hands of the enemy, but on 13 August the regiment was accidentally bombed. Their losses, which included the death of Ted's commanding officer, Lieutenant-Colonel Robert Cracroft MC, were so heavy that the regiment was broken up and its survivors sent to other units.[1]

Ted went through the rest of the war with the 5th Royal Tank Regiment, and lost his second commanding officer, Lieutenant Colonel Charles Holliman DSO MC,[2] to what Ted and others believed was a 'friendly' shell, in January 1945.[3]

'He was a good CO. This shell burst over their heads, and it killed all the four in that jeep. I was about fifty yards away from it.'

Ted was one of a handful of men from 148th Regiment who had made it all the way from the beaches. I asked him if he felt the amount of action he saw slackened off after Normandy.

'Not a lot, no.'

'How did people cope with it?'

'They had to,' he smiled patiently.

Ted's war came to an end at the devastated city of Hamburg. 'Terrible, it was,' he said of the plight of the locals, 'they'd just moved in where they could.'

Assigned as a driver and armed escort to a mobile canteen of the Church Army, Ted met Valerie, whose husband had been killed in service with the Royal Navy. They fell in love and returned to England with Max, a fully grown German Shepherd who had approached them one day when they were walking in the woods.

Ted went back into joinery after the war and became a standard bearer for his local branch of the British Legion in Mansfield. He attends Remembrance Sunday every year, laying the wreath at the town's church, and believes that its importance should be known by younger generations today.

Ted's contribution to the liberation of Europe has been recognized with awards presented by heads of state, and the waves of local children who pass by his window. It is with a mixture of emotions that I leave his home. Pride and gratitude, to have inherited the legacy that he and his comrades fought to give us. Sadness, that we will one day be without them.

My journey then took me Holland to meet Olaf, a resident of Den Bosch who wrote a touching online tribute to Bob Atkinson of the East Lancs. Olaf first met Bob at a celebration of the town's liberation, and they remained friends thereafter. At lunch, Olaf, gregarious and full of enthusiasm, hands me a book full of signatures. I recognize others beside Bob's – Owen Butcher, the East Lancs sniper. Bruce Coombs, 6 RWF. After a long moment I hand the precious papers back to Olaf and ask him about the liberators who became his friends.

'I realized as an adult that I never knew war or occupation. They fought and suffered for the freedom I enjoy. For me it's an honorary obligation to not take that for granted.

'They were great people and I miss them.'

I part ways with Olaf later that afternoon and drive to a memorial outside of the town's centre. It is dedicated to the 53rd (Welsh) Division, and I am staring at its stone and wondering about the friends and comrades lost to Bob, and Owen, and Bruce and all those like them who fought for victory and peace in Europe, when a voice speaks over my shoulder.

'They are gone but not forgotten.'

I turn and see a lady of perhaps fifty, the truth of her words clear in her eyes.

'I come here every day,' she tells me, and I believe her, and I trust her, and there is nothing I can add.

They are gone but not forgotten.

NOTES

INTRODUCTION

1 MacDonald Fraser, *Quartered Safe Out Here*, p. 10

CHAPTER 1: THE LONELIEST CLUB IN THE WORLD

1 National Archives: WO 373/53/105
2 *The Oxford Companion to World War II*
3 https://www.cwgc.org/find-records/find-war-dead/casualty-details/2198565/george-dodd/
4 https://www.cwgc.org/find-records/find-war-dead/casualty-details/2081745/james-wylie/
5 Tim Saunders, *Breaking the Siegfried Line: Rhineland, February 1945*, p. 12
6 Sir Brian Horrocks, *Corps Commander*, p. 240
7 Horrocks, *Corps Commander*, p. 240
8 IWM Archive: 1969
9 https://internationalbcc.co.uk/about-ibcc/news/memories/a-pilots-story-one-hell-of-a-bombing-run/

CHAPTER 2: HIGHLANDERS

1 Horrocks, *Corps Commander*, p. 243
2 Report on Operation Veritable, 21st Army Group
3 National Archives: WO 171/5160
4 https://www.cwgc.org/find-records/find-war-dead/casualty-details/2646511/thomas-macdonald/

5 Patrick Delaforce, *Monty's Highlanders: 51st Highland Division in the Second World War*, p. 207
6 Sir Martin Lindsay, *So Few Got Through: With the Gordon Highlanders From Normandy to the Baltic*, p. 178
7 Lindsay, *So Few Got Through*, p. 179
8 National Archives: WO 171/5160
9 National Archives: WO 171/5160
10 https://www.cwgc.org/find-records/find-war-dead/casualty-details/2842382/peter-mcgrory/
11 https://www.cwgc.org/find-records/find-war-dead/casualty-details/2646964/alfred-stronach/
12 Whitehouse, *Fear Is the Foe*, p. 168

CHAPTER 3: BREAK-IN

1 https://www.15thscottishdivisionwardiaries.co.uk/war-diaries
2 https://www.15thscottishdivisionwardiaries.co.uk/war-diaries
3 https://www.cwgc.org/find-records/find-war-dead/casualty-details/2645698/douglas-alexander-hutton/
4 https://www.cwgc.org/find-records/find-war-dead/casualty-details/2046161/thomas-stevenson/
5 National Archives: WO 373/53/448
6 National Archives: WO 373/53/799
7 The Military Medal was discontinued in 1993, from which time the Military Cross became an award for all ranks.
8 https://www.15thscottishdivisionwardiaries.co.uk/war-diaries
9 Saunders, *Breaking the Siegfried Line*, p. 107
10 https://www.15thscottishdivisionwardiaries.co.uk/war-diaries
11 Horrocks, *Corps Commander*, p. 245
12 Saunders, *Breaking the Siegfried Line*, p. 128
13 Saunders, *Breaking the Siegfried Line*, p. 152
14 https://www.15thscottishdivisionwardiaries.co.uk/war-diaries
15 https://www.15thscottishdivisionwardiaries.co.uk/war-diaries
16 Horrocks, *Corps Commander*, p. 245
17 Render, *Tank Action*, p. 254
18 James Holland, *Brothers in Arms: One Legendary Tank Regiment's Bloody War from D-Day to VE-Day*, p. 368
19 Major-General H. Essame, *The 43rd Wessex Division at War 1944–1945*, p. 208

20 https://www.15thscottishdivisionwardiaries.co.uk/6-kosb
21 https://www.15thscottishdivisionwardiaries.co.uk/6-kosb
22 https://www.15thscottishdivisionwardiaries.co.uk/15-recce
23 Essame, *The 43rd Wessex Division at War 1944–1945*, p. 213
24 Horrocks, *Corps Commander*, p. 242

CHAPTER 4: ONE OF THE MOST UNPLEASANT WEEKS OF THE ENTIRE WAR

1 National Archives: WO 373/53/816
2 Patrick Delaforce, *Red Crown & Dragon: 53rd Welsh Division in North-West Europe 1944–1945*, p. 169
3 https://www.cwgc.org/find-records/find-war-dead/casualty-details/2048146/alfred-lawrence-mead/
4 https://www.cwgc.org/find-records/find-war-dead/casualty-details/2048146/alfred-lawrence-mead/
5 https://www.cwgc.org/find-records/find-war-dead/casualty-details/2647100/arthur-crawford-white/
6 https://www.cwgc.org/find-records/find-war-dead/casualty-details/2619410/frank-whiteoak/
7 Delaforce, *Red Crown and Dragon*, p. 176
8 Wagstaff survived his wounds and went on to become a surveyor on the Electricity Board in Wrexham.

CHAPTER 5: MOYLAND

1 https://www.cwgc.org/find-records/find-war-dead/casualty-details/2042104/peter-mcdowell-spafford/
2 National Archives: WO 373/53/453
3 Patrick Delaforce, *Monty's Northern Legions: 50th Tyne Tees and 15th Scottish Divisions at War 1939–1945*, p. 182
4 https://www.cwgc.org/find-records/find-war-dead/casualty-details/2055774/benjamin-charles-jackman/
5 National Archives: WO 373/53/814
6 Delaforce, *Monty's Northern Legions: 50th Tyne Tees and 15th Scottish Divisions at War 1939–1945*, p. 182

CHAPTER 6: GOCH

1. Ford, *Campaign: The Rhineland 1945*, p. 43
2. Ford, *Campaign: The Rhineland 1945*, p. 43
3. National Archives: WO 171/5290
4. National Archives: WO 171/5290
5. National Archives: WO 373/53/900
6. National Archives: WO 373/53/851
7. Essame, *The 43rd Wessex Division at War 1944–1945*, p. 215
8. Essame, *The 43rd Wessex Division at War 1944–1945*, p. 215
9. National Archives: WO 373/56/792
10. https://www.cwgc.org/find-records/find-war-dead/casualty-details/2042067/thomas-george-smith/
    https://www.cwgc.org/find-records/find-war-dead/casualty-details/2055726/john-hutchinson/
11. Essame, *The 43rd Wessex Division at War 1944–1945*, p. 216
12. National Archives: WO 171/4691
13. National Archives: WO 171/4685
14. Ford, *Campaign: The Rhineland 1945*, p. 48
15. https://www.cwgc.org/find-records/find-war-dead/casualty-details/2645344/victor-wallace-day/
16. https://www.scotsman.com/news/obituary-thomas-j-renouf-black-watch-veteran-and-physicist-1472708
17. Renouf, *Black Watch*, p. 243
18. Renouf, *Black Watch*, p. 244
19. Renouf, *Black Watch*, p. 247
20. Renouf, *Black Watch*, p. 248
21. Stanley Whitehouse, *Fear is the Foe: A Footslogger from Normandy to the Rhine*, p. 151
22. Lindsay, *So Few Got Through*, p. 202
23. Lindsay, *So Few Got Through*, p. 201

CHAPTER 7: IRON SIDES

1. https://www.cwgc.org/find-records/find-war-dead/casualty-details/2040453/albert-daniel-moat/
2. National Archives: WO 373/53/409
3. National Archives: WO 373/56/262
4. National Archives: WO 373/53/887

5   https://www.cwgc.org/find-records/find-war-dead/casualty-details/2056458/christopher-loughran/
6   Reginald W. Thompson, *The Battle for the Rhineland*, p. 215
7   Thompson, *The Battle for the Rhineland*, p. 217
8   https://www.cwgc.org/find-records/find-war-dead/casualty-details/2031430/herbert-william-fox/
9   https://www.cwgc.org/find-records/find-war-dead/casualty-details/2046193/james-stokes/
10 Thompson, *The Battle for the Rhineland*, p. 221
11 https://www.keymilitary.com/article/battle-billiard-table
12 National Archives: WO 373/56/737
13 National Archives: WO 373/53/450
14 John Lincoln, *Thank God and the Infantry: From D-Day to VE-Day with the 1st Battalion, The Royal Norfolk Regiment*, p. 184
15 https://www.bbc.com/history/ww2peopleswar/stories/12/a2069912.shtml
16 https://www.cwgc.org/find-records/find-war-dead/casualty-details/2040375/harold-miles/
17 https://www.cwgc.org/find-records/find-war-dead/casualty-details/2047034/adrian-needham-wilson/

CHAPTER 8: ANOTHER TASTE OF HELL

1   Delaforce, *Red Crown & Dragon*, p. 182
2   Delaforce, *Red Crown & Dragon*, p. 182
3   Delaforce, *Red Crown & Dragon*, p. 182
4   National Archives: WO 373/53/481
5   Delaforce, *Red Crown & Dragon*, p. 184
6   Holland, *Brothers in Arms*, p. 385
7   Delaforce, *Red Crown & Dragon*, p. 185
8   Stuart Hills, *By Tank into Normandy: A Memoir of the Campaign in North-West Europe from D-Day to VE Day*, p. 218
9   National Archives: WO 373/54/295
10 https://www.cwgc.org/find-records/find-war-dead/casualty-details/2619193/george-frederick-thomas-dickson/
11 Major Richard Hughes MC, *Sheldrake*, p. 122
12 https://www.cwgc.org/find-records/find-war-dead/casualty-details/2765853/albert-lee/

13 Horrocks, *Corps Commander*, p. 242
14 Hughes, *Sheldrake*, p. 122

CHAPTER 9: REACHING THE RHINE

1 Murray Walker, *Unless I'm Very Much Mistaken*, p. 21
2 https://www.cwgc.org/find-records/find-war-dead/casualty-details/2232190/william-a-miller/
3 https://www.cwgc.org/find-records/find-war-dead/casualty-details/2232115/tom-marshall/
4 https://www.cwgc.org/find-records/find-war-dead/casualty-details/2036246/frank-dossett/
5 https://www.cwgc.org/find-records/find-war-dead/casualty-details/2961850/ronald-horn/
6 https://www.cwgc.org/find-records/find-war-dead/casualty-details/2054633/leslie-john-smith/
7 Anon, *BAOR Battlefield Tour – Operation Plunder, Directing Staff Edition*, p. 5
8 Horrocks, *Corps Commander*, p. 251

CHAPTER 10: OPERATION PLUNDER

1 Lindsay, *So Few Got Through*, p. 208
2 Lindsay, *So Few Got Through*, p. 209
3 Tim Saunders, *Operation Plunder: The British and Canadian Rhine Crossing*, Chapter 3
4 Arthur Beardsley, *Trooper: From Barnard Castle to Berlin*, Chapter 21
5 Anon, *BOAR, Battlefield Tour – Operation Plunder, Directing Staff Edition*, p. 26
6 Render, *Tank Action*, p. 260

CHAPTER 11: OPERATION TURNSCREW

1 Lindsay, *So Few Got Through*, p. 215
2 National Archives: WO 373/54/668
3 Horrocks, *Corps Commander*, p. 263
4 Delaforce, *Monty's Highlanders*, p. 221
5 Delaforce, *Monty's Highlanders*, p. 221

6   Renouf, *Black Watch*, p. 268
7   Renouf, *Black Watch*, p. 268
8   Delaforce, *Monty's Highlanders*, p. 222
9   Lindsay, *So Few Got Through*, p. 218
10 Anon, *The Story of the 79th Armoured* (Naval & Military Press, 24 July 2013), p. 323
11 https://www.cwgc.org/find-records/find-war-dead/casualty-details/2046419/geoffrey-harwick-thompson/
12 Ken Ford, *Campaign: The Rhine Crossings 1945*, p. 33
13 Lindsay, *So Few Got Through*, p. 222
14 Lindsay, *So Few Got Through*, p. 223
15 Renouf, *Black Watch*, p. 274
16 Renouf, *Black Watch*, p. 276
17 Lindsay, *So Few Got Through*, p. 226

CHAPTER 12: OPERATION WIDGEON

1   RAF Bomber Command Campaign Diary
2   https://www.cwgc.org/find-records/find-war-dead/casualty-details/2041700/jack-sanderson/
3   RAF Bomber Command Campaign Diary
4   National Archives: WO 218/86
5   Peter Caddick-Adams, *1945 Victory in the West*, pp. 228–9
6   Carl Shilleto, *The Fighting Fifty-Second Recce: The 52nd (Lowland) Divisional Reconnaissance September 1944 to March 1946*, p. 127
7   https://www.cwgc.org/find-records/find-war-dead/casualty-details/2040823/bertram-kenneth-ord/
8   National Archives: WO 373/47/70
9   National Archives: ADM 202/83
10 Derek Mills-Roberts, *Clash by Night*, p. 168
11 Based on Commonwealth War Graves Commission (CWGC) lists
12 Mills-Roberts, *Clash by Night*, p. 168

CHAPTER 13: OPERATION TORCHLIGHT

1   Vaughan-Thomas went on to become a prolific writer after the war. His book *Anzio* was the basis for the Hollywood film of the same name. He also wrote several volumes about the Welsh countryside. His recordings from the war are available to listen to online.

2   https://www.cwgc.org/find-records/find-war-dead/casualty-details/041731/reginald-sayer/
3   https://www.cwgc.org/find-records/find-war-dead/casualty-details/2040251/william-thomas-mashford/
4   https://www.15thscottishdivisionwardiaries.co.uk/war-diaries
5   https://www.cwgc.org/find-records/find-war-dead/casualty-details/2036688/ronald-victor-baker/
6   https://www.15thscottishdivisionwardiaries.co.uk/war-diaries
7   https://www.cwgc.org/find-records/find-war-dead/casualty-details/2040533/david-pender-morris/

CHAPTER 14: RED DEVILS

1   Saunders, *Operation Varsity*, p. 111
2   Saunders, *Operation Varsity*, p. 111
3   https://www.cwgc.org/find-records/find-war-dead/casualty-details/2035807/harry-copeland/
4   https://www.cwgc.org/find-records/find-war-dead/casualty-details/2055510/william-hobson/

CHAPTER 15: NOTHING IS IMPOSSIBLE

1   https://emmalathamwriter.com/category/non-fiction-articles/interviews/operation-varsity/
2   *Liverpool Echo*, 2 October 1944
3   Aside from the interviews given to Liverpudlian newspapers in October 1944, the author could find no further record of Staff Sergeant Penketh in his own words, which is a great tragedy.

CHAPTER 16: MASS MURDER

1   Denis Edwards, *The Devil's Own Luck: Pegasus Bridge to the Baltic, 1944–45*, p. 181
2   Edwards, *The Devil's Own Luck*, p. 221
3   Edwards, *The Devil's Own Luck*, p. 222
4   https://www.cwgc.org/find-records/find-war-dead/casualty-details/2046869/dennis-john-ernest-white/ https://www.cwgc.org/find-records/find-war-dead/casualty-details/2031381/denis-fogarty/
5   Edwards, *The Devil's Own Luck*, p. 222

6   National Archive: WO 373/54/588
7   Edwards, *The Devil's Own Luck*, p. 237
8   Edwards, *The Devil's Own Luck*, p. 224
9   Edwards, *The Devil's Own Luck*, p. 224

CHAPTER 17: THE MOSAIC OF VICTORY

1   Max Hastings, *Armageddon: The Battle for Germany, 1944–1945*, p. 437
2   https://www.telegraph.co.uk/news/obituaries/military-obituaries/army-obituaries/8733804/Lt-Col-Joe-Cetre.html
3   https://www.cwgc.org/find-records/find-war-dead/casualty-details/2040781/thomas-oddie/; https://www.cwgc.org/find-records/find-war-dead/casualty-details/2056306/richard-lee/
4   National Archives: WO 373/54/350
5   National Archives: WO 373/55/297
6   Delaforce, *Red Crown & Dragon*, p. 193
7   Desmond Milligan, *View from a Forgotten Hedgerow*
8   Milligan, *View from a Forgotten Hedgerow*
9   Wilson, *Flame Thrower*, p. 229
10 Wilson, *Flame Thrower*, p. 231
11 Wilson, *Flame Thrower*, p. 234
12 Wilson, *Flame Thrower*, p. 236
13 https://www.cwgc.org/find-records/find-war-dead/casualty-details/2037374/ivor-buttle/
14 This may have been Trooper Pollard, 5th Royal Inniskilling Dragoon Guards, who was the only soldier killed in action in the regiment that day. https://www.cwgc.org/find-records/find-war-dead/casualty-details/2041161/stanley-william-pollard/
15 Moses, *The Gateshead Gurkhas: A History of the 9th Battalion the Durham Light Infantry 1859–1967*, p. 349
16 Moses, *The Gateshead Gurkhas: A History of the 9th Battalion the Durham Light Infantry 1859–1967*, p. 349
17 https://www.cwgc.org/find-records/find-war-dead/casualty-details/2646860/ronald-mervyn-sheehan/
18 https://www.telegraph.co.uk/news/newstopics/wfdeedes/1581172/Deedes-at-war-a-legacy-of-loss-and-bitterness.html
19 https://www.cwgc.org/find-records/find-war-dead/casualty-details/2646637/barry-stuart-newton/

20 https://www.telegraph.co.uk/news/newstopics/wfdeedes/1581172/Deedes-at-war-a-legacy-of-loss-and-bitterness.html
21 Shiletto, *The Fighting Fifty-Second Recce*, p. 129
22 George Blake, *Mountain and Flood: The History of the 52nd (Lowland) Division*, p. 171
23 Blake, *Mountain and Flood*, p. 174
24 Blake, *Mountain and Flood*, p. 178
25 Horrocks, *Corps Commander*, p. 265
26 Horrocks, *Corps Commander*, p. 265

CHAPTER 18: FOR VALOUR

1 Patrick Delaforce, *Onslaught on Hitler's Rhine: Operations Plunder and Varsity, March 1945*, p. 238
2 Patrick Delaforce, *The Black Bull: From Normandy to the Baltic with the 11th Armoured Division*, p. 213
3 Delaforce, *The Black Bull*, p. 215
4 Delaforce, *The Black Bull*, p. 215
5 National Archives: WO 171/5246
6 Delaforce, *The Black Bull*, p. 214
7 https://www.southwalesargus.co.uk/news/4618550.poignant-farewell-to-a-true-hero/
8 https://www.cwgc.org/find-records/find-war-dead/casualty-details/2055590/john-hopkinson/
9 https://www.cwgc.org/find-records/find-war-dead/casualty-details/2035871/john-richard-cox/; https://www.cwgc.org/find-records/find-war-dead/casualty-details/2036173/david-dickson/
10 Delaforce, *Red Crown & Dragon*, p. 200

CHAPTER 19: MORE BLOODY BRIDGEHEADS

1 https://www.cwgc.org/find-records/find-war-dead/casualty-details/2041701/thomas-sanderson/
2 https://www.cwgc.org/find-records/find-war-dead/casualty-details/2037118/robert-james-brand/
3 A. W. Taylor, *Shine Like a Glowworm*, p. 117
4 Taylor, *Shine Like a Glowworm*, p118
5 Patrick Delaforce, *The Invasion of Hitler's Third Reich*, p. 222
6 Bell, *From the Beaches to the Baltic*, p. 105

7 Bell, *From the Beaches to the Baltic*, p. 109
8 John Russell, *Theirs the Strife: The Forgotten Battles of British Second Army and Armeegruppe Blumentritt, April 1945*, p. 173
9 Bell, *From the Beaches to the Baltic*, p. 109
10 https://www.paradata.org.uk/people/walter-w-tanner
11 Russell, *Theirs the Strife*, p. 193
12 Mills-Roberts, *Clash by Night*, p. 177
13 https://www.cwgc.org/find-records/find-war-dead/casualty-details/2042220/john-alderson/
14 Mills-Roberts, *Clash by Night*, p. 179
15 https://film.iwmcollections.org.uk/record/468
16 Mills-Roberts, *Clash by Night*, p. 179
17 Ned Thornburn, *After Antwerp, The Long Haul to Victory: The Part played by 4th Bn King's Shropshire Light Infantry in the Overthrow of the Third Reich, September 1944 to May 1945*, p. 105
18 Bell, *From the Beaches to the Baltic*, p. 111

CHAPTER 20: FOR FREEDOM

1 John Russell, *No Triumphant Procession: Forgotten Battles of April 1945*, p. 82
2 https://www.cwgc.org/find-records/find-war-dead/casualty-details/2040555/jack-spencer-morrison-jones/
3 National Archives: WO 373/54/989
4 Russell, *No Triumphant Procession*, p. 92
5 http://www.desertrats.org.uk/WarDiaries/5th_RTR/5thRTR1945.htm
6 Russell, *Theirs the Strife*, p. 254
7 Russell, *No Triumphant Procession*, p. 96
8 Anon, *The History of the 6th Battalion, The Royal Welch Fusiliers – Europe 1944–45* (Unknown publisher, 1946), p. 168
9 George Forty, *Tanks Across the Desert: The War Diary of Jake Wardrop*
10 Urban, *Tankies: Tank Heroes of World War 2*, Part 2, BBC
11 Delaforce, *Red Crown & Dragon*, p. 204
12 Russell, *No Triumphant Procession*, p. 107
13 Russell, *Theirs the Strife*, p. 330
14 Russell, *No Triumphant Procession*, p. 109

15 Julian Thompson, *Imperial War Museum Book of Victory in Europe: The North-West European Campaign, 1944–1945*, p. 220
16 Hughes, *Sheldrake*, p. 139
17 Russell, *No Triumphant Procession*, p. 117
18 Hughes, *Sheldrake*, p. 140
19 Russell, *Theirs the Strife*, p. 349
20 Russell, *No Triumphant Procession*, p. 126
21 Russell, *Theirs the Strife*, p. 351
22 Russell, *Theirs the Strife*, p. 361
23 Russell, *Theirs the Strife*, p. 356
24 Hughes, *Sheldrake*, p. 142
25 Major Henry d'Avigdor-Goldsmid DSO MC, OC B Squadron, 53rd Reconnaissance Regiment
26 https://www.cwgc.org/find-records/find-war-dead/casualty-details/2389794/paul-peter-rockfield/
27 Delaforce, *Red Crown & Dragon*, p. 212
28 Mills-Roberts, *Clash by Night*, p. 181
29 Mills-Roberts, *Clash by Night*, p. 184
30 Mills-Roberts, *Clash by Night*, p. 185
31 Mills-Roberts, *Clash by Night*, p. 185
32 https://www.cwgc.org/find-records/find-war-dead/casualty-details/75191289/keith-james-griffith/

CHAPTER 21: LIBERATION

1 One report has it that Harries was later charged with treachery and cowardice for his decision to cede Belsen to British forces, and executed. Another says that he later marched his German and Hungarian troops across the Elbe, and was then taken into captivity as a POW in Schleswig Holstein. It is difficult to imagine how both could be true, unless his execution was an 'unofficial' one carried out by die-hards while Harries was a prisoner.
2 http://www.bergenbelsen.co.uk/pages/Timeline/TimelinePUTruce.html
3 https://www.cwgc.org/find-records/find-war-dead/casualty-details/2101574/frank-cecil-phillips/
4 Leon Goldensohn and Robert Gellatley (ed.), *The Nuremberg Interviews: Conversations with the Defendants and Witnesses*, p. 358

CHAPTER 22: DIE-HARDS

1 https://www.cwgc.org/find-records/find-war-dead/casualty-details/2107343/albert-henry-claxton/
2 https://www.cwgc.org/find-records/find-war-dead/casualty-details/2390141/john-charles-vines/
3 https://www.cwgc.org/find-records/find-war-dead/casualty-details/2389718/albert-edward-ramsden/
4 Essame, *The 43rd Wessex Division at War 1944–1945*, p. 255
5 Patrick Delaforce, *Monty's Iron Sides: From the Normandy Beaches to Bremen with the 3rd Division*, p. 202
6 https://etheses.whiterose.ac.uk/3626/1/486464.pdf, p.208
7 https://www.cwgc.org/find-records/find-war-dead/casualty-details/2107561/hugh-smiley-elgar/
8 National Archives: WO 373/55/307
9 National Archives: WO 373/55/307
10 Peter White, *With the Jocks*, p. 328
11 Blake, *Mountain & Flood*, p. 198
12 Organisation Todt was a joint German civil–military engineering conglomerate, responsible for a variety of engineering and industrial projects in occupied territories. It was infamous for using forced labour.
13 https://www.cwgc.org/find-records/find-war-dead/casualty-details/2199109/william-houston/; https://www.cwgc.org/find-records/find-war-dead/casualty-details/2199407/martin-mcdowall/
14 Delaforce, *Monty's Iron Sides*, p. 214

CHAPTER 23: FINAL DAYS

1 National Archives: WO 373/54/843
2 Hansen, *Disobeying Hitler*, pp. 301–03
3 https://www.15thscottishdivisionwardiaries.co.uk/war-diaries
4 Hansen, *Disobeying Hitler*, p. 306
5 Walker, *Unless I'm Very Much Mistaken*, p. 23

CHAPTER 24: VICTORY IN EUROPE

1 https://www.cwgc.org/find-records/find-war-dead/casualty-details/2389999/george-stewart-beat-stirling/; https://www.cwgc.org/

find-records/find-war-dead/casualty-details/2390046/james-edwin-taylor/
2　https://www.cwgc.org/find-records/find-war-dead/casualty-details/2716243/brian-glyn-hickey/
3　Commonwealth War Graves Commission
4　https://www.royal.uk/king-george-vis-ve-day-broadcast

CHAPTER 25: THE PRICE OF VICTORY

1　https://pmc.ncbi.nlm.nih.gov/articles/PMC6293353/
2　Whitehouse, *Fear is the Foe*, p. 158
3　Whitehouse, *Fear is the Foe*, p. 165
4　https://www.cwgc.org/find-records/find-war-dead/casualty-details/2074886/robert-walker-miller/
5　Stockman, *Seaforth Highlander 1939–45: A Fighting Soldier Remembers*, p. 226

EPILOGUE

1　https://www.cwgc.org/find-records/find-war-dead/casualty-details/2847858/robert-george-cracroft/
2　https://www.cwgc.org/find-records/find-war-dead/casualty-details/2961563/charles-alexander-holliman/
3　Urban, *The Tank War*, p. 331

BIBLIOGRAPHY

Anon, *Report on Operation Veritable: 8 February – 10 March 1945, Part 1* (BiblioGov Project, 2013)

Anon, *The History of the 6th Battalion, The Royal Welch Fusiliers – Europe 1944–45* (unknown publisher, 1946)

Anon, *The Story of the 79th Armoured Division* (The Naval & Military Press, 2013)

Arthur, Max, *Forgotten Voices of the Second World War* (Ebury, 2005)

BAOR: *Battlefield Tour – Operation Plunder Directing Staff Edition* (The Naval & Military Press, 2021)

BAOR: *Battlefield Tour – Operation Varsity Directing Staff Edition* (The Naval & Military Press, 2021)

BAOR: *Battlefield Tour – Operation Veritable Directing Staff Edition* (The Naval & Military Press, 2021)

Beardsley, Arthur, *Trooper: From Barnard Castle to Berlin* (Arthur Beardsley, 2013)

Bell, Noel, *From the Beaches to the Baltic: 'G' Company 8th Battalion The Rifle Brigade* (The Naval & Military Press, 2023)

Blake, George, *Mountain and Flood: The History of the 52nd (Lowland) Division* (Jackson, Son & Company, 1950)

Borthwick, Alastair, *Battalion: A British Infantry Unit's Action from El Alamein to the Elbe 1942–1945* (Bâton Wicks, 1994)

Burkinshaw, Philip, *Alarms and Excursions* (Davis Brothers, 1991)

Caddick-Adams, Peter, *1945 Victory in the West* (Hutchinson Heinemann, 2022)

Carver, Brigadier R. M. P, *The History of the 4th Armoured Brigade in the Second World War* (The Naval & Military Press, 2023)

Delaforce, Patrick, *Monty's Highlanders: 51st Highland Division in the Second World War* (Pen & Sword, 2016)

Delaforce, Patrick, *Monty's Iron Sides: From the Normandy Beaches to Bremen with the 3rd Division* (Amberly, 2010)

Delaforce, Patrick, *Monty's Northern Legions: 50th Northumbrian and 15th Scottish Divisions at War 1939–1945* (Sutton, 2004)

Delaforce, Patrick, *Onslaught on Hitler's Rhine: Operations Plunder and Varsity, March 1945* (Fonthill, 2015)

Delaforce, Patrick, *Red Crown & Dragon: 53rd Welsh Division in North-West Europe 1944–45* (Lume Books, 2021)

Delaforce, Patrick, *The Black Bull: From Normandy to the Baltic with the 11th Armoured Division* (Pen & Sword, 1993)

Delaforce, Patrick, *The Invasion of Hitler's Third Reich* (Fonthill Media, 2014)

Edwards, Denis, *The Devil's Own Luck: Pegasus Bridge to the Baltic 1944–45* (Pen & Sword, 2016)

Elstob, Peter, *Battle of the Reichswald* (Hazell Watson & Viney Ltd, 1970)

Essame, Major-General H., *The 43rd Wessex Division at War 1944–45* (The Naval & Military Press 2020)

Ford, Ken, *The Rhine Crossings 1945: The Final Push into Germany* (Osprey, 2007)

Ford, Ken, *The Rhineland 1945: The Last Killing Ground in the West* (Osprey, 2000)

Forty, George, *Tanks Across the Desert: The War Diary of Jake Wardrop* (Sutton Publishing, 2003)

Gill, Robert and Groves, John, *Club Route: 30 Corps in Europe* (The Naval & Military Press, 2014)

Goldensohn, Leon, *The Nuremberg Interviews: Conversations with the Defendants and Witnesses* (Pimlico, 2007)

Hansen, Randall, *Disobeying Hitler: German Resistance in the Last Year of WWII* (August Books, 2024)

Hastings, Max, *Armageddon: The Battle for Germany 1944–45* (Macmillan, 2004)

Hills, Stuart, *By Tank into Normandy* (Cassell Military Paperbacks, 2003)

Holland, James, *Brothers in Arms: One Legendary Tank Regiment's Bloody War From D-Day to VE Day* (Bantam, 2021)

Horrocks, Lieutenant-General Sir Brian, *Corps Commander* (Lume Books, 2023)

Hughes, Major Richard, *Sheldrake: Memories of a World War II Gunner* (Pen & Sword, 2016)

James, Lucas, *The Last Days of the Reich: The Collapse of Nazi Germany, May 1945* (Arms & Armour Press Ltd. 1986)

Kemp, Lieutenant-Commander P. K. and Graves, John, *The Red Dragon: The Story of the Welch Fusiliers 1919–1945* (Gale & Polden Ltd, 1960)

Lindsay, Martin, *So Few Got Through: With the Gordon Highlanders from Normandy to the Baltic* (Pen & Sword, 2012)

Longden, Sean, *To The Victor The Spoils: Soldiers Lives from D-Day to VE Day* (Robinson, 2007)

Lucas, James, *The Last Days of the Reich: The Collapse of Nazi Germany, May 1945* (Book Club Associates, 1986)

MacDonald Fraser, George, *Quartered Safe Out Here* (Harper Collins, 2000)

Milligan, Desmond, *View from a Forgotten Hedgerow* (Desmond Milligan, 1993)

Mills-Roberts, Brigadier Derek, *Clash By Night* (William Kimber, 1956)

Moses, Harry, *The Gateshead Gurkhas: A History of the 9th Battalion, The Durham Light Infantry 1859–1967* (County Durham Books, 2001)

Render, David with Tootal, Stuart, *Tank Action: An Armoured Troop Commander's War 1944–45* (Weidenfeld & Nicolson, 2016)

Renouf, Tom, *Black Watch: Liberating Europe and Catching Himmler, My Extraordinary WWII with the Highland Division* (Abacus, 2011)

Russell, John, *No Triumphant Procession: Forgotten Battles of April 1945* (Arms & Armour Press Ltd, 1994)

Russell, John, *Theirs the Strife: The Forgotten Battles of British Second Army and Armeegruppe Blumentritt, April 1945* (Helion & Company, 2020)

Saunders, Tim, *Breaking the Siegfried Line: Rhineland, February 1945* (Pen & Sword, 2023)

Saunders, Tim, *Operation Plunder: The British and Canadian Rhine Crossing* (Pen & Sword, 2006)
Saunders, Tim, *Operation Varsity: The British & Canadian Airborne Assault* (Pen & Sword, 2023)
Saunders, Tim, *The Battle of the Reichswald: Rhineland, February 1945* (Pen & Sword, 2023)
Shilleto, Carl, *The Fighting Fifty-Second Recce: The 52nd (Lowland) Divisional Reconnaissance Regiment RAC in North-West Europe, September 1944 to March 1946* (Eskdale Publishing, 2001)
Stockman, Jim, *Seaforth Highlanders 1939–45: A Fighting Soldier Remembers* (Crecy Books, 1987)
Taylor, A. W., *Shine Like a Glow-Worm* (Serendipity, 2002)
Thompson, Julian, *Imperial War Museum Book of Victory in Europe: The North-West European Campaign, 1944–1945* (Sidgwick & Jackson, 1995)
Thompson, Reginald W., *The Battle for the Rhineland* (Westholme, 2012)
Thornburn, Ned, *After Antwerp, The Long Haul to Victory: The Part Played by 4th Bn King's Shropshire Light Infantry in the Overthrow of the Third Reich, September 1944 to May 1945* (4th Bn KSLI Museum Trust, 1990)
Urban, Mark, *The Tank War: The British Band of Brothers – One Tank Regiment's World War II* (Abacus, 2013)
Verney, Major-General G. L., *The Desert Rats: The History of the 7th Armoured Division* (Hutchinson, 1954)
Walker, Murray, *Unless I'm Very Much Mistaken* (Collins Willow, 2003)
White, Peter, *With the Jocks: A Soldier's Struggle for Europe 1944–1945* (Sutton, 2002)
Whitehouse, Stanley, and Bennet, George G., *Fear is the Foe: A Footslogger from Normandy to the Rhine* (Robert Hale, 1997)
Wilson, Adrian, *Flame Thrower: Memoir of a Crocodile Tank Commander, D-Day to the Rhine* (Spitfire, 2022)
Zaloga, Steven J., *Downfall 1945: The Fall of Hitler's Third Reich* (Osprey, 2016)

ACKNOWLEDGEMENTS

Voices of Victory would not have been possible without the cooperation of the Imperial War Museums, and I am incredibly grateful to Lara Bateman and Madeleine James, and senior curator Stephen Walton for reading the manuscript. Special thanks go to all those involved in the recording and archiving of the interviews that formed the basis of this book, and to Charlie and Lucas for their help in transcribing hundreds of hours of audio.

One of the most enjoyable parts of writing a book is reading other people's. Special thanks to Tim Saunders, John Russell and Patrick Delaforce for their many works on this period, and to all authors listed in the bibliography.

I am deeply indebted to Roel Dekkers, International Guild of Battlefield Guides, who provided me with excellent tours concerning Operations Veritable, Plunder and Varsity, and who kindly took the time to look over the manuscript with an expert eye.

My deepest thanks to Ted Rutland for his service, and for inviting me into his home. It was a very special day for me, and I am indebted to Martin and Jane for making it possible.

My thanks to Olaf, who shared his time and stories, and to the many kind people I met in Holland and Germany whilst researching the book.

For access to war diaries, I chiefly relied upon Mark Hickman, curator of the Pegasus Archive. I am deeply thankful to him, and to Adam Bruce-Watt, who has made the diaries of the entire 15th (Scottish) Division available online in memory of his grandfather, Reverend Alek William Sawyer OBE, MC, TD, DD. My thanks also to the curators of desertrats.org, who have done the same for 7th Armoured Division's war diaries, and my apologies that I cannot thank you by name.

Thank you as ever to my friend and agent, Rowan Lawton, and the Soho Agency, for setting me on this path. My thanks to Martin Lubikowski for creating the book's maps, and to Justin Avoth for his dramatic narration of the audiobook. I am hugely grateful to all involved at my publisher, Pan Macmillan, and I would particularly like to thank Rosie Friis, Jiri Greco, Nick Griffiths, Neil Lang, Lindsay Nash, Holly Sheldrake, Kate Tolley and Ingrid Connell, my friend and editor, who has gone above and beyond in making this book possible. A big thank you is also due to my friends and family for bearing with me as I disappeared into my bunker for prolonged periods, and for your continuing support.

My final thanks is to you, the reader. Thank you for trusting me with your time, thank you for allowing me to do what I do, and thank you for caring about those who gave so much, for theirs was not a victory of conquest but of peace, and we will remember them.

Geraint Jones

PICTURE ACKNOWLEDGEMENTS

Page 1 *top* © IWM (BU 1732)
Page 1 *bottom* © IWM (BU 1785)
Page 2 *top* © IWM (BU 1716)
Page 2 *bottom* © IWM (B 14413)
Page 3 *top* © IWM (B 14499)
Page 3 *bottom* © IWM (B 14454)
Page 4 *top* © IWM (B 14419)
Page 4 *bottom* © IWM (B 14638)
Page 5 *top* © IWM (B 14678)
Page 5 *bottom* © IWM (B 14833)
Page 6 *top left* © IWM (B 15007)
Page 6 *top right* © IWM (B 14459)
Page 6 *bottom* © IWM (B 14972)
Page 7 *top* © IWM (B 15235)
Page 7 *bottom* © IWM (BU 2505)
Page 8 *top left* © IWM (BU 2152)
Page 8 *top right* © IWM (BU 2150)
Page 8 *middle* © IWM (BU 2090)
Page 8 *bottom* © IWM (BU 2091)
Page 9 *top* © IWM (EA 59364A)
Page 9 *bottom* © IWM (BU 2277)
Page 10 *top* © IWM (BU 2305)
Page 10 *bottom left* © IWM (BU 7670)
Page 10 *bottom right* © IWM (BU 2333)
Page 11 *top* © IWM (BU 2440)
Page 11 *bottom* © IWM (BU 2542)

Page 12 *top* © IWM (A 27929)
Page 12 *bottom* © IWM (BU 2783)
Page 13 *top* © IWM (BU 2889)
Page 13 *middle* © IWM (BU 3569)
Page 13 *bottom* © IWM (BU 3419)
Page 14 *top* © IWM (BU 3947)
Page 14 *bottom* © IWM (BU 4434)
Page 15 *top* © IWM (BU 5238)
Page 15 *middle* © IWM (BU 5308)
Page 15 *bottom* © IWM (BU 5138)
Page 16 *top left* © courtesy of Olaf
Page 16 *top right* © Bodmin Keep: Cornwall's Army Museum, The Keep, Bodmin, Cornwall, PL31 1EG
Page 16 *bottom* © Geraint Jones

VOICES FROM THE IMPERIAL WAR MUSEUMS

Excerpts from the following interviews are taken from the IWM Sound Archive. All © IWM.

Abbot, Joseph (20670)
Absalom, James (12523)
Adams, Albert (21129)
Ashton, Raymond (22624)
Atkinson, Robert (18738)
Baines, David Alan Talbot (20062)
Baker, Austin Edward (31328)
Baldwin, Arnold (18475)
Bigland, Walter (20617)
Blizzard, Arthur (17979)
Boardman, Thomas (17498)
Bone, William (21011)
Boxall, Paul (17725)
Brodie, Frank (19047)
Brown, Andrew Alfred (20942)
Brown, Peter (13854)
Bryan, Thomas (21188)
Buchanan, John (19867)
Burton, Francis (21014)
Burton, Victor (18204)
Butcher, Owen (18727)
Butler, Cyril (27262)
Cakebread, Derrick (20484)

Cammack, Harold (18832)
Campbell, James (20983)
Capon, Sidney (21061)
Carney, John Joseph (22927)
Cêtre, Ferdinand 'Joe' (30134)
Chandler, Raymond (21107)
Clack, Ronald (21287)
Clark, Henry (11357)
Colgan, Anthony (21658)
Coombs, Aubrey 'Bruce' (21106)
Cooper, Fredrick 'Fred' (21118)
Corbyn, John 'Josh' (17680)
Cosgrove, Henry (10177)
Cosgrove, Travers (20841)
Crawshay, William Robert (12521)
Crookenden, Napier (16395)
Dane, Roland (24618)
Day, John (20895)
Dobbs, John (27302)
Donnelly, John (19799)
Duddle, John (17943)
Edwards, Dave 'Dai' (32384)
England, Sidney (17268)
Essex, William Charles (21610)
Evans, Ivor (21277)
Eves, James (18739)
Fieber, Alex (15553)
Fink, John (16594)
Follett, Ronald (12402)
Fussell, Peter (10242)
Gibbons, Harry (22381)
Gibson, Leslie (20935)
Goddard, Douglas (20982)
Gore, Thomas (20144)
Gray, William (11478)
Griffin, Norman (18615)
Griffiths, Tom (32383)
Hammerton, Ian (8939)

Handley, Cyril (20783)
Hann, Ronald (20812)
Hanna, William (13949)
Hardman, Leslie (17636)
Harris, Fredrick 'Fred' (21288)
Hartle, Fred (22114)
Henderson, Ronald 'Ronnie' (17632)
Hicketts, Arthur John (22596)
Holdsworth, Albert (13652)
Hope, Tom (14971)
Hubbard, Roy (21104)
Hutchison, J. D. (20315)
Irwin, Stewart (18210)
Jones, Arthur (18346)
Keenan, Robert (20785)
Leatherbarrow, Richard (8253)
Leigh, Alfred (18548)
Leppard, Ernest 'Ernie' (19057)
Lindsey, John (30641)
MacDonald, Leonard (27235)
Markwell, Ivan (20368)
McDonough, Bernard (16344)
Meaney, Gertrude (17112)
Meredith, Berkeley (18577)
Mole, Ronald (13420)
Myers, Thomas (10166)
Neary, Thomas (18252)
Nelson, Ian (25277)
New, Kenneth (20948)
Newsom, Donald (20302)
North-Lewis, Christopher (16643)
O'Brien, Thomas (20587)
Ohlson, Kenneth (33890)
Old, Douglas (23146)
Palmer, Edward (14800)
Parr, Walter Robert (11073)
Pemberton, Alan Brooke (19043)
Petts, Ronald John (9732)

Pond, Hubert (13143)
Poulter, Charles (20362)
Powter, Kenneth (16648)
Rayner, Raymond (27350)
Rayson, George (18004)
Reid, George (17823)
Riches, Frederick (9937)
Ridout, Fredrick (22655)
Robinson, Raymond (20306)
Rouse, Arthur (14255)
Sassoon, Agnes (9093)
Sayer, Victor John (34594)
Scott, Stanley Wilfred (20940)
Scottson, Geoffrey 'Geoff' (20976)
Simpson, Fredrick (12168)
Simpson, Harry (18560)
Sinclair, Jack (21019)
Smith, Richard 'Sandy' (11333)
Smith, Robert (18575)
Snell, William (13580)
Stein, Philip (8848)
Summers, Robert (20949)
Swan, Mary Haddie (18571)
Symes, Laurence (13952)
Tanner, Walter (11448)
Tate, Alan (21296)
Taylor, Nelson (22135)
Tichard, William (20620)
Topliss, Arthur (12093)
Trafford, Kenneth (26094)
Treacher, Edward 'Eddie' (20609)
Vallance, Royston (19074)
Waller, Douglas (23447)
Warren, Cecil (15605)
Watson, John (12417)
Watson, Leonard Alfred (29543)
Welch, Godfrey (20610)
Wheeler, Eric (21059)

Whitbread, Alfred (27788)
White, Charles (22127)
White, Frederick 'Chalky' (20591)
Whybro, Denis (20008)
Wigmore, Raymond John (20589)
Wilkinson, James (23196)
Williams, William (15437)
Wilson, John (17985)
Wooltorton, Alfred (20958)